A VIEW

OF THE

ORGANIZATION AND ORDER

OF

THE PRIMITIVE CHURCH,

AS PRESENTED IN

SCRIPTURE AND HISTORY,

TO THE END OF THE SECOND CENTURY:

WITH THE

APOSTOLIC SUCCESSION TO THE PRESENT DAY.

BY THE LATE

REV. A. B. CHAPIN, D. D.

NEW HAVEN:

PUBLISHED BY HENRY H. BABCOCK.

1873.

TO

THE RIGHT REVEREND

THOMAS CHURCH BROWNELL, D.D. LL.D.

BISHOP OF CONNECTICUT,

WORTHY SUCCESSOR

OF

SEABURY AND JARVIS,

THIS WORK

IS RESPECTFULLY DEDICATED,

IN TOKEN

OF REGARD FOR HIS OFFICE AND CHARACTER,

BY THE AUTHOR.

"O ALMIGHTY GOD, who hast built thy Church upon the foundation of the Apostles and Prophets, JESUS CHRIST himself being the head Corner Stone, grant that all thy children may be so joined together in unity of spirit, by their doctrine, that we may be made an holy temple, acceptable unto Thee, through JESUS CHRIST our LORD. *Amen.*"

PREFACE

TO THE STEREOTYPE EDITION.

THE favorable reception with which the *View of the Organization and Order of the Primitive Church* has been received, since its publication in 1842, has induced the author and publisher to put it in a permanent form, by having it stereotyped. In preparing the present edition for the press, no pains have been spared, which would tend to enhance its value, or increase its usefulness. The whole work has been thoroughly revised, both as it regards the facts, and the manner of representing them. In doing this, the author has availed himself of whatever assistance might be derived from a careful comparison of authorities, from the suggestions of friendly and the cavils of opposing reviews, and from the views and opinions set forth in the many works which have appeared within the last three years, on some of the topics treated of in this volume.

The principal changes to which these have led, have been the omission of a few unimportant considerations, the condensation of some arguments that were carried out more in detail than seemed necessary, and the expansion of some others that were too brief to be well understood. But, in no instance has it led to the omission of any fact which was before deemed important, or to the modification of any conclusion whatever. Several important facts have been added, chiefly in *notes*. But, in regard to the early translations of the word *baptize* and *baptism*, and in regard to the *consecrations of the consecrators* of the Archbishops of Canterbury from Augustine to Cranmer, and in a few other instances, important matter has been added to the text. The last chapter of the previous edition, on the relative strength of Christianity now and fourteen hundred years ago, has been omitted; not from any doubt of the correctness of the opinions there expressed, but because the brevity with which it was necessary to consider the subject in a work like this, necessarily impaired the force of the arguments adduced. He trusts the evidence on this point, may some day be presented to the public in a more satisfactory manner. The important words from foreign languages, on which any argument depends, have been printed in the appropriate letter.

The principal points which distinguish this work from all others on the same subject, are: (1,) It is not a book of controversy, as most works on this subject have been, but an inquiry into the early organization of the Church, as a simple matter of history. (2,) It is confined to a consideration of that organization and worship, as it existed previously to the commencement of the third century, and before there could have been any considerable departure from the Apostolic practice. And, (3,) it has brought out more fully than any preceding work, the evidence that the succession of ministers, established by the Apostles, has been continued in the Church of England, as an independent Church, to the present day. Its importance has, therefore, been in no degree lessened by the books which have recently appeared; but is rendered the more necessary, to fill up a chasm, and supply a desideratum, which no other has attempted to fill. And that it may tend to do this, while it advances the Apostolic order of the Church, is the sincere prayer of

THE AUTHOR.

New Haven, March 10, 1845.

EPISTLE TO THE READER.

No apology need be offered for an inquiry into the subject of this volume: for, next in importance to that of personal holiness, is the question, *How shall that Gospel, which has produced this holiness in us, be best preserved and perpetuated, that it may produce the like holiness in generations yet to come?* Nor is this duty to be made out by inference alone, for we are commanded, to "walk about Zion, to go round about her; to tell the towers thereof; to mark well her bulwarks, to consider her palaces; that we may tell it to generations following." (Ps. xlviii. 12, 13.) But the reasons for considering this subject, the reasons for presenting the public with a new work upon a topic already so fully discussed, may not be uninteresting.

The substance of this work was written several years since, under the following circumstances. The author was born and educated among the Congregationalists; and it was not until he had entered upon the duties of a professional life, that the subject of the organization and order of the Church attracted his attention. He then resolved to examine the question thoroughly, according to principles of legal evidence, drawing his conclusions according to the same, not dreaming of its producing a change in his own views on the subject. For this purpose he read the New Testament through, with the utmost care and attention, marking every passage that seemed to bear upon the organization or order of the Apostolic Church. These he classified under their appropriate heads, arranging them according to their several subordinate topics, upon principles hereinafter detailed. This forms *the Scriptural evidence,* as drawn out, except on the single topic of Baptism, not only before the author entered the Ministry, but before he had conformed to the Episcopal Church. His conclusions, therefore, are to be regarded as those of a layman, who, up to the time of compiling the evidence embodied in this work, had no partialities in favor of Episcopacy; but whose prejudices, partialities, and supposed interests, were all in opposition to it. In this examination, it was designed to bring together all the Scriptural evidence; and thus to develop, *A Scriptural Draught of the Apostolic Church.* Hence, no time was spent in discussing the peculiarities of existing denominations, nor any allusion made to their principles or practices, except as they fell necessarily within the scope of the inquiry. Thus, controversy with all preceding writers, and with all existing sects, has been avoided.

To the Scriptural evidence, thus drawn out, *A brief Historical view of the Church, to the end of the second century,* has been added, in which the author has endeavored to examine *all the evidence,* afforded by the extant writings of the Primitive Christians, within that period. It has been his design, under both heads, to give all *the direct* evidence there is on this subject, whatever might be its weight; and also, to add such *presumptions* as bear upon the subject under consideration. Consequently, the reader will find that while some arguments are strong, others are, comparatively, less so. The author's plan required him to notice all the arguments, weak or strong;—to bring forward all the evidence, direct or indirect, that the whole might be judged of, in connection. And it is in this way, he asks that it may be judged. To enable the reader to do this, with more clearness and certainty, the principles upon which all investigations of the kind must be conducted, have been stated and explained. In this way alone, can we ever arrive at any *certain* conclusions.

To these topics, the author has added a few chapters on other subjects, growing out of the preceding, which seemed necessary to give application to the principles discussed, and the conclusions drawn. Without these, it was impossible to connect the Church of the present day, with the Church in the times of the Apostles. And unless this were done, one end of our inquiry would be lost. These chapters, the author flatters himself, will often be found of peculiar service to Churchmen, under a great variety of circumstances; and he hopes they will not be devoid of interest to others.

In conclusion, the author would remark, that he neither courts nor deprecates criticism. But he may be permitted to say to those who differ from him, that, if they attempt either to review, or reply to him, they ought to show, (1,) that the principles he has proceeded upon are unsound; or, (2,) that he has departed from those principles in the investigation; or, (3,) that the mass of evidence has been misrepresented or misapplied. It will not be enough for them to show, that he may have been mistaken on some points, even could that be done, if the principles on which he has proceeded are sound. Or, (4,) they ought to show that he has omitted to mention other important proof, sufficient to outweigh all the evidence adduced. Unless one of these four points can be shown, the conclusions drawn in this volume, must be received as proved. If the author has failed upon any one of these points, he will be much obliged to those who will point it out to him, in that spirit of kindness and charity, with which this work is presented to the public. Truth has in some instances required the author to state facts that will not be acceptable to all; but he has endeavored to do it in the way that would be the least offensive to such brethren as dissent from him.

In order to put it into the power of every one who desires to test the accuracy of *the facts* stated in this volume, as well as the soundness of the conclusions drawn from the facts, the author has given full and careful references to his authorities, and, as far as possible, to the *original* authorities. He has thus put it into the power of those who wish, to subject his arguments to the most rigid scrutiny, with the least possible labor, while at the same time it furnishes the reader with a sort of guaranty, that the facts are fairly stated, on sufficient authority. The author also trusts, that in addition to other advantages which may be derived from this volume, it will be found a general index to the authors from whom all facts and arguments on this subject must be drawn.

That those who are unwilling to lay aside the prejudices of early education; or who are not resolute enough to ask unhesitatingly, "What is truth?" nor bold enough to dare fearlessly to follow it; or who are unwilling to relinquish the pride of opinion, or the interest of place: that those will be convinced, is not expected. But it is hoped, that the sincere inquirer after truth will find essential aid in this volume; and that he who is anxiously seeking to know what is that Church which hath been declared to be "the body of Christ," will be helped forward in his investigation. That it may do this; and also tend to lead "those who profess and call themselves Christians, into the way of truth, and to hold the faith in unity of spirit, in the bond of peace, and in righteousness of life,"—until the whole of GOD's elect shall be "knit together in one communion and fellowship, in the mystical body of his Son our LORD," is the hearty prayer of

THE AUTHOR.

VIEW

OF THE

PRIMITIVE CHURCH.

CHAPTER I.

STATE OF THE QUESTION.

From the days of the Lutheran Reformation to the present time, the question; *What was the organization and order of the Apostolic Church*, has excited much discussion and interest among the various religious denominations, each claiming to be exclusively patterned after the Apostolic model. A large proportion, indeed, believe this model to be binding on succeeding generations. Even the few who deny it, show by their endeavors to prove their conformity to that model, that they consider its sanction very desirable. Since this subject is deemed by Christians to be of such magnitude, its consideration cannot fail to be both interesting and useful.

This examination, it should be remembered, is one of mere history, and must be considered like any other question of that nature. Consequently, we have nothing to do with the supposed tendency of any organization; nor with existing organizations, unless to compare them with the results obtained.

In this examination there are two kinds of evidence, independent of each other—equally relevant;—the Scriptures, and the writings of the primitive Christians, usually referred to by the appellation of the Fathers. The writings of the Fathers are equally pertinent with the Scriptures, in an inquiry into the organization of the *primitive* Church, when they speak of *facts* within their own knowledge, provided they were honest men; and that they are so considered, is sufficiently proved by the fact, that all Christians appeal to their testimony to ascertain what should constitute the canon of Scripture. But there are some, at the present time, who deny the relevancy of the testimony of the Fathers; and insist that we must confine ourselves entirely to the evidence of Scripture, in attempting to determine the Constitution of the Apostolic Church. Out of respect to the feelings of those entertaining this opinion, we shall confine our examination to such points as may be made out by Scripture, citing the Fathers merely in confirmation, and as proof of what was the Constitution of the Church, in the age *immediately succeeding* that of the Apostles. For the same reason, we shall confine ourselves to the time when it is acknowledged that the Church remained uncorrupt; that is, to the two first centuries. The full object of our inquiry is, (1,) to ascertain, *What is the Scriptural account of the Apostolic Church;* and, (2,) *What is the historical account of the primitive Church, to the end of the second century;*

Before proceeding to examine the evidence in the case, we must acquaint ourselves with three things: (1,) *The things to be proved;* (2,) *The manner of proving them;* and, (3,) *The testimony by which they are to be proved.* But in every subject which men discuss, or examine, there must be certain things which are *assumed*, or agreed upon, by all parties. These, like axioms in mathematics, are the starting points of the argument. Their necessity is self-evident, for if men do not agree upon certain first principles, they cannot reason together at all.

One of the points thus assumed, or agreed upon in this matter, and which the common sense of every person must approve, is, that the Apostolic history, as contained in the Acts of the Apostles, was written to inform us that the Gospel was preached, and *Churches were formed;* but not to detail peculiarities of organization;—that the Apostolic Epistles were written to confirm the Churches in the faith; not to give a *platform of Church organization and order.* Hence, we might infer, as we know the fact to be, that *the New Testament gives, in no one place, a detailed account of the organization and order of the Apostolic Church.* This point being assumed, it is necessary to assume another, before we can proceed:—that the Apostolic Churches, when fully established, had a uniform system of organization; and that the Apostles, in their writings, allude to, and speak of that form, with sufficient distinctness, to enable us to determine what it was.

It will be seen from this, that the scriptural evidence on this subject, is, mainly, of that indirect kind, which will render some portions of the examination rather difficult. The precise nature of it may be best illustrated by an example. Suppose a man, born and educated in one of the South Sea islands, grown up without any communication with, or knowledge of, any civilized nation. Put into the hands of such a man, *the military correspondence of Washington, during the American Revolution,* and require him, from that alone, to determine the organization of the American army; and we should impose upon him a task of no small magnitude. It is true, he would find letters *to* and *from* the officers of the army, accounts of acts performed by various persons; but nowhere, an enumeration of the ranks and grades of officers; nowhere a distinct account of the power and duty incident to each; and for a very satisfactory reason—both the writers of the letters, and the persons to whom they were written, were familiar with every rank and grade, with all the power and duty of every office and officer in the army, of which they were speaking.

But this supposition does not present a parallel to the case we are to consider, inasmuch as the subject of the supposed letters is the same with the question to be determined. But suppose further, instead of the military correspondence, this man should receive only *the letters written by Washington to such familiar friends, during the same period,* as had left the army, and were residing in a remote part of the country, *accompanied by a few proclamations, issued by the General to the army.* The task of determining the constitution of the army, would now be far more difficult; and yet, such a man, under such circumstances, would be situated very much as we are, when attempting to determine the entire Constitution of the *Apostolic Church, from Scripture alone.* This will be evident upon slight reflection, for it will not be believed for a moment, that General Washington, when writing to men who had been soldiers or officers under him, and who were as familiar with the organization of the army as himself, would enter into a detail of facts, with which he knew them to be conversant; nor is there any greater reason for believing, that the Apostles would give a detailed account of the organization and order of the Churches they had established, when writing to the members of such Churches. The nature of the evidence in the two cases is similar; and what would be proof of the Constitution of the American army, to a South Sea islander, situated as supposed, must be proof to us of the Constitution of the Apostolic Church.

Hence the necessity of ascertaining, with as much certainty as possible, the precise nature of the *evidence* to be considered, that we may confine our attention to questions of *history.* For this purpose, we shall reduce these fundamental principles to propositions, that we may refer to them without difficulty.

PROPOSITIONS.—1. It is agreed, then, that the Churches planted by the Apostles, when fully established, had a uniform system of organization.*

2. That, whatever this form was, it must have been tangible and visible; known to all the members of the Churches; and, therefore, could not be mistaken or forgotten.

3. For this reason, the Apostles did not address Epistles to the Churches in relation to ecclesiastical organization; that being a subject about which there was no possibility of mistake. But they did address Epistles to the various Churches, on matters of faith and doctrine, which not being visible and tangible, but depending on recollection and memory for their transmission, were liable to be forgotten or misremembered.

4. These Epistles contain allusions to that organization, sufficiently distinct to enable us to determine what it was.

5. That form only can plead the authority of Apostolic sanction, to which these allusions are all applicable.

CHAPTER II.

RULES OF EVIDENCE.

THE truth of the propositions contained in the foregoing Chapter, will not be doubted or denied, by those giving their assent to the correctness of the view we have taken, and the nature of the evidence by which it is to be determined. Indeed, it is only by supposing them true, that the subject can be discussed at all; since, if the organization of the

* This is denied by a few Independents, but their number is too small to require any notice.

Apostolic Churches was not *uniform*, all inquiry concerning it is useless; for, unless they were so, we could not quote an Epistle to one Church, to prove what was the organization of another. Hence, unless we allow this uniformity, the Epistle to the Corinthians would be no evidence of what was the organization of the Church at Ephesus. And so of the rest. And further; if the Apostolic writings do not allude to that organization, with sufficient distinctness to enable us to determine what it was, all attempts to ascertain the fact from Scripture, are visionary.

Having ascertained those general principles, upon which all are agreed, and which must, therefore, form the basis of all argument, we must establish some *rules of evidence*, or *principles of interpretation*, which will enable us to give to each circumstance the precise force it deserves.

We can not, perhaps, better illustrate the necessity and nature of these rules, than by resuming our former supposition. We may then imagine our South Sea islander, reading the familiar correspondence of Washington, and there finding accounts of a Major General commanding two or more Brigadier Generals; a Brigadier General commanding two or more Colonels; a Colonel commanding two or more Captains, and so down to privates. The most natural, and the only reasonable inference he could draw from these accounts, would be, that the officer who commanded two or more officers, was of a higher rank or grade than those over whom he had command; and consequently, that a Major General ranked higher than a Brigadier General, a Brigadier General higher than a Colonel, and so on. By carefully collating and comparing the passages in which the various officers were spoken of, or alluded to, he might determine the rank, grade, and duty of every officer in the army.

But he would need some rules for weighing the evidence contained in those letters, that he might decide correctly as to what was *proof* of a fact in reference to the organization of the army. Satisfied that the person writing the letters, and the persons to whom they were written, were well acquainted with its organization, and that the writer was ***honest,*** he would see that it was impossible for him to state facts, or allude to things which did not exist; and, therefore, that the bare mention of an office, officer, custom, or regulation, as existing in the army, and forming a part of it, was conclusive evidence of its existence. He would also find things directly alluded to, when not expressly mentioned; and indirect allusions to what he would have reason to suppose formed a part of the same.

Hence, he would classify his proof into express mention of facts in reference to the organization of the army, and into direct and indirect allusions to them. The first of these would be conclusive evidence of the fact thus mentioned; the second, or direct allusions, would be, unless contradicted or explained, proof of the fact; and the third, or indirect allusions, would raise a presumption of the existence of the fact apparently alluded to, liable to be confirmed or contradicted. If, however, the fact apparently alluded to, existed in the army, it never could be contradicted by the correspondence of Washington.

At first, it would be difficult for him to determine, whether a thing spoken of was part of the ordinary discipline and practice of the army, or some peculiar and extraordinary service, performed by special command. To do this, however, it would only be necessary for him to bear in mind, that as the persons to whom these letters were written, were at a distance from the army, acquainted only with its *ordinary* duties and discipline; it would be necessary for Washington, when speaking of any thing *extraordinary* or unusual, to tell what it was, and for what purpose ordered; or he would be unintelligible to his correspondent. If, therefore, he found a distinct statement of the performance of an act, unaccompanied by any intimation that it was unusual, he would conclude it was an ordinary practice, or a regulation of the army. Thus, suppose he should find Washington, in one of his letters, telling his friend, that he was "awoke that morning, by the beating of the revellie;" and in another place should say, he "awoke at daylight;" and there should be no further allusion to the "revellie" in all the letters, our South Sea islander would necessarily infer, that it was a custom or regulation of the American army to beat the revellie at daylight. Again, suppose that, among the proclamations submitted to his examination, he should find one addressed to a branch of the army, in which mention was made of their disorderly and mutinous conduct, concluding with a command, that all things should hereafter be done *according to rule;* the inference would be, that certain *rules* existed, well known to the persons whom he addressed, the transgression of which had made them obnoxious to the charge of disorderly conduct.*

All this is most emphatically true, in reference to the Epistles of St. Paul, from which we are obliged to gather nearly all the evidence on the subject. This has been so clearly and forcibly stated by Mr. Locke, in his *Essay for the Understanding of St. Paul's Epistles,* in reference to another point, that we can not better express our ideas, than by copying a passage from him.

"The nature of epistolary writings in general, disposes the writer to pass by the mentioning many things, as well known to him to whom his letter is addressed, which are

* An attempt has been made to evade the force of this illustration, by pretending to carry out the supposition, and applying it to the *present* sectarian division of the world, (New Eng. I. 396, 397.) But that is to substitute a question of sectarian gloss, for a question of pure history.

necessary to be laid open to a stranger, to make him comprehend what is said; and it not seldom falls out, that a well-penned letter, which is very easy and intelligible to the receiver, is very obscure to a stranger, who hardly knows what to make of it. The matters St. Paul writ about, were certainly things well known to those he writ to, and which they had a peculiar concern in; which made them easily apprehend his meaning, and see the tendency or force of his discourse. But we, having now, at this distance of time, no information of the occasion of his writing, little or no knowledge of the temper and circumstances those were in he writ to, but what is to be gathered out of the Epistles themselves; it is not strange that many things in them lie concealed to us, which, no doubt, they who were concerned in the letter, understood at first sight."

It can not be necessary for us to pursue the subject further. Every reader will see the parallelism of the evidence to be relied on by the South Sea islander, in his attempts to discover the organization of the American army, from such materials, and that to be employed by us, in attempting to determine *what is the Scriptural Draught of the Apostolic Church.* The evidence is of the same general nature; the circumstances under which it was written, in the main, analogous, and the difficulties to be encountered in the investigation, exactly similar.

It will be convenient for future reference, to reduce the foregoing illustration to propositions, applicable to the question under consideration. We also add a few, growing out of the subject, so plain and obvious, as to require no argument in their support; and which every writer does, in effect, *assume*, in every similar inquiry.

RULES OF EVIDENCE.—1. The references made in Scripture to the form of the organization of the Apostolic Church, are of three kinds; *positive statements*, *direct allu-*

sions, and *indirect allusions ;* each possessing a different degree of force.

2. *A positive statement*, in regard to any office, officer, or regulation in the Apostolic Church, as forming a part of it; is *conclusive evidence* of its existence.

3. *A direct reference* to any office, officer, or regulation in the Apostolic Church, as forming a part of it, is *prima facie evidence*, that is, full proof, unless contradicted or explained away, of its existence.

4. *An indirect allusion* to any office, officer, or regulation in the Apostolic Church, as forming a part of it, is *presumptive evidence*, but not of itself, *proof* of its existence.

5. Evidence of an inferior, may confirm, but can not contradict, that of a higher degree.

6. Several presumptions, arising from different sources, tending to prove the same fact, uncontradicted by other evidence, are sufficient to establish the existence of the fact.

7. No name designates an office in the Church, unless some particular power be assigned to, or some person to whom it is applied exercised some power, or performed some duty in the Church, by virtue of it.

8. The nature of an office in the Apostolic Church, can not be learned from its name, but must be determined by the nature and extent of the power ascribed to the office; or exercised by the officer filling the office.

9. The grade or rank of an officer, is to be determined by the extent of power appertaining to the office, or exercised by the officer.

10. The application of several names to the same person, is not evidence that they all designate the same, or a similar office.

One other subject deserves notice in this place, the *reason* and *extent* of the relevancy of the testimony of primitive writers on this subject. This may be illustrated by an example. Polycarp of Smyrna, one of the writers we quote, was the disciple of St. John. He must have known, therefore, *from St. John*, what was the order and faith of the Apostolic Churches. Irenæus of Gaul, who flourished from A.D. 175 to A.D. 200, was the disciple and pupil of Polycarp, and must have known, *from Polycarp*, what was the faith and order of the Church, in the time of the Apostles; and *from personal observation*, what was the faith and order of the Church, in his own day. In regard to the latter—the order and organization of the Church—it was impossible he could be mistaken. It was a thing of public notoriety, tangible and visible, and about *which* there could be no dispute. The testimony of Irenæus, therefore, as to the order of the Church in his own day, is conclusive evidence on that point; and that which he received from Polycarp, was conclusive on the same point, in his day. Ignatius, another writer whose writings will be employed as evidence, was also the disciple of St. John, and a fellow pupil with Polycarp. Justin Martyr, another, was conversant with those who had lived in the days of the Apostles, and so, also, was Hegesippus, both of whom lived in Palestine.

CHAPTER III.

MODE OF INTERPRETING SCRIPTURE.

We are now ready to proceed in our examination by a rigid application of the principles and rules of evidence already established. It must, however, have been obvious to the most casual reader of the New Testament, that there is not only a dearth of facts, in reference to many things in the Constitution of the Apostolic Church; but also, that in some cases, the language is such as to render it doubtful to what the Apostles intended to refer. In many instances, however, much of the ambiguity may be removed, by a more full and free translation of the original. But as this generally involves some disputed point, it is difficult to give a version which shall satisfy all. Inasmuch, however, as we have consented, out of respect to the feelings of others, to leave out of consideration some important testimony on the subject, that might be drawn from the general consent of the Fathers of the third and fourth centuries; for the same reason, we shall take the interpretation of one of their own men, in those instances where a deviation from the common version is made. In other words, where we find occasion to propose a translation different from the standard version, we shall follow the "Greek and English Lexicon of the New Testament, by Edward Robinson, D. D., late Professor Extraordinary of Sacred Literature, in the Theological Seminary at Andover, Mass.;" a man whose acquaintance with the Greek, and with what has been written in Germany, on the peculiar Greek of the New Testament, qualify him, in an eminent degree, to judge of the exact meaning of the language of the New Testament. If any have a right to complain of this course, it is certainly *not* those whose opinions on this subject are similar to Prof. Robinson's.

As a general rule, however, Scripture must be its own interpreter; and no reference will be made to any existing form of Ecclesiastical organization, unless by way of illustration. Nor can any appeal to human opinions be allowed, except to determine the sense of words and phrases made use of by the writers of the New Testament. Nor shall we appeal to the Old Testament, as authority on this subject, except in those cases where the New contains some reference or appeal to it; or where both treat in common of the same subject, as is the case in regard to the character of our Saviour; or where the writers of the New have used words and phrases which have a determinate Ecclesiastical meaning in the Old Testament. Bearing these things in mind, we shall now proceed to inquire,

1. What was the Apostolic Church?
2. Who composed that Church?
3. What were the powers and duties of its members?
4. What were its officers? and,
5. What were the qualifications required of, and the power and duty belonging to each?

CHAPTER IV.

THE CHURCH A REGULARLY ORGANIZED SOCIETY.

We proceed now to inquire, *What was the Apostolic Church?* We answer, *a regularly organized society.** This appears from the language of Scripture.

1. *It is one fold, having one shepherd.* This is expressly declared by the Great Head of the Church himself, (John x. 16,) "Other sheep I have, which are not of this [the Jewish] fold; them also I must bring, and there shall be *one fold* and *one shepherd.*" And in another place, (John xvii. 21–23,) Christ prayed that his disciples might be one, "even as he and his Father were one." So Paul, in his Epistle to the saints at Rome, assures them, that though many, they "were *one body* in Christ," (Rom. xii. 5,) and he proclaims to the Ephesians, that Christ has broken down the wall of partition

* Recently attempts have been made to overthrow and set aside this position, but as seems to us, entirely without success. Indeed, if the language of Scripture under this head, does not imply *unity* and *organization*, we know not what construction to give it.

between Jew and Gentile, and "has made both *one*." (Eph. ii. 14,) or, as in 1 Corinthians, (xii. 13,) were "baptized into *one body*," i. e. "the Church." (Col. i. 18.) So also St. Paul assures the Church of the Romans, that they are a wild olive-tree, grafted into the root of that true olive, which before had been the Jewish Church. (Rom. xi. 13–24.)

2. *It is one body, having one head.* In Ephesians, (i. 22,) CHRIST is said to be "*head* over all to the Church." In Colossians, (i. 18,) he is called "*the head* of the body—the Church," and in Romans, (xii. 4,) the Church itself is called "one body." So in 1 Corinthians, (xii. 13,) it is said that Jews and Gentiles are "baptized into *one body*," that is, into the Church. (Col. i. 18.)*

3. *But having many members.* This is asserted in Romans, (xii. 4,) "We are many members, IN ONE BODY;" and also in 1 Corinthians, (xii. 12,) "For the body is one, and hath many members, and all the members of that one body are one body." And again, (xii. 20,) "Now are they many members, but ONE BODY."

4. *The members having various offices.* Thus St. Paul says to the Romans, "we have many members in the same body, but all members have not the same office." (Rom. xii. 4.) And in 1 Corinthians, (xii. 18,) he writes, "GOD hath set the members in the body, as it pleased him," every one to perform some distinct office, or appropriate duty. And reasoning in the same manner in reference to the Church, (comp 1 Cor. i. 2; xii. 12, 27,) he calls the Church one body, in which; "GOD hath set, first, Apostles; secondarily, Prophets; thirdly, Teachers; after that, miracles," &c. (vv. 28, 29.) So in Ephesians, (iv. 11, 12,) he declares, that "he gave

* This doctrine of the Church's being the body of CHRIST, was universally prevalent. Ignatius says, (Ep. Smyr. c. 8,) "where JESUS CHRIST is, there is the Catholic Church." Tertullian (De Bap. c. 6,) calls the Church, "the body of the three" persons of the Trinity.

some Apostles, and some Prophets, and some Evangelists, and some pastors and teachers, for the perfecting of the saints, for the work of the ministry, for the edifying of the body of CHRIST;" i. e. "the Church."

5. But having "*one faith, one baptism, one Lord and Father of all.*" (Eph. iv. 5, 6.)

6. Again, *The head is called a king.* Gen. xiv. 18; Ezek. xxxvii. 24, 25; Hos. iii. 5; Matt. xxi. 5; John i. 49; xii. 13–15, and elsewhere often.

7. *And the Church itself is called a kingdom.* That the phrase, "the kingdom of heaven," and the phrase, "the kingdom of GOD," often denote the Church of "the living GOD," will be hereafter shown, so that we shall only enumerate some of the passages referred to by Prof. Robinson, (p. 130,) where it is so used. Matt. vi. 10; xii. 28; xiii. 24, 31, 33, 41, 47; xvi. 28; Mark iv. 30; xi. 10; Luke xiii. 18, 20; Acts xix. 8, etc.

The common practice of the Apostle, of comparing the Church to the human body, seems to have been designed to intimate that it is deserving of careful consideration. If the Church be "one body," having "one head," "with many members," the members having "various offices," we should expect to find it attended by the following particulars:

(1.) The head would be *the eye*, that is, the *overseer* of the body. This follows, both from the analogy of the Apostle's figure, and from the office and object of the eye. Hence the duty of *overseeing* can reside nowhere but in the head.

(2.) The head would be *the ear* of the body. And if the ear, must have the power of *hearing*, and consequently of *judging* all matters relative to the wants and duties of the body.

(3.) The head would be *the mouth* of the body. And if the mouth of the body—the Church—must have power of *speaking on behalf* and in the name of the Church.

From the foregoing it follows, that in every Apostolic Church we should expect to find *a head*, having the power of *overseeing*, *hearing*, *judging*, and *speaking*, for and in behalf of the Church. No Church, therefore, can be formed after the Apostolic pattern, to which these allusions are not applicable, or which has not such a head, having these powers, and performing these duties.

(4.) It would also follow, that if every Church must have such a head, then there can be no such thing as a head over these heads. Each head must be the highest authority, on earth, over the body. Hence, the doctrine taught by some, that Christ has one visible head on earth over all Churches, is opposed to the opinion of St. Paul, and therefore can not be true.

Thus much the language of the Apostle clearly authorizes us to infer. It is, indeed, a *positive statement* of facts, which inevitably leads to this conclusion; and as *he* has nowhere limited the application of the figure, *we* may not take it upon ourselves to do so. If any are unwilling to rely on this as proof, they can not object to its introduction, as assisting to develop the *Apostolic idea of the Church.*

It may be asked, whether the Apostle's language necessarily supposes any *head of the Church* on earth? We think it does, clearly so. Thus he says, (1 Cor. xii. 12,) "For [or *according*] *as* the body is one, and hath many members, and all the members of that one body, being many, are one body; so *also* [i. e. *in like manner*] is Christ:" by which, as appears from the same chapter, is meant the body of Christ, (v. 27,) which in Colossians (i. 18) he calls "the Church." And again he says, "The eye can not say unto the head, I have no need of thee; nor again, *the head* unto the foot, I have no need of you." (xii. 15–17.) This language naturally, if not necessarily, implies, that *the head* was of the same nature as *the eye*, *the ear*, *the foot*, and *the hand.* Hence, although Christ is the Great Head of the Church, (Eph. i. 22; iv. 15; v. 23; Col. i. 18,) and "the Bishop of our souls," (1 Pet. ii. 25,) still he hath constituted visible heads of his visible Church, to act as his representatives and ministers here on earth.

The propriety and appropriateness, if not necessity of this, will be seen more clearly by attending to the *nature of the Church.* It appears on reading the New Testament, and especially the Epistle to the Hebrews, that the Apostolic idea of the kingdom of heaven, or of the Church, was, that it included all the *actual* and *professed* subjects of the King of heaven, whether on earth or in heaven. And further, they seem to have regarded the *visible* things of the Church, in some sense at least, as *types of the invisible;* and not only as types, but also as *means* of producing the things of which they were types. This idea seems to have been copied from the Apostles by the primitive Christians, and to have formed the basis of their *systematic theology.* Not that they ever embodied these ideas in so many words, but, that a perception of them, as existing in the mind, lay at the foundation of what they wrote upon the subject. From these general principles the following system was developed:—

The Church is one; but two fold in its nature;—

1. *Outward and visible:*—THE CHURCH MILITANT:—a type of, and designed to prepare us for—

2. *The invisible and spiritual:*—THE CHURCH TRIUMPHANT.

I. *The Church is one.* This is a prime article of faith with the greater part of Christians. In the Creed called Apostolic, we profess our faith in "one Catholic (or Universal) Church;"*

---

* The phrase "*the Catholic Church,*" first occurs in the Epistle of Ignatius to the Smyrneans, A. D. 107, (c. 8.) It is also used in the *Circular Epistle* of the Church of Smyrna, A. D. 168, Itd. and c. 16, and in Clement of Alexandria, A. D. 180, (Stron. vii. p. 764,) in Cyprian, and in numerous later writers.

and in the Nicene Creed, in "one Catholic and Apostolic Church." That this is the doctrine of Scripture, has already been shown; to which may be added, the following testimonies:—"The disciples were all of one heart and one soul," (Acts iv. 32; xiii. 11; Phil. i. 27; 1 Pet. iii. 8; Rev. xvii. 13;) "being one body," (1 Cor. x. 17; xii. 13,) "espoused to one husband," (2 Cor. xi. 2,) having "one faith, one Lord, one baptism, one God." (Eph. iv. 5, 6.) This language is decisive of the *oneness* of the Church.

This was the sentiment of the primitive Church, as we shall see in the course of this inquiry. We shall, therefore, only quote a passage from Cyprian, Bishop of Carthage.—Thus he says,* "The Episcopate; it is a whole, in which each enjoys a full possession. The Church is likewise one, though she be spread abroad, and multiplies with the increase of her progeny; even as the sun has many rays, yet one light. . . . . . Thus the Church, flooded with the light of the Lord, puts forth her rays through the whole world, yet with one light, which is spread upon all places, while its unity is not infringed." There is also other language of Scripture, which implies the same thing. This is clearly evident from the Scripture usage of the phrases, "the kingdom of heaven," and "the kingdom of God." These are applied—

1. *To the Church on earth.* "They demanded when the kingdom of God should come." (Luke xvii. 20.) "The kingdom of heaven is likened unto a man which sowed good seed in his field; but while men slept, the enemy came and sowed tares among the wheat." (Matt. xiii. 24.) "The kingdom of heaven is like a net cast into the sea, and gathered of every kind." (Mat. xiii. 47.) And again: "I will give you the keys of the kingdom of heaven." (Matt. xvi. 19.)

2. *The Church in heaven.* "I will drink no more of the

* Unit. Church, c. 4, Ep. 55.

fruit of the vine, until I drink it new in the kingdom of God." (Matt. xxvi. 29.) "The unrighteous shall not inherit the kingdom of God." (1 Cor. vi. 9.) "Extortioners shall not inherit the kingdom of God." (1 Cor. vi. 10.) "Flesh and blood can not inherit the kingdom of God." (1 Cor. xv. 50.)

By *the kingdom of God*, or *the kingdom of heaven*, is meant, therefore, *all the actually, or professedly obedient subjects of the King of heaven.* Metaphorically and figuratively, the same language is used to signify—

1. *That spiritual principle* which produces this obedience.

2. And also the *doctrines* which tend to produce this principle of obedience.

3. And, finally, the *gospel* which proclaims those doctrines.

If, then, by the phrases, *the kingdom of God*, and *the kingdom of heaven*, is meant, all who actually are, or who profess to be, obedient subjects of the King of heaven, then it follows, that it includes all the saints in heaven, and all professed Christians on earth. In other words, the kingdom of God, as spoken of in the New Testament, includes both the Church militant, and the Church triumphant. Hence it follows, that although—

The Church is one, IT IS TWOFOLD IN ITS NATURE.

1. *Outward and visible* :—THE CHURCH MILITANT.

2. *Invisible and spiritual* :—THE CHURCH TRIUMPHANT.

II. The Church Militant is *a type* of the Church Triumphant. So St. Paul: "For if he, (Christ,) were on earth, he should not be a priest, seeing that there are priests that offer gifts according to the law: *who serve unto the example and shadow of heavenly things:* as Moses was admonished by God, when he was about to make the tabernacle: for see, saith he, that thou make *all things according to the pattern shown to thee in the mount.*" (Heb. viii. 4, 5.) And again: "The Holy Ghost this signifying, that the way into the holiest of all was not yet made manifest, while as *the first tabernacle* was yet standing: *which was a figure for the time then present.*" (Heb. ix. 8, 9.) And still again: "It was, therefore, necessary, that *the patterns of the things in the heavens* should be purified with these, [the blood of sacrifices;] but the heavenly things themselves with better things than these." (Heb. ix. 23.) Now it follows, necessarily, that the priests who "served unto the example and shadow of heavenly things," and also the tabernacle which "was a *figure* for the time then present," "a *pattern* of the heavenly things," and "an *example* and *shadow* of heavenly things," were *types* of those things of which they were "examples," "shadows," and "patterns." We may conclude, therefore, that the Church Militant, *under the Jewish dispensation,* WAS A TYPE of the Church Triumphant. Its rites and ordinances being, in the mean time, types of the redemption.

From the foregoing we infer, that the Church Militant under the Christian dispensation, is a type of the Church Triumphant, *because* the Jewish and Christian Church is the same Church, under different dispensations. Thus St. Paul: "For *the law* [the Jewish dispensation] having a *shadow* of good things to come, and not the very *image* of the things." (Heb. x. 1.) The words here translated "shadow" and "image," would convey a fuller idea of the sense of the original, were they rendered "an outline," like the first draft or plan of a picture; and "a full representation," like the plan or outline completed. And this "fuller representation," the Apostle tells us, is contained in the gospel. But neither the "outline," nor yet the fuller representation of a thing, is the thing itself. We have, then—

1. *The law*, which has a brief *outline of;* and,

2. *The Gospel*, which has a full *representation of*—

3. *The substance,* or salvation that awaits the faithful in heaven.

Both, therefore, refer to the same thing; differing only in

their fullness:—the one presenting a mere ***sketch;*** the other *the filling up* of the picture. Both, therefore, came from the same source; both have the same end in view, and both point to the same thing. Hence we are not at liberty to consider the two dispensations as distinct and independent Churches. The former covenant is not done away, nor abrogated. It is *fulfilled*, but not destroyed. (See Matt. v. 17; Luke xxii. 44.) Now a *fulfillment* is not destruction nor abrogation. The filling up of a picture causes it to present a different appearance, but does not change the outline. It is the completion of the picture, not the destruction of it. So the Gospel is the fulfillment, not the destruction of the law.

The same doctrine is still more clearly asserted by St. Paul, in other places. Thus he tells the Roman Christians, (Rom. xi. 17,) that they are "a wild olive grafted in among the natural branches." In this figure, the Christian Church is represented as standing in the same place, growing out of the same tree, and drawing its nourishment from the same source, and through the same channels as the Jewish Church which preceded it. It is, therefore, the same tree still,—planted in the same soil, watered by the same streams, and refreshed by the same dews. It is not, therefore, a *new*, but the same Church.

The same conclusion must be drawn from the language of the Apostle to the Ephesian Christians. (c. ii.) Thus he tells them, while they were of the "Uncircumcision," they were "*aliens* from the commonwealth of Israel; and *strangers* from the covenants of promise." But now he tells them, that Christ "*hath broken down the middle wall of partition*, between Jew and Gentile." It would be impossible to assert the identity of the two dispensations in stronger language than this; and since it has been shown that the Church Militant under the former dispensation, was a type of the Church Triumphant, it follows, necessarily, that the Church Militant under the present dispensation, must also be a type of the Church Triumphant.

The conclusion here drawn, is fully sustained by the interpretation of Primitive writers. This will appear from a single passage from Clement, of Alexandria, A. D. 175. In speaking of the marital relation, he quotes the language of the Apostle in Ephesians 5th, and Colossians 3d ; and in connection with it says: "*The Terrestrial Church is the image* (εικον or *likeness*) *of the Celestial.*"* And in another place† he says: "I imagine the progressions in the Church, of Bishops, Presbyters, and Deacons, to be *imitations* (μιμηματα) of the Angelic glory." The same idea was recognized and acted upon by other Primitive writers, especially by Ignatius, Bishop of Antioch, in his Epistles. Thus he exhorts the Trallians to "reverence the Deacons as Jesus Christ, and the Bishop as the Father, and the Presbyters as the Council of God."‡ But by this he does not design to exhort them to pay divine honors to these men, but to "reverence" the former, as holding places in the visible Church, analogous to those held by the latter in the invisible. In other words, he uses language in the same sense in which St. Paul used it, when he said to the Galatians, "ye received me as an angel of God,—even as Jesus Christ." (Gal. iv. 14.) So also he speaks of the "Bishops as presiding in the place of God," that is, holding the headship of the Church on earth, as the Father holds the headship of the Church in heaven ; and is "the Bishop of us all." And so in many other places, to which we shall have occasion to allude in other parts of the work.

From these considerations, (to which many more might be added,) it follows, that the Church on earth, which is an image of the Church above, must have such a visible head, as shall constitute it a perfect visible body. And it also

* Strom. iv. 500. † Strom. vi. 667. ‡ c. 3.

follows, that as there is no head over any other heads, in that spiritual and invisible Church, so there can be no such thing as a head over other heads, in the Church on earth. Each Church, within a particular portion of country, forms a complete and distinct Church, independent of every other Church; but it is still a representation, or image of the one Church in heaven. Consequently, every complete and perfect Church on earth, is "an image of the heavenly," so that the various Churches in the several countries, are so many copies of the same heavenly pattern; and hence all must be essentially the same—must be constituted in a similar manner, and be independent of every other. Yet, as being parts of the same great body, they must be in communion with each other, and are bound mutually to assist and support each other.

These descriptions all necessarily imply, that the Apostolic Church was *a regularly organized Society*, with officers and laws. They are, indeed, a direct statement of facts, incompatible with any supposition, but that of a regular uniform system of organization; and this inference is nowhere contradicted in Scripture. We may, therefore, set it down as an incontrovertible fact, that the Apostolic Church was a regularly organized Society. For this reason we conclude, that the Church in all ages, should be a regularly organized Society, and as such, must be endowed with perpetual duration.

But, though in a general sense, the Church was *one*, Universal, or Catholic, yet, in a limited sense of the word, there were many Churches; as the Church of Jerusalem, of Rome, of Ephesus, of Colosse, of Thessalonica, of Crete, of Smyrna, and the like. And that each Church was complete and perfect in itself, is clearly deducible from the language of the Apostle, since he speaks of these several Churches as distinct, and, at the same time, as complete. But it is to be observed, that he never speaks of more than one Church in the same place. Hence we must conclude, that every Church was so complete and perfect in itself, that it would remain a complete and perfect Church, though every other Church in the world had been destroyed. Consequently, the head of a Church, within any given territory, was not only ruler over those within his territory, but was also, so head of the Church, that in case the head of the Churches in all other districts should be taken away, he would be the visible head over all the Church on earth.

CHAPTER V.

WHO COMPOSED THE APOSTOLIC CHURCH—BAPTISM.

HAVING ascertained what the Church is, we proceed to inquire, who compose it? To this inquiry but one answer has ever been given, viz., those who have received Christian baptism, and have not been rightfully excommunicated. Though men have differed widely as to the mode of baptism, they have ever held that, to be the only rite of initiation into the Christian Church. The unanimity on this point would excuse us from offering any proof of it, were we not inquiring as to the *scriptural draught of the Apostolic Church.*

There are several distinct arguments in proof of this; but one of them must be sufficient. Christ instituted but two ordinances—baptism and the Lord's supper; and that baptism was the rite of initiation, appears expressly from the language made use of by St. Paul in his Epistles: "There is one Lord, one faith, one baptism," (Eph. iv. 5,) by which "we are all baptized into one body," (1 Cor. xii. 13,) which "body is the Church," (Col. i. 18.)

But though men agree as to the nature and design of baptism, they differ widely as to what constitutes baptism; and, also, as to who are proper subjects of baptism. And as these are important inquiries, laying at the foundation of the Church, they must be examined with care and attention. We shall first consider the mode of baptism; and then inquire, who are proper subjects of it? In this inquiry, there are four kinds of evidence to be considered.

1. The meaning given to the language used, in the dictionaries.

2. Its usage in the Old and New Testaments.

3. The allusions made to the mode of performing the rite, in the New Testament.

4. The account given of it by the Primitive Christians.

The words used in the New Testament in reference to this subject, are, (βαπτιζω,) *to baptize;* and the derivative, (βαπτισμος,) *baptism.* Our first inquiry, therefore, is, what is the meaning of the word *baptizo?* But *baptizo* is a derivative from *bapto;* and both are so frequently referred to in discussing this subject, that we must inquire into the meaning of both.

1. Of the meaning given to *bapto* and *baptizo,* in the dictionaries. These give various meanings, as *dipping, washing, bathing, wetting, moistening, dyeing,* and the like; so that we must have recourse to some other kind of proof to settle the question. Now it is agreed on all hands, that the native Greeks are the best authority for the meaning of their own language, and we shall refer the question to them. We give, therefore, only the definitions of native Greek lexicographers.

The oldest native Greek lexicographer is Hesychius, who lived in the fourth century of the Christian era. He gives merely the root; and the only meaning he gives the word is (αντλεω) "*to draw,* or *pump* water." Next in order comes

SUIDAS, a native Greek, who wrote in the tenth century. He gives only the derivative, *baptizo;* and defines it by (πλυνω) "*to wash.*" Passing over the intermediate Greek lexicographers, we come down to the present century, at the beginning of which we find GASES, a learned Greek, who, with great labor and pains, compiled a large and valuable Lexicon of the ancient Greek language. His book, in three volumes quarto, is a work deservedly held in high estimation by all, and is generally used by native Greeks. The following are his definitions of *bapto* and *baptizo.**

ΒΑΠΤΩ, βρεχω, *to wet, moisten, bedew.*
πλυνω, *to wash,* (viz. clothes.)
γεμιζω, *to fill.*
βυθιζω, *to dip.*
αντλεω, *to draw, to pump* water.
ΒΑΠΤΙΖΩ, βρεχω, *to wet, moisten, bedew.*
πλυνω, *to wash.*
λυω, *to wash, to bathe*
αντλεω, *to draw, to pump* water.

These are the definitions of a native Greek, "whose opinion is entitled to the highest deference."

* Ed. Venice, 3 vols. 4to. The work of *Gases* was based on that of *Schneider*, he only making such alterations and additions as were deemed necessary. The definitions of Gases were followed by *Hilarion*, a learned Archimandrite, of Mount Lebanon, who, in 1819, with the approbation of his archbishop, revised the translation of the Bible made by the British and Foreign Bible Society. In this translation, νιπτα, πλυνω, βαπτιζω, are used interchangeably.

ANTHIMIS GASES, the author of this work, was a native of Melias, in Magnesia, in the province of Thessaly. He was educated at Venice. He resided in that city several years, and subsequently travelled extensively in Germany and Italy, and formed an acquaintance with many of the principal scholars in both countries. He was one of the most learned men of Greece before the Revolution, and was a member of the body that framed, and a signer of the Grecian Declaration of Independence.

2. Of the Scriptural usage of *bapto* and *baptizo*. It is often taken for granted, that the Hebrew word, (טבל,) *tabal;* the Greek, (βαπτο,) *bapto;* and the Latin, *mergo*, uniformly rendered *dip* in the English Bible, are corresponding words, and signify *to dip, to immerse, to plunge*. This assumption is unfounded, for reasons we shall lay before our readers. But we ought to remark, that *dip* and *immerse* are not, as many seem to suppose, synonymous words. A body is not *immersed* in water, until it is entirely covered by the water; but it is *dipped in* or *into* water, when any part of it comes in contact with the water. Thus, a man *dips* his pen, that is, *the point* of his pen, in ink, and "*dips* his finger, that is, *the tip* of his finger, in water," but in neither case is there any *immersion*. The question, therefore, is, do the foregoing words signify, *to immerse*, in the sense claimed, that is, *a complete immersion* of the thing dipped? This question must be decided by Scriptural usage alone, to which, therefore, we now turn our attention.

According to *the Scriptural usage*, the Hebrew and Greek words above mentioned, denote *a partial dipping, or wetting*. "And as the feet of the priests that bare the ark *were dipped* (טבל, βαπτω) *in the brim* of the water." (Josh. iii. 15.) There was plainly no immersion here, but simply a touching of the soles of the feet. Similar to this was the language of Dives to Abraham: "Send Lazarus, that he *may dip the tip* of his finger in water." (Luke xvi. 24.) So in the various Jewish purifications, none of the *dippings* were *immersions*. Thus the priest is told that "he *shall dip his finger*, or a bunch of hyssop, that is, *the end* of his finger, or the end of the bunch of hyssop, in the water." (Ex. xii. 22; Lev. iv. 17; ix. 9; xiv. 6, 16, 51; Numb. xix. 18; Deut. xxxiii. 24.) So Jonathan "put forth *the end of his rod and dipped* in the honey-comb." (1 Sam. xiv. 27.) To the same effect in Ruth, (ii. 14:) "And *dip* thy morsel in the vinegar." So also the language of Christ to Judas denotes a partial dipping: "He that *dippeth* (Matt. xxvi. 23; Mark xiv. 20; John xiii. 26) with me in the dish." In one place in Job, (ix. 31,) these words have the sense of *to plunge*, in the common acceptation of the word, that is, to cast headlong; as, "Thou shalt plunge me into the ditch."

If there were any room for doubt, after considering the foregoing, the following would entirely settle the question. Thus, when Nebuchadnezzar was driven from the abodes of men, it is said that "his body *was wet with the dew* of heaven." (Dan. iv. 33; v. 23; or iv. 30, and v. 21, of the Hebrew and Greek.) Here *bapto* does not signify *to dip*, in any sense, but merely *to wet*, or *moisten*, and is therefore synonymous with *brecho*, (βρεχω,) as defined by Gases. In one place in 2 Kings, (viii. 15,) and in one in Leviticus, (xi. 32,) it appears to have the sense of *to immerse*, which are the only places in the Bible where it has that signification. In Psalms (lxviii. 23, or lxviii. 24, of the Greek) and in Revelations, (xix. 13,) it has the meaning of *to tinge*, *dye*, or *stain*, which may be done either by *sprinkling* or *immersing*. These, we believe, are all the places in the Bible where *bapto* occurs in any form; and we see, that out of twenty-three instances, it has the sense of immersion but twice.

From *bapto* comes *baptizo*, which, being a frequentive in form, ought to signify a repeated action,* and is, in fact, so defined by Schneider,† *I dip in often*. But, though it has the *form* of a frequentive, most lexicographers are not willing to allow that it has that *signification*.‡ We shall, therefore, examine the Scriptural use of this word, as we have the root

* Butt. Gr. Gram., § 119, 1, 2

† Gr. Lex., 2 vol. 4to. "Ich tauche oft ein."

‡ Rob. Gr. Lex. N. T.

from which it is derived, in every case where it occurs in the Bible.

The word *baptizo*, it is claimed by some, signifies exclusively, "*to immerse, to submerge, to sink.*" The point of inquiry, therefore, is, does the Scripture usage sustain this assertion? This word occurs in the Old Testament *four times;* twice in the Canonical books, and twice in the Apocrypha. It first occurs in 2 Kings, (v. 11, 14:) "And Elijah sent a messenger unto Naaman, saying, Go and *wash* (λουω) in Jordan seven times. . . . . Then he went and *washed himself* (βαπτιζω) in Jordan seven times." Here the word is used in accordance with what, judging from its form, should be its meaning, to signify *a repeated action*, which action was a washing of purification. In Ecclesiasticus, (xxxiv. 25, or xxxi. 30, or xxxiv. 27,) it is used in the same manner: "If he that *washeth himself*, (βαπτιζω,) after touching a dead body, touch it again, what availeth his *washing*, (λουτρω?)" In both of these instances, *baptizo* is synonymous with LOUO, *to wash;* and, therefore, according to the principles of those who hold immersion alone to be baptism, "it is not essential how it was performed." But, as some may say that the original Hebrew would lead to another conclusion, we shall dwell a moment upon that.

Louo is the word used in the Septuagint as the equivalent of the Hebrew *rahats*, (רחץ) to denote the washings of purification, and is found in the places mentioned in the note.* It occurs in but one other place in the Bible, (Psalms vi. 6,) where it has the sense of *to wet*, or *moisten:* "I *wet* my

---

* Ex. ii. 5; xxix. 4; xl. 12. Lev. viii. 6; xv. 5, 6, 7, 8, 10, 11, 12, 13, 16, 21, 26; xvi. 4, 24, 26, 28; xvii. 15, 16; xxii. 7. Numb. xix. 7, 19. Deut. xxiii. 11. Ruth iii. 3. 2 Sam. xi. 2; xii. 20. 1 Kings xxii. 38. 2 Kings v. 10, 12, 13. Cant. v. 13. Is. i. 16. Ezek. xiv. 4, 9 xxiii. 40. In Apoc., Susanna 15, 17.

couch *with tears*." A few examples will show its general meaning. "A *little* water *to wash* the feet." (Gen. xviii. 4.) "He *washed* his face." (Gen. xliii. 31.) "Thou shalt bring Aaron and his sons unto the door of the tabernacle, and *shalt wash* them." (Ex. xxix. 4, and xl. 12.) "And Moses brought Aaron and his sons, [to the door of the tabernacle,] and *washed* them with water." (Lev. viii. 6.) The same language is used in reference to all the purifications. An unclean person was "*to wash himself* in water;" (Lev. xv. 5, 7, 8, 10, 11, 21, 22, 27; xvii. 15; Deut. xxiii. 10; Numb. xix. 19;) also, "*to wash* his flesh in water." (Lev. xi. 13, 16; xvi. 4, 24, 26, 28; xvii. 16; xxi. 16; Numb. xix. 7, 8.) "And one *washed* the chariot in the pool." (1 Kings xxii. 38.) "His eyes, like doves', with new milk *washed*." (Cant. v. 12.) "Thou wast not *washed* in water in the day of thy nativity." (Ezek. xvi. 4, 9.) These examples are sufficient to prove, that *rahats*, in the Hebrew, and *louo*, in the Septuagint, denote *washings* performed by the application of water *to the person*, and not by putting the person *into the water*. And, as *baptizo* is the equivalent of these words, it must have the same meaning.

Besides, St. Paul expressly calls these *washings* of purification, *baptisms*. (Heb. ix. 9, 10.) "Which was a figure for the time then present, ... which stood only in meats and drinks, and divers washings, (βαπτισμοις, '*baptisms*.')" So all the primitive writers understood him.

The next place in the Canonical books of the Old Testament, where this word occurs, is Isaiah, (xxi. 4:) "My heart panteth; fearfulness *fills* me." In this case, *baptizo* is synonymous with *to fill*, (γεμιζω,) according to one of the definitions of Gases, quoted above. The other place is Judith, (xii. 7:) "And Judith went out by night and *washed herself* in a fountain, (that is, in a *spring*,) by the camp." There is no reason why the word in question should not be understood in this case as in the former cases of washing, and if so, there was no immersion. We are, therefore, authorized to say, that the *authority of the Septuagint is decidedly against the opinion*, that *baptizo* means "to immerse, submerge, or sink." We turn now to the New Testament, and inquire how *baptizo* is used there.

1. This word is used as synonymous with words which denote *washing*. "The Pharisees and the Jews, except they *wash hands*, (νιπτω,) eat not. . . . . When they come from the market, except they *wash*, (βαπτιζω,) they eat not. And many other things there be, which they have received to hold, as the *washing* (βαπτισμος or *baptism*) of cups and pots, brazen vessels and tables. . . . . Why do thy disciples eat bread with *unwashen* (ανιπτω) hands." (Mark vii. 3, 4, 5.) So, "The Pharisees marvelled that Jesus had not first *washed* (βαπτιζω or *baptized*) before dinner." (Luke xi. 38.) That *nipto* does not *mean* to immerse, is admited by all; but every reader may satisfy himself of the fact by examining the places where it occurs in the New Testament. (Matt. vi. 17; xv. 2; John ix. 7, 11, 15; xiii. 5, 6, 8, 10, 12, 14; 1 Tim. v. 10.) *Baptism* is also called *the washing* (λουτρω) of *regeneration*, or "the new birth." (Titus iii. 5.)*

2. In a majority of instances in the New Testament, the word is used without any qualifying words to denote the manner of its performance, and we must therefore interpret it according to the customary usage of the Scriptures, to signify, *a washing*.†

* The Ethiopian version calls it "the washing of baptism."

† It is thus used in Matt. iii. 6, 13, 14, 16; xxviii. 19. Mark i. 4, 5, 8; vi. 14; xvi. 16. Luke iii. 7, 12, 21; vii. 29, 30; xi. 38; xiii. 38. John i. 25, 28; iii. 22, 23, 26; iv. 1, 2; x. 40. Acts ii. 38, 41; viii. 12, 13, 16, 36, 38; ix. 18; x. 47, 48; xi. 16; xvi. 15, 33; xviii. 8; xix. 3, 4, 5; xxii. 16. 1 Cor. i. 13, 14, 15, 16, 17; xii. 13; xv. 29. Gal. iii. 27.

3. It is sometimes construed with words denoting the *instrument* WITH which baptism was performed, in such a manner as to negative the idea of *immersion*. Thus St. Luke says: "John baptized WITH *water*, but CHRIST baptized WITH *the* HOLY GHOST." (Luke iii. 16; Acts i. 5; xi. 16.) Similar phraseology, but accompanied by a preposition, occurs in Matthew, (ii. 11;) Mark, (i. 8,) and John, (i. 26, 31, 33.) Some, however, claim that these passages should all of them be translated so as to read; "I baptize you *in* water, but he shall baptize you *in* the HOLY GHOST." They ground their argument for this, on the meaning of the Greek preposition εν, which primarily denoted *in*. However well this argument might hold in reference to the writings of Matthew, Mark, and John, it has no force when applied to the writings of Luke, as, *water*, (υδατι,) is, "the dative of the instrument,"* or "in the instrumental case,"† without the preposition, and consequently could not be rendered *in*. But further, *en* does not always mean *in*. It frequently denotes "the manner or mode, that is, the state or circumstances by which an action is accompanied,"‡ as may be seen by comparing Matt. xxii. 37, and Rom. xv. 6, where it has the force of *with*.

4. It is construed with words denoting the *effect* of baptism, in such a manner as to negative the idea of *submersion*. Thus CHRIST says of himself: "I have a *baptism to be baptized* with." (Luke xii. 50.) And he inquired of two of his

* Rob. Gr. Lex. New Testament.

† Hist. Crit. View of Ind. Europ. Cases, 7. III. 3. [2.] Q. C. Spec. IX. 425. The proper instrumental case does not occur in the Greek, being supplied by the Dative, though it is common to many of the Indo-European languages,—as Sanscrit, Zend, Armenian, Old Slavic, Russian, Polish, &c., and existed in fact, though not in form, in all the old Gothic languages, as well as in the Greek. It is always equivalent to *by* or *with*.

‡ Rob. Gr. Lex. New Testament.

disciples; "Are ye able *to be baptized* with the *baptism* that I am *baptized* with," (Matt. xx. 22, 23; Mark x. 38, 39.) So also, persons were said to be baptized "*into* (εις) Moses," (1 Cor. x. 2,) and "*into* CHRIST," (Gal. iii. 27,) and "*into* repentance," (Matt. iii. 11,) and "*into* death," (Rom. vi. 3.) To substitute "immerse, submerge, or sink," as the meaning of *baptizo*, in any of these places, would be absurd. Indeed, these passages can not be construed so as to make sense, except by considering baptism as *a symbolical washing* or *purification*.

The allusions made in the New Testament to the mode of performing baptism, are such as to negative the idea of *immersion*. CHRIST, a short time before his ascension, promised his disciples that they "should be baptized with the HOLY GHOST, not many days hence." (Acts i. 5.) This promise was fulfilled upon the day of Pentecost, and at subsequent times upon those who afterwards believed, at the "laying on of an Apostle's hands." The language chosen by the sacred historian, in giving an account of this baptism, is descriptive of his view of it. Thus when the HOLY GHOST fell upon the Gentiles, or when they were "baptized with the HOLY GHOST," he says, "they of the circumcision were astonished, because the gift of the HOLY GHOST was *poured out* (εκχεω) upon the Gentiles also." (Acts x. 45.) This is the only direct reference in the New Testament, to *the mode* in which baptism of any kind was performed, and in this the *act* was that of *pouring*, or, as the language was figurative, and as every metaphor must have something to sustain it, the obvious inference is, that the *instrument* WITH which baptism was performed, *was poured* upon those who were baptized. Hence, we conclude, that baptism was probably performed by *pouring*, of which *sprinkling* is a species.

We have now gone over with the Bible, and examined every place where either *bapto* or *baptizo* occurs, (unless some instance has been overlooked by accident,) and have found, that out of twenty-three instances where *bapto* occurs, it signifies to immerse but twice; and that in seventy places where *baptizo* is found, there is not one where it means to immerse. We are therefore authorized to say, that whatever may be the classic meaning of these words, they do not in Scripture signify *to immerse.*

CHAPTER VI.

MODE OF BAPTISM CONTINUED.

HAVING shown that the Scriptural usage of the words denoting baptism, and the mode of their construction with other words, as well as the direct allusions to the rite, do not harmonize with the idea of immersion, in the modern sense, that is, of total submersion, we shall now consider two forms of expression, on which some rely with confidence: "Buried with him by baptism," and "they went down into the water, and they came up out of the water."

"*Buried with him* BY *baptism.*" 1. This phrase occurs in the New Testament but twice: in Romans vi. 4, and "*buried with him* IN *baptism,*" Colossians ii. 12. In the fifth chapter of Romans, St. Paul having shown, that GOD overrules the wicked acts of men to his own glory, and that, where sin had reigned, grace did now abound, proceeds, in the sixth, to answer an objection which might be made: "What shall we say then?" that is, if grace now abounds where sin formerly reigned, "Shall we continue in sin, that grace may abound?" To this inquiry he replies, "God forbid;" and to show the absurdity of the supposition, he asks, "How shall we who ARE DEAD to sin, live any longer therein?"

This inquiry, then, is equivalent to an affirmation, that every Christian is *dead* to sin. The Apostle then proceeds to show why Christians are dead to sin. "Know ye not," says he, "that so many of us as were baptized into Jesus CHRIST, were baptized *into his* DEATH?" Now, in order to make the Apostle consistent with himself, we must give this question such a construction as shall correspond with the preceding. The death of CHRIST, then, into which we are baptized, must be such a death as has been described—"*a death unto sin*." That this was the Apostle's meaning, he has expressly told us. Thus, in verse tenth, he says, "for, in that CHRIST died, *he died unto sin*;" when he proceeds to write the passage on which the argument turns: "Therefore, (that is, because *He died* unto sin,) we are buried with him BY baptism into *a death* to sin, that, like as Christ *was raised up* from the dead by the glory of the Father, even so we also should walk in newness of life." (Romans vi. 4.)*

That the whole *effect* of the death and burial here spoken of, is spiritual, no one denies; but some suppose there is here an allusion to *the mode* of administering baptism by immersion. The sense of the first part of this passage, according to this interpretation, is, "Therefore, as CHRIST was buried *in the earth*, so in a similar manner are we buried *in water* at our baptism." To this construction, there are several weighty objections.

(1.) The Greek word, translated "*buried with him*," (συνθάπτω,) will not admit that construction.† In the classic writers, the same word is used to denote being buried *in the*

* This verse is quoted by several of the ancient Baptismal Liturgies, but most of them omit the first part of it. Thus it is with the Greek, Syriac, Jerusalem, and Antiochan. Ass. II. 132, 139, 222, 250.

† Rob. Gr. Lex. p. 786. "Συν, in composition, implies society, companionship, consort, *with*, in connection with." Butt. Gr. Gram. § 147. 2. n. 11.

same grave, as when Herodotus says, "the wife *is buried with* the husband."* To give, therefore, the phrase, "buried *with* him," the sense of "buried *in like manner as* he was," when the *modes* of burial were unlike, is to change the meaning of the original, if not to make nonsense. Besides, if this verse determines *the mode* of baptism, it should also determine *the mode* of the resurrection, which no one pretends.

(2.) So also the prepositions employed in this narrative, contradict the interpretation sought to be put upon it. In the phrase, "buried with him *by* (δια) baptism," baptism is represented as *the instrument* BY *which* we are "buried," and not *the thing* IN *which* we are "buried." And, although in the corresponding passage in Col. ii. 12, the preposition *in* (εν) is employed, it is the *dative of the instrument*, and must bear the same construction.†

(3.) But, there is no such similarity as is claimed. The construction which supposes that the Apostle alluded to an actual, physical burial of the person under water, in the act of immersion, assumes, that the burial of CHRIST was like the ordinary burials of modern days, when the person *is covered with the earth* in which he is buried. Now CHRIST was not so buried, his body being simply laid in the chamber of "a sepulchre," (Luke xxiii. 33;) and there is no analogy whatever, between the act of laying away a body in the tomb, and the *act of plunging* the person under water, so that there is no such analogy between these acts, as this interpretation supposes.

* Her. v. 5. See also authorities cited Rob. Gr. Lex. *in loco.*

† In the *Peshito*—old Syriac version, dating from the beginning of the second century, the language is the same in both passages, and may be rendered either "buried with him BY baptism," as an instrument, or "buried with him *from* baptism," that is, "from *the time* of baptism."

(4.) The language used in the latter part of the same verse, is inconsistent with the idea that the Apostle had an actual, *physical burial* in his mind. By every rule of grammar and rhetoric, the different parts of a figure should correspond. Now, had the Apostle been intent on the *mode* of baptism, and known that mode was *immersion*, and from this drawn the metaphor in this verse, the least he could have said, would have been; "Therefore we are buried with him at our baptism into death, that in like manner as he was raised from the dead by the glory of the Father, so also we should be raised to newness of life." Hence it is evident, that it was not the *burial* on which the Apostle dwelt, but the *death to sin*, which every true believer undergoes. It should also be remarked, that if the Apostle had such a physical burial in his mind, as is pretended, then baptism must of necessity be a *saving ordinance*, that is, *the mere act of receiving baptism would procure pardon of sin.* This conclusion is inevitable, for, if "we are buried in water at baptism, *in order that* we may be raised to newness of life," then, such a burial, if it has its legitimate effect, must enable us to walk in that newness of life. Either, therefore, it must be allowed that baptism procures salvation for us, or the idea that a physical burial is denoted in this place, must be considered doubtful.

2. A similar form of expression occurs in Colossians, which, in connection with what precedes, reads as follows: "Ye are complete in CHRIST, who is the head of all principality and power; in whom also ye are circumcised with the circumcision made without hands, in putting off the body of the sins of the flesh, by the circumcision of CHRIST; *buried with him* IN *baptism*, wherein also ye are risen with him through the faith of the operation of God, who hath raised him from the dead." (Col. ii. 10–12.)

In these verses there is a direct reference to two distinct

rites, *circumcision* and *baptism;* and, consequently, both must be construed alike. Now it is sometimes claimed, that when the Apostle speaks of being "buried with him in baptism," he alludes to an actual and physical burial of the person under water. But we have already shown that this form of expression will not bear that construction. Besides, if the allusion to baptism is to be construed as having reference to a physical act representing the mode of baptism, then the allusion to the physical act of circumcision, must have a similar reference to the actual mode of performing it. This, however, can not be allowed, as the language of the Apostle confines the circumcision to a putting off, or more properly "a renunciation* (απεδυσει) of the sins of the flesh in (εν) the circumcision of CHRIST." Now there is no analogy between the *mode* of a physical and metaphorical, or spiritual circumcision; the whole resemblance being in its effects; for, as a physical circumcision is the taking away of the impurities of the natural man, so a spiritual circumcision is a putting away of the impurities of the spiritual man.†

The same rule of construction must be applied to the other part of the Apostle's argument, "buried with him in baptism." We are not, therefore, to understand him as alluding to a physical burial, as the unity of his argument will not allow it; but as referring to a spiritual burial "of the sins of the flesh," which were put off in our spiritual circumcision. No reference is, therefore, made to *the mode,* either of circumcision or baptism, *the effect* being the thing

---

* Rob. Gr. Lex. p. 74. Cyprian on this passage, says, "the former carnal circumcision is made void, and a second spiritual one assigned." Adv. Jud. i. 8.

† President Beecher has undertaken to show, that βαπτιζω in the New Testament, always signifies "to purify or cleanse thoroughly, without any reference to the mode in which it is done." Bib. Rep 2d series, III. pp. 40–66, 322–371; V. 24–47; VI. 28–55.

the Apostle intended to bring into view. But we are said in this place, not only to be buried with him, but also to be "*raised* with him." Now in no literal sense is it true that we are raised with him in baptism. If this might ever be true, it could not be admitted in this place, as the means *by* which, or the immediate and efficient cause *through* which, we are raised from this burial, is faith. "Buried with him in baptism; *wherein* ye are also *risen* with him *through* the faith of the operation of God." Here, then, we have a burial and resurrection answering to each other, and a resurrection purely *spiritual*, such as would follow the spiritual circumcision already described. Inasmuch then, as the resurrection was spiritual, the burial must have been spiritual; and, as no allusion is made to the mode of circumcision, we are not at liberty to infer, that any allusion is made to the mode of baptism. We see, therefore, that the phrase, "buried with him in baptism," does not, and can not authorize the inference, that baptism was performed by immersion.

We shall now proceed to examine the meaning of the phrases, "they went down into the water," and "they came up out of the water." As great stress is laid upon these forms of expression, to prove immersion the Apostolic mode of baptism, we shall briefly inquire whether they authorize the inference. It is sufficient in English to justify the expression, we "go into the water," that we merely step into the water. Indeed, our phrases, "he is in the water," and "he has gone into the water," do not, without some additional words, imply that the person is immersed, or put all over under water. So when a person who has stepped into the water, steps out again, he "comes out of the water," or, if he stepped into a brook, "he comes up out of the brook, or up out of the water." These are common-sense every-day modes of expression, found alike in the speech of the unlettered rustic, and the composition of the classic scholar. These forms of expression will not, therefore, sustain the interpretation sought to be given them, unless the genius and idiom of the Greek language differs from ours in this respect, concerning which we shall now inquire.

(1.) And first, does the phrase, "they went down *into* the water," denote that "they went down under the water?" To this inquiry there can be but one answer, and that in the negative. The Greek preposition *eis*, (εις,) denotes *into*, but never *under*. If, therefore, St. Luke had intended to say that the Eunuch was immersed, (Acts viii. 38,) he would have said, "he went down under the water," and not "into the water." But the narrative will not allow this alteration, for it is said, that "both went down into the water, both Philip and the Eunuch." If, therefore, the narrative proves the Eunuch went down under the water, it proves that Philip went down under the water, and that Philip was as really immersed as the Eunuch. Besides, *katabaino*, (καταβαινω,) from *baino*, "to go, or walk," and *kata*, "down," implies that they walked down into the water, as a person would now walk down into a brook, and that after having so walked into the water, Philip baptized the Eunuch, but whether by immersion or no, is not intimated.

(2.) Second, does the phrase, "they came *up out of* the water," denote that "they came *up from under* the water?" This question must also be answered in the negative, as αναβαινω, *to come up*, *to ascend*, is the opposite of καταβαινω, *to go down*, *to descend*; and, consequently, can denote only an *ascent*, from a *descent* previously made. Nor can the preposition (εκ) *out of*, *from*, authorize any other inference, for though used in Acts, (viii. 39,) in the account of the baptism of the Eunuch, its place is supplied in Matthew, (iii. 16,) in the account of the baptism of our Saviour, by *apo*, (απο,) which has the general meaning of *from*, *away* *from.** The passage in Matthew, (iii. 16,) therefore, might properly be translated: "And Jesus, when he was baptized, straightway *went up from* the water;"† that is, he ascended from the place where he stood when he was baptized, which might have been either on the bank of the Jordan, or in the edge of the river. But in neither case does it furnish any ground to infer an immersion. We have now examined all the strong arguments and proof texts, which are urged in favor of the exclusive validity of immersion, and have found, that not one of the arguments is sound, and not one of the positions tenable.

We come now to consider, The usage of the Primitive Christians, which is such as to negative the idea of immersion.

BARNABAS. One of the earliest Fathers, was Barnabas, supposed by many to be the Apostle Barnabas, probably without sufficient reason. He wrote, as appears from his epistle, (cited by Clement, of Alexandria,‡ and Tertullian, in the second century;§ by Origen,‖ in the third, and by many subsequent writers,) after the destruction of Jerusalem. The

---

* The Apostolic Liturgy, so called, in the Syriac, represents CHRIST at his baptism, as *standing* and "*bowing his head*" into the water. Ass. I. 257, II. 287. The monuments of the Greek Church represent CHRIST and John as *standing* in the water, and John *pouring* water on the head of Jesus. And in the old Syriac, the common language of Palestine in the time of our Saviour's sojourn here, the word denoting *baptism*, (ܥܡܕ,) was a root which signified *to stand*, in all the kindred languages. Heb. עמד—Arab. عمد. Hence Michaelis (Ed. Castell. Syr. Lex.) and Gesenius (Hebrew Thesaurus) suppose it was so called, because the candidate *stood* in the margin of the water, when baptized

† The *Peshito*—old Syriac, is clearly to this purport; the verb (ܣܠܩ) signifying *to go up*, in the sense of the Hebraism, "*he went up* into the mountain—his own house—Jerusalem—Antioch," &c. &c.

‡ Strom. ii. p. 410. Strom. v. p. 571.

§ De Pud. c. 20. ‖ Cont. Cel. I.

whole of his epistle is in a strain of allegory; but we copy all that has any bearing on the mode of baptism.

"Let us now inquire whether the Lord foretold any thing of the water and the cross. Now of the water, it is written to Israel, how that they would not receive that *baptism*, (βαπτισμα,) which brings to remission of sins, but would institute another to themselves; as saith the Prophet: 'Be astonished, O Heaven! and let the earth tremble at it, because this people have done two great and wicked things; they have left me the living fountain, and dug for themselves broken cisterns.'" (c. 10.)

In this place, *baptism* has no direct reference to any mode of washing, but refers to the partaking of that "*well* or *fountain of living water*," of which every man, who desires eternal life, *must drink*. (John iv. 10–15.) If it has any indirect reference to the mode of washing, it is to those ceremonial washings denoting purification. That these were not performed by immersion, is evident from Barnabas, as well as from what we have before said on this point. In c. 8, he explains the Jewish mode of purification, described in Numbers, (xix.) Thus, he says, "The heifer to be offered by wicked men, is JESUS CHRIST; but the young men [in Numb. xix. the clean men] that performed the *sprinkling*, (ραντιζοντες,) [i. e. of the people, that they should be clean from their sins,] signify those who preach to us the remission of sins and the purification of the heart, to whom the Lord gave authority to preach his gospel, being at the beginning, twelve."

Here we have "remission of sins and purification of heart," wrought by "the *sprinkling* of the twelve," that is, Apostles. So in c. 5, (of the Old Latin Version, the Greek of that place being lost,) it is said, that "the Lord gave his body to destruction, that we might be sanctified, through the remission of sins, which is by the *sprinkling* (*sparsione*) of is blood." In all these cases "remission of sins and purication of heart," are said to be wrought by *sprinkling*; and as these purifications are also called *baptisms*, the inference is, that, in the days of Barnabas, *baptism was performed by sprinkling*, or, as the words may signify, *by pouring*. There are, however, two other passages in the Epistle of this writer, which have been claimed in favor of immersion, and we give them both entire:

"Consider how he has joined the cross and the water, for this he saith: Blessed are they who when they have trusted in the cross, *descend into the water*. . . . . And there was a river running on the right hand, and beautiful trees grew up by it, and he that shall eat of them shall live forever. The signification of which is, that we descend into the water full of sins and pollutions, but *ascend*, bearing fruit, having in our hearts hope and fear in Jesus by the Spirit." (c. 10.)

In respect to the sentences in these extracts printed in italics, we need only say, that they are quoted from Acts, (viii. 38, 39,) where this language is applied to both Philip and the Eunuch, and must, therefore, be construed in a similar manner. We need, therefore, only refer our readers to the remarks made upon that place, to show that they do not denote immersion. We add, however, the remark; these phrases authorize us to infer that the candidate took his stand on, or probably in, the edge of the water, when the water was poured upon him, as we have seen was probable from the Scripture account.

Hermas. Another allegorical writer of the early ages of Christianity, was Hermas. He has been supposed by some to belong to the first century; but this is probably a mistake. He seems to have written a little before the middle of the second century. He represents the Church under the similitude of "a great tower built upon the water, with bright square stones."* The building of the tower he describes as performed by six young men, or angels; who first "drew up from the deep, stones so well polished, that they exactly fitted together, so that the tower seemed to be built of one stone."† The stones thus drawn up from the deep, denoted men of the former ages, "who died in righteousness and great purity, only the seal [of baptism] was wanting to them, without which they could not enter the kingdom of God."‡ With them ascended certain other stones, representing the Apostles and teachers, "who [having received the seal of the Son of God, and] dying after they had received his faith and power, preached to them who were dead, and gave them the same seal," that is, "the seal of baptism." These [i. e. the Apostles and teachers] went down into the water with them, [i. e. those who died in righteousness and great purity,] and again came up. But these [the Apostles, &c.] went down alive, and came up alive; whereas those who were before dead, went down dead, but came up alive."§

Thus far, there is nothing which at first sight appears to bear directly upon the question under consideration. Yet it is not irrelevant, for we see that those righteous men who died before the coming of Christ, are represented as descending into the water, *dead*, that is, not having received the seal of the Son of God in baptism; while the "Apostles who had received this seal, it is said, descended into the water alive," and then administered the rite to those who had gone down dead. From this, therefore, we learn that the "descent into the water," was not, in the opinion of Hermas, *baptism*. This is also in conformity with the baptism of the Eunuch by Philip. In the language of Hermas, Philip, who had received the seal of the Son of God in the ordinance of bap-

* L. i. Vis. iii. c. 2, 3.
† L. i. Vis. iii. c. 2, L. iii. Sim. ix. c. 16.
‡ L. iii. Sim. ix. c. 16.
§ L. iii. Sim. ix. c. 16.

tism, and was therefore alive, went down into the water with the Eunuch, who, not having received that seal, was dead; and while both were in the water, the rite of baptism was administered. In both of these cases, the descent into the water was no part of the baptism.

The building of the tower proceeded thus far, when "the stones ceased to ascend from the deep, and they which built, rested a little. Then those six men commanded the multitude that they should bring stones out of the mountains for the building of the tower. So they cut out stones of divers colors, from all the mountains, and brought them to the virgins, which, when they received, being [round, were cut away and made square,* and delivered to] those who built the tower."† But the stones which had been so cut, and which represented the persons then living, and who were to compose a part of the tower of the Church, were required "to be cleansed before they could be put in the building,"‡ which was done by the virgins, as follows: "Then those virgins took besoms, and cleared all the place around, and took away all the rubbish, and *sprinkled* (*sparserunt*) water, and the place became delightful, and the tower beauteous."§

Here we have a cleansing, which can be applied only to baptism, performed by sprinkling, or pouring, *spargo* being capable of both senses. As far, therefore, as any inference can be drawn as to the mode of baptism, it is in favor of applying the instrument used in performing the rite, to the person, and not of applying the person to the instrument, as is done in cases of submersion. There are, however, a couple of passages which are usually cited in favor of immersion; both of which are quotations of the language of the Acts, (viii. 38, 39,) already spoken of, and must, there-

* L. i. Vis. iii c. 6.

† L. iii. Sim. ix. c. 4.

‡ L. iii. Sim. ix. c. 7.

§ L. iii. Sim. ix. c. 10.

fore, be construed in accordance with what has already been said of that place. We give them that our readers may see all the evidence on which the claim of the exclusive validity of immersion rests. The first passage* is used in reference to the righteous men who died before the coming of CHRIST, of which we have already spoken.

"Before a man receives the name of the Son of GOD, he is ordained unto death, but when he receives that seal, he is freed from death, and assigned unto life. Now that seal is the water, into which men descend ordained unto death, but ascend assigned unto life."

The other passage is in the Commands,† "I have heard from certain teachers that there is no other repentance than that, when we descend into the water and receive remission of sins." Now as the whole of Hermas is allegorical, it is not certain that the water is to be understood literally; the more so, as the water into which men are represented as descending, is that "by which their lives are saved."‡ Besides, the descent into the water is not baptism, in the language of Hermas, as he speaks of men descending into the water who had not received the seal of baptism, and of others descending, who had received that seal.§ There is not, therefore, in these passages, any thing which at all militates against the conclusion before drawn from the language of Hermas.

JUSTIN MARTYR. Next to Hermas, and probably cotemporary with him, was the learned and accomplished JUSTIN, the Martyr. He was a native and resident of Syria, acquainted with the common or spoken Greek of Palestine, and had been educated in the most refined schools of classic literature. He is, therefore, an important witness as to the

* L. iii. Sim. ix. c. 16.

† L. ii. Com. iv. c. 3.

‡ L. i. Vis. iii. c. 3.

§ L. iii. Sim. ix. c. 16.

mode of baptism. The most full description he has given, is contained in his first Apology, or *Defence of the Christian Religion*, addressed to the Roman Emperor, about A. D. 150.*

"We then lead them [the candidates for baptism] to a place where there is water, and they are regenerated, (αναγεννεω,) in the same mode of regeneration as we were regenerated; for they *are washed* (λουτρον) in water, in the name of GOD, the Father and Lord of the Universe, and of the Son, and of the HOLY GHOST; for CHRIST has said, except ye *be regenerated*, (αναγεννεω,) ye can not enter into the kingdom of GOD." He also quotes, in immediate connection with this, and as bearing directly upon the same point, Isaiah i. 16: "*Wash you*, (λουω,) make you clean." "And this *washing*," (λουτρον,) he says,† is "called illumination."

That this is a description of baptism, admits not of doubt, and there is a remark which naturally arises from the language of Justin, too important to be omitted in this place. It is claimed and admitted, that, *in classic* Greek, *baptizo*, more generally denotes a washing performed by applying the thing baptized to the element in which the baptism was performed, and that *louo* is the proper word to be used to signify washing of a general nature, or, more properly, when it is performed by applying the water to the person washed. Now as Justin was a thorough classic scholar, and also familiar with the spoken Greek of Palestine, it is evident that he is the most competent witness that can be produced, concerning the common meaning of *baptizo*, in Palestinian Greek, in accordance with which it is used in Scripture, as is now admitted by all critics.‡

---

* We quote from p. 94 of the Paris edition; p. 89 in the edition of Thirlby, Lond. 1722, c. 79, translation of Chevalier.

† Page 94, or 90, and c. 80.

‡ Stuart Gr. Gram. N. T. Gerard, Inst. Bib. Crit. P. I. c. i. § 5.

The first thing to be observed, is, that Justin, in writing to the Roman Emperor Pius, who was also versed in classic Greek, but knew nothing of any peculiarities of the Palestinian, never uses *baptizo*, to denote baptism, which word, as understood by the Emperor, would signify, that the candidate was put into the water; but always uses *louo*, from which he would understand that the water was applied to the person. Hence, if baptism was performed by immersion in the days of Justin, he intentionally avoided language which would have been understood, and used such as he knew would mislead, and that, when he could gain nothing by it, and could have no motive to do it. Not so when he writes against Jews, familiar with all the peculiarities of the dialects of Palestine; for in his *Dialogue with Trypho the Jew*, he uses *baptizo* and *louo* as synonymous terms.* The authority of Justin, therefore, sustains the conclusion drawn from our examination of the Scripture lexical usage, that *baptizo* and *louo*, in the common Greek of Palestine, were words of similar import; and hence the use of this word in Scripture, to denote baptism, can not even raise a presumption in favor of *immersion*.†

There is another passage in Justin, still more decisive; in which he declares that baptism was performed by sprinkling. To a full understanding of the passage, we must bear in mind, that Justin, in his *Apology*, was attempting to show, that the various heathen mysteries were *imitations* of

---

* This will be seen by comparing pp. 163, 164, 173, 174, 193, 194, Lond. Ed.; pp. 231, 232, 236, 246, Par. Ed.

† The old Syriac word for *baptism*, ([illegible],) had also a *peculiar usage*, as will be seen when we come to speak of the Syriac translations of βαπτιζω. The first distinct trace of baptism by immersion, is in Cyril, about A. D. 330, who employs the word καταδυνω, instead of βαπτιζω, and gives as a reason, that we *submerge* three times, because CHRIST was in the earth three nights. Cat. ii. 286.

the rites and ordinances instituted by GOD; that "they erroneously imitated what was really performed, because they did not perfectly understand the prophecy."* Thus he says, the story of the ascent of Bacchus and Bellerophon into heaven, were *imitations* of the prophecies concerning CHRIST; also, that some of the stories of Hercules and Esculapius,† were copied from the character of the same being. So also he says, that the *demons* raised up false Christs, to deceive the people,‡ and that the practices of the priests were imitations of what Moses did.§ Hence, he says: "It is not, therefore, that we hold the same opinion with others, but that all others speak *in imitation* (μιμουμενοι) of ours."‖ Then, after giving the account of baptism, quoted above, he says:

"This *washing* (λουτρον) is called illumination, since the minds of those who are thus instructed, are enlightened. And he who is so enlightened, *is washed*, (λουω,) [i. e. *baptized*,] also in the name of JESUS CHRIST, who was crucified under Pontius Pilate, and in the name of the HOLY GHOST, who, by the prophets, foretold all things concerning Jesus. The demons, also, who heard that this *washing*, (λουτρον,) [i. e. of *baptism*,] was predicted by the prophet, caused, that those who entered into their holy places, and were about to approach them, to offer libations and the fat of victims, should *sprinkle* (ραντιζω) themselves."

Two things are asserted by Justin, in this place: (1,) that the baptism of demons was *by sprinkling*, and, (2,) that this was *in imitation of Christian baptism*. Hence, it follows, that *Christian baptism was sometimes at least performed by sprinkling*.¶ Justin also distinguishes the "going down into the

---

* C. 70. † C. 71. ‡ Cc. 73, 75. § C. 81.

‖ C. 78, p. 93. Par. Ed., Apol. I.

¶ St. Cyprian, A. D. 256, says, the sacrament is equally efficacious, whether the person be plunged in water, or whether it be sprinkled upon him. Ep. 66.

6

water," from the baptism. Thus he says, that "Jesus coming to the river Jordan where John was baptizing, he (John) went down with Jesus into the water."*

CLEMENT of Alexandria, about A. D. 190. The works of this Father, that have come down to us, contain very little on this subject. But what they do contain, is in accordance with the testimony of Justin. Thus, when speaking of the symbolical meaning of the external rites of religion, he says:† "But the purification we are to seek and observe, is that of a holy heart. That also, of which *baptism* (βαπτισμα) was the image, and which Moses taught the Poets, was in in this wise:

"'When she *had washed herself* (υδραινο) in water, having ornaments in all her garments, Penelope came to prayers.'

"'And Telemachus, *having washed his hands* (νιπτω) in the sea, offered vows to Minerva.'

"This was the custom of the Jews; and often they *baptized* (βαπτιζω) in bed. Well, therefore, is it said, 'Be not *washed* (λουτρω) in body, but in mind.'" And in another place, he says:‡ "But if he [CHRIST] was perfect, wherefore, then, was he *baptized*, (βαπτιζω)? It became him, say they, to fulfil the human profession. Well, I concede this. As soon, therefore, as he was *baptized* (βαπτιζω) by John, he was perfected? True. Then he learned nothing more from him? Nothing. He was complete, save only *washing*, (λουτρω,) and the Spirit coming, he was sanctified." This indiscriminate use of *louo*, *nipto*, *loutro*, and *baptizo*, and the application of this latter word to all the Jewish washings, is conclusive evidence that Clement did not suppose the word *baptizo* to signify immersion only, and that he used it in the same general sense in which Justin employed it.

---

* Dial. Tryph. P. II. p. 331. † Strom. iv. 531. ‡ Pædag. i. 6.

TERTULLIAN. We proceed to examine Tertullian on *the mode* of baptism. But, before we do this, we must premise: (1.) Though the earliest of the Latin Fathers, Tertullian was a Carthagenian by birth, and Latin was not his mother tongue. Consequently, we can not look for that nice discrimination in the choice of words, we should naturally expect in a native Latin. (2.) Another cause of obscurity in the writings of Tertullian, is to be found in the character of his figures, which are often far-fetched and unnatural, and frequently clothed in high-sounding, pompous epithets.* (3.) Tertullian led the way in adapting the Christian literature of the Greeks, to the genius of the Latin tongue.†

Tertullian uses several words to denote baptism. (1.) When quoting from the Bible, where the original is *baptizo*, he either transfers the word, or uses *tingo*, which, Valpy‡ says, signifies *to wet, dye, tinge, stain.*§ Thus, in citing the command to the Apostles, "commanding that they *should baptize* (*tinguerent*) in the name of the Father, and of the Son, and of the HOLY GHOST."|| (2.) When speaking of baptism, and not quoting from the Bible, he uses *tingo* much oftener than any other word.¶ Occasionally he uses *lavo,*

---

* Dupin. Hist. Ecc. Writ. I. p. 83. † Gies. Ecc. Hist. Div. iii. § 64.

‡ Etym. Dic. p. 475.

§ And Forcellini, an Italian lexicographer, of the Latin tongue, (Lat. Dic., 2 vols. 4to. Lond., 1828,) defines it by *to dip, immerse, wet, moisten, bathe,* and gives us its equivalent in Greek, τεγγω, βρεχω, υδραινω, βαπτω. The same author defines *mergo,* "to dip, plunge, sink, immerse, and overwhelm."

|| Adv. Prax. c. 26, &c.

¶ Tertullian's favorite word was *tingo,* probably from the idea that *baptism* impressed upon us a new and peculiar *hue* or *color* of character. Indeed, this opinion is found in all the African writers, as Tertullian, Cyprian, and Augustine. See Tert. *On Baptism;* Cyp. *On the Grace of God,* 2. 3; *Testimonies against the Jews,* iii. 25–28; Bing. xi. 1. § 7. The same idea also occurs in the Ethiopian version of the Scriptures.

"to wash, bathe, sprinkle;" *mergo*, "to sink, or plunge," according to classic usage—but *to wash* simply, in vulgar Latin, to which Tertullian approximates; and *abluo*, "to wash, to purify." (3.) He also denotes baptism by *aspergo*, "to sprinkle."* Thus, speaking of the hypocrisy of those who desired baptism without true repentance, he says; "No man should grant to such false penitents, one *sprinkling* (*asperginem*) of water."† A similar usage occurs in cc. 5, 12, of his treatise *On Baptism*. From all this, the necessary inferences are, that Tertullian does not use the Latin language with perfect classic certainty; and that the practice in regard to baptism, in his time, was various—the quantity of water being considered unessential. This is a fact, expressly asserted by Tertullian. Thus,‡ "There is no difference whether we are *washed* (diluvatur) in the *sea*, (mari,) or a *pond*, (stagno,) in a *river*, (flumine,) or *spring*, (fonte,) in a *standing pool*, (lacu,) or *running brook*, (alves.) Nor is there any difference between those whom John *baptized* (tinxit) in Jordan, and Peter in the Tiber!" This language of Tertullian is the more conclusive, as he seems to have placed a higher estimate upon the effect of baptism, than was authorized by the Church at that time.

We have now, we believe, examined every passage in the Scriptures, and every passage in the Fathers of the two first centuries, that bears upon the mode of baptism, and upon a review of the whole evidence on this subject, we are authorized to say, that there is not, either in the Bible, or the writings of the Christians to the end of the second century, any thing which will establish the claim that baptism was performed by the Apostles and Primitive Christians by immersion, in the modern sense of the word.

---

* And so does Cyprian, his disciple. Ep. 69, § 11–15.

† De Pœnit. c. 6.

‡ De Bap. c. 4.

CHAPTER VII.

SUBJECTS OF BAPTISM.

THAT believing adults are proper subjects of baptism, all allow. But is baptism to be administered to any but adults? To this, some reply in the negative; we, in the affirmative. We proceed, therefore, to the proof.

1. "Go ye, therefore, teach all nations, baptizing them in the name of the Father, and of the Son, and of the HOLY GHOST; teaching them to observe all things whatsoever I have commanded you." (Matt. xxviii. 19, 20.)

In this commission, three things are to be observed:—

(1.) The Apostles were *to teach* all nations.

(2.) They were *to baptize* all nations.

(3.) They were *to teach* all nations whatsoever had been commanded them.

In reference to the *teaching* all nations, we observe, that the original (μαθητευω) does not signify *to teach*, in the present sense of that word. Its proper signification is, if we may be allowed the word, *to disciple*. This may be done, in some measure, by teaching and instructing, and generally, though not necessarily, implies some degree of it. The *teaching*, however, mentioned under the third head, (διδασκω,) is distinct from that under the first head, and denotes that kind of instruction given by a master to his pupils. A literal rendering of the foregoing passage, would be: "Go ye, *disciple* all nations, *baptizing* them in the name of the Father, and of the Son, and of the HOLY GHOST; *teaching* them to observe all things whatsoever I have commanded you."

From this it is evident, that the first clause, "*disciple* all nations," includes, in *general* terms, what is more *particu-*

larly pointed out in both of the others; that is, "*baptizing*" and "*teaching*," as the means of making disciples. The first idea which occurs upon reading this passage, is, that it is not to be understood in its most literal sense, as no one pretends that "all nations" were to be baptized in a mass or body. We are therefore obliged to seek some rule of interpretation, which will enable us to give it a consistent and reasonable construction. The rule must also be one which will apply both to *baptizing* and *teaching*, as both are clothed in the same general terms. Some construe the command to mean; "Teach all *who are capable of being taught*, and baptize *those whom* ye teach." But this is framing a rule applicable only to one clause; and, from the construction of that clause, deducing a rule by which to construe the other. We are willing to abide the rule of interpretation our opponents have framed, if they will be consistent, and apply it to all the clauses, in the order in which they are given by the Evangelist. It will then read: "Go ye, disciple all *that are capable of being discipled;* baptizing all *who are capable of receiving baptism*, and teaching all *who are capable of being taught.*"

If this be the meaning of the passage, it does not devolve upon those who believe in the necessity and authority of *infant baptism*, to do more than show that *infants are capable of receiving baptism;* a point so self-evident, that those who deny it assume the burden of proof; for, though it is a sound rule, that no man shall be bound to prove the negative of a *general* proposition, it is no less a sound rule, that he who limits the language of such a proposition, must prove the limitation. If, then, it be affirmed that infants are *not* included in this general language, it is the duty of those who make the affirmation, to prove its truth. And if they can not prove its truth, then infant baptism is not only lawful, but is commanded. The language of St. Mark clearly sustains this conclusion:—"Go ye into all the world, and preach the gospel *unto every creature*," that is, *to all human creatures*. (Mark xvi. 15.)

2. The next passage which authorizes "infant baptism" is; "Suffer little children to come unto me, and forbid them not, for of such is the kingdom of heaven." (Matt. xix. 14; Mark x. 14; Luke xviii. 16.) It is worthy of remark, as a singular, as well as an unusual coincidence, that the three Evangelists considered this passage of sufficient importance to be recorded at full length in each of their gospels, and all have given it in the same language, except that Mark and Luke have "the kingdom of God," instead of "the kingdom of heaven." Upon this, two questions arise:—

(1.) What is meant by "the kingdom of heaven?"

(2.) And what, by coming to Christ?

First, what is meant by "the kingdom of God," and "the kingdom of heaven," in these passages? These phrases may denote two things—either the Church Triumphant above, or the Church Militant on earth, or both together. As to the first of these significations, there will be no doubt; nor is there any more room for doubt as to the second, as we have already shown, in a former chapter. It is clear, therefore, that by the phrase, "the kingdom of heaven," and "the kingdom of God," the Church on earth *may* be meant. Whether that be the meaning in this passage, depends upon the construction to be put upon it, to which we shall soon refer.

Second, what is meant by coming to Christ? The answer to this, as to the other inquiry, is twofold. We are said "to come to Christ," when we submit ourselves to him, giving up our souls and bodies to him and to his service, by repentance, faith, and obedience. We are also said to come to

CHRIST, when we enroll our names upon the list of his professed disciples and followers, by publicly professing his name before men. No man can come to CHRIST in the first of these senses, except by that true and living faith, which qualifies for admission into the New Jerusalem above; but many come to CHRIST, by such a public profession of his name, and thus enter the Church on earth, who are nevertheless to be reckoned among the *bad,* who, when "the net is drawn ashore," will be cast away. If, therefore, by "the kingdom of heaven," in the foregoing places, the Church on earth is meant, then coming to CHRIST in baptism, must be the mode designated, and if this mode of coming to CHRIST be the one intended, then the Church on earth must be the one referred to.

Now nothing can be plainer, than that *little children* were "to come to CHRIST," and that such were to enter into "the kingdom of heaven." If, then, by "the kingdom of heaven" is meant *the Church,* it follows necessarily, that they were to enter the Church *by baptism;* for it is admitted by all, that baptism is the only rite of initiation into the Church. Hence, if it be shown that a person has received baptism, then we know that he is a member of the Church; or if it be shown that a person is a member of the Church, then we know that he has been baptized. If, then, it be shown that children are members of the Church, or are considered fit subjects to become members, then we have shown that they have been baptized, or are fit subjects for baptism. It follows, therefore, from the foregoing passages, either that children are to come to CHRIST by being received into his Church by baptism; or that being *unworthy* to join the Church Militant, they are to be transported immediately to the abodes of blessedness, in the Church Triumphant—a conclusion they can not avoid. Unless, then, we are willing to abide this absurdity, we must allow that little children are to be made members of the Church, and that *infant baptism* is, therefore, commanded.*

3. The foregoing passages prove that little children were to receive the ordinance of baptism; we shall now show that they actually were baptized in the days of the Apostles. Thus, St. Paul says to the Corinthians; "The unbelieving husband is sanctified by the wife, and the unbelieving wife is sanctified by the husband; else were your children unclean, but now are they holy." (1 Cor. vii. 14.) It is admitted by all, that this passage is not to be interpreted in its most *literal* sense, as those words are now understood, for then the faith of the wife would become the faith of the husband, and the faith of the husband would become the faith of the wife, and the faith of either would become the faith of the whole family, so that the whole family would be finally saved by the faith of one of its members, which is not only absurd, but contrary to the declarations of Scripture.

It will assist us in the interpretation of this text, to ascertain what the Apostle took for granted, and what he desired to prove. When, therefore, the Apostle says; "The unbelieving husband is sanctified by the wife, and the unbelieving wife is sanctified by the husband; else were your children unclean, but now are they holy," he assumes, that "children whose parents were both believers, were sanctified, or holy," and reasoning from that assumption, assures the Corinthians, that "children who had one believing parent, were placed in the same situation; else, (επει,) *for otherwise*,† they would be *unclean*, that is, *unsanctified* and *unholy*." Our first inquiry must be, therefore, what is the Scriptural meaning of

* This passage was so universally understood to apply to baptism, in the days of Tertullian, that he felt himself called upon to explain it away. De Bap. c. 18. See Apos. Cons. vi. 15.

† Rob. Gr. Lex. p. 296; Butt. Gr. Gram. § 149.

agiazo, (αγιαζω,) *to sanctify?* and *agios*, (αγιος,) "*holy?*" and when, and in what sense, could the children of believing parents be said to be sanctified?

(1.) What is the meaning of *agiazo*, "to sanctify?" The usual signification of this word is, *to set apart*, or *consecrate to the service of* God. Thus, in Matthew, (xxiii. 17, 19:) "Whether is greater, the gold, or the temple that sanctifieth the gold." So St. Paul addresses his Epistle; "Unto the Church of God which is at Corinth, unto them that are sanctified in Christ Jesus." (1 Cor. i. 2.) And again he says to the same Church; "But ye *are washed*, (απολουω,) i. e. in baptism, but ye *are sanctified*, i. e. set apart, or consecrated to the service of God by baptism." (1 Cor. vi. 11.) Neither of these passages from Corinthians, can be confined to that sanctification of heart, which is wrought "by the renewing of the Holy Ghost;" for both are addressed to all the individuals composing the Church at Corinth, among whom were *some* bad men, as we learn from the epistle itself. Another, and a more conclusive proof, that this word does not mean purification of heart alone, is to be found in the fact, that the same language is applied to Christ himself; "Say ye of him, whom the Father hath sanctified, and sent into the world." (John x. 36.) In no sense could Christ be said *to be sanctified*, except as he was set apart to the office of Mediator, &c. This is indeed its more usual sense, both in the New Testament and in the Septuagint, where it is used for the Hebrew קדש, "*to consecrate, to make holy by consecration.*" The language of St. Paul "to the *saints* at Ephesus," is decisive on this point:—That he *might sanctity* (αγιαζω) and cleanse it *with the washing* (λουτρο) of water." (Eph. v. 26.) This can mean nothing but baptism, and hence, when *agiazo* is applied to the members of the Church collectively, including, of course, the good and bad members, it means that they have been *sanctified*, i. e. ***set apart to the*** *worship and service of* GOD BY BAPTISM.*

The same conclusion must be drawn from an examination of the word *agios*. This word, says Tittman,† "is rarely or never used by the Greek writers, for that purity of mind, which theologians have called sanctity, but it constantly denotes that which is consecrated to the Gods." In the New Testament it is applied to both persons and things. As the Prophets, (Luke i. 70; Acts iii. 21; 2 Peter i. 21;) to the priesthood of the Christian, (1 Peter ii. 5;) to the Apostles, (Eph. iii. 5;) to the Angels, (Matt. xxv. 31;) to places, (Acts vii. 33;) and especially to Jerusalem, (Matt. iv. 5;) to the Temple, (1 Cor. iii. 17;) and also to all who professed the Christian name. (Acts ix. 13, 32, 41; xxvi. 10; Rom. i. 7; viii. 27.) It is clear, therefore, that the children of Christians were holy, and, as must follow from these considerations, in the sense of having been consecrated to GOD.

(2.) Our next inquiry is, how the children of believing parents had been sanctified. They were certainly not sanctified "by the renewing of the HOLY GHOST," in consequence of the faith of either or both of the parents; nor were they sanctified in the sense of being consecrated to GOD, by the simple act of the parents' faith. Something more is necessary, as a sanctification or consecration requires a public act of dedication to GOD, which, in reference to Christians, is done in baptism. But still, the sanctification of the children, is said by the Apostle to be in consequence of the faith of the parent. Now the parent could in no way sanctify the child, except by offering him, through faith in the LORD JESUS, in the ordinance of baptism, that he might be sanctified; that

---

* Origin says, Ep. Rom. v. 9, "The Church derived from the Apostles the tradition to give baptism to infants." See also Hom. Lev. viii. 3.

† Synom. N. T. c. 2, p. 37.

is, be set apart and consecrated to the service of God, in that holy rite. Our only alternative, therefore, is to conclude that the Apostle uses the same language in the same sense here as elsewhere in his epistles, and if he does so, then this passage contains an unequivocal declaration of the blessed Apostle Paul, that the children of the Corinthian Christians had received the ordinance of baptism.

In accordance with this conclusion, is the language of St. Paul, Eph. vi. 1, and Col. iii. 20, "Children, obey your parents in the Lord," etc., thereby showing that these were included in the number of "the saints" to which these epistles were addressed, (Eph. ii. 1, Col. i. 1,) and must, therefore, have been baptized.

CHAPTER VIII.

SUBJECTS OF BAPTISM CONTINUED.

To the Scriptural evidence on this subject, we shall add the testimony of the earliest Fathers.

Hermas describes the subsequent conduct of all who had received this rite, under the similitude of twelve mountains. The *first* mountain was "black," and was composed of "those who had revolted from the faith, that is, had apostatized, for whom there was no repentance."* The *second* was "smooth," and composed of "hypocrites, for whom there was no repentance."† The *third* was "covered with thorns and brambles," and was composed "of those who had been choked with the affairs of the world, to whom a "space for repentance was allowed."‡ The *fourth* had herbs, "with

* L. iii. Sim. ix. c. 19. † C. 19. ‡ C. 20.

dry roots and green tops, which withered in the sun," and denoted the "doubtful, who live in words, but are dead in works." To these "space of repentance was also given."* The *fifth* was "steep and craggy, but had green grass," and signifies "those who believed and were faithful, but were bold and self-conceited."† The *sixth* was "filled with small clefts," and denoted those "who had had controversies among themselves, by reason of which their faith languished."‡ The *seventh* "was green and flourishing," and denoted "those who were always good and upright."§ The *eighth* was "filled with abundance of springs, by which all creatures of God were watered," and denoted "the faithful teachers of the word of God."‖ The *ninth* "was desert, and covered with serpents," and denoted such "ministers as had discharged their ministry amiss," but to whom "space of repentance was allowed."¶ The *tenth* was "covered with trees affording shade for the cattle," which were "the faithful Bishops and Governors of the Church."** The *eleventh* had "trees of divers sorts of fruits," and denoted "those who had suffered for the name of the Lord."†† The *twelfth* mountain was *white*, and denoted "such as have believed as sincere *children, into whose thoughts no malice ever came, who had never known what sin was, but had always continued in their integrity.* Wherefore this kind of mortals shall without doubt enter into the kingdom of God."‡‡ "Wherefore because those who had believed of that mountain were very innocent, the Lord of the tower commanded that they which were of the roots of this mountain should be placed in the building; for he knew that if they were put into the building, they would continue bright, nor would any of them become black."§§

* C. 21. † C. 22. ‡ C. 23. § C. 24. ‖ C. 25.
¶ C. 26. ** C. 27. †† C. 28. ‡‡ C. 29. §§ C. 30.

We have given a full account of these symbolical mountains, that our readers might see for themselves, that the *twelfth* mountain is descriptive only of children, and can denote nothing but children and infants, who, having received the seal of baptism, died before they had known sin. Hence it follows, that *children and infants, in the days of Hermas, received the rite of baptism, and that, too, by sprinkling or pouring.* When this rite was administered to adults, the candidates seem to have stood in the edge of the water, if they were baptized in a brook or river, or by the side of the water in other cases, when the water was poured upon them.

JUSTIN MARTYR. There is one passage in Justin, which the principles of just criticism require us to apply to *infants*, as subjects of baptism. Thus he says: "There are many of both sexes, sixty or seventy years of age, who *had been discipled* (μαθητευω) to CHRIST in *childhood*, (παις.)"*

To this it is objected by some; (1,) That *pais* does not always signify *children*, but sometimes youths, and that these might have been made disciples upon their own faith. We grant that *pais* does not necessarily, though it does usually, signify a child, in the *strictest* sense of the word, but it is admitted that it is nearly or quite equivalent to *child*, according to its common meaning. The word *childhood*, therefore, by which we have rendered *pais*, is the true meaning of the original. They also object, (2,) That *to disciple*, does not mean *to baptize*, and does not necessarily imply that *baptism* was performed in childhood. In answer to this objec-

* P. 22, Lond. Ed. p. 62, Par. Ed. c. 18, Trans. Chevalier. In the old Syriac version of the New Testament, the vernacular of Justin, and which was made some time before he wrote, this word, παις, in Matt. xix. 14, Mark x. 14, Luke xviii. 16, is rendered ܛܠܝܐ, (*thalo*,) which, according to Castell and Michaelis, signifies, "infans, puer, adolescens, parvulus."

tion, we may say, *first;* It is evident, *if* they had been baptized, they were baptized when they were discipled, which no one doubts; and, *second,* The language does imply that they had become Christians, and, consequently, must have received the rite of baptism.

IRENÆUS, bishop of Lyons, in Gaul, lived and wrote about A. D. 175. His work *Against Heresy,* has ever been held in high repute. He says:* "CHRIST came to save all persons by himself; all, I mean, who are *regenerated* (*renascuntur,* i. e. baptized†) unto GOD; *infants,* (*infantes,*) and *little ones,* (*parvulos,*) and *children,* (*pueros,*) and *young persons,* (*juvenes,*) and *old persons,* (*seniors.*) Therefore he went through all ages; and for infants, became an infant, that he might sanctify infants; and for little ones, became a little one, that he might sanctify those of that age; and also give them an example of goodness, justice, and dutifulness."

The only objection which it has been possible to raise against this passage, is to doubt whether it has reference to baptism. But such an objection can have no force, even with the merest tyro in ecclesiastical history. Those who are not familiar with it, we refer to the language of Justin, above quoted, and to the following, from Irenæus:‡ "And because the renunciation of *baptism*—of *that regeneration* (baptismatis ejus regenerationis) which is unto GOD." And,§

---

* L. ii. c. 39.

† On the meaning of *renascor,* see Orig. ad Rom. 6. Cyp. Ep. Ad. Fidum, Cyr. Jerus. Cat. Mys. 1. Greg. Naz. Orat. Sanc. Lav. Basil Exhor. Bap. and Chrys. Jerom. Augus. Theod. &c. Also, all the ancient Baptismal Liturgies, as, Lit. Ant. Ass. II. 220, Armenian, Ib. II. 198, Apos. Jerus. Ib. II. 266, Alex. Copt. Ib. II. 165, Old Gallic, Ib. II. 42, Syriac, Ib. II. 258, &c. The difficulty is not to find proof in favor of this interpretation, but to find authorities against it.

‡ L. i. c. 18.

§ L. iii. c. 19.

"CHRIST gave his disciples the power *of regeneration* (regenerationis) into GOD, saying to them, 'Go, teach all nations, baptizing them,'" &c.

We must here add a word concerning the knowledge of Justin and Irenæus upon these subjects, and of the means they had of acquainting themselves with the practices of the Apostolic age. Justin tells us, that when he wrote, A. D. 150, persons were living seventy years of age, who became Christians in their childhood. Such persons must have been born as early as A. D. 80, or twenty years before the death of St. John, and, consequently, they must have known what was the practice of the Apostles. From these, Justin could obtain the most satisfactory information. Nor were the means of information possessed by Irenæus, less satisfactory, for he tells us himself, that he was a pupil of Polycarp, bishop of Smyrna,* and Polycarp we know was a pupil of the Apostle and beloved disciple, St. John.† Polycarp, therefore, knew personally, and Irenæus knew from Polycarp, what was the Apostolic practice, and the bare mention of the existence of infant baptism, by Irenæus, unaccompanied by any intimation that it was an innovation, in a work written expressly to point out all innovations, is conclusive evidence that it had been practised from the days of the Apostles. The testimony of these two writers, does, therefore, render it certain, that infant baptism was practised in the Primitive and Apostolic Church. No evidence could be more entirely decisive on this point.

TERTULLIAN. We will consider next the case of Tertullian, a presbyter in the Church at Carthage, who was contemporary with Irenæus, and wrote about A. D. 195. He was a man of ardent temperament, something wanting in sound judgment, and in the latter part of his life, not en-

* Ep. Flor. in Euseb. Ecc. Hist. v. 20. † Martyr. Ign. c. 3.

tirely sound in the faith. Among other strange notions that he fell into, one was, that sin, after baptism, could hardly be pardoned; or, in other words, that all sin, after baptism, was sin against the HOLY GHOST. Hence he advised the delay of baptism. The following is from his treatise *On Baptism.**

"Therefore, according to the condition and disposition of persons, and also their age, the delay of baptism is more advisable; especially in the case of *little children, (parvulos.)* . . . . Our LORD says, indeed, 'Forbid them not to come unto me.' Therefore let them come when they understand; when they are instructed why it is that they come."†

Two remarks are suggested by this quotation; first, that Tertullian, in advising the *delay* of infant baptism, recognizes the existence of the practice in the Church at that time; and, second, that he understood the passage, "Suffer little children to come unto me, and forbid them not," (Matt. xix. 14; Mark x. 14; Luke xviii. 16;) as did the Primitive Church generally, and as the principles of common-sense interpretation now require us to construe it, to denote coming to CHRIST in baptism. Tertullian also understands the passage, (1 Cor. vii. 14,) of which we have before spoken, to denote baptism. Thus he quotes the passage: "*Of either parent sanctified, the children that are born are holy;*" by reason of the prerogative of that seed, and also the instruction in their education; *else*, says he, *were they unclean.*

---

* C. 18.

† In the days of Cyprian, A. D. 250, a council was held at Carthage, at which sixty-six African bishops were present, when the propriety of baptizing before the eighth day was considered, and all were of opinion that it might be done before that. (Ep. Fidus.) Now, as Cyprian was the pupil and an admirer of Tertullian, (Jerom. Script. Ecc.,) the language of the pupil may fairly be quoted, to show the opinion of the master on this subject.

But yet meaning to be understood thus: that the children of the faithful, are designed for holiness;* that is, "baptismal holiness."† That Tertullian was opposed to infant baptism, no one doubts, and this fact is the most conclusive evidence of the existence of the practice, as no one would oppose a thing which had no existence.

We have now examined all the passages in the Bible, and the Fathers of the two first centuries, which have any direct bearing on the question touching the subjects of baptism; and are authorized to say, that the evidence is conclusive in favor of the right of infants to baptism.

There are several other arguments in proof of the conclusion here drawn, but we have extended this examination so much beyond our original intention, that we shall barely enumerate them.

I. That the quantity of water is not essential to the ordinance, we infer:—

1. Because baptism being symbolic of purification, the rule given by CHRIST to Peter, (John xiii.,) he that was washed in part, was clean every whit, is applicable.‡

2. From the cases of household baptism, as in the cases of Cornelius, (Acts x.;) of Lydia, (Acts xvi.;) of the Jailer, (Acts xvi.;) of Crispus, (Acts xviii. and 1 Cor. i.;) of Stephanus and Gaius, (1 Cor. i.;) and of the baptism on the day of Pentecost, (Acts ii.;) and at Samaria, by Philip, (Acts viii.;) which alone would render infant baptism highly probable.

II. That infants are to be admitted to baptism and the privileges of the new covenant, we also infer:—

1. From the fact that the Christian Church has succeeded

---

* De Anima, c. 39. † De Bap. c. 12.

‡ This text was understood by Tertullian, as having especial reference to baptism. De Bapt. c. 12.

the Jewish Church, into which infants were received by express command. That it has so succeeded, is evident from what we have before said; and also,

(1.) Because the blessings promised to Abraham, at the institution of the covenant, of which circumcision was the seal, were intended for the Gentiles also, through faith in JESUS CHRIST. (Gen. xvii.; Gal. iii. 19–29.)

(2.) Because the covenant made with Abraham, was not disannulled by the fulfilling of the law given at Sinai; and must, therefore, continue in force. (Gal. iii. 17.)

(3.) Because all persons who have been baptized into CHRIST, are Abraham's seed, and heirs to the promises contained in the covenant made with him. (Gal. iii. 27, 29.)

2. We also infer that infants should be offered to GOD in baptism, upon the faith of the parent, or master, because the blessings which CHRIST conferred upon men, were frequently given to children and servants, on the faith of the parents or master. Thus, the servant of the centurion was healed, upon the faith of his master. (Matt. viii.) The ruler's daughter was restored to life and health, on account of her father's faith, (Luke viii.;) and the woman of Samaria, by her faith, obtained the like blessing for her daughter. (Matt. xx.) And the little children, on whom CHRIST bestowed his blessing, were presented to him on the faith of believing parents. In view of these, and many other facts of a similar character, it is impossible for us to see how any servant of CHRIST can reject from his covenant, those to whom He extended those blessings while on earth, and of whom He said, "of such is the kingdom of GOD."

CHAPTER IX.

INCIDENTAL PROOF AS TO THE MODE OF BAPTISM.

In the discussion of this question, reference is often made to the present practice of the Oriental Churches. We add, therefore, the customs of those Churches, to satisfy the curiosity of such as lay any stress upon it.

Armenians. . . . . "The Priest then asks the name of the child, and taking him on his left arm, and supporting his feet with his right, he puts him into the font, *his head being kept out of the water.** Then with the hollow of his hand, he *pours water upon* the child three times, baptizing him,"† &c.

Syro-Jacobites. . . . . "The child is then put into the font with his face toward the East, and *his head being supported by the right hand of the Priest, the water is taken up in the hollow of his left hand, and poured three times upon the head,* while he says, 'N. is baptized,'"‡ &c.

Copts and Abyssinians. "Among the Copts and Abyssinians, baptism is administered as among the Syrians;" that is, by the priest's *pouring water upon the head of the candidate,* while the body of the person is in the water, the head

---

* Yet the Armenian Liturgy uses the language, "descending into the water," as applied to our Saviour. Ass. vol. II. p. 199.

† This account of the mode of baptism among the Armenians, is from Rev. Dr. Jarvis' Report to Board of Missions of Prot. Epis. Ch., U. S. That given in Schrœder's Thesaurus Linguæ Armeniacæ, p. 328, on the authority of an Armenian Priest, (the Bishop of Erivan) varies little from this. It is there said that the Priest holds the child *over* the font and *pours*, or *sprinkles* water upon the top of his head, three times, saying the words of baptism, and afterwards putting him into the water three times, *washes* his whole body.

‡ Ass. Bib. Orient. IV. 241–245.

being out. Consequently, baptism among them is *accompanied* by immersion, in one sense of the word, but not in the sense contended for; while at the same time, the immersion is not regarded as a part of the baptism.

THE SYRO-CHALDÆANS, improperly called Nestorians, use the same formula of baptism as the Syro-Jacobites, and the Priest puts the child into the font in the same manner as among them, that is, *he puts the candidate into the water up to the neck, and pours water upon him three times, imposing hands upon him while in the water.**

GREEK CHURCH. The practice of this Church is not uniform. In Greece proper, some hold immersion necessary; others not; but the whole Russian Church holds it immaterial. We give an extract from a very scarce book; *An Account of the Greek Church*, by Thomas Smith, B. D.†

"The infant, if well, is brought into the Church; in the entrance of which is the font, usually large, *and about a foot and a half deep*. . . . . In the winter, that the tender body of the infant may not suffer by cold, they for the most part warm the water, upon which the Priest breathes and makes a cross, and then poureth oil upon it in the form of a cross, three times, with which having anointed the child, *and holding him upright with his hands,* his face toward the east, he performs the mystical rite, ... and at the mention of each person of the Trinity, the Priest dips the child into the water; . . . . which threefold immersion, they for the most part rigidly retain; . . . . though they do not scruple to vary from it upon occasion, being content sometimes to pour water upon the face of the infant three times."‡

It is not said in this work, whether the head of the person is put under the water or not, but the account gives us such

---

* Chal. Rit. in Ass. Bib. Orient. IV. 241–245.

† 8vo. Oxford, 1680.

‡ See Ch. Mag. iii. 71, 2.

particulars, as to show it is impossible it could be done.* Besides, the fact that pouring is sometimes substituted, shows conclusively that this must be somewhat connected with the practice of the other Oriental Churches, which we have mentioned.

We give, on the other side, a quotation from "Theocletus Pharmacides, 'Secretary of the Holy Synod of Niece.' It is taken from a pamphlet published in Athens, in 1839, entitled, *O pseudonumos Germanos*, and is a reply to an article in a religious periodical in Athens, which was attributed to Constantine Œconomos, who wrote under the assumed signature of Germanos, the editor of the periodical. Hence the appellation *pseudonumos*, false." . . . . "It appears that Œconomos, following the Russian theologians, held that *the mode of Christian baptism is twofold, being either immersion or ablution*. On this point, the Secretary of the Synod of Greece says,†

"But we ask the very pious Russian divines, where they found this twofold mode of baptizing? Was it in the New Testament? But in that *baptizo*, in the command of our LORD JESUS CHRIST, (Matt. xxviii. 19,) signifies nothing else than that which the *same Greek word properly signifies;* and this is manifest from the baptism of our LORD himself, who, when he was baptized, *went up out of the water*, (Matt. iii. 16;) but he who goes up out of the water, goes down first into it; that is, he is all baptized in it. We learn, therefore, from the New Testament, one mode of baptizing, that by *immersion*, (καταδυσεως,) and immersion is no other than an entire covering *by means of*, or *in* water. . . . . . Then again the

* The fonts of the Greek Church, even in Greece, are often, if not generally, so small that immersion is impracticable, being frequently not more than a foot deep.—E. A. S.

† We quote from a periodical that allows nothing but immersion to be baptism, and give *its* translation.—*Bap. Advocate.*

Russians were taught Christianity by us, and from their teachers they learned *one and only one* mode of baptizing; that by a threefold immersion and emersion of the entire person baptized in the water; and this is baptism, according to the most proper and Scriptural meaning of the word." (p. 36.)

Here then we have an immerser's *version* of a foreign writer; which proves that thirty-five millions of "the Greek Church," out of forty-five millions, hold, that *it is indifferent whether baptism be performed by immersion, or any other washing.* Second, the "Secretary of the Holy Synod of Niece," writing especially to contradict this opinion, tells us, that baptism "is no other than an entire covering *by means of*, or *in* water;" that is, water enough must *be poured on to* the person, to wet him all over, or he must be *put into* the water. Hence the strongest advocate of immersion, according to his own translation of the author, places the covering of the person *by means of* POURING water on to him, before that of putting the person into the water, which is in accordance with the conclusion before drawn, as to the proper mode of applying the element.

We add another species of evidence, hitherto overlooked, which can hardly fail to carry convincing evidence to the minds of intelligent men. In early times, when Christianity was first preached to the different nations, different practices were pursued, in regard to ecclesiastical phraseology. Technical terms were either transferred from the Greek, as in Latin, or the Greek was translated, as in most of the languages of Europe. Where this was done, the translator would select that word in his own language, which would give the leading and prominent idea of the original, as it was then understood. This argument, as applied to Baptism, is especially appropriate, for if the word *baptizo* had once been introduced and naturalized, it would have held its place.

PESHITO, or *Old Syriac*. The oldest of all the versions, and the one most important in reference to this point, is that which was made into the common language of Palestine, and which is known as the *Peshito*, or *Literal Version*. This, too, was the vernacular tongue of Justin Martyr, and hence, is of deep interest, as confirming or contradicting the inferences drawn from his writings. This version *translates* "baptizo" and its derivatives, by *Amad*, (ܥܡܕ.) which signifies in all the cognate languages, *to stand, to cause to stand*, but in Syriac, (1) *to be washed*, and (2) *to be baptized*. The derivative *amodo*, signifies *ablution, baptizing, baptism*, or *washing*, indiscriminately. It is worthy of note, that in the Syriac, neither the common words for *immersion*, or *sprinkling* are ever employed to signify baptism, and also, that while *amad* and its derivatives are used interchangeably with those words which signify *washing*, they do not seem ever to have been used as synonymous with words denoting *immersion* or *submersion*.*

---

* Castell, Heptaglot. Lex. *in loco*. Kirschius, Syriac Lexicon, 93. Tyschen's Syriac Lexicon, 149, and Michaelis' Edition of Castell's Syriac Lexicon, II. 655.—The inquiry, why the Syrians employed *amad*, which, in the kindred languages,—the Hebrew, Ethiopian, and Arabic,—signifies *to stand, to cause to stand, to be firm, to constitute*, and which in Hebrew never signifies washing of any kind, is a curious and important one. It is impossible for us, however, to give more than a conjectural answer. Michaelis (Cast. II. 655) supposes it was, because the candidate *stood in the water*, at the administration of the rite. This seems at first to be altogether too slight and insufficient a reason, but when we recollect the ancient usage of this class of words, it is not so improbable. Thus the Latin *Sto*, (*to stand*,) signifies "*to stand* to make a set speech," and hence it came to mean, "*to make a set speech*;" also "*to stand* to fight," and hence, *to fight*. The Greek has also a similar usage of *ιστημι*. So the Hebrew *amad*, signifies *to stand* before one to serve or minister; and hence, *to serve, to minister*. In the same manner the Syriac *amad* may signify "*to stand* to be baptized," and hence, *to be*

Brittano-Celtic. The ancient Britons, as we shall show in a subsequent chapter, were certainly converted to Christianity in the second, in all probability in the first, century. In this language, the word *baptizo* was translated, not transferred. The Brittano-Celtic word for *baptism*, was *bedyz;* which denotes primarily "a giving, a gift, a preparation, a setting apart, or consecration." No reference whatever is made *to the mode* of baptism in the use of this word, which denotes "consecration or setting apart." The derivatives are, *bedyza* and *bedyzvan*, "a font, or baptistry;" *bedyzian*, "to baptize." So also, *bedyz yr Ysbryd Glan*, was "baptism of the Holy Ghost," or "the gift of the Holy Ghost," and *bedyz esgob*, confirmation, or *Bishop's baptism*.* The mode of baptism could not have been the leading idea in the minds of the Britons, as no reference is made to it, in the words denoting the rite.

Hiberno-Celtic. Christianity was propagated from Britain into Ireland, and had made considerable progress there before the time of St. Patrick, who was ordained Bishop of Ireland, A. D. 433. They used words in their own language to denote the several rites and ceremonies of religion, and *baptism* was called "*baiste;*" to *baptize*, "*baisd-im.*" The original and proper meaning of this word may be inferred from the fact, that a derivative from the same root, and the only one in common use in that language, "*baist-each*," is used to denote rain. Hence, among the ancient Irish, the

---

baptized,—a conclusion in accordance with all the evidence we have been able to discover in regard to *the mode* of receiving this rite.

* Owen's Geiriadur Cymraeg a Seasong, 2 vols. 4to. London, 1793. This reference to the gift of the Holy Ghost in confirmation, is an interesting fact, and worthy of consideration. It is worthy of note also, that the quotations from Scripture, made by the British historian Gildas, are not from the Latin Vulgate, though he wrote in Latin.—Pref. to *Works of Gildas*, viii.

mode of baptism was thought of, and reference is made to it; consequently, baptism must have originally been performed in Ireland, by *sprinkling* or *pouring*.*

Scoto-Celtic. Christianity was preached in Scotland about the same time as in Ireland, and the same words are employed to denote the rite of *baptism; baist,* "*to baptize:*" *baisteadh,* "baptism." The kindred words from the same root, are, *baistidh,* "drops of water from the eaves," and *baiseach,* "a shower of rain."†

Egyptian. The New Testament was translated into the Egyptian tongue at an early period, certainly as early as the third century, and hence, is of high authority on this point. It is of importance, also, as tending to confirm or contradict the conclusions we have drawn, in regard to the usage of *baptizo,* by the Egyptian, Clement of Alexandria. The common word to denote *baptism* in all the Egyptian dialects, is ⲱⲙⲥ, (*oms,*) to which Tattam‡ gives no signification but *to baptize;* while Peyron§ supposes it to signify primarily, *to stand in the water, to cover with water.* The root, however, seems to be merely *om,* as appears from the noun ϫⲓⲛ-ⲱⲙ, (*jin-om,*) signifying *baptism* and *baptizing,*|| and, consequently, signifies *water,* or *wet;* and, as a verb, *to*

---

* O'Brien's Focaloir Gaoighilge-Sacs-Bhearla, 8vo. Dublin, 1832

† Dictionarum Scoto-Celticum, 2 vols. 4to. Lond. and Edin. 1836. Our English word *to baste,* used in cookery, to signify moistening by pouring on a fluid, is a Brittano-Saxon word, and comes from the same root.

‡ Lexicon of the Languages of Egypt.

§ Grammar of the Coptic Language, 79.

|| The prefix *jin-,* is the common Egyptian prefix, added to verbs to form nouns, signifying the name of the action, (Peyron, Copt. Gram. 29;) and *s* final is often a *servile* letter, (Pey. 23.) The root, *om,* occurs in ⲓⲟⲙ, (*iom,*) *the sea,* Heb. ים; in ⲡⲓ-ⲟⲙ, (*pi-om,*) *the water, the sea,* etc.

wet, moisten, water. No distinct allusion is made to the mode of performing baptism in the Egyptian versions, and all apparent reference there is, sustains the views we have taken of Clement's language.

Ethiopian. The Ethiopian version of the New Testament was made in the fourth century, in all probability at Alexandria, from whence this people received Christianity, and, consequently, furnishes a valuable commentary upon the Alexandrine views of baptism at that time. The word employed in this version to denote the ordinance, is ጠመቀ, (*ta-ma-ka,*) from ጠመሀ, (*ta-ma-a,*) *to tinge, dye, color, stain,* rarely *to dip.* But the ordinary words signifying *immersion* and *submersion* are never applied to baptism. Hence we must conclude, that the mode of baptism was not prominent, if at all, present in the mind of the Ethiopian translator.*

Mœso-Goths. The Goths appear to have been converted to Christianity some time before A. D. 300, as the signature of the Gothic Bishop, *Theophilus of Bosphorus, Metropolitan of the Goths,* stands to the decrees of the Council of Nice, A. D. 325.† But the Bible was not translated into that language until about A. D. 400, when it was done by Ulfilas, Bishop of the Mœso-Goths.‡ He employs *daup,* cognate with our word *dip,* to denote baptism.§ From the Gothic, this word was adopted into German, and several other north-

---

* Waunsleb's Ed. Ludolf Ethiop. Lex. col. 414, Castell, in טמק. It is worthy of remark, that טמא, which in Hebrew and Syriac signifies *to be unclean, impure, foul,* in the Ethiopian signifies *to dye, color, stain;* so that *tamaka,* is precisely like Tertullian's use of *tingo,* to signify the same thing. See ante p. 63.

† Soc. Ecc. H. ii. 41.

‡ Soc. Ecc. H. iv. 27, Sozem. vi. 37, and Hug. Intd. N. T., P. I. § 138.

§ Zahn's, Ulfilas, Weissenfels, 4to. 1805, in Glossar., and Matt. ii. 11; Mark i. 4; vii. 4, 8; Luke iii. 3, 21; John xiii. 26.

ern languages, at a much later period: Dutch, *doopen;* German, *taufen.* But that Ulfilas did not use *daupen,* to denote dipping, is evident from his language. Thus, he says, (Mark i. 8,) "Ik *daupja* izwis in watin, is *daupeith* izwis in Ahmin Weihamma; I baptize (dip) you in water, he shall baptize (dip) you in the HOLY GHOST."

ARMENIAN. The Armenians, until about A. D. 430, made use of the Syriac Scriptures and Liturgy, when the Bible was translated into the language of Armenia, from Greek manuscripts, and *baptizo* was translated. The word ordinarily employed was մկրտել, (*mekerdiel,*) which is a derivative, compounded, as would seem, of մաքրիլ, (*makhriel,*) and զտել, (*zdiel,*) both of which signify *to purify,* in a neuter sense, after the analogy of the oriental usage. But we do not find the word signifying baptism, ever used interchangeably, either with words signifying *immersion* or *sprinkling.* No allusion, therefore, is here made to *the mode* of baptism, the idea being that of purification.*

ANGLO-SAXON. The Anglo-Saxons were converted from A. D. 590 to 610, and they also used a word in their own language to denote this rite. The word chosen by them was "*fullian,*" "to whiten, cleanse, purify," from whence came "*fulluht,*" baptism; and "*fulluhtere,*" a baptizer.† Nothing can be certainly learned from this language, concerning the *mode* of baptism; but this we may certainly learn, that the Anglo-Saxons regarded *the moral signification,* and not *the mode,* as important. Some of the Lexicons give "*dyp-pan,*" to dip,‡ as one of the words used by the Anglo-Saxons, sig-

---

* Schrœder's Thesaurus Linguæ Armeniacæ, iii. 3, v. 6. Aucher's Armenian Dictionary, *in loco.*

† Matt. iii. 1, 11; xxi. 25. Sax. Chron. 24, 25, 26, 28, 29, 32, 39, etc. Bede, Ecc. Hist. i. 27; ii. 2; iii. 21. Elf. Ep. i. c. 20, 23, 40.

‡ *Dyp-pan* is the common word in the Saxon Scriptures, where *dip* occurs in English; *fulluht,* when the word *baptism* is found. Another

nifying *to baptize ;* but we have never seen an instance of its use in that sense. "*Fulluht*" is used in the Creeds, in the Scriptures, and such of the Homilies as we have been able to examine.

DUTCH. The Dutch version of the Scriptures has been appealed to by some, as evidence on this subject. But that is altogether too late to be pertinent. Besides, the Dutch were converted by Anglo-Saxon missionaries; Willibrod, the first missionary there, having been consecrated bishop by Wilfred, for some time Archbishop of York, A. D. 692,* and founded the See of Utrecht, A. D. 697.† The Dutch, therefore, derived Christianity from the Anglo-Saxons, who did not regard *the mode* of baptism as essential; and they copied their translation of *baptizo* from the Mœso-Gothic, where *daupen* could not signify *immersion*. Besides, *doop* does not signify *immersion*. Thus in the Rubric to the baptismal service, it is said; "He shall *dip* ('dompelen') the child in the water;" or "pour water upon it," and shall say: "*I baptize* (doop) thee," &c. Here is a distinction made between *dipping* and *baptizing* ;‡ and, consequently, they can not mean the same thing. The same may be said of the German "taufen," *to baptize* ; and "eintunken," "eintauchen," *to dip, to immerse*. In addition to this, we give the following words in the Dutch, as tending to illustrate the same point: *doopen*, "to baptize;" *dooping*, "washing;" *dompelen*, "to

---

word employed by the Saxons to denote baptism, was *Cristnian*, from whence comes our word *to christen*, which denotes literally, *to make a Christian*, according to the Scriptural use of the word. The Icelandic *Kristna*, has the same signification.

* Bede, v. 11, 12. Alcuin. Vit. Will.

† Hist. Episc. Ultraj. p. 1, in Boss. Diss. Orig. Germ. Lang. p. xciv.

‡ Het. Boek der Gewone Gebeden. See also, Vander Kemp. Catechismus, p. 516.

dip, to cover with water, to dip in water;" *dompeldoop*, "to baptize by immersion."*

These considerations prove most conclusively, to our minds, that the mode of baptism was not regarded as important by the early Christians, for had it been, it is perfectly incredible that those who received Christianity, if not from the Apostles themselves, from their immediate disciples, should make no allusion to it, in the words employed to denote it.

CHAPTER X.

REQUISITES OF BAPTISM—CREEDS.

HAVING ascertained who were proper subjects of baptism, and how it was to be administered, we shall inquire, *What was required of those who came to baptism?* To this inquiry the answer is obvious, in all parts of the New Testament—*faith and repentance.* What were *all* the articles of faith required by the Apostles, we are not told. But, in the case of the Eunuch, it was required that he should profess his faith in the Son of GOD. (Acts viii. 37.)

In the age next succeeding the Apostles, the articles of belief were embodied in what is called a *Creed.* Among the Latin Fathers, it was called *The Rule of Faith,* (*regula fidei.*)† It was called the *Canon*, or *Rule of Faith*, by the Council of Antioch, about 265.‡ In later writers it has still other names.

---

* Nederduitsch, Wortel-Worden, and Kilian.

† Iren. i. 19. Tert. De Præs. c. 13. De Veland. Virg. c. i. Jerome, Ep. 54. Ad Marcel.

‡ Euseb. vii. 30.

This, Irenæus says,* was an "unalterable Canon," which "the Church, though it be dispersed over all the world, from one end of the earth to the other, received from the Apostles, and their disciples."† And Tertullian frequently mentions its being used at baptism.‡ Several of the early writers have given *the substance of the creed*, as it was in their day. Some have erroneously supposed that these writers give the words of their creeds. But this they do not profess to do. They merely give *the sense*, or substance of it, in their own language; and generally, only so much of it as is pertinent to the particular subject under consideration. The following are some of the earliest accounts of it.

Substance of the Creed, as given by Irenæus, A. D. 175:§ "The Church, though it be dispersed over all the world from one end of the earth to the other, received from the Apostles and their disciples, the belief in one GOD the Father Almighty, Maker of heaven, and earth, and sea, and all things in them: and in one CHRIST JESUS, the Son of God, who was incarnate for our salvation: and in the HOLY GHOST, who preached by the prophets the dispensations of GOD: and the advent, and nativity of a virgin, and passion, resurrection from the dead, and bodily ascension of the flesh of his beloved Son, CHRIST JESUS our Lord, into heaven; and his coming again from heaven in the glory of the Father, to consummate all things, and raise the flesh of all mankind: that, according to the will of the invisible Father, every knee should bow, of things in heaven, and things in the earth, and things under the earth, to JESUS CHRIST, our Lord, and GOD, and Saviour, and King; and that every tongue should confess him; and that He shall exercise just judgment upon all, and send spiritual wickedness, the transgressing and apostate

* Adv. Hær. i. 1.

† i. 2.

‡ See De Bap. c. 6; De Præs. c. 13, 14, 21, 27.

§ L. i. c. 2.

angels, with all ungodly, unrighteous, and blaspheming men, into everlasting fire; but grant life to all righteous and holy men, that keep his commandments and persevere in his love, some from the beginning, others after repentance, on whom he confers immortality, and invests them with eternal glory."

Substance of the Creed, as given by Tertullian, about 195:* "There is," says he, "one rule of faith only which admits of no change or alteration, that teaches us to believe in one GOD ALMIGHTY, the Maker of the world; and in JESUS CHRIST, his Son, who was born of the Virgin Mary, crucified under Pontius Pilate, the third day arose again from the dead, received into heaven; he sitteth now at the right hand of GOD, who shall come again to judge both the quick and the dead, by the resurrection of the flesh."

In his book *De Præscriptis,* and also in that against Praxeas, he has other forms substantially the same, with the addition of the doctrine of the procession of the HOLY GHOST, the Sanctifier and Comforter.†

Substance of the Creed, as given by Origen, about A. D. 230:‡ "The things," says he, "which are manifestly handed down by Apostolical teaching, are these: First, That there is one GOD, who created and made all things, and caused the whole universe to exist out of nothing; the GOD of all the just that ever were from the first creation and foundation of all; the GOD of Adam, Abel, Seth, Enos, Enoch, Noe, Sem, Abraham, Isaac, Jacob, the twelve Patriarchs, Moses and the Prophets; and that this GOD, in the last days, as he had promised before by his Prophets, sent our LORD JESUS CHRIST, first to call Israel, and then the Gen-

* De Veland. Virg. c. 1. Adv. Prax. c. 2. † C. 13, Prax. c. 2.

‡ *Peri Archon,* in Pref. Tom. i. p. 665, in Bing. Ant. Ecc. B. x. c. 4, § 2.

tiles, after the infidelity of his people Israel. This just and good God, the Father of our Lord Jesus Christ, gave both the Law and the Prophets, and the Gospels, being the God of the Apostles, and of the Old and New Testament." The next article is, "That Jesus Christ, who came into the world, was begotten of the Father before every creature, who ministered to his Father in the creation of all things, (for by him all things were made,) in the last times made himself of no reputation and became man; he who was God, was made flesh, and when he was man, he continued the same God that he was before. He assumed a body in all things like ours, save only that it was born of a virgin by the Holy Ghost. And because this Jesus Christ was born and suffered death common to all, in truth, and not only in appearance, he was truly dead; for he rose again truly from the dead, and after his resurrection conversed with his disciples, and was taken up into heaven. They also delivered unto us, that the Holy Ghost was joined in the same honor and dignity with the Father and the Son."

In another place he gives it more briefly, thus:* "I believe there is one God, the Creator and Maker of all things; and one that is from him God the word, who is consubstantial with him, and co-eternal, who in the last times took human nature upon him of [the Virgin] Mary, and was crucified, and raised again from the dead. I believe also the Holy Ghost, who exists from all eternity."

The substance of the Creed, is given by Cyprian, about A. D. 250, in which he enumerates all the articles included in the foregoing, but in the form of questions.†

Substance of the Creed, as far as it relates to the Holy Trinity, as given by Gregory Thaumaturgus, about A. D.

* Cont. Marc. Dial. i. Tom. 2, 815.

† Ep. 69, 70, 76.

270.* "There is one GOD, the Father of the living Word, the subsisting wisdom and power, the eternal express image of GOD, who is a Perfect begetter of a Perfect, a Father of an only begotten Son. And one LORD, one of one, GOD of GOD, the character and image of the Godhead, the word of power, the wisdom that comprehends the whole system of the world, the power that made every creature. The true Son of the true Father, invisible of invisible, incorruptible of incorruptible, immortal of immortal, eternal of eternal. And one HOLY GHOST, who has his existence from GOD, who was manifested to men by the Son, the perfect image of the perfect Son, the living cause of all living, the fountain of holiness, essential sanctity, who is the author of holiness in others. In whom GOD the Father is manifested, who is above all and in all, and GOD the Son, whose power runs through all things. A perfect Trinity, whose glory, eternity, and dominion is no way divided or separated from each other. In this Trinity, therefore, there is nothing created or servile, nothing adventitious or extraneous, that did not exist before, but afterward came into it. The Father was never without the Son, nor the Son without the Spirit, but the Trinity abides the same, unchangeable and invariable forever."

Substance of the Creed, as given by Lucian the Martyr, about A. D. 280.† "We believe, according to the tradition of the Gospels, and Apostles, in one GOD, the Father, Almighty, Creator, and Maker, and Governor of all things, of whom are all things: and in one LORD JESUS CHRIST, his only begotten Son, who is GOD, by whom are all things, who was begotten of the Father, GOD of GOD, Whole of Whole, One of One, Perfect of Perfect, King of King, Lord of Lord, the Word, the Wisdom, the Life,

---

* Greg. Thaum. 42.

† Athan. De Synod. Armin. et Seleuc. i. 869–929. Socr. Ecc. His. ii. 10.

the true Light, the true Way, the Resurrection, the Shepherd, the Gate, the incommutable and unchangeable image of the divine essence, power and glory, the first-born of every creature, who was always from the beginning, God, the Word with God, according to what is said in the Gospel; 'and the Word was God,' by whom all things were made and in whom all things subsist, who in the last days descended from on high, and was born of a virgin according to the Scriptures, and being the Lamb of God, he was made the Mediator between God and man, being fore-ordained to be the author of our faith and life: for he said, 'I came not from heaven to do my own will, but the will of him that sent me.' Who suffered and rose again for us the third day, and ascended into heaven, and sitteth on the right hand of the Father; and he shall come again with glory to judge the quick and the dead. And we believe in the Holy Ghost, which is given to believers for their consolation, and sanctification, and consummation, according to what our Lord Jesus Christ appointed his disciples, saying, 'Go, teach all nations, baptizing them in the name of the Father, and of the Son, and of the Holy Ghost.' Whence the properties of the Father are manifest, denoting him to be truly a father, and the properties of the Son, denoting him to be truly a Son, and the properties of the Holy Spirit, denoting him to be truly the Holy Ghost: these names not being simply put and to no purpose, but to express the particular subsistence, or hypostatic substance, of each person named, so as to denote them to be three in hypostasis, and one by consent."

Creed of the Church of Jerusalem, A. D. 300.* "I believe in one God, the Father Almighty, Maker of heaven and earth, and of all things visible and invisible; and in one

* Cyril. Cat. 6, 77.

Lord Jesus Christ, the only begotten Son of God, begotten of the Father before all ages, the true God, by whom all things were made, who was incarnate and made man, who was crucified and buried, and the third day he rose again from the dead, and ascended into heaven, and sitteth on the right hand of the Father, and shall come to judge the quick and dead, of whose kingdom there shall be no end. And in the Holy Ghost, the Comforter, who spake by the Prophets. In one baptism of repentance, in the remission of sins, in one Catholic Church, in the resurrection of the flesh, and in the life everlasting."

Creed of the Church of Alexandria, about the same time.* "We believe in one God, the Father Almighty, and in Jesus Christ his Son, our Lord, God the Word begotten of Him before all ages; by whom all things were made, that are in heaven and in earth; who came down from heaven, and was incarnate, and suffered, and rose again, and ascended into heaven, and shall come again to judge the quick and the dead. And in the Holy Ghost, and in the resurrection of the flesh, and in the life of the world to come, and in the kingdom of heaven, and in one Catholic Church of God, extended from one end of the earth to the other."

Creed of the Church of Antioch, about the same time.† "I believe in one only true God, the Father Almighty, Maker of all creatures visible and invisible; and in Jesus Christ our Lord, his only begotten Son, the first born of every creature, born of Him before all ages, and not made, very God of very God, [consubstantial] with the Father; by whom the world was framed and all things made; who for our sakes came, and was born of the Virgin Mary, and was crucified under Pontius Pilate, was buried, and the third day

* Soc. i. 26.

† Cass. De Incar. L. iv.

rose according to the Scriptures, and ascended into heaven, and shall come again to judge the quick and the dead."

We have given these several Creeds, to show how general they were, and also to show what was the faith of the primitive Church, on some of the most important doctrines of the gospel. The first, however, are to be regarded rather as the substance of the Creeds, than as the Creeds themselves. From this collection of primitive Creeds, it will be seen, that those who came to baptism, were required to profess their faith in all the great fundamental doctrines of the gospel; especially in the following: In one GOD, the Father Almighty, the Creator of all things. In JESUS CHRIST, begotten of the Father before all ages; in his nativity, passion, burial, resurrection, ascension, and future coming to judgment. In the HOLY GHOST, the Sanctifier and Comforter. That this Trinity of persons constitutes one only GOD, the same in substance, and all equally eternal. In one baptism, one Catholic Church, the resurrection of the dead, and a future judgment.

The candidate was also required to make a public and formal renunciation of the devil and all his works, of the pomps and vanities of the world, and of all of the lusts of the flesh;* to give his consent to the Creed† when water was applied three times,—in the name of the Father, and of the Son, and of the HOLY GHOST,‡ some person standing sureties or sponsors for them.§ In some Churches the newly baptized person was given a mixture of honey and milk, in token of his spiritual infancy.|| After this, it was deemed impro-

* Tert. De Cor. cc. 3, 13. De Icedol. c. 6, De Spect. c. 4.

† Tert. De Cor. c. 3.

‡ Tert. De Cor. c. 3, Apos. Can. 42.

§ Tert. De Cor. c. 3.

|| Tert. De Cor. 3, Clem. Alex. Pæd. i. 6, Jerom. Adv. Lucif. c. 8. Conc. III. Carth. Can. 24.

per for them to strive after the honors or offices of the world, or to seek its praises and glories,* to attend the circus, the theatre, the gladiatorial camp, or the wrestling gallery.† Nor were the baptized permitted to engage in any trade or occupation which ministered directly or indirectly to the practice of idolatry, by making idols, or assisting in the erection of idol temples, or in the adornings for either, or any other business, whereby God was dishonored.‡

Having ascertained who composed the Apostolic Church, we proceed to inquire, *who were communicants in that Church?* We answer, only those who had received, or were desirous of receiving the rite of Confirmation. By *Confirmation,* we mean a rite which existed in the Apostolic Church, sometimes called "receiving the Holy Ghost," at others, "Confirmation," and at others, "the doctrine of the laying on of hands," and which consisted in *the laying on of an Apostle's hands upon those who had been baptized,* accompanied by a *public profession* of the faith of the person confirmed. As the examination of this point belongs properly to the "power and duties of an Apostle," we shall only remark here, that if we find this rite existing in the various Churches, it was the *duty* of those who had received baptism, to receive this also, for we are not at liberty to suppose that the Apostles established any thing unmeaning or unnecessary.

---

* Tert. De Cor. c. 13.

† Tert. Apol. c. 38.

‡ Tert. de Spect. cc. 6–8.

CHAPTER XI.

POWERS AND DUTIES OF THE MEMBERS OF THE CHURCH.

1. It was their duty to assemble on the first day of the week, for the purpose of public worship, religious instruction, and the celebration of the Eucharist. This is manifest from the Apostolic history. Thus, they *were assembled*, "with one accord, in one place, when they received the Holy Ghost." (Acts ii. 1, 4; iv. 31.) And this, as one may see, by reference to the Jewish festivals, was on the first day of the week. So at Antioch, Paul and Barnabas "*assembled with the Church*, for the space of a year," (Acts xi. 26;) and Paul commands the Hebrews not to "*forsake the assembling of themselves together*." (Heb. x. 25.)

That this *assembling was on the first day of the week*, we learn from the same source. St. Paul, in one of his journeys through the cities of Asia, "stopped at Troas *seven days*. And *on the first day of the week*, when the disciples came together to break bread, Paul preached." (Acts xx. 6, 7.) That this assembling of the Church at Troas was no extraordinary or unusual meeting, but the common and ordinary one, appears from the language, "on the first day of the week, *when the disciples came together to break bread*;" that is, to partake of the Lord's Supper. (Acts ii. 42;* 1 Cor. x. 16, 17; xi. 23.) Besides, the fact that it is not said to be an unusual or extraordinary thing, is conclusive evidence that it was usual and customary.

To the same effect is the command of St. Paul, to the

---

* The Peshito, or Old Syriac Version, made at the close of the first, or beginning of the second century, renders this passage, "breaking of the Eucharist," as also Acts xx. 7, quoted below.

Church at Corinth: "*On the first day of the week*, let every one of you 'lay up in store,'* as GOD hath prospered him; *that there be no gatherings when I come*." (1 Cor. xvi. 2.) "That there be no gatherings *when I come*," implies that there should be a gathering before he came; that is, when the alms were laid by in the treasury, or, on *the first day of the week*.

The same account alludes to the object of this assembling. At Troas, "the disciples came together on the first day of the week *to break bread*, and Paul *preached* unto them." (Acts xx. 7.) At Antioch, also, Paul and Barnabas, when "assembled with the Church, *taught the people*," (Acts xi. 26,) things suitable only for *public* assemblies, and belonging mainly to *religious worship*. In the absence of every thing opposed to the conclusion, we may affirm, that these *direct references* prove, that the members of the Apostolic Church *assembled on the first day of the week*, for *public worship*, *religious instruction, and celebrating the Lord's Supper*; and hence, that it was their duty to do so.

Such, too, was the practice of the Church in the age next succeeding the Apostles. Pliny, Governor of Bithynia, A. D. 110, tells the Roman Emperor,† that the Christians "met on a certain stated day," for religious worship. This day, Ignatius, A. D. 107, calls "the LORD's day,"‡ the name by which it is designated by St. John. (Rev. i. 10.) It is called by Justin Martyr, "Sunday," because it is the first day, in which "GOD changed darkness and matter, and made the world." On "the same day, also, JESUS CHRIST rose from the dead,"§ on which day "they assemble for public worship."‖ The same thing is noticed by Tertullian, A. D. 185,¶ and by numerous subsequent writers.

---

* Rob. 374. † Ep. L. x. Ep. 97. ‡ Ep. Mag. c. 9.
§ Apol. i. 89. ‖ C. 87. ¶ De Cor. Mil. c. 3, etc.

2. When assembled, *all were to take part in the services*, according to some order or form which was made use of in the Church. The Colossians were directed "to teach and admonish one another," or, as Professor Robinson renders it, *one to another*,* "in psalms, and hymns, and spiritual songs." (Col. iii. 16.) This "teaching and exhorting one to another," could only be performed when assembled together; and if when assembled, must have been done according to some form or order previously established or agreed upon, or be productive of disorder and confusion. That it was not to be done according to every man's fancy, but agreeably to some established system, is a necessary inference from the censure cast upon the Corinthians for irregularities in this particular, as also from the language made use of by the Apostle in condemning those practices. "How is it, brethren," saith he, "when ye come together, every one of you hath a psalm, a doctrine, a tongue, a revelation, or an interpretation? God is not the author of confusion, but of peace, as in all the Churches of the saints. Let all things be done decently, *and in order.*" (1 Cor. xiv. 26, 33, 40, κατα ταξιν, "*according to arrangement, disposition, or series.*")† The existence of a *series*, or an *order*, implies *pre-arrangement*, and the language in this case, like the one put in chapter second, is intelligible only by supposing the existence of some *form*, previously established, to which reference is here made.

The Ephesians, also, were directed to be "filled with the spirit; *speaking among themselves*," or, as Robinson says, "*one to another*,‡ in psalms, and hymns, and spiritual songs." (Eph. v. 18, 19.) These "psalms, and hymns, and spiritual songs," were of necessity *precomposed forms*, and the persons using them "spoke and exhorted one to another, ac-

* Rob. 215. † Rob. 420, 806. ‡ Rob. 470 and 215

cording to [some] arrangement, disposition, or series." Now the only "arrangement or series," by which public worship could be carried on by the whole assembly, without producing "confusion in the Churches," is, that one or more should speak, and the rest reply by way of response. This, however, applies only to those portions of worship, which were conducted by means of "psalms, and hymns, and spiritual songs;" for, in praying and giving thanks, the speakers were directed to use "words easy to be understood," (1 Cor. xiv. 9–15;) or else how, saith the Apostle, "shall he that is unlearned,* say AMEN?" (v. 16.) This allusion to the practice of responding *Amen* to the prayers of the speaker, is the only thing on the subject in all the New Testament, and is, therefore, precisely parallel to the supposed case of "beating the revellie," before put; and for reasons there given, compels us to believe it was the custom in the Apostolic Church for the people to respond, *Amen*, to the prayer of the speaker. Justin Martyr, A. D. 150, says that this was then the universal practice in the Church.†

Should there be any doubt whether the Apostle, in writing to the Ephesians and Colossians, referred to *public worship*, it will vanish at once, if a comparison is instituted between that, and the account in Corinthians. In Ephesians and Colossians, the argument is not only similar, but the language is also the same. To the Colossians, he says: "Teach and exhort, one to another, in psalms, and hymns, and spiritual songs, singing with grace in your hearts to the Lord. And whatsoever ye do, in word or deed, do all in the name of the LORD JESUS, giving thanks to GOD, and the Father by him. Wives, submit yourselves unto your own husbands, as it is fit in the LORD." (Col. iii. 17, 18.)

To the Ephesians, he says: "Speaking one to another, in

---

* Rob. 52.

† Apol. i. 87.

psalms, and hymns, and spiritual songs, and (ψάλλοντες) *chanting*,* in your hearts to the LORD; giving thanks always for all things unto GOD and the Father, in the name of our LORD JESUS CHRIST. Wives, submit yourselves unto your own husbands, as unto the LORD." (Eph. v. 19, 22.)

In Corinthians, the argument is parallel, and the language very similar; and here the Apostle speaks *expressly* of public worship. "How is it, then, brethren? when ye come together, [in the Church,] (vv. 23, 28, 34,) every one hath a psalm, hath a doctrine, hath a tongue, hath a revelation.† Let all things be done unto edifying. Let your women keep silence in the Churches, for they are commanded to be under obedience, as also saith the law; and if they will learn any thing, let them ask their husbands at home." (1 Cor. xiv. 26, 34, 35.)

In all three Epistles the argument is the same, saving that in the two first, the language is that of direction, in the last, of censure;—the mode of conducting it the same, and the language similar; and, as one refers expressly to public worship, the only reasonable inference is, that the others relate to the same thing.‡ These passages, therefore, in the absence of all contradiction, *prove the use of precomposed forms in the Apostolic Church;* and they refer directly to the practice of *responsive worship*. And from the nature of the evidence by which these questions are to be decided, this is as much as we have a right to expect.

That much, if not all, of the public worship of the Primi-

---

* Rob. 904.

† St. Cyprian passes sentence of condemnation upon those "who dare to build another altar, and *to offer another prayer with unlicensed words*." Unit. Ecc. c. 14.

‡ Compare Paley's *Horæ Paulinæ*, on this mode of analysis, and also on the synchronism of the Epistles to the Ephesians and Colossians.

tive Church, was by way of response, is proved by the earliest writers. Clement, of Rome, about A. D. 83, says:* "We ought to take heed, that looking into the depths of divine knowledge, we do all things *in order*,† whatsoever our LORD hath commanded us to do. That we perform our offerings and services [i. e. the offering of the Holy Communion and public worship] to GOD, at their appointed seasons; for these he hath commanded to be done, not rashly and disorderly, but at certain determinate times and hours."

So the Roman Governor, Pliny, A. D. 110, informs us, that the Christians "met *on a certain stated day*, and sung *by turns*, (invicem,) a hymn to CHRIST, as GOD."‡ Tertullian often mentions forms of prayer, and expressly attributes them to CHRIST. That the public worship of the Synagogue was by *a form of prayer*, is so well known, that it is needless to spend time in proof of it. Hence Tertullian says: "Our LORD JESUS CHRIST gave his disciples of the New Testament, *a new form of prayer*."§ He also speaks of "the *appointed* prayer," and "the *ordinary* prayer."‖ And Cyprian¶ says: "Christ did himself give a form of prayer, and himself advise and instruct us, what we ought to pray for." He also mentions the "Sursum Corda," or, *Lift up your hearts*, as used in the Communion Service to this day.**

Concerning the *order of worship* in the Church, in the second century, but very little has been preserved. We gather, however, from that, especially from a letter of Pliny, A. D. 110, and the Apology of Justin Martyr, A. D. 150, compared with the New Testament and subsequent writers, that it was nearly as follows: The ancient service consisted of two parts—that which was common to all, and is now called the

* Ep. Cor. c. 40.
† Comp. 1 Cor. iv. 40.
‡ Plin. Ep. L. x. Ep. 97.
§ De Orat. c. 1.
‖ De Orat. c. 9.
¶ On Lord's Prayer, c. 1.
** Ibid. 20.

Ante-Communion Service, and that used in the administration of the Communion.

Order of the Ante-Communion Service.

1. A responsive psalm or hymn, addressed to CHRIST, as GOD.* This was also the practice in the time of Jerome,† though in some places they read the Old Testament first.‡

2. Reading of the Scriptures, of the Old and New Testaments,§ intermingled, as we know, a while after, with the reading or singing of psalms.‖

3. The sermon,¶ which was generally delivered sitting.**

4. Next, prayers by the minister, and to each petition the people responded, *Amen.*†† A while later, the people also responded, *Kyrie eleison,* "Lord have mercy on us," to the shorter petitions.‡‡

Order of the Communion Service.

1. The kiss of peace.§§

2. [A. D. 330. The *Sursum Corda* followed, though not mentioned in Justin's brief account. *Minister.*—"Lift up your hearts." *People.*—"We lift them up unto the Lord."‖‖ This is mentioned by Cyprian,¶¶ Chrysostom,*** and Augustine.]†††

3. [The hymn *Tersanctus,* or, as it is sometimes called, the *Trisagion,* "Holy, holy, holy, LORD GOD of Sabaoth, heaven and earth are full of thy glory," though not expressly mentioned by Justin, was used in Cyril's time, 330.]‡‡‡

---

* Plin. B. x. Ep. 97.

† Ep. 22, Ad Eustach. c. 15.

‡ Apos. Cons. ii. 57, v. 19.

§ Jus. Apol. i. 87.

‖ Aug. Serm. 10, Hom. 33; Counc. Laod. Can. 17.

¶ Jus. Apol. i. 87.

** Bing. B. xiv. c. 4, § 24.

†† Jus. Apol. i. 87.

‡‡ Apos. Cons. viii. 5, 6.

§§ Jus. Apol. i. 85.

‖‖ Cyril, Cat. Myst. v. 4.

¶¶ Orat. Dom. c. 20.

*** Hom. De Euchar.

††† Hom. 83, De Divers.

‡‡‡ Myst. v. 5.

4. The commemoration of our LORD's words, in consecrating the elements.*

5. The oblation, or offering.†

6. Prayers, [including the LORD's prayer,] the people responding, *Amen.*‡

7. Breaking of bread, and distribution of the elements, by the Deacons.§

8. The Communion.||

9. Collection of the alms of the Church.¶

These are the more important parts of the early public worship, but there were, no doubt, some particulars that have not come down to us.

There are presumptions of the strongest kind, arising from other sources, that the public worship of the primitive Church was by means of a Liturgy. If we examine the most important of the present Liturgies, and trace them back to their sources, we shall find four ancient Liturgies, bearing the names of St. Peter, St. James, St. John, and St. Mark; to one of which every Liturgy in all the Churches in the world can be traced; and there does not now exist, and never has existed, more than four independent forms of Liturgies; and these four resemble each other too much, to have grown up independently, and too little, to have been copied from each other. We shall consider each of these as briefly as can be consistently done.

Liturgy of Jerusalem, or St. James, called also the Liturgy of Antioch.—The Patriarchate of Antioch originally included that of Jerusalem, and comprised the countries of Judea, Mesopotamia, Syria, and some of the provinces of Asia Minor. The Liturgy which prevailed in these countries is de-

---

* Jus. Apol. i. 85, 86, 87.

† Ib. 85, 86, 87.

‡ Pal. Orig. Lit. I. pp. 15–45.

§ Jus. Apol. i. 85, 86, 87.

|| Ib.

¶ Ib.

serving of particular attention, for several reasons: (1,) because the Church of Jerusalem was the Mother-Church of Christendom,* and the faithful first received the title of Christians at Antioch, (Acts xi. 26;) (2,) because the Liturgy there used prevailed over a large extent of country; and (3,) because we have more ancient and numerous notices of this Liturgy in the writings of the Fathers, than of any other.

This Patriarchate has for a long time been chiefly inhabited by two denominations of Christians, the Melchites or Orthodox, who hold the true faith concerning the divine and human nature of CHRIST; and the Monophysites or Jacobites, who hold that the human nature of CHRIST is entirely absorbed in the divine, and made one with it. This error was condemned by the Council of Chalcedon, A. D. 451, and a separation between the parties took place at that time. They have held no communion with each other since. The orthodox of this Patriarchate have long used a Liturgy called the *Liturgy of St. James*, because they believe him to have been the original composer of it.† The Syrian Monophysites also use a Liturgy which they call that of St. James, and which they say was composed by him.‡ These Liturgies now teach the doctrines held by the respective parties; yet, *they agree in the order of the parts, in the rites by which they are accompanied, and the general nature of the ideas* in those parts where there is no difference of doctrine: so that whoever compares the two will be surprised at their minute agreement in sentiments and expressions, when he recollects that near fourteen centuries have elapsed since the separation took place.§ The *Liturgy of St. James*, therefore, must be older than the Council of Chalcedon, 451, and was then held in such estimation, as coming down from Apostolic

* Gies. Ecc. Hist. c. 2, § 29.

† Palm. Orig. Lit. I. § 1.

‡ Ibid.

§ Orig. Lit. I. p. § 1.

days, that on a separation in the Church, each party retained both the *title* and *substance* of the same Liturgy. This Liturgy still continues to be used by the Monophysites, but has been supplanted, among the orthodox, by that of Constantinople, except on the festival of St. James, when the Liturgy bearing his name is used.

The allusions to this Liturgy are frequent among the Fathers of the fourth and fifth centuries. It is particularly described, or evidently alluded to, by Theodoret, Bishop of Cyrus,* by Jerome,† by Chrysostom, afterwards Bishop and Patriarch of Constantinople,‡ Ephrem of Syria,§ and Cyril, Bishop of Jerusalem. In a work of the last, written between 330 and 340, he describes the Liturgy which was celebrated after the dismissal of the Catechumens with a minuteness which proves its identity with the Liturgy of St. James.‖ These writers living in different parts of the Patriarchate of Antioch, agree in describing a Liturgy essentially the same, and which was called the Liturgy of St. James, before the Council of Chalcedon, 451, being the same then, as 120 years before, or A. D. 330. If from this time we ascend to A. D. 150, and compare the account given by Justin Martyr, of the order of worship in the Syrian Churches in his day, with the Liturgy of St. James, we shall find that as far as he goes, he agrees with the order of the Liturgy which we know was used in the same place 150 years after.¶ There is, therefore, every reason to believe, that the Liturgy of St. James has come down from the most primitive times; not, indeed, precisely as we now have it, since the origin of many things contained in it can be shown; but much of the substance of

---

* Ep. Œcon. † Adv. Pelag.

‡ Hom. vii., ix., xviii., xxviii., lxxii. Ep. Ad. Cor.

§ De Sacerdot. ‖ Cyr. Op. 296–300

¶ Apol. i. p. 96, 7. Ed. Thir. Dial. Tryp. p. 386.

it, in the same order in which it now occurs, is certainly as old as the second, and probably as old as the first century.

Liturgy of Cæsarea, or St. Basil.—The Exarchate, or Patriarchate of Cæsarea, extended from the Hellespont to the Euphrates, and with the exception of Proconsular Asia, Phrygia, and a few maritime provinces, included the whole of Asia Minor. Cæsarea, in Cappadocia, was the metropolis of this country, and corresponded to the civil diocese of Pontus. Basil, surnamed "the Great," was consecrated Bishop of this city, A. D. 370. The unanimous voice of antiquity ascribes to him the composition or enlargement of a Liturgy; and one bearing his name, has long been used in Asia Minor. The existence of a Liturgy, bearing the name of Basil, is testified to by Charles the Bold, in the ninth century;* by the Council of Constantinople, 691;† by Leontius, of Byzantium, 590;‡ by Peter, the Deacon, 520,§ and by Gregory Nazianzen, the cotemporary and intimate friend of St. Basil;‖ and after a lapse of near 1500 years, this same Liturgy, without any substantial variation, is used from the northern shore of Russia, to the extremities of Abyssinia, and from the Adriatic and Baltic seas, to the furthest shore of Asia.¶ In many respects, this is the most valuable Liturgy extant, as we can trace back most of *the words and expressions* contained in it, to about the year 370.

It becomes, therefore, an interesting inquiry—to what extent was Basil the composer of this Liturgy? That it was more than merely reducing to writing a Liturgy previously in use, is evident; but that it extended to the composition of an entirely new one, is improbable; and if not improbable, is contradicted by the writers of that age. Indeed, he in-

* Imp. Ep. Ad. Cler. v. † Can. 32. ‡ Adv. Nestor. iii. 18.
§ De Incar. c. 8. ‖ Orat. 20.
¶ Orig. Lit. I. § 2. Bing. Ant. Ecc. i. c. 17, § 2, 9, 10.

forms us himself, that "the customs" which he had appointed, were "consonant and agreeable to all the Churches of God;"* whence it must be inferred that these customs had been settled long before his day. Now if we compare the *Liturgy of St. Basil* with that of *St. James*, in the fourth century, we shall find *the order and substance* of both exactly the same.† Hence, the most reasonable conclusion is, that the part performed by Basil, consisted only in enriching the ancient formularies of Cæsarea, by the addition of new fervor and sublimity to their devotion, and greater beauty and correctness to their diction.‡ Hence, also, it is reasonable to infer, that previous to the time of St. Basil, the *Liturgy of Cæsarea* was essentially the same as that of St. James. Upon no other supposition can we account for their great similarity. Antioch and Cæsarea were independent Patriarchates, covering extensive tracts of country; and as the Bishops in both, not only possessed the authority to compose new Liturgies, but also to change and modify old ones, the Liturgies of the two countries would be unlikely to agree, unless they had been the same at the beginning. And if they had been the same at the beginning, the *Liturgy of St. Basil*, both *in substance and order*, has certainly existed from the second, and probably from the first century. This Liturgy, or one bearing the same name, still exists, and is used in three languages, the Greek, Coptic, and Syriac. The oldest

* Ep. 207.

† Orig. Lit. I. 71.

‡ It is uncertain whether the Liturgy of St. Basil had been reduced to writing before his time, and he has been understood by some in one place, (De Spir. Sanc. c. 27. Opp. T. III. p. 55,) to say as much. But his language in that applies only to a small portion of the Liturgy, and not to all, as the objector assumes, and it is doubtful whether he intended to say, as he has been understood, even of that small portion. At any rate, it recognizes the existence of the very prayer alluded to, previous to his own day.

manuscript of this Liturgy is supposed to be above 1180 years old, or to have been written before A. D. 660.*

Liturgy of Constantinople, or, *Chrysostom*.—The Church of Byzantium, afterwards Constantinople, originally subject to the Metropolitan of Heraclea, in the civil Diocese of Thrace, was elevated to dignity and power by the Emperor Constantine, about the middle of the fourth century; and the second General Council held at Constantinople, A. D. 381, raised the Bishop of that Church to the dignity and precedence of the Second Metropolitan See. Subsequently, his jurisdiction was extended over the whole of Thrace, Ephesus, and Cæsarea, and these were formally placed under him by the Council of Chalcedon, 451. The whole of Greece, also, became subject to him, and remained under him, until the recent revolution in that country.

In the Churches of this Patriarchate, a Liturgy has long been used, bearing the name of Chrysostom. At what period it was introduced, we are not able to say, as there is very little mention of it, before the tenth century. It was translated into Latin about 1180. In all the main features, the *Liturgy of St. Chrysostom* agrees with that of *St. Basil*, the former expanding and carrying out the ideas contained in the latter. The *Liturgy of St. Chrysostom*, therefore, appears to be nothing more than an expansion of that of St. Basil, and in all its important features—in *its substance and order*—must be equally ancient with that and the *Liturgy of St. James*.†

These Liturgies, taken together, may justly be called the Great Oriental Liturgy; one recension of which, in the fourth century, prevailed from Arabia to Cappadocia, and from the Mediterranean to the Euphrates, and which may be traced back nearly or quite to the Apostolic age,—another, at the same time prevailing throughout nearly all Asia Minor,

* Orig. Lit. I. § 2.

† Orig. Lit. I. § 3.

having existed there from time immemorial; and the third, at the same time, with the same antiquity, prevailing in Greece and Macedonia. When, therefore, we reflect on the vast extent of these countries, the independence of the Churches existing there, the power possessed and exercised by each Bishop, of improving the Liturgy of his own Church; the *circumstantial* varieties, but *substantial* agreement of all; it seems difficult, if not impossible, to account for this identity and uniformity in any other manner, than by supposing that the Apostles themselves originated the order and substance of the Oriental Liturgy, and communicated it to all those Churches at their very foundation. The *uniformity* of these Liturgies, as extant in the fourth and fifth centuries, bespeak a *common* origin; while their *diversity* is such as to prove the *remoteness* of the period at which they were originated. To what remote period, then, can we refer, as exhibiting a general uniformity of Liturgy, except to the Apostolic age? And why not to that age, since we have proved the existence of such a Liturgy in the time of Justin Martyr, who was removed but a single link from the Apostles?

Liturgy of Alexandria, or St. Mark.—The patriarchate of Alexandria, where Christianity was first planted by St. Mark,* has been in possession of the Monophysites, or Jacobites, eleven hundred years. The Jacobites took their rise in the fifth century, and soon became numerous in Egypt. But, owing to the favor of the Emperors, the Orthodox kept possession of the See until the invasion of the Mohammedans, in the seventh century. From that period to the present, the Monophysites have possessed nearly all the Churches in Egypt, the Orthodox being but a small minority. The Egyptian Monophysites use three Liturgies, written in the ancient Coptic language, all of which prevailed in Egypt *at,*

* Euseb. Ecc. His. ii. 16.

and probably *before*, the time of the Mohammedan invasion. They are called the Liturgies of St. Basil, of Gregory Nazianzen, and of Cyril, Patriarch of Alexandria. They do not appear, however, to have been originally written in Coptic, but to have been translated from the Greek, as appears from the occurrence of Greek phrases in the Coptic Liturgies, now extant, and by the existence of ancient Greek manuscripts of those Liturgies.*

The precise time when the Coptic language began to be used in the celebration of divine worship, is not known, though it must have been at an early period, as we read of Egyptian clergy in the fourth century, who could read no language but their own, and yet, who read the Scriptures daily, and celebrated divine service.† Now it appears from a comparison of the Liturgies of St. Basil and Gregory Nazianzen, that they were introduced, as they profess to have been, from Cappadocia, or the surrounding dioceses. But the Liturgy of Cyril does not seem to have come from any foreign Church. Some of the Alexandrian historians call it "The Liturgy of St. Mark, which Cyril perfected;"‡ and it is clear that the Liturgies of Cyril, and that of St. Mark, used by the Orthodox, as they now exist, had a common origin, or one was borrowed from the other. There is reason to believe, that both have proceeded from the ancient Liturgy of the Egyptian Church, used before the Council of Chalcedon, 451. On no other supposition can we account for the fact, that these two Liturgies, professing to have come from the same source—used by two bodies of men holding no communion with each other since that time—should agree with each other both in *substance and order*, and yet differ from the Liturgies of all other Churches in the world, except

* Orig. Lit. I. § 4.

† Hug. Intd. N. T. Par. I. viii. § 91

‡ Renaud. Tom. I, p. 171.

the Ethiopian. The chief difference between the Liturgy of St. Mark and that of Cyril, is confined to the introduction, and to differences of doctrine. The Ethiopian Liturgy was evidently borrowed from Alexandria, from whence the first missionaries were sent to the former country, about A. D. 330; and was clearly copied from that of St. Mark.* Yet it has so many things unlike the others, that it must have been compiled at an early period. Indeed, it is hardly possible there should have been much, if any, copying of Liturgies after the schisms which occurred in the fifth century.

It is not certain at what time the Liturgy of St. Mark was composed. Some believe it was composed by St. Mark himself; but, because it contains some things of a later date, and some which the Evangelist could not have written,

* Soc. Ecc. His. i. 19. Soz. Ecc. His. ii. 24. Theod. Ecc. His. i. 23. The whole of the calendar of the Ethiopian Church, by which all its services were regulated, was copied from the peculiar calendar of the Egyptians, as will be seen by the following comparison.

Fixed year of Egyptians.	*Ethiopian year.*	*Begins.*	*Length.*
1 Thoth,	Maskarram,	Aug. 29,	30.
2 Paophi,	Tekemt,	Sept. 28,	30.
3 Athor,	Hedar,	Oct. 28,	30.
4 Choiak,	Tahsas,	Nov. 27,	30.
5 Tobi,	Ter,	Dec. 27,	30.
6 Mechir,	Yekatit,	Jan. 26,	30.
7 Phamenoth,	Magabit,	Feb 25,	30.
8 Pharmuthi,	Meaziah,	Mar. 27,	30.
9 Pachon,	Genbot,	April 26,	30
10 Paoni,	Sanne,	May 26,	30.
11 Epiphi,	Hamle,	June 25,	30.
12 Mesori,	Nahasse,	July 25,	30.
Epagomenæ,	Pagmen,	———	5.

Every *fourth* year an additional day was intercalated. This calendar of the "fixed year" was first adopted about twenty years before the Christian era.

others have supposed it all a forgery. This *name* is not known to be older than the fourth century, but the *substance and order* of the Liturgy must be much more ancient. If it were not so, it is inconceivable why the Orthodox and Monophysites, who separated in 451, should both retain the same Liturgy; or, why a Church, that was planted by missionaries from that Church 120 years before, should also have the same Liturgy. We are, therefore, able to trace *the words* of the Liturgy of St. Mark, to about 451, and the *order* of it, to about 330, accompanied by the tradition, that it had come down from the Apostles. Hence, the probability is, that the *order and substance* of this Liturgy have come down from the Apostles, and if so, it was originally derived from the institutions of *St. Mark*, or composed by St. Mark himself.

Liturgy of the Exarchate of Ephesus, or *St. John.*—The Exarchate of Ephesus included the provinces of the Hellespont, Phrygia, Asia, Lycaonia, Pamphylia, and the maritime cities included within that limit. The Exarch of Ephesus was independent until 451, when by decree of the Council of Chalcedon, it was made subject to the Patriarch of Constantinople. For a long time, the Liturgies of Basil and Chrysostom have been used in this region; but there is reason to believe that another form was used there at an early period. Some time in the fourth century, a Council was held at Laodicea, composed of the bishops of this Exarchate. One of the canons enacted by this Council, gives minute directions for the use of the Liturgy.* Such a canon would not have been made without cause, and the only probable supposition is, that the object of the canon was *to change* the existing practice in reference to this subject. This canon appoints an order, the same, or similar to that ever since

* Coun. Laod. can. 19.

used in those Churches, that is, in conformity with the order of St. Basil and St. Chrysostom. What the precise difference between the old Liturgy, and that introduced by the Council of Laodicea, was, it is not easy to say. This much, however, may be inferred, that they differed only where directions were given to alter it. We have no copy of the Ephesian Liturgy before that Council, but we have one which seems clearly to have been derived from it.

The Gallican Liturgy.—It has long been known, that the ancient Liturgy of Gaul differed from that of Rome, though the precise nature of the difference was unknown, until some ancient monuments of that Liturgy were discovered in the seventeenth century. The composition of this Liturgy, either in whole or in part, has been ascribed to different individuals. Musæus, a Presbyter of Marseilles, who died about the middle of the fifth century, is said to have composed a book of Sacraments, for Eustasius, Bishop of that city.* Sidonius, Bishop of Auvergne, who died about A. D. 494, also composed a book of Sacraments.† A preface was written to this by Gregory, of Tours, in the sixth century. Hilary, Bishop of Poicters, who died about 368, composed a book of Sacraments and Hymns.‡ These, as far as can be ascertained, were nothing more than modifications of an older *Liturgy*. They seem to have constituted the *Missal* of the Gallican Church, or the Liturgies adapted to the various feasts. That this was different from the Liturgy of Rome, is evident from the questions proposed by Augustine, after his arrival in Britain, to Gregory, Bishop of Rome.§ They remained in use in Gaul, until Pepin introduced the Roman mode of chanting, and finally *Charlemagne* substituted the whole body of the Roman service. The introduc-

* Bona. Rer. Lit. I. 12.

† Greg. Turo. His. France, i. 22.

‡ Hieron. De Scrip. c. 100.

§ Bd. i. 27.

tion of this Liturgy was opposed by the Gallican clergy, as they were unwilling to give up the use of a Liturgy which they believed to be coeval with the introduction of Christianity into that country.

There are numerous reasons for supposing the Gallican Liturgy to be of Eastern origin. Lyons was the oldest Church in Gaul, and Irenæus, consecrated Bishop of that city, A. D. 176, was an Eastern man, and several of the missionaries to that place were also from the East.* So, also, Pothinus, the predecessor of Irenæus, came from the East.† Several of these, and Irenæus, the most prominent of all, were the disciples of Polycarp, who was himself the disciple of St. John. A community of interest and feeling between the Churches of Gaul and Asia, is proved by the fact, that at the time of the great persecution of 175, the Churches of Lyons and Vienne wrote an account of their sufferings to the Churches of Asia and Phrygia, and to no others. It was, therefore, from Asia that the Gallican Church received her ecclesiastical rites and customs, which early historians ascribe to St. John.‡ And it is reasonable

---

* Iren. Adv. Hær. iii. 3. Ep. Ad. Flor.

† Greg. Tuor. i. 28, 29.

‡ Strong evidence of this is to be found in the fact, that the technical language of the Gallican Church came from Greece, and not from Rome. Thus, the word *Church*, (from the Greek κυριακον,) employed by the Gothic Churches—Old German, *chirihh;* German, *kirche;* Dutch, *kerk;* Scottish, *kirk;* Anglo-Saxon, *circ*, and *cyric;* Icelandic, *kyrkia;* Swedish, *kyrka;* Danish, *kirke;* English, *Church,* —is also found in the Slavonic languages: Russian, *tserkov;* Bohemian, *cyrkew;* Lusatian, *zirkwa;* Dalmatian, *czrikwa;* Polish, *cerkiew*, denoting the Greek Church, and [*kasciol*, (Russian and Bohemian, *kostel;*) denoting the Romish:]—could never have been derived from the Latin. This word is certainly as old as the time of *Ulphilas*, A. D. 400, and probably much older. In all places where this word prevails, the ecclesiastical rites must have come from the Greeks, and not from the Ro-

to infer, that, as the *Liturgy of St. James* contained *the rites and customs* of the Churches over which *St. James* originally exercised ecclesiastical jurisdiction; and that of *St. Mark*, the customs of the Churches planted by him; so the Liturgy of Ephesus, from which the Gallican Liturgy was copied, contained the rites and customs adopted by the Churches over which *St. John* exercised a supervision. And as these can all be traced up to a very early period, it is reasonable to conclude, such *rites and customs* had their origin with the Apostles themselves.

Tradition, from the earliest period, has always ascribed the Gallican Liturgy to St. John. Thus an Irish writer of the seventh century, says: that "John the Evangelist first chanted the Gallican course, [i. e. Liturgy;] then afterwards the blessed Polycarp, the disciple of St. John; then afterwards, thirdly, Irenæus, who was Bishop of Lyons, in Gaul, chanted the same course in Gaul."* Now, though the tes-

---

mans, as they uniformly employed the Greek word *Ecclesia*. The Portuguese *igreja* may have come from the same root, though generally derived from the Latin *Ecclesia*. It is the same word as the Hindostane *girja*, which we know is from this root, as that has also *kulesa*, from *Ecclesia*.

The Goths copied very little, if any, of their ecclesiastical language from the Romish Church, as we have already seen in regard to the word *Church*, and the words employed to signify baptism. So also, their languages did not adopt either *Eucharist* from the Greek, nor *Sacrament* from the Latin, but used a word of their own to signify the same thing. Thus, Mœso-Gothic, *hunsle*, (signifying both *sacrifice* and *Eucharist*;) A. S. *husel*; Icelandic, *husl*, *hunsl*; old English, *housel*; which seems to be from the root *hus*, "to protect;" with reference to the *effect* of a participation of this Sacrament.

So also *Confirmation*, was expressed in their own language, by the verb "to be bishopped;" and *Ordination* or *Consecration*, by the word "to be hallowed," or made sacred.

* Spel. Concil. I. 176.

timony of this author is not conclusive evidence of the truth of these facts, it is, as to what was then the *universal belief* respecting them. This Liturgy always differed, both from the Roman and Oriental, but approximated much nearer the latter than the former.

Liturgy of Rome, or *St. Peter.*—It has been much debated, whether the Roman Liturgy can justly claim any considerable antiquity. Some suppose it to have been composed by Gregory "the Great," about 590. Others think it impossible at this day, to ascertain the text, even as it stood at that time. The subject has been confused, by confounding the *Missal*, formerly called *Sacramentary*, with the *Liturgy*. It is perhaps impossible to ascertain the true text of the Roman *Missal*, as it existed in any of the early centuries; but this is not the case with the *Liturgy*. All the manuscripts of this, give the same number of prayers, in the same order, throughout the *invariable* part of the Liturgy, or, as it is usually termed, *the Canon*. The only difference consists in the introduction of short petitions, or the name of some person to be commemorated.

It has been said that this was *composed* by Gregory,* but this can hardly be, as history gives a minute account of his alterations and improvements. These consisted in collecting, arranging, abbreviating, and improving the collects and prayers. He introduced one petition into the Canon, and joined the Lord's Prayer to it. These facts prove that Gregory was not the *composer*, but the compiler and improver of the *Roman Liturgy*.†

Others suppose that this Liturgy was composed by Vigilius, who lived near fifty years before Gregory, about A. D 540.‡ The reason for this, is the fact, that Gregory himself

* Brett. Liturg. p. 331.
† Orig. Liturg. I. § 6.
‡ Ep. Ad. Profotur.

speaks of the Canon extant in his time, as having been com posed by a scholastic, or learned man, which some have understood to refer to Vigilius. But it is nowhere said that Vigilius was this "scholastic," and besides, Vigilius says of the Liturgy in his time, "that they had received it from Apostolical tradition." Whoever, therefore, was the "scholastic" referred to by Gregory, it is probable that he was no otherwise the composer of this Liturgy, than Gregory was the composer of the *Sacramentary* that bears his name; and hence, that he only collected, arranged, and modified existing materials, supposed to have come down from the Apostolic age.

Still earlier than this, mention is made of a Liturgy of the Church of Rome, and history informs us, that about 492, Gelasius performed a work somewhat similar to that of Gregory. An ancient *Sacramentary* has also been discovered in modern times, which is believed by learned men, to represent the *Roman Sacramentary*, as it was in the time of Gelasius. There is also a manuscript of the Roman Liturgy in existence, supposed to have been written *before* the time of Gelasius, or as early as 483. It is generally known by the appellation of the *Leonian Sacramentary*, from an opinion that it represents the offices of that Church in the time of Leo "the Great." This author, who lived at the time of the Council of Chalcedon, 451, is said to have *added* certain passages to the Liturgy, whence it is evident that the remainder was in existence before his time. Besides, there are certain passages in his writings, which seem to have been transcribed almost verbatim, into this *Sacramentary*. In addition to this, Innocent, Bishop of Rome, about 410, makes mention of *the rites* of that Church, and describes them as having descended from St. Peter. Here the *direct* evidence to the antiquity of the Romish Ritual ends. There is, however, reason to believe, as many suppose, that the so-called *African Liturgy*, which was used at Carthage and its vicinity, was originally the same as the Roman, and that it was *probably* copied from it.

African Liturgy.—The civil Diocese of Africa comprised the Provinces of Proconsular Africa, Numidia, Tripoli, Byzancium, and the two Mauritanias. At what time Christianity was first preached at Carthage, the chief city of this portion of country, or by whom preached, is uncertain. It is not improbable, however, when we recollect the situation of Carthage, in reference to Rome, and the intercourse between the two countries after the death of Hannibal, B. C. 183, that the earliest missionaries to Carthage, should go from Rome; and if so, they would of course carry the Roman Liturgy with them. This supposition will account for the fact, that the African Fathers, when professing to give an account of their own rites, have seemed to some ritualists, to be describing the Roman customs. On this point we are only able to obtain probabilities, as all those Churches, once conspicuous for their numbers, their learning, and their piety, have long ceased to exist. And with them, has gone every copy of their Liturgy; so that now we have only the allusions made to it, in the writings of those Fathers who lived in Africa, to inform us concerning its nature and character.*

The Roman Liturgy differed in some respects from all the Liturgies of the East. One of these points consisted in directing "the kiss of charity," as it was called, to be given *after* the consecration of the elements; whereas, in all the Eastern Liturgies it was given *before*. In this respect, the African corresponded with the Roman Liturgy, as we learn from Tertullian† and Augustine.‡ We learn also from Augustine, that the custom of singing anthems from the Book

* Orig. Lit. I. § 8. † Adv. Marc. i. c. 23. Ad. Scap. c. 2.
‡ Retract. ii. c. 11. Serm. 45, 49, 176.

of Psalms, before the Liturgy began, was introduced at Carthage in his time; and we know that this practice was introduced at Rome by Cœlestine, A. D. 423. Then came reading of the Scriptures, which sometimes began with a Lesson from the Prophets, followed by one from the Epistles, and sometimes began with one from the Epistles. After reading the first Lesson, followed a Psalm, which order corresponded with the Roman customs, but has no other parallel either in the East or West, except in the Liturgy of Milan, which is supposed by many to have been copied from that of Rome. Indeed, the whole order of service in the African Church, as described by Tertullian, Cyprian, Augustine, and Optatus, is in every essential point, the same as in the Roman. These striking coincidences render it almost certain, that these two Liturgies came from the same source, or that one was copied from the other. But as Christianity was planted at Rome, before at Carthage, it is not probable the Liturgy of Rome came from Africa; yet, the Liturgy of Africa, in the second and third centuries, corresponded with the Roman in the fifth. Consequently, both must be as old as the second century, and hence there is reason to believe, that the *order and substance* of those Liturgies, is as ancient as in other Churches, and if so, it must have come down from the Apostles.

Liturgy of Spain.—We remarked, when speaking of the Gallican Liturgy, that its use was abolished in France, by Charlemagne. The old Spanish Liturgy, however, was not abolished until three centuries after, when the Spanish monarchs obliged the Churches in their dominions to relinquish their own, and adopt the Roman Liturgy. It was abolished in Arragon, A. D. 1060, but was used considerably later in Navarre, Castile, and Leon. From that time to the sixteenth century, this Liturgy ceased to be used, when Cardinal Ximenes endowed a College and Chapel at Toledo, for the celebration of the ancient rite. This is probably the only place where the primitive Liturgy of this country continues to be used.

This Liturgy agrees in most particulars with the Gallican.* The number and order of the invariable parts maintain a close correspondence, though the introductions are various. So great is their similarity, that Charles the Bold, in the ninth century, writing to the clergy of Ravenna, speaks of the clergy of Toledo as using the Gallican Liturgy, abolished by his ancestor, Charlemagne.† And Isidore, Bishop of Seville, in the sixth century, described the Spanish Liturgy so minutely as to leave no doubt that it was the Liturgy used in that country some centuries after.‡ It also appears from a letter of Vigilius, of Rome, to Profuturus, Bishop of Braga, in 538, that the Spanish Bishops were *not* familiar with the Roman Liturgy at that time.§ And as we know the Spanish Liturgy differed from the Roman in the sixth century, there is reason to believe it had from the beginning.

Before this time, there was no power over them that would be likely to introduce a new Liturgy. Rome had not the power, and if she had possessed it, would not have introduced one different from her own. Nor is there any reason to believe the Pagan Goths introduced a new Liturgy when they overran Spain, as some contend; nor any reason to believe, had they done it, that the Spanish Churches would have relinquished their own Liturgy, and adopted one introduced by their barbarous invaders. Nor is there any reason to suppose that the Gallican Liturgy was introduced into Spain, or the Spanish into Gaul, at any period *near* the sixth century. There is no trace, either in history or tradition, of any such

---

* Orig. Lit. I. § 10.
† Imp. Ep.
‡ De Ecc. Offic. i. c. 11–15.
§ Ad. Profuturus.

introduction. It is, however, apparent, that this Liturgy was derived from the Gallican, at a very early period, or that both came from the same source.

The probability seems to be, that, though Christianity was introduced into some portion of Spain, even in the times of the Apostles, it did not make much progress there, until the second century. The first mention of the Spanish clergy, is by Cyprian, about 250, a hundred years after Pothinus was Bishop of Lyons, in Gaul.* The first Spanish Martyr, of which we have any *undoubted* account, suffered in A. D. 259.† In the absence of all positive *proof* on the subject, it seems probable that Spain, or a large portion of it, was converted by Gallican Missionaries, and that they took along with them the Liturgy of their own Church; whence, the correspondence of the two. That the Spanish Liturgy was at any time introduced into Gaul, is improbable. Christianity was in a flourishing condition there, before it was in Spain; and we have already seen that the Gallican Liturgy came from Ephesus. Hence, then, either the Spanish Liturgy was copied from the Gallican, which is probable, or, it was brought from Ephesus to Spain, of which there is no proof.

Liturgy of Britain and Ireland.—The period when Christianity was introduced into England, has been the subject of much debate. It is *probable*, that the gospel was preached there in the first century; it is *certain*, that there were Christians there in the second; and the Bishops of Churches there, attended the Council of Arles, 315, perhaps of Nice, 325, and of Sardica, subsequent to that time. At the time Augustine came to England, the Liturgy of the British Churches was different from that of Rome. From whence the British Churches derived their Liturgy, we can not certainly say; but as that of Gaul prevailed in the vicinity, and as there

---

* Ep. 67

† Ruinart, Acta Martyr. p. 219.

was no other in that region, which differed essentially from that of Rome, it is reasonable to conclude, they used the Gallican, or one resembling it. It also appears from an ancient catalogue of Irish saints, written, as is supposed, in the seventh century, that from the time Patrick was Archbishop in Ireland, to the middle of the sixth century, the Irish had but one Liturgy, and that this Liturgy was different from that used in Britain; and if, as some suppose, the Irish Liturgy *corresponded* with that of Rome, it follows that the British Liturgy was *different* from it.

Liturgy of Milan.—The Liturgy of the Church of Milan, known by the name of the *Ambrosian Liturgy*, differs in several particulars from that of Rome, but is nevertheless believed by many to have been copied from it. Others, however, believe it to have been different from the beginning. In either case, it was probably copied from some other Liturgy, and hence, no conclusive argument can be drawn from it relative to the subject of primitive Liturgies.

We have now gone over with a brief view of the several Liturgies, and have found in the East, a great *Oriental Liturgy*, used in Antioch, Cæsarea, and Constantinople, capable of being traced nearly, or quite up to Apostolic times, and *from the earliest ages attributed to St. James.* We have found in Alexandria, a Liturgy reaching back nearly to the same period, and *from very early ages bearing the name of* St. Mark. In Britain, Spain, and Gaul, a Liturgy derived from that of Ephesus, the substance of which *has descended*, as is believed, *from the time of* St. John; and we have also found one in Rome, Milan, and the Civil Diocese of Africa, extending back, we can not tell how far, but certainly to a very early period, *owing its origin*, as many believe, to St. Peter. In all these Liturgies, there are these several parts in which they resemble each other.

I. All the ancient Liturgies now existing, or which can be

proved ever to have existed, now resemble one another in the following points:—

1. All of them direct, that previous to communion, those who intend to communicate, shall exchange "the kiss of peace."

2. In all of them, the more particularly solemn part of the service commences with the words exactly answering to the English, "Lift up your hearts," &c., as far as "HOLY FATHER, almighty, everlasting GOD."

3. All contain the Hymn, "Therefore with Angels and Archangels," &c., with very trifling varieties of expression.

4. Also, a commemoration of our LORD's words and actions in the institution of the Eucharist, which is the same, almost word for word, in every Liturgy, but is not taken from any of the four Scriptural accounts.

5. A sacrificial oblation of the Eucharistic bread and wine.

6. A prayer of consecration, that GOD will "make the bread and wine the Body and Blood of CHRIST."

7. Also, they all contain a prayer, answering in substance to ours, "for the whole state of CHRIST's Church militant."

8. And likewise another prayer, (which has been excluded from the English Ritual,) "for the rest and peace of all those who have departed this life in GOD's faith and fear;" concluding with a prayer for communion with them.*

9. The Lord's Prayer.

10. Direction to the Priest for breaking the consecrated bread.

11. Communion.

---

* This prayer is often confounded with prayers *for* the dead, which were not strictly Primitive; and also with prayers *to* the dead, which are far more recent. The earliest trace of this commemoration is in *The Martyrdom of Ignatius*, written about A. D. 108, and that of

II. These parts are always arranged in one of the four following orders.

ST. JAMES' LITURGY.

Oriental.

1. The kiss of peace.
2. Lift up your hearts, &c. [Sursum Corda.]
3. Therefore with Angels, &c. [Trisagion.]
4. Commemoration of our Lord's words.
5. The Oblation.
6. Consecrating Prayer.
7. Prayer for the Church Militant.
8. Commemoration of departed saints.
9. The Lord's Prayer.
10. Breaking of bread.
11. Communion.

ST. MARK'S LITURGY.

Egyptian and Ethiopian.

1. The kiss of peace.
2. Lift up your hearts, &c. [Sursum Corda.]
7. Prayer for the Church Militant.
8. Commemoration of departed saints.
3. Therefore with Angels, &c. [Trisagion.]
4. Commemoration of our Lord's words.
5. The Oblation.
6. Consecrating Prayer.

Polycarp, written about 168. But no account is given of the manner in which it was done, and we only learn that it was *annually*. Tertullian, A. D. 200, is more particular; he says, "We offer on one day in every year, oblations for the dead, *as birth-day honors*." (De Cor. 3.) Cyprian calls it an "anniversary commemoration." (Ep. 39.) Cyril, of Jerusalem, says, the offering was "*in memory* of those who had fallen asleep." (Cat. Myst. 5.)

10. Breaking of bread.
9. Lord's Prayer.
11. Communion.

St. John's Liturgy.

Gallican, Ephesian, and Mozarabic.

7. Prayer for the Church Militant.
8. Commemoration of departed saints.
1. Kiss of peace.
2. Lift up your hearts, &c. [Sursum Corda.]
3. Therefore with Angels, &c. [Trisagion.]
4. Commemoration of our Lord's words.
5. The Oblation.
6. Consecrating Prayer.
10. Breaking of bread.
9. Lord's Prayer.
11. Communion.

St. Peter's Liturgy.

Roman, Milanese, African.

2. Lift up your hearts, &c. [Sursum Corda.]
3. Therefore with Angels, &c. [Trisagion.]
7. Prayer for the Church Militant.
6. Consecrating Prayer.
4. Commemoration of our Lord's words.
5. The Oblation.
8. Commemoration of departed saints.
10. Breaking of bread.
9. The Lord's Prayer.
1. The kiss of peace.
11. Communion.

The American Liturgy, adopted with alterations from the English, has the following:—

AMERICAN LITURGY.

United States, Texas.

7. Prayer for the Church Militant, containing also,
8. Commemoration of departed saints.
2. Lift up your hearts, &c. [Sursum Corda.]
3. Therefore with Angels, &c. [Trisagion.]
4. Commemoration of our Lord's words.
10. Breaking of bread.
5. The Oblation.
6. Consecrating Prayer.
11. Communion.
9. The Lord's Prayer.

One remarkable circumstance in these several Liturgies, is, that although the language, in consecrating the elements in the Eucharist, in commemoration of our LORD's words and actions, is almost the same, word for word, in them all, it does not agree in words, with any of the Scripture accounts of it. Indeed, it would almost seem, that this is an original and independent account of the transaction, by the Apostles themselves, incorporated into these Liturgies, and that it has come down to us unchanged.

A similar conclusion must be drawn from the substantial agreement of the Baptismal Liturgies. Thus, if we examine the various copies of the several Liturgies, we shall find them using the same Scripture, giving it the same interpretation, describing it by the same terms, and pleading the same authority for their interpretations and practices. A few coincidences will be mentioned.

1. The text, John iii. 5, "Except a man be born of water and the Spirit, he can not enter into the kingdom of God," is universally applied to baptism.* It is read as a lesson in

---

* This is also done by all the early fathers.

the Armenian Baptismal Service, (Ass. Bib. Lit. ii. 196–206,) the Malabar, (i. 188,) Greek Liturgy of James of Edessa, (ii. 274,) Apostolic Liturgy revised by Severus, (ii. 154,) that of Gelasius, (i. 9, 10,) Gregory, (i. 35,) Gaul, (i. 40,) Gellone, (i. 57,) Poictiers, (i. 63–69,) Naples, (i. 75,) Vienne, (i. 77–80,) and Liege, (i. 83.) It is also referred to in the prayers, in the Old Gothic Baptismal Service, (ii. 34,) Old Roman, (ii. 4, 8, 63, 68, 75,) Old Gallican, (ii. 38,) Chrysostom, (ii. 138,) Antioch and Jerusalem, (ii. 220, 231,) Coptic and Ethiopic, (ii. 166, 7,) Maronite, (ii. 344,) Armenian, (ii. 198,) and in that of James of Edessa, (i. 256.)

2. The passage in Titus, (iii. 5,) "the washing of regeneration," is universally understood of baptism.* It is part of the lesson in the Baptismal Service of the Alexandrian Church, (Ass. ii. 152,) as also in the Coptic and Ethiopic, (ii. 152,) and Syriac Liturgies, (i. 228.) It is recited in the Gothic and Gallican Service, (ii. 34, 35,) Alexandrian, Coptic, and Ethiopic, (ii. 173,) in the Greek, (ii. 138,) in that of Jerusalem and Antioch, (ii. 220, 231, 259, 219,) and in the Armenian, (ii. 169–172.)

3. All the Liturgies refer to the baptism of CHRIST, as their authority for praying, that "the water might be sanctified, to the mystical washing away of sin." Thus it is in the Old Roman, (Ass. ii. 4, 8, 53,) the Gothic, (ii. 34, 5,) Greek, (ii. 132,) Armenian, (ii. 197,) Coptic, (ii. 166, 167, 180,) Syriac, (i. 262, ii. 268,) Maronite, (ii. 314,) Malabar, (i. 178,) Antioch, (i. 226, ii. 268,) James of Edessa, (i. 241,) Jerusalem, (ii. 244–7.) Now this interpretation is not based on any express words of Scripture, and, consequently, we must conclude that it has come down from the earliest times; since there has been no time subsequent to the days

* The same is done by all the early fathers, and one ancient version, the Ethiopian, translates the passage, "the washing of baptism."

of the Apostles, that such an interpretation could begin and become universal, much more find its way into every ancient Liturgy.

4. All the Liturgies agree in calling baptism *a seal.* Thus it is in the Old Gallican, (Ass. ii. 40,) Old Gothic, (ii. 37,) Coptic, (i. 164,) Greek, (i. 337,) Syriac, (i. 220,) Malabar, (i. 178,) Apostolic by James of Edessa, (i. 263,) Antioch, (ii. 282,) Maronite, (ii. 316,) Ambrosian, (ii. 45,) Maronite, (ii. 330–337.)

5. Very many of them quote or refer to the language of St. Paul, in Galatians, (iii. 27:) "As many of you as have been baptized into CHRIST have put on CHRIST;"—as the Armenian, (Ass. ii. 196,) Syriac, (ii. 249,) Greek, (ii. 299,) Old Roman, (ii. 3,) Old Gallican, (ii. 3, 38,) and appears to have been referred to in the rest.

6. The language of St. Paul, in Colossians, (ii. 10, 11,) on which we have commented, is also recited or spoken of in the Baptismal Liturgies; as in the Malabar, (Ass. i. 196,) Old Roman, (i. 57,) Greek, (ii. 138,) Antioch, (ii. 222,) Jerusalem, (ii. 230,) Coptic, (ii. 151,) Maronite, (ii. 329,) and in several others.

7. They agree, in renouncing "the devil and all his works." It is in the Service for making Catechumens, in the Gelasian Liturgy, (Ass. i. 17,) Gregorian, (i. 22,) Greek, (i. 114, 137,) Armenian, (i. 172,) Coptic, (ii. 158.) It is also in the following Baptismal Liturgies: Gallican, (ii. 39,) Roman, (ii. 17,) Syriac, (ii. 251,) Coptic, (ii. 150,) Armenian, (ii. 194,) and is implied in the Malabar, (ii. 183.)

There are many other points of agreement; but these are sufficient to show, that *the substance* of all the Baptismal Liturgies is the same. As we have already seen, that the Liturgies of the Communion Service must have been composed back nearly or quite in Apostolic times, so we are also led to conclude, that the same is true of the Baptismal

Liturgies. These conclusions give a peculiar force to the language of St. Paul to Timothy: "Hold fast the form of sound words thou hast heard of me." (2 Tim. i. 13.) Upon a view, therefore, of the foregoing summary of evidence, it does not seem to admit of question, that the worship of the Church has been by a Liturgy from the very days of the Apostles.

But there is still further evidence, that the Apostles used *a form of prayer*. Indeed, we have one of the Apostolic prayers on record. (Acts iv. 24–30.)

An Apostolic Form of Prayer.—"LORD, thou art GOD, which has made heaven and earth, and the sea, and all that in them is; who by the mouth of thy servant David has said:

Why did the heathen rage,
And the people imagine vain things?
The kings of the earth stood up,
And the rulers were gathered together
Against the LORD, and against his CHRIST.
For of a truth against thy Holy Child JESUS,
Whom thou hast anointed,
For to do whatsoever thy hand
And thy counsel determined before to be done,
Both Herod and Pontius Pilate, with the Gentiles,
And the people of Israel were gathered together.

And now, LORD, behold their threatenings, and grant unto thy servants that with all boldness they may speak thy word, by stretching forth thine hand to heal, and that signs and wonders may be done by the name of thy Holy Child JESUS."

The occasion upon which the use of this prayer is recorded, was the extraordinary escape of Peter and John from the hands of the Jews. And yet, there is no allusion to the circumstance. It is such a prayer as they would be likely to use on every occasion of meeting together; one that would be applicable to *their* case, at all times. Hence, as this *general* prayer was used upon a *special* occasion, it is but reasonable to infer, that it had been precomposed, and formed a part of their daily worship.

3. To return; the third duty of the members was to contribute of their goods, to supply the wants and necessities of the poor of the Church. To the Corinthians, says St. Paul: "Concerning the collection for the saints, as I have given order in the Churches of Galatia, so do ye." (1 Cor. xvi. 1.) There are numerous accounts of contributions for the saints, at Achaia and Macedonia, (Rom. xv. 26; 2 Cor. viii. 1–5; ix. 1;) at Rome, (Rom. xii. 13;) at Corinth, (1 Cor. xvi. 1, 2;) and in many other places. The same custom also prevailed in the next age. Dionysius, Bishop of Corinth, writing to Soter, Bishop of Rome, A. D. 160, says: "For the practice has prevailed with you from the beginning, to do good to all the brethren in every way, and to send contributions to many Churches in every city."* And this practice Eusebius assures us had continued to his day.†

4. It was their duty to support those who preached the gospel to them. "The Lord hath ordained, that those who preach the gospel, should live of the gospel." (1 Cor. ix. 14.) The money for the support of the clergy was at first raised by voluntary oblations, made every Sunday, and a special oblation made once a month.‡ This practice is mentioned in the second century by the Apostolical Canons,§ and by Tertullian;‖ in the third century by Cyprian,¶ and by numerous subsequent writers.

5. It was their duty to send assistance or support to those

* Euseb. iv. 23.

† Ecc. Hist. iv. 23.

‡ Bing. Ant. B. v. c. 4, § 1

§ Can. 3, 4, 5.

‖ Apol. c. 39.

¶ Of Alms, c. 12. Ep. 34 or 39, 66 or 1, 28 or 35.

who preached the gospel in regions where there was no Church. When St. Paul first preached the gospel of CHRIST at Corinth, those of his necessities which his own hands could not supply, were ministered to by the Church of Macedonia, so that he was not chargeable to the Corinthians. (Acts xviii. 1, 3; 2 Cor. xi. 9, 12, 13.) In the same manner, he was not chargeable to the Thessalonians when he first preached to them, (1 Thess. ii. 9; 2 Thess. iii. 8;) and after he left Macedonia, the Church at Philippi communicated with him about giving and receiving. (Phil. iv. 15.) These facts are abundant proof of the existence of this custom in the Apostolic Church; to which there is nothing analogous at the present time, save the contributions by the Churches, for the support of those who preach the gospel in places where there is no Church.

6. It was their duty, by mutual kindness and assistance, to do all in their power to promote the Christian character and welfare of the brethren. If a brother were overtaken in a fault, it was the duty of the brethren to endeavor to reclaim him, (Gal. vi. 1;) having the promise that if they succeeded they should "hide a multitude of sins." (James v. 19, 20.) The Apostle exhorts the Christians not to seek their own happiness only, but also that of the brethren. (Col. iii. 13.) They were also directed to "exhort and admonish such as neglected their duty; to comfort the feeble-minded; to support the weak; and to exercise patience towards all men," (1 Thess. v. 14;) "to stir up each other unto good works," (Heb. x. 24;) "and to confess their faults to each other," (James v. 16;) to "submit themselves one to another, and be clothed with humility." (1 Pet. v. 5.)

This duty of Church members is called by some the mutual watch, and, if nothing more is intended by the expression, than is implied in the above, we do not object to the phrase. But when it is urged as an *official duty* of each member, appertaining to them, because the discipline of the Church resides in the congregation; we must say, that we find no evidence of any such duty, nor can we imagine, that a custom likely to produce so much evil, would be made *a duty*. We say, "likely to produce so much evil," because such is the frailty of human nature, and such the power of habit, that it is impossible for men who have not more grace than often falls to the lot of humanity, to become overseers, prosecutors, judges, and executioners of their fellow-men, and remain unaffected by it. They will neglect the discipline of the Church, especially of leading and influential men, or become spies upon their neighbors' conduct, and busy-bodies in other men's matters.

It is not merely because this supposed "mutual watch" tends to produce an inquisitorial and unchristian spirit, that we can not admit its claim; but because it is not authorized in Scripture. The principal argument urged in favor of the supposed *official duty* of the members, is based on the language of our Saviour, (Matt. xviii. 15, 16, 17,) where he gives direction concerning our treatment of an offending brother, founded on the false assumption, that the interviews we are commanded to seek with those who have injured or offended us, are part of a judicial proceeding; or necessary to lay the foundation for one. When, however, the language is duly considered, it only proves, that we are to seek reconciliation before complaining. And if we can not effect it alone, we are to call in the aid and mediation of friends to assist in bringing it about. It is then, and only then, that we are at liberty to complain. It is not till we have done this that we are at liberty to "tell it to the Church." And having told it to the Church, the fairest inference is, that our personal duty has been fulfilled.

7. It was the duty of the members frequently to communicate with each other in the Holy Sacrament of the Lord's

Supper. The agreement on this point renders it unnecessary to do more than merely refer to some places where it is spoken of.* Among the Fathers of the second century, the frequent celebration of the Eucharist is often mentioned, as by Ignatius, Justin Martyr, Tertullian, and many others, by whom abstinence from it was considered a departure from Christian duty.†

8. They were to obey those who had the rule over them in the Church. St. Paul's command to the Hebrew Christians, was, "obey them that have the rule over you; for they watch for your souls." (Heb. xiii. 17.) Timothy and Titus were both directed to "let no man despise them." (1 Tim. iv. 12; Tit. ii. 15.) It will also be seen, in its appropriate place, that the various officers in the Apostolic Church, had a right *to rule* in the Church; and this necessarily implies a corresponding duty on the part of the people to obey.

9. It was their duty to assist their rulers in executing the discipline of the Church. This view of the subject will reconcile, in some degree, the contradictory interpretations put by different persons, upon the case of the offending Corinthian. (1 Cor. v.) The order in which the different members of ver. 3, chap. v. stand in the common version, is such as to prevent a ready apprehension of the precise force of the language. Changing these to the natural order of the English, in that verse; and omitting "concerning," which is not in the original, and the verse will read, for though "absent in body, (but present in spirit,) *I have judged* (that is, in a judicial sense)‡ *him* that hath so done this deed, as though I were

---

* Matt. xxvi. 26–29. Mark xvi. 22–25. Luke xxii. 19–20. 1 Cor. xi. 23–25. Acts ii. 42, etc.

† Ignat. Ad. Smyr. c. 7. Con. Apos. 7, etc.

‡ Comp. vv. 12, 13, and Rob. 460.

present;" that is, *as I would have judged, had I been present.* This *judgment* was, that the Church when gathered together in the name of the LORD JESUS CHRIST, should, "with the power of the LORD JESUS CHRIST, and his spirit, deliver such an one to Satan;" that is, cast him out of the Church.* The sentence was by the Apostle; but the *execution* by the Church, either as part of their official duty, or in consequence of the Apostle's absence; and we learn from 2 Corinthians, (ii. 6,) that they carried it into effect. "Sufficient to such a man, is this punishment which *was inflicted by the many.*"†

There is another interpretation of this passage, which may be, after all, the true one, and which we must not overlook. Here was a case that seems not to have been provided for, either by the customs or canons of the Corinthian Church, and hence they address the Apostle as the *law-giver* of the Church, for direction in the matter. In this view the decree of the Apostle would have the force of a canon, and the office of the Church would be, *the execution* of the law, whether that power resided in the members or in the officers. The act of the Church, therefore, in either point of view, was that of *execution.* This case proves, therefore, that it was the practice in the Apostolic Church for the members of the Church to assist in *executing* the discipline of the Church.

The language of St. Paul to the Thessalonians, implies the same thing:—"Now we command you, brethren, in the name of our LORD JESUS CHRIST, that ye withdraw yourselves from every brother that walketh disorderly, and not after the tradition which he received from us. And if any man obey not our word by this epistle, note that man, and have no company with him;" or, as others translate the passage, "signify, or point him out to me."‡ (2 Thess. iii. 6, 14.)

*** Hammod. Bloomfield, etc. But others understand it of some greater punishment. See *Pole. Synop. Criticor.* † Rob. 851. ‡ Rob. 749**

10. They were to give their testimony, or testimonials, to the character of candidates for the office of Deacon, or Presbyter. This point will be considered when speaking of the qualifications requisite in Deacons and Presbyters; to which reference is made.

11. To give their assent to canons framed for the government of the Church. The only instance we have on record, of such an occurrence in the Apostolic Church, is in the fifteenth chapter of Acts, which is briefly this. Dissension had arisen at Antioch, in consequence of certain Jews insisting that the Gentile converts ought to be circumcised. The controversy becoming strong, Paul and Barnabas, with certain brethren, were sent up to Jerusalem to the Apostles and Elders on the subject. When the delegation arrived, they were received by the Apostles and Elders and the whole Church, to whom they declared the nature of their errand. But a difference of opinion existed here; and the Apostles and Elders came together to hear and decide the matter. Much debate ensued between the Elders; and when there seemed no likelihood of an agreement, Peter addressed the assembly; and after him, Paul and Barnabas. The discussion being ended, James gave judgment, or pronounced sentence.

To this sentence of James, the people gave their assent, as is clearly proved by the narrative. It does not appear that the laity took part in the debate; but that it took place *in their presence*, is proved by the narrative. (vv. 12, 22, 23, 25, 28.) "And *the multitude* kept silence," while Paul and Barnabas recounted the wonders wrought among the Gentiles. So after sentence was pronounced, it is said, that "it pleased the Apostles and Elders and *the whole Church*, to send chosen men to Antioch," to bear the decree of the council. An Epistle was also sent, beginning, "The Apostles and Elders, and brethren, greeting;" and in it they say, "it seemed good unto *us*, [i. e. Apostles, Elders, and *brethren,] being assembled with one accord,*" which language could not have been used, had the debate not taken place in presence of the Church.*

But not only was the debate in their presence; they gave their assent to "the decree of the Apostles and Elders," (xvi. 4,) else how could they say in truth, "it seemed good unto the HOLY GHOST, and *to us,*" that is, the persons who wrote the letter, or to the Apostles and Elders, and brethren, "to lay upon you no greater burden than was necessary?" This language is evidence of the fact, that *the members of the Apostolic Church gave their assent to new canons framed for the government of the Church.*

CHAPTER XII.

OFFICERS OF THE CHURCH.

THE Church being a regularly organized society, must have had regular officers to administer and execute its laws and ordinances.† These officers were of three ranks or grades; and were called *Apostles, Presbyters* or *Bishops, and Deacons;* and each were ministers in the Church. It has been doubted by some, whether the Apostles were officers of the Church, and also whether Deacons were ministers of the Word; but the view we have taken of the Scriptural evidence, has led us to conclude, that all were both officers

---

* The attendance of the laity in Councils of the Church is mentioned by Cyprian. Ep. 30.

† This is conceded by all; even those who deny that the Primitive Church had any *ministry,* allow that it had *officers.*

and ministers. We shall, however, postpone the examination of these questions for the present; as we shall be obliged to discuss them when we come to consider the power and duty of each.

CHAPTER XIII.

DEACONS.

Deacons were officers in the Church.

1. The existence of Deacons in the Apostolic Church is proved by positive statements of Scripture. "Paul and Timotheus to all the saints which are at Philippi, with the Bishops and *Deacons*," (διακονος, Phil. i. 1.) "Likewise the *Deacons*." (1 Tim. iii. 8, 10.) The passage from Philippians is not only evidence of the existence of persons called *Deacons* in the Apostolic Church; but also that they were *an order* distinct from the saints, or body of the people composing the Church, and is also *presumptive* evidence that they were officers of the Church. And this presumption is in exact accordance with the positive statement in 1 Timothy, (iii. 10:) "Being first proved, let them use the OFFICE *of a Deacon*."

2. Deacons are also mentioned as *ministers* in the Church, by Polycarp,* and by Ignatius, frequently;† also by Justin Martyr,‡ Clement of Alexandria,§ and by Tertullian, in numerous places. Indeed, from the days of Irenæus and

---

* Ep. Phil. c. 5.

† Ep. Eph. c. 2. Ep. Mag. cc. 2, 6, 13. Ep. Trall. cc. 2, 3, 7. Ep. Phil. Intd. cc. 4, 7, 10. Ep. Smyr. cc. 8, 12. Ep. Poly. c. 6.

‡ Apol. i. cc. 85, 87.

§ Strom. 6. p. 667

Tertullian, it is admitted that Deacons were ministers and officers in the Church. And the language of Polycarp and Ignatius leaves no doubt that they were so, in their days.

The qualifications of Deacons.

1. A Deacon must be a man in whose character are mingled "gravity, perfect honesty, temperance, and charity." (1 Tim. iii. 8.)

2. He must be a sincere Christian, "holding the mystery of the faith in a pure conscience." (1 Tim. iii. 9.)

3. He must be a man "who ruled his house and children well." (1 Tim. iii. 12.)

4. He must have but one wife, and she must be a woman of "gravity, strict probity, sobriety, and perfect uprightness of character." (1 Tim. iii. 11, 12.)

5. He must have received *the testimony of the Church, or testimonials from the Church*, to his unblemished and Christian character, and to his fitness for the office. This is a legitimate inference from, or rather proved by, the language used in giving an account of the appointment of "the seven," in the sixth chapter of Acts; and who, from the *nature of the office* they filled, "the *ministry of tables*," as distinguished from the exclusive "*ministry of the word*," have ever been called *Deacons*.

The command of the Apostles to the brethren was, "Look ye out, (i. e. seek out,)* seven men of *honest report*, full of the Holy Ghost and wisdom, whom we may appoint over this business." "And they chose (selected, chose, or gave the preference† to) Stephen," and others.

The word rendered, *of honest report*, (μαρτυρουμενους,) conveys a much stronger idea than our translation, and literally signifies, that they were to be persons to whose unblemished and Christian character they could bear "honorable testi-

* Rob. 314. † Comp. Luke x. 42; xiv. 7. Rob. 251.

mony;"* or, as Professor Robinson says, in this place, men who were *lauded* for their excellent character. This testimony, or laudation, as the word implies,† and as the narrative requires us to believe, was to be borne by the "multitude of the disciples," composing the Church; and hence, the direction of the Apostles to the Church was, Select from among yourselves seven men, to whose unblemished and Christian character you can bear "honorable testimony;"—which testimony was borne by the Church in the act of selecting according to the direction of the Apostles. No matter, therefore, by what means it was carried into effect, *it was the testimony of the Church, or testimonials from the Church, to the Christian character of the seven.*

This interpretation reconciles the different constructions put upon this passage by opposing parties, as it points out the part borne by all. The *people* selected; or, if it be preferred, elected, certain persons to be *Deacons*; and the *Apostles* ordained them.

Manner of making Deacons

1. It was requisite for a candidate for the order or office of Deacon, to present himself *to an Apostle*, and "be proved," that is, to satisfy the Apostle that he possessed the requisite qualifications. He must "be proved," (1 Tim. iii. 10,) that is, "examined, or put to trial,"‡ and "be found blameless;" in a judicial sense, *irreprehensible*.§ This necessarily implies *a trial*, or by analogy, *an examination*. Besides, the word used by the Apostle in this place, (δοκιμαζεσθοσαν,) was a technical term, denoting *the examination of a candidate for an office*.

2. A Deacon was to be ordained by an Apostle, that is, be appointed to the office, and be set apart by prayer, and

* Rob. 495.
† Rob. 497. Comp. μαρτυρεω.
‡ Rob. 203, 204
§ Rob. 56

the imposition of the hands of an Apostle. We might presume this, from the tenor of the language used by Paul in his Epistle to Timothy ; but the *positive statements* made in Acts, (vi. 3, 6,) leave no room for inference. The Apostles direct the brethren to select seven men, "*whom* WE *may appoint.*" And when the brethren had selected the seven, "they set them before the Apostles, who prayed, and laid their hands upon them."

Of the powers and duties of Deacons.

1. The first duty of a Deacon was to receive and distribute the alms of the Church. That the primary object in the appointment of *Deacons* was to provide suitable persons to take care of the alms of the Church, is *proved* by the narrative in Acts vi. : "And there arose a murmuring among the Grecians against the Hebrews, that *their widows were neglected in the daily ministrations ;*" wherefore the seven were appointed "to this business."

That this ministration was not of common property, by which the whole Church was supported, as has sometimes been supposed, is evident from two considerations: (1.) "*Widows*, who were widows indeed," who were in an emphatical sense "bereaved," if over sixty years of age, were to be received into the number of those who were maintained at *the charge or expense of the Church*, (1 Tim. v. 3, 9, 16;) but it does not appear that any others were thus supported, or that any others "were neglected in the daily ministration" of the alms. (2.) Though the Church at Jerusalem *enjoyed*, it did not possess "all things in common." This is, in effect, asserted in the narrative itself. Thus in Acts ii. 44, 45, it is said, that "they that believed were together, and *had all things common ;* and sold their possessions and goods, and *parted them* to all men, *as every man had need.*" The sale and partition therefore, was not of the whole estate ; but only of so much as they had need.

So again in Acts iv. 32, it is said, that "the multitude of them that believed were of one heart and of one soul; *neither said any of them that aught of the things he possessed was his own;* but they had all things common." This is an express assertion, that property was *possessed* by individuals; though *used or enjoyed* for the common benefit. The same conclusion must be drawn from Peter's language to Ananias: "While *thy* property remained, was it not *thine own?* and after it was sold, *was it not in thine own power?*" (Acts v. 3.)

It may be said, that the language in Acts iv. 34, 35, is opposed to this opinion: "Neither was there any among them that lacked, for as many as were possessed of houses and lands, sold them, and brought the prices of the things that were sold; and laid them down at the Apostles' feet, and distribution was made *to every man according as he had need.*" In reference to this, however, it must be borne in mind, that in Acts ii. 44, 45, the "sale and partition of possessions and goods," is expressly limited to the need or wants of the Church; and that only two verses preceding the ones quoted above, the individual *possession* of property is no less distinctly recognized; neither of which could be true, if these verses prove a community of goods.

And further, the partition, which prevented any from lacking, was only as every man *had need*, that is, to such as were *in want*, or *had need of such a division;** and hence, the sale was only for that purpose—of so much as was needed to supply the wants of the Church. These passages compel us to believe, that, though the property of the Saints at Jerusalem was enjoyed by all in common, it was not possessed by all; that the sale and partition of their estates was only of so much as they had need; and that this was

* Rob. 897.

voluntary, and not by the command of the Apostles, and that no such thing as a community of goods existed among the Christians at Jerusalem. Hence it necessarily follows, that the Deacons could only have the distribution of the alms of the Church.

2. Though the first business of the Deacons was to take charge of the alms of the Church, *they were also to preach, as occasion offered.* The qualifications required of a Deacon, lead directly to this inference. They were not only to possess all the ordinary virtues, but also to have a "strong testimony" that they were men "full of wisdom and the Holy Ghost." In conformity with this conclusion, was the conduct of the newly-ordained Deacons. "And Stephen, full of faith and power, did great wonders and miracles among the people," (Acts vi. 8;) and that this was accompanied by *preaching* is evident, from the course pursued by his enemies. At first they *disputed* with him, (vi. 9,) and then suborned men to say they had "heard him speak blasphemous words." (Acts vi. 11, 13.) And when those at Jerusalem were scattered abroad, Philip, who was one of the seven, "went down to Samaria, and *preached* Christ and the kingdom of God," (Acts viii. 5, 12,) working miracles among them. And from Samaria, he went to Azotus, "*preaching* from city to city, until he came to Cæsarea," (viii. 40.)

That preaching was part of the duty of Deacons, in the age next succeeding the Apostolic, there can be no doubt. Polycarp calls them "the ministers of God in Christ."* And Ignatius speaks of them, as "the ministers of the mysteries of Jesus Christ."†

3. They were to baptize. Philip "*baptized*" those who believed at Samaria, (Acts viii. 12,) and also the eunuch of

* Ep. Phil. c. 7.

† Ep. Mag. c. 6. *etc.*

Ethiopia, (viii. 36, 38.) Though Deacons *baptized* in the age following the Apostolic, it was only with the consent of the Bishop. Thus Ignatius says: "It is not lawful without the Bishop, either *to baptize*, or to celebrate the Holy Communion."* And Tertullian says: "The highest priest, that is, the Bishop, hath the right of giving *baptism;* after him the Presbyters and Deacons, but not without authority of the Bishop."†

4. They were to assist their superiors in ruling in the Church. It is not easy, perhaps not possible, for us to decide what *authority* the Deacons had in the Apostolic Church; but the language of Paul to Timothy compels us to believe that they had some authority, in some cases. Of a Bishop, Paul says, "He must be one that *ruleth well his own house*, having his children in subjection;" and of a Deacon, he says, "Let him be one who rules his children and his own house well." (1 Tim. iii. 4, 12.) The language in reference to both officers is the same; and in reference to the former, the Apostle, by way of explanation, or as assigning a reason why this qualification was necessary, says in parenthesis: "For if a man know not how to rule his own house, how shall he *take care of* [literally, how shall he be fit *to have the care over*]‡ the Church of GOD?" (1 Tim. iii. 5.) Inasmuch, then, as the ability to rule one's house was necessary to qualify a Bishop to rule in the Church of GOD; the same qualification was required in a Deacon, evidently for the same purpose.

5. They were to assist in the administration of the Eucharist. This is nowhere expressly asserted in Scripture; but in the days of Justin Martyr, A. D. 150, it was a common practice. Thus he says:§ "Those whom we call *Deacons* give to each of those present a portion of the bread

---

* Ep. Smyr. c. 8. † De Bap. c. 17. ‡ Rob. 312. § Apol. i. c. 85.

which hath been blessed, and of the wine mixed with water; and carry some away for those who are absent." And in another place he says:* "The consecrated elements are then distributed and received by every one; and a portion is sent by the *Deacons* to those who are absent." The same thing is abundantly witnessed to in later times.

6. To render obedience to the command of an Apostle. For a consideration of the question, whether an Apostle had authority over Bishops and Deacons, the reader is referred to the appropriate head, where we shall consider *the power of an Apostle;* only remarking, that if the Apostles had authority over Deacons, then were Deacons bound to obey.

CHAPTER XIV.

PRESBYTERS OR BISHOPS.†

It is evident from a comparison of certain passages of Scripture, that *the terms Presbyter and Bishop are often used in the Bible to designate the same class of officers.* Thus in Acts, (xx. 17,) it is said that when Paul was at Miletus, "he sent to Ephesus and called the *Presbyters of the Church;*" and in his address to them, (ver. 28,) he tells them, "to take

---

* Apol. i. c. 87.

† The English word *Bishop,* is derived from the Greek *Episcopos.* This word was adopted into Latin without change, *Episcopus,* but in most languages it has undergone some modification; Anglo-Saxon, *Bisceop;* Dutch, *bischof;* Swedish, *biskop;* Russian, *Episcopi;* Armenian, *Iepiscuepues;* Syriac, *Episkopo;* Polish, *Biskupa;* Welsh, *Esbog;* Gaelic, *Esbuig;* Irish, *Easbog;* Portuguese, *bispo;* Spanish, *obispo;* Italian, *vescovo;* French, *évêque.*

The word *Presbyter,* contracted into *Priest,* is also from the Greek;

heed to themselves and to all the flock, over which the Holy Ghost hath made them *Bishops*." So the Apostle "ordained *Presbyters* in every Church," (Acts xiv. 23;) but the direction of the Epistle to the Philippians is, "to the *Bishops and Deacons*."*

This indiscriminate use of the words Bishop and Presbyter, is never found *out* of the New Testament, nor later than about A. D. 65. In the days of Ignatius, 107, the name Bishop was exclusively used to designate the Apostolic Bishop, and the name Presbyter, as the name of an office to denote that which St. Paul calls a Presbyter or Bishop. There are a few passages, however, in the Fathers, in which it is said the words are used indiscriminately. Two of these will fall under other heads; the remainder we shall consider in this place. The passages in question are from Irenæus.

"When we refer them [the heretics] to that tradition which is from the Apostles; which by succession from the Fathers, (*Presbyterorum*,) hath been preserved in the Church, we provoke them; they oppose the tradition, saying that they are wiser than, not only the Fathers, (*Presbyteris*,) but the Apostles also."†

"It becometh those who are in the Church, to learn from those Fathers (*Presbyteris*) who have their succession (or

---

Latin, *Presbyter;* Spanish and Portuguese, *presbitero;* French and Italian, *prêtre:* German and Dutch, *priester;* Danish, *præest;* Swedish, *prest;* Icelandic, *prestr;* Russian, *Presbyteri.*

It is worthy of remark, that these words, in all these languages, are technical terms of ecclesiastical phraseology, and that they always denote distinct offices, never being used interchangeably.

* It is remarkable that this community of names does not occur in the old Syriac version of the New Testament, which dates as far back as the beginning of the second century. In this, the word is *chasiso,* "Presbyter," in all the passages in dispute.

† Adv. Hær. iii. 2.

inheritance) from the Apostles; who with the Episcopate (*Episcopatus*) have received the gift of certain truth."*

"From all such, therefore, it becometh us to keep aloof, and truly to adhere to those [Fathers] who maintain the doctrine of the Apostles, and according to the custom of the Fathers, (*Presbyteris*,) do show forth sound speech and conversation without offense."†

In these passages, which are all there are to this purpose in Irenæus, he uses *presbyter* in the same sense in which we now use the phrase "the Fathers," to denote eminent men who had gone before, or aged and honorable men then living. Nor is this usage peculiar to him. Thus Papias, Bishop of Hierapolis, who was "the hearer of St. John,"‡ tells us that "he had treasured up in his memory what he had received from the Fathers, [Presbyters,] and had recorded it."§ Among those *presbyters*, or elders, or Fathers, were the Apostles, Peter, James, John, Matthew, Philip, Thomas, and Andrew. Now Irenæus was an admirer of Papias,‖ and would therefore be *likely* to use language in a similar manner, as we know he did. Thus he tells us¶ that "Polycarp was ordained Bishop (επισκοπος) of Smyrna." But when writing to Florinus he calls him "that blessed and Apostolic Father," (Presbyter.)** And in the same letter he speaks of those "Fathers (Presbyters) who were the immediate disciples of the Apostles." So also this same Irenæus writing to Victor, Bishop of Rome, speaks of "those Fathers (Presbyters) who governed the Church before Soter."†† These "Fathers" were Anicetus, and Pius, and Hyginus, and Telesphorus, and Sixtus, whom, in another place, he tells us were Bishops, (επισκοπος,) and "successors of the Apostles in

---

* Adv. Hær. iv. 43. † Adv. Hær. iv. 44. ‡ Iren. Adv. Hær. v. 33.
§ Pref. Interp. Lord's Dec. in Euseb. iii. 39. ‖ Euseb. iii. 39.
¶ Adv. Hær. iii. 3. ** Euseb. v. 20. †† Euseb. v. 24.

the government of the Churches."* And he speaks of *John* and the other Fathers, (Apostles.)†

That this mode of expression was common in the days of Irenæus, is also evident from other primitive writers. Thus Clement of Alexandria speaks of Pantaneus, his master, as "the blessed Father, (Presbyter.")‡ He also applies the same epithet to all the eminent men who had preceded him, whether clergymen or laymen.§ And Alexander, Bishop of Jerusalem, writing to Origen, calls Pantænus and Clement those "blessed Fathers."|| And Dionysius, Bishop of Alexandria, calls his predecessor, Heraclas, "the blessed Father," (παπα.)¶ This title was also given to Cyprian, Bishop of Carthage,** and was indeed, in the fourth century, a name common to all Bishops.†† The same language is also incorporated into many of the ancient Liturgies, as that of St. Basil,‡‡ of Alexandria,§§ of Ethiopia,|||| etc. If further proof were necessary as to the primitive understanding of this language, it may be drawn from Eusebius. Thus, those whom Clement of Alexandria had called "the blessed Presbyters," in the sense of Ancients, or Fathers, Eusebius in one place calls "the oldest Presbyters" or Fathers,¶¶ and

---

* Adv. Hær. iii. 3.

† Adv. Hær. iii. 39.

‡ Hypot. in Euseb. vi. 14.

§ Strom. vi. 667, and Apud Euseb. vi. 13. From the first of these it has been argued, that Clement made no distinction between clergy and laity. Cong. Catechism, p. 69. But such an inference is unauthorized, as he enumerates the three orders of clergy on the same page, and says he supposes them to be "imitations of the angelic glory."

|| Euseb. vi. 14.

¶ Euseb. vii. 7.

** Ep. 23, 31, 36.

†† Aug. Com. Ps. 44, Chrysos. Hom. 3. Ad. Pop. Bing. ii. c. 2, § 7

‡‡ Brett. Coll. Lit. 79.

§§ Pal. Orig. Lit. I. 86

|||| Brett. Coll. Lit. 84.

¶¶ E. H. vi. 14.

in another place, "the Ancient Fathers."* These facts prove abundantly the correctness of this interpretation.

But there is other evidence, that Irenæus did not design to speak of the *office* of Presbyter, as the same as Bishop, as will be evident upon examination of the places where he speaks of the succession of Bishops. Thus he says: "We can enumerate those whom the Apostles appointed Bishops (επισκοπι) in the Churches, and their successors, even to us. . . . *In this order and by this succession* that tradition in the Church, which is from the Apostles, hath come uninterruptedly to us."† Again: "True knowledge is the doctrine of the Apostles, and the ancient customs of the Church throughout the whole world—the characteristic of the body of CHRIST *next to the succession of Bishops,* to whom they delivered the Church in every place."‡ And again: "For all these [heretics] are far later than the Bishops to whom the Apostles delivered the Churches, as we have carefully shown in the third book."§

Those who compare carefully the language here applied to Bishops, with what Irenæus says of "the Fathers" (Presbyters) before quoted, must be satisfied that he is not speaking of the same *office* in both cases, whatever sense the reader may prefer to put upon "Presbyter." The language applied to Bishops is clearly *official;* that applied to Presbyters, is not so. Those who differ from us on this point, must apply it to another office than that of Bishop. We may also quote a passage from Jerome on this subject, in proof of our conclusion, rendered famous for its always being quoted on ordination by Presbyters, which we shall have occasion to consider more at large, He says:‖ "The name of Presbyter denotes *age,* that of Bishop, *office;*" the sense we have given it.

---

* E. H. iii. 3. † Adv. Hær. iii. 3.
‡ Adv. Hær. iv. 63. § Adv. Hær. v. 20. ‖ Ep. 85.

That Bishops or Presbyters, or, for convenience, Presbyter-bishops, were *officers in the Apostolic Church*, follows from what has been offered under the preceding head. And so St. Paul's language to Timothy, (1 Tim. iii. 1,) "If a man desire *the office of a Bishop*," &c.

Of the qualifications of Presbyter-bishops.

1. The candidate for the office of Bishop in the Apostolic Church, was to possess *an unblemished character.* "He must be blameless and of good behavior." (1 Tim. iii. 2.) He must not only be of "good behavior," having "his appearance, conduct, and carriage, decent, grave, and correct, but he must be one who was *perfectly irreprehensible*."*

2. He must be a man who was "vigilant, sober, given to hospitality, not given to wine, no striker, not greedy of filthy lucre, but patient, not a brawler, not covetous." (1 Tim. iii. 2, 3.) That is, he must be a man whose conduct was watchful and prudent; whose practices were hospitable and liberal, charitable and temperate; and whose demeanor was quiet, peaceable, and patient.

3. He must be an experienced Christian; not "a novice," (νεοφυτον,) "*a young or new convert*."† But he must be one who was "settled and grounded in the faith," whose character had become established, "lest he be lifted up with pride and fall into condemnation."

4. He must be capable of teaching and instructing. "Apt to teach," (1 Tim. iii. 2,) that is, *able to teach and instruct others*.

5. He must have *but one wife*, (1 Tim. iii. 2;) which command was necessary in those days, as polygamy was

---

* Rob. 57.

† 1 Tim. iii. 6. Rob. 537. It was decreed by the Apostolical Canons, (Can. 72,)—by the Council of Nice, (Can. 2,) and the Council of Gangre (Can. 3,)—that a new Convert should not be ordained to the ministry.

allowed by the laws of the Greeks and Romans, but forbidden by the law of CHRIST.

6. He must be a man "who ruled his children and house well." (1 Tim. iii. 4.)

7. He must have received the testimony of, or testimonials from, the Church. "He must have a *good report* of them which are without." (1 Tim. iii. 7.) In the ambiguous language of the English version of this text, it is not easy to determine what is the Apostle's meaning. Much of the difficulty, however, may be obviated by a more literal translation. "He must have *an honorable testimony*,* from those without;" and the only difficulty is, to determine, who are intended by the phrase, "*from without*."

Most commentators and lexicographers explain this passage, by saying that the phrase "from without," designates those who were without the Church, or not Christians, citing in proof, (Col. iv. 5,) "Walk in wisdom, *towards those without*." But this appears to us misinterpretation, and derives no sanction from the text quoted. The epistle of Paul to the Colossians, was *addressed* "to the saints and faithful brethren at Colosse," (i. 2,) and the command to walk in wisdom toward those "without," signifies those not included within, or among the saints and faithful brethren, and who therefore were not Christians. Apply the rule furnished by this passage, in construing the one under consideration, and it supports our position.

Paul, in this part of his Epistle to Timothy, is speaking generally of *officers of the Church*, and in this passage, particularly of *Bishops*, who were one class of those officers; and hence, "from without" must denote those not included

---

* Rob. 496. The Peshito, or old Syriac, shows that it was *testimony*, not *report*, that was intended, the word being ܣܗܕܘܬܐ, (*soduto*,) which is rendered "testimonium, testificatio, obtestatio."

within the class of persons of whom he was speaking, that is, who were not officers in the Church. Should it be said that this interpretation includes all who were not officers in the Church, whether Christians or not; we answer, that though in English it might seem to have this signification, it is limited in its application, by the idiom of the Greek, to those who were Christians. The preposition απω, is used in the New Testament only in reference "to such objects as before were *on*, *by*, or *with* another, but now separated from it; and when, as in this case, it follows a verb of *having* or *receiving*, denotes the origin or source from whence the thing proceeded."*

Now the relation borne by a Christian to the world, was not changed by his appointment to an office in the Church, but it was changed in reference to the members of the Church with whom he had before been associated merely as private Christian, but from whom he was, in a sense, now separated, by being made a public officer. The term "without" would seem, therefore, to be limited to those with whom the officer had been associated, and in reference to whom his relation was changed by his appointment to office, that is, to the members of the Church; and it was from them, therefore, that this honorable testimony was to come.

In confirmation of this conclusion, we have also the improbability of the contrary supposition. That a candidate for the office of Bishop in the *Christian Church*, should be obliged to have "an honorable testimony from those who were not Christians," is contrary to all our notions of probability. Besides, it is not easy to imagine how Timothy and Titus could know whether those they were to ordain in Ephesus and Crete, had been of "good report" among those who were not Christians, before their conversion to Chris-

---

* Rob. 77, 99.

tianity, unless they obtained the information from the Church. And if the *testimony of the Church* was to be the evidence of this fact, it would still be what we suppose—the testimony, or *testimonials of the Church.*

This hypothesis relieves the passage, (Acts xiv. 23,) "And they ordained them Presbyters in every city," of the difficulties hitherto supposed to attend it. We learn from the Apostolic history, that after Paul and Barnabas had preached the gospel in certain cities of Asia, "they returned again to Lystra, and Iconium, and Antioch, *confirming* the souls of the disciples, *exhorting* them to continue in the faith, *ordaining* Presbyters for them in every Church; having prayed with fasting, they commended them to the LORD, on whom they believed, and *passing* through Pisidia, they came to Pamphylia." (Acts xiv. 22–24.)

We give this literal rendering, that the English reader may see the force and connection of the language of the historian. The course of the narrative, therefore, compels us to believe, that the "confirmation, exhortation, and *ordination*," or whatever it might have been, were performed by the same persons, that is, by Paul and Barnabas. It is objected, however, by those who assert the absolute independency of each particular congregation, that the word translated *ordaining*, (χειροτονεσαντες,) denotes *an election by the people*, and that it must be so understood in this passage; alleging that the verb from which it comes, signifies *to stretch out* or *lift up the hand, as in voting.** The word, however, is defined by Professor Robinson,† *to choose by vote, to appoint;* and as the connection will not allow us to adopt the former,

* Coleman's Prim. Church, 62–64; where he has cited the leading authorities in his favor. But all this proves nothing to the purpose, until he has shown that it was the brethren, and not the Apostles that *stretched forth the hand,* since the text does not say which it was.

† Gr. Lex. 893.

we will substitute the latter word for ordaining. The account will then read, "*confirming* the souls of the disciples, *exhorting* them [the disciples] to continue in the faith, *appointing* Presbyters for them [the disciples] in every Church, having prayed with fasting." The *appointment* was, therefore, made by the Apostles, *with prayer and fasting*.*

It is worthy of remark, that this word is used in the subscriptions to the Epistles to Timothy and Titus, supposed to have been added about the third or fourth century, when there could be no doubt that it signified ordination by a Bishop, and that it is used in the same sense in the Greek Church to the present day.†

We are willing to grant, though the narrative does not require it, that *the people* took part in the selection of persons appointed to the office of Presbyters. Indeed, the history authorizes us to infer, that the people selected persons to whose unblemished and Christian character they could bear honorable and strong testimony, and that the Apostles *appointed* or ordained such to the office of Deacons; and subsequently, upon receiving another testimonial, to the office of Presbyter. Whether this *selection* was made by holding up of hands, as in voting, or by some other means, the narrative furnishes no information, nor is it of any importance.

---

* It is worthy of observation, that the *Peshito*, or old Syriac version of the New Testament, which is the very highest authority in regard to customs and practices in Palestine, makes no allusion to any participation of the *people* in this transaction; employing the verb ܩܘܡ, (*kom*,) *to stand, to raise up, to cause to stand;* hence, *to constitute*, or *appoint*. The same language is also employed in reference to the appointment of the seven *Deacons*, Acts vi. 3; and also in regard to those *Presbyters* whom Titus was to ordain. Tit. i. 5. This language was also employed by later writers, to signify *ordination* or *consecration*, whether by Bishops, Patriarchs, or others. Mich. Cast. ii. 784, 785.

† Suicer, *in verbo*.

This conclusion is sustained by the testimony of the earliest Fathers. Clement of Rome, about A. D. 83, speaks of ministers appointed by the Apostles and their successors, "with the consent of the whole Church."* That is, the whole Church knowing of, and consenting to the appointment, and thus bearing testimony to the fitness of the persons appointed. This practice continued for a long time, and is mentioned by many writers. Cornelius, Bishop of Rome, in his epistle to Fabius, Bishop of Antioch, alludes to the same custom.†

Origen, about 230, speaking of the ordination of a Bishop, says: "The presence of the people is necessary in the ordination of a Bishop, that all may know, and be assured that he who is chosen to that office, is distinguished among the people, for his pre-eminence in learning and holiness, and a virtuous life; and this is done in the presence of the people, that there may be no room for mistake or objection."‡ So also in his last book against Celsus, he says, that "rulers of the Church are chosen to their office by those over whom they rule."§

Cyprian, about 250, says: "In compliance with divine tradition and Apostolical usage, the custom should be diligently observed and maintained, which is established among us, and in almost all other provinces, that for the due celebration of ordinations, the Bishops of all the adjoining provinces are to repair to the people, over whom a Bishop is to be ordained; and then a Bishop shall be chosen, in the presence of the people, who have had the fullest knowledge of the life of each one, and been thoroughly acquainted with their manners, and whole conversation."|| In another place, he speaks of Cornelius as having been made Bishop, "by

* Ep. Cor. c. 44. † Apud Euseb. vi. 43

‡ Hom. 6. Levit. § Ad Finem. || Ep. 78.

the testimony of the clergy, and the suffrage of the people present."* And again, "That ordination is just and lawful, which shall have been determined by the suffrage and sentence of all."†

Later writers also testify to the existence of the same custom in their times. Thus, Gregory Nazianzen, 370, says, that Athanasius was "*elected by the suffrage* of all the people."‡ Ambrose, 374, says the election is by the whole Church.§ Again, "Ye are my fathers who chose me to be Bishop."|| Jerome, 378, "The Watchman of the Church, either a Bishop or Presbyter, who was chosen by the people."¶ And so late as 440, Leo the Great lays it down as a standing rule of the Church, that "He who is to preside over all, should be chosen by all."**

The right and duty of the people to elect their clergy, and of the Bishops to ordain them, was distinctly recognized by all the early Councils, among which we may mention that of Nice, Antioch, Alexandria, Carthage, Chalcedon, Arles, Barcelona, Toledo, Constantinople, &c. The foregoing language, in most instances, was used in reference to Bishops, but it is evident from many circumstances, that what was done by the Church of a diocese, at the ordination of a Bishop, was done by a particular congregation, at the ordination of Presbyters and Deacons.

8. He must have been a Deacon, and have acquitted himself honorably in that station. There is no *positive statement* in Scripture, that this was the fact; but there is a *direct allusion* to the existence of such a custom in Paul's Epistle to Timothy. "They that have used the office of a Deacon well, purchase to themselves a good degree, and great bold-

* Ep. 52, or 55.
† Ep. 67, or 68.
‡ Orat. 21.
§ Ep. 82.
|| Com. Luc. viii. c. 1.
¶ Com. Ez. lx. c. 33.
** Ep. 84.

ness in the faith which is in Jesus Christ." (1 Tim. iii. 13.) The language in which the common version presents this text to the reader, renders it difficult to say what was intended by the Apostle; but a more literal translation will remove much of the doubt and uncertainty. "They that fill *the office of a Deacon*, (or perform the duties of a Deacon,) faithfully, shall acquire for themselves an excellent degree, (or *step of dignity*,) and *great* authority, (or *license*,) in the faith which is in Christ Jesus."* This language evidently implies, that he who has filled the office of a Deacon well, should be promoted to an office of higher grade, where he should have greater license or authority to preach and proclaim the faith or gospel of Christ Jesus.

Of the manner of making Bishops or Presbyters

1. He must have been examined and tried by an Apostle, and found to possess the requisite qualifications. Paul, after enumerating the principal qualifications of a Deacon, adds: "Let *these also* first be proved." (1 Tim. iii. 10.) The language of the Apostle, "*and these also*, being first proved," implies, that this trial or proof was not applicable to Deacons alone, but to them *in addition*† to others, which here can signify nothing but Bishops, of whom he had just been speaking. In what manner this *trial or examination* was conducted, the Scripture furnishes no means of determining; but that the Apostles considered something of the kind necessary to prevent the introduction of improper persons into the ministry, is sufficiently evident.

We may, however, obtain some light on this subject, by reference to the practice of those times. The word used by the Apostle in this place, (δοκιμαζω,) signifies *to prove, to try,*

*** Rob. 123, 650, 631. Clement of Alexandria supposed this text to refer to gradation of office. Strom. vi. 667.**

† Rob. 406.

—also, *to make trial of, to put to the proof, to examine*;* and the noun derived from this verb, (δοκιμασία,) denotes *a trial, or examination.* In this sense, it was used *technically* by the Greeks, and no man could be admitted to a seat in the Senate of Five Hundred, until he had been proved, had undergone a strict *dokimasia,* as to his life and conduct. To a Greek of those days, the language of the Apostle would convey the same idea as that signified by our phrase, "the examination of a candidate." There can be no doubt, therefore, that in the Apostolic Church, both Presbyters and Deacons were to be examined by the Apostles, or those to whom they had committed Apostolic authority before ordination.

2. Must be ordained by an Apostle. The similarity of qualification required in Bishops and Deacons, and the similar manner of making them, would lead us to infer that Bishops must be ordained, as well as Deacons. But we are not left to inference. Titus, whom St. Paul called an Apostle, (2 Cor. viii. 23,) was left at Crete, "that he should *ordain* Presbyters in every city." (i. 5.) So Timothy, who was also an Apostle,† was directed "*to lay hands suddenly on no man.*" (1 Tim. v. 23.) If, in connection with the fact, that Timothy himself was ordained by the laying on of an Apostle's hands, (2 Tim. iii. 6,) we consider the particular direction given him concerning the necessary qualifications of Bishops and Deacons; we can not doubt that by the "laying on of hands," (1 Tim. v. 23,) was meant ordination. The same is also asserted in Acts xiv. 23. "The Apostles ordained Elders [Presbyters] in every Church."

The language of Clement, of Rome, is decisive on this point. "Our Apostles knew from our LORD JESUS CHRIST,

* Lys. Orat. Evander, Æschin Contra Tim. Arch. Græca, 32.

† Compare 2 Cor. i. 1–8, 23; Phil i. 1; Col. i. 1; 1 Thess. i. 1; 2 Thess. i. 10; and post. c. xv. § 1.

that contentions should arise on account of the ministerial office. And therefore, having a perfect knowledge of this, *they appointed* persons, as we have before said, and then gave direction in what manner, when they should die, other approved men should succeed in their ministry."* We have, therefore, the authority of an associate, friend and fellow-laborer of St. Paul, for declaring, that the ministerial office was constituted and appointed by God; that the Apostles, in consequence of revelations made to them, appointed men to the ministerial office; and that the Apostles gave direction about their successors.

Of the power and duties of Presbyter-bishops.

1. To teach and instruct the people, by preaching the gospel. One of the first qualifications of a Bishop mentioned by the Apostle, was, "He must *be able to teach and instruct others;*" from whence we conclude, that one duty of a Presbyter-bishop was to teach and instruct; or, *to preach.* The same is implied in St. Paul's charge to the Presbyters (Acts xx. 17) of Ephesus. "Take heed, therefore, *to feed the Church of God,*" ("to feed, i. e. *to lead, to cherish, to provide for,*"† which implies *instruction, teaching, preaching.*) The same language is used by St. Peter, in reference to the same subject. (1 Pet. v. 2.) A Bishop would also possess this authority as a Deacon, though raised to a higher rank or grade in the ministry; the power of the latter being included in the former; even as the power of an Apostle included that of both Presbyters and Deacons. Thus St. Peter, who was an Apostle, calls himself a Presbyter, (1 Pet. v. 1,) and St. Paul and Apollos, who were both Apostles, are called Deacons. (1 Cor. iii. 6.)

2. To rule in the Church. "Let the Presbyters that *rule* well, be counted worthy of double honor." (1 Tim. v. 17.)

* Ep. Cor. c. 44. † Rob. 683.

The same doctrine is also taught in 1 Timothy iii. 4, 5. "A Bishop must rule his own house well, lest he know not how to take care of the Church of GOD." The language of Peter implies the same thing. "I exhort the Presbyters to take the oversight, not as *lords*," (1 Pet. v. 1–3.)

3. To administer the sacraments. The Presbyter would possess power and authority *to baptize*, by virtue of having been a Deacon; the Bishop not only having the same power, but "greater license and authority" than the Deacon. Authority to administer the Eucharist would be included in the command "to feed the Church," (Acts xxvi. 18; 1 Pet. v. 2;) for, as it was the business of an earthly shepherd *to feed his flock*—that is, to see that all their wants were supplied; so it is the duty of a spiritual shepherd and pastor, to take care that the spiritual necessities of his flock—"*the Church of God*"—are supplied. In doing this, he must administer all those ordinances which CHRIST had ordained to be their spiritual food and sustenance, and the means of their spiritual edification. That this includes the administration of the LORD's Supper, no one can doubt, that carefully considers the account given of it by Paul, in 1 Corinthians xi. This last, however, could only be derived from the Apostles, or their successors; authority to consecrate the elements in the Eucharist having been originally given only to the twelve. This power was granted at the time of its institution, but did not take effect until after the crucifixion. Thus, at the time of the celebration of the last Supper, JESUS said to his Apostles, "I appoint you a kingdom, as my Father hath appointed unto me, that (or, *in order that*) ye may eat and drink at my table, in my kingdom." (Luke xxii. 29, 30.) The language here made use of, makes evident allusion to bequest, as the word frequently signifies,* and is tantamount

* Comp. Heb. ix. 16, 17.

to saying, I make over, or appoint to you, *as by bequest*, the kingdom I have received from my Father. And the reason given is, *in order that* they might be able to eat and drink at that table which he had spread; that is, might have power and authority to consecrate and set apart the elements of bread and wine, so that they should become *sacramentally* his body and blood, as he himself had declared them to be. (Matt. xxvi. 26, 28; Mark xiv. 22, 24; Luke xxii. 19, 20; 1 Cor. xi. 24, 25.)

In consequence of the authority to consecrate the Eucharist being derived from the Bishop, it has been held from the days of the Apostles, not to be lawful to celebrate it without the Bishop's consent.* The oldest Canon, or Liturgy, for the administration of the Communion, in which we know the precise words made use of, belongs to the fourth century. We have, however, the substance of several others, still earlier. The words of consecration, as they stood in the *Clementine Liturgy*, about A. D. 400, were as follows:—

"For in the night in which he was betrayed, taking bread into his holy and immaculate hands, and looking up to Thee, HIS GOD and Father, he brake it and gave it to his disciples, saying: This is the mystery of the New Testament; take, eat, this is my body, which is broken for many, for the remission of sins. Likewise, also, having mingled the cup with wine and water, he blessed it, and gave it to his disciples, saying: Drink ye all of it; this is my blood which is shed for many, for the remission of sins. Do this in remembrance of me; for as oft as ye eat this bread and drink this cup, ye do show forth my death until I come."†

The words of consecration in the *Liturgy of St. James*, the very *words* of which we know to be as old as 450, the

---

* Ign. Ep. Smyrn. c. 11. Bing. B. xi. c. 3, § 3.

† Apos. Const. viii. c. 12.

substance of it as ancient as 300, and the *order* as early as 150, are as follows :—

"In the same night that he was offered, or rather offered up himself for the life and salvation of the world; taking bread into his holy, immaculate, pure, and immortal hands, looking up to heaven, and presenting it to Thee, His God and Father, he gave thanks, blessed and brake it, and gave it to his disciples and Apostles, saying: Take, eat, this is my body, which is broken and given for you, for the remission of sins. Likewise after supper he took the cup, and mixed it with wine and water, and looking up to heaven and presenting it to Thee, His God and Father, he gave thanks, sanctified, blessed it, and filled it with the Holy Ghost, and gave it to his disciples, saying: Drink ye all of it; this is my blood of the New Testament, which is shed and given for you, and for many, for the remission of sins. Do this in remembrance of me; for as oft as ye eat this bread and drink this cup, ye do show forth the death of the Son of Man, and confess his resurrection, until his coming again."*

The *Liturgy of St. Basil*, arranged about 370, and the *Liturgy of St. Chrysostom*, arranged 381, were both based upon the *Liturgy of St. James*, and agree with the foregoing in every thing but some slight verbal alterations.

The words of consecration in the *Liturgy of St. Mark*, as they stood 451, and the substance and order of which is known to have existed before 330, are as follows :—

"For in the same night wherein he delivered himself for our sins, and was about to suffer death for mankind, sitting down to supper with his disciples, he took bread in his holy, spotless, and undefiled hands, and looking up to Thee, His Father, but our God, and the God of all, he gave thanks, he blessed, he sanctified, and brake it, and gave it to them, say-

---

* Brett. Col. Lit. p. 16, from Biblioth. Patr. T. II.

ing: This is my body which is broken and given for the remission of sins. In like manner he took the cup after supper, and mixing it with wine and water, and looking up to heaven, to Thee, His Father, but our God, and the God of all, he gave thanks, he blessed it, and filled it with the Holy Ghost, and gave it to his holy and blessed disciples, saying: Drink ye all of this, for this is my blood of the New Testament, which is shed and given for you, and for many for the remission of sins; do this in remembrance of me, for as oft as ye shall eat this bread, and drink this cup, ye show forth my death, and confess my resurrection and ascension until my coming again."*

The *Ethiopian Liturgy*, which was drawn from that of St. Mark, about 330, agrees with it in all important particulars, but abridges the language somewhat.

The language of the *Roman Liturgy* is peculiar in some points. In 1647 it stood thus:

"The day before he suffered, took bread into his holy and venerable hands, and lifting up his eyes to heaven, to Thee, His God, and Father Almighty, giving thanks to Thee, he blessed it, brake it, and gave it to his disciples, saying: Take and eat ye all of this, for this is my body. In like manner, after he had supped, taking also this glorious cup into his holy and venerable hands, giving thanks likewise unto Thee, he blessed it and gave it unto his disciples, saying: Take and drink ye all of it, for this is the cup of my blood of the New and Eternal Testament; the mystery of faith; which shall be shed for you, and for many, for the remission of sins. As oft as ye shall do these things, ye shall do them in remembrance of me."†

We have given this last, in order to show, that the modern

---

* Brett. Col. Lit. pp. 36, 37, from Renaudot, Lit. Orient. Coll. Tom. I.
† Bret. Coll. Lit. 123, 124.

notion of transubstantiation, so clearly alluded to in the modern Roman Canon, is wanting in all the Ancient Liturgies.

4. To watch over and inspect the conduct of the members of the Church where they were placed. The etymology of the word rendered *Bishop*, (Επισκοπος,) signifies literally, "an overseer or inspector;"* and we must therefore infer, that part of the duty of a Bishop was to take the *oversight*. This conclusion is strengthened by the direction of Paul to the Presbyters of Ephesus. "After my departure, grievous wolves shall enter in among you, not sparing the flock. Also of your own selves shall men arise, speaking perverse things, to draw away disciples. Therefore watch." (Acts xx. 29, 30, 31.) So Peter "exhorts the Presbyters to take the *oversight* of the flock of God." (1 Pet. v. 2.) Paul, also, to the Hebrews directs them to "obey them that have the *rule* over you, for they watch for souls." (Heb. xiii. 17.)

5. To sit in council with the Apostles at the formation of *new canons* for the government of the churches, and to assent to such as were made. The only account of an occurrence of this kind in the Apostolic Church, is contained in the fifteenth chapter of the Acts of the Apostles, on the exciting and important question, *whether the Gentile converts should be required to receive the Jewish rite of circumcision*. The difficulties attending this question were then considered so great, that Paul and Barnabas, with certain brethren at Antioch, were sent up to Jerusalem, to obtain a "*decree*" of "the Apostles and elders on the subject." (Acts xiv. 26; xv. 2; xvi. 4.) On their arrival at Jerusalem, "the Apostles and Presbyters came together to consider of the matter." Here was much debate, as would seem, among the elders, before the Apostles delivered their opinions; when Peter, and after

---

* Rob. 314.

him Paul and Barnabas, took part in the discussion; and when they had finished, *James declared sentence.* This sentence, judgment, or decree of James, was *approved* by the Apostles and *elders*, (Presbyters.) (Acts xv. 22, 23, and xvi. 4.) That the elders took part in the debate, is inferred from the fact, that there is no mention of the presence of any of the Apostles except those just named; and no intimation that any thing was said by them before the speech of Peter. That their assent was given to the decree, we have already shown, when speaking of the part borne by the people in this transaction.

6. The Presbyter-bishops owed obedience to the commands of an Apostle. If the Apostles exercised authority over the Presbyters, it follows that they had a right so to do; and if they had a right to exercise such power, then it was the duty of those over whom the power was exercised, to *obey*. But an examination of this point belongs to another place—a consideration of *the power of an Apostle*—to which the reader is therefore referred.

CHAPTER XV.

APOSTLES—APOSTOLIC BISHOPS.

We come now to speak of the third and last class of persons, who were *ministers and officers* in the Apostolic Church, that is, who possessed *executive*, *judicial*, and, in conjunction with others, *legislative powers* in particular Churches. It is not to be concealed that there is great difference of opinion on this point, nor, that it has excited controversy, which we wish to avoid. This question is interesting, important, and fundamental; but we hope to be able to show, that it is not difficult to decide. We say it is *fundamental*, because, if the Apostles were not *officers*, but simply *ministers* at large,* there were but *two orders of official ministers* in the Apostolic Church. If, on the contrary, they had official authority in particular Churches, superior to Presbyters and Deacons, there were THREE ORDERS *of official ministers* in the Apostolic Church.

This part of our subject, therefore, involves two questions: first, were the Apostles *officers?* And, second, if *officers*, did they possess authority *superior* to Presbyters? These questions must be examined and decided in accordance with the rules of evidence already established,† and which are repeated here, that they may be the more strongly borne in mind.

"7. A name designates an office in the Church, when some person to whom it is applied, exercised some power in the Church by virtue of it.

"8. The nature of an office in the Church, must be determined by the nature and extent of the power ascribed to the office, or exercised by the officer filling the office.

"9. The grade or rank of an officer is to be determined by the extent of the power appertaining to the office, or exercised by the officer."

If, then, the Apostles exercised executive, judicial, or legislative authority in the Church, by virtue of their Apostleship, they were *officers in the Church;* and if the extent of power appertaining to the Apostleship was superior to that exercised by Presbyters, or if the Apostles exercised official authority over Presbyters, they were superior to Presbyters, and the Apostolic Church contained *three orders of officers and ministers.*

---

* This is the position taken by those who deny the *three orders* in the ministry.

† Ante. p. 22

Our attention will now be directed to an examination of these questions. But we are not left to make out by inference, from brief ambiguous references, the nature of the *Apostolic office;* for we have the *Apostolic commission,* in which they received their authority to act in CHRIST's stead, and by virtue of which they acted. We shall, therefore,

1. *Inquire into the nature of that commission, and the extent of power therein granted.*

2. *Endeavor to ascertain the power exercised by the Apostles under that commission.*

OF THE APOSTOLIC COMMISSION.—This commission, which is generally regarded as dating from the appearance of CHRIST to the eleven after his resurrection, as collected from the Evangelists who have recorded it, reads as follows:—

" Go ye into all the world and *preach the gospel* unto every creature, *baptizing* them into the name of the Father, and of the Son, and of the HOLY GHOST; *teaching* them to observe all things whatsoever I have commanded you. And unto you *I give the keys of the kingdom of heaven,* and whatsoever ye shall bind on earth, shall be bound in heaven; and whatsoever ye shall loose on earth, shall be loosed in heaven; and whosesoever sins ye remit, they are remitted unto him, and whosesoever sins ye retain, they are retained; AS THE FATHER HATH SENT ME, EVEN SO SEND I YOU; *and lo, I am with you alway, even unto the end of the world.*" (Matt. xvi. 19; xviii. 18; xxviii. 19, 20; John xx. 21, 23.)

This commission, as it here reads, is one of the most important things of which we can conceive, and yet the rule of construction furnished by the Scriptures, tends rather to enlarge than to limit the powers granted in it. It is a sound rule of evidence, tnat *when one instrument contains an express reference to another instrument, for further description, the description contained in the instrument referred to, thereby becomes a part of the description of the instrument in which the* *reference is contained.* Now the phrase, "*As the Father hath sent me,* EVEN SO SEND I YOU," contains a direct reference to the *manner** in which CHRIST was sent by the Father, accompanied by the declaration that the Apostles were sent in like manner. The manner in which CHRIST was sent by the Father, thus becomes descriptive of the powers granted in the Apostolic commission; and reference to that must be had, in order to ascertain the full extent of the powers conferred by that commission. But lest it be said that we overestimate the authority conferred upon the Apostles, we shall first show, that the things included in the phrase "even so," most, or all of them, had been actually promised before; and that this was, therefore, only a renewal of previous grants, accompanied by *an enlargement of the field of action.* The powers granted in this commission, are :—

1. *Of preaching.* That this was given in the early part of their Apostleship, is acknowledged by all, and a simple reference to the gospel history will be sufficient.†

2. *Of baptizing.* We are told, at the very outset of our Saviour's ministry, that the "Pharisees heard that JESUS made and baptized more disciples than John; though himself baptized not, but his disciples." (John iv. 1, 2.)

3. *The power of the keys;* that is, of admitting to, or rejecting from, the Church.‡ "Unto you *I will give the keys of the kingdom of heaven;* and whatsoever thou shalt bind on earth, shall be bound in heaven; and whatsoever thou shalt loose on earth, shall be loosed in heaven." (Matt. xvi. 19.) And this power, which was first *promised* (not, as some erro-

---

* This must not be confounded with the *object for which* he was sent, as is often done.

† Matt. x. 7, 27; xi. 5. Mark iii. 14; vi. 12. Luke ix. 2, 6, 60; xvi. 16; xxiv. 27.

‡ Rob. 445.

neously say, *given*) to Peter, was shortly after promised to all of the twelve. (Matt. xviii. 18.)

There are several other points of comparison which will be seen to best advantage by contrast. Indeed, without bearing this in mind, we shall hardly feel the full force of the language made use of in this commission.

4. CHRIST was set apart to his ministerial office, by the HOLY GHOST descending upon him, (Matt. iii. 16;) and he caused the Apostles to be set apart in like manner. (John xx. 22; Acts ii. 3, 4.)

5. He had a kingdom appointed unto him, and he appointed one to his Apostles, in like manner. (Luke xxii. 29.)

6. CHRIST had power to forgive sins, (Matt. ix. 2; Mark ii. 5, 10,) and he gave authority to his Apostles to absolve and remit the sins of repenting sinners: "Whatsoever ye shall loose on earth, shall be loosed in heaven, (Matt. xviii. 18,)* and whosesoever sins ye remit, they are remitted unto him." (John xx. 23.)†

7. The Father committed all judgment to the Son, (John v. 22;) and at the time he instituted the sacrament of the Holy Communion, he appointed to his Apostles, (διατιθεμαι, *made over* or *committed* to them, as *by devise* or *bequest*,) the kingdom which the Father had appointed or committed to him, (Luke xxii. 29;)‡ (ινα) *in order that*§ they might eat and drink at his table, and sit on thrones, (*the emblems of power*,)‖ judging (*in a judicial sense*)¶ the twelve tribes (or *persons composing "the commonwealth*) of Israel," (Eph. ii. 22;) which in the New Testament signifies *the Church*.

---

* Rob. 176.

† Rob. 458, and comp. Matt. vi. 12, 14, 15; ix. 2, 5, 6; xii. 31, 32. Mark ii. 2, 5, 7, 9, 10; iii. 28; iv. 12; xi. 31, 32. Rob. 119.

‡ Rob. 191; comp. ix. 16, 17.

§ Rob. 388.

‖ Rob. 376. Matt. xix. 28

¶ Rob. 460 Comp. Matt. xix. 28. 1 Cor. v. 12; vi. 2, 3.

8. He consecrated bread and wine, and declared them to be his "body and blood;" or, as others understand the language, "made them the authoritative and acknowledged signs of his body and blood;" and he gave his Apostles authority to do the same. (Matt. xxvi. 26–30; Mark xiv. 22–26; Luke xxii. 17–30; 1 Cor. xi. 23–27.)

There are several other points in which the conduct of CHRIST *before*, and of the Apostles *after* his ascension, were similar; but, as some of them involve questions concerning the extent of the powers of an Apostle, we shall proceed to inquire how the Apostles understood the commission which they had received; which must be gathered from the acts they performed under it. This must be conclusive evidence concerning the meaning of their commission; for, as they were inspired men, it was impossible that they could be mistaken about *the meaning* of the commission under which they acted, or the *extent of powers* granted by it. Hence, whatever they *did*, they had *a right* to do; and what they had a right to do, that *was granted* to them in the commission, or followed by force of the phrase, "even so." In the *Acts of the Apostles*, then, we have an *inspired commentary* upon a *divine commission.*

OF THE POWERS EXERCISED BY THE APOSTLES UNDER THEIR COMMISSION.

1. The Apostles alone possessed the power of conferring Apostolic authority on others. This is a natural, if not a necessary inference, from the tenor of their commission, and that CHRIST intended they should do this, is evident from the language, "Lo, I am with you alway, even unto the end of the world;" which could not be true, if limited either to the Apostles, or the Christians then living, personally. This leads us, therefore, to inquire, whether the Apostles ever committed this authority to others. We have already seen, that the power to judge in the Church was exclusively

an Apostolic right; and hence, imparting this authority to others, is evidence of a transmission of Apostolic authority.

This authority was conferred on TITUS by Paul. "For this cause, *I left thee* at Crete, that thou shouldst set in order the things that are *lacking*, (or *wanting*,)* and *ordain Presbyters* in every city." (Titus i. 5.) All antiquity testifies to the fact, that Titus was ordained Bishop of Crete, by St. Paul. Thus Eusebius, out of the records of the Church, tells us, that "Titus was appointed over the Churches in Crete,"† and Chrysostom,‡ and Theodoret,§ Jerome,|| and the Apostolical Constitutions,¶ tells us the same thing, adding, that he was ordained by St. Paul.

The same authority was also conferred upon TIMOTHY. To Timothy he says, "The things that thou hast heard of me among many witnesses, do thou *give in charge* (*commit*, or *entrust*)** the same to faithful men, who shall be able to teach others also;" but "lay hands suddenly on no man." (2 Tim. ii. 2; 1 Tim. v. 22.) Timothy, also, is said by the ancients to have been ordained by St. Paul, the first Bishop of Ephesus, which some say, was the metropolitan Church of Asia Minor. Mention is made of this by Eusebius,†† by the author of the *Life of Timothy*, in Photius;‡‡ and by the Bishop present at the Council of Chalcedon, who was the twenty-seventh in descent from Timothy.§§ The same thing is also asserted by Chrysostom,|||| by Theodoret.¶¶ by the Apostolical Constitutions,*** and indeed, by all the ancient historians.

* Rob. 478.
† Ecc. H. iii. 4.
‡ Hom. Tit. i. 1.
§ Arg. Ep. ad Tit.
|| Cat. Ecc. Scrip.
¶ B. vii. c. 46.
** Rob. 624.
†† Ecc. H. iii. 4.
‡‡ Biblio. No. 254.
§§ Coun. Chal. Act. 11.
|||| Hom. 1 Tim. iii. 1, 5, 9.
¶¶ Com. 1 Tim. iii. 1.
*** B. vii. c. 46.

These facts furnish conclusive evidence, that Paul gave Timothy and Titus authority to ordain, and of course that he committed to them at least one point of Apostolic authority. There is also, as we shall show under the proper heads, evidence that Timothy and Titus were clothed with various other functions of Apostolic authority; but we propose now to show, that both are called *Apostles.** That there were other Apostles beside the twelve, is conceded by all. Thus Matthias, (Acts i. 26,) Paul, and Barnabas, were *Apostles*, (Acts xiv. 4, 14;) and also Andronicus and Junia, (Rom. xvi. 7,)† were Apostles; and in 2 Corinthians viii. 23, the term Apostle is applied to Titus and several others whose names are not mentioned.‡ It would seem also, from the language of Paul to the Thessalonians, that Timothy was called an Apostle. We learn from his first Epistle to them, that both Paul and Timothy had been at Thessalonica; and the Epistle is addressed, "Paul, and Sylvanus, and Timotheus, to the Church of the Thessalonians," (i. 1;) and in it they say, (ii. 6,) "*We* were not burdensome to you as *Apostles of* CHRIST." And the language of St. Paul, in 2 Corinthians (i. 1) and Colossians, (i. 1,) leads to the same conclusion. "Paul, an Apostle, and Timothy, *our* brother." Now the word *our*, used in the English version, is not in the original. Hence, a literal translation would be, "Paul, an Apostle, and *brother* Timothy." But in what sense was Timothy

* The word *Apostle* was not considered, in primitive times, so peculiarly appropriated to the twelve, as to be inapplicable to any one else. Thus, Clement of Alexandria says, (Strom. vi. 667:) "It is lawful now, to enroll in the company of the Apostles, those who are well versed in the commands of the LORD, and live perfectly and intelligently according to the gospel."

† Rob. 91.

‡ Rob. 91. This passage is quoted by Areus, Archbishop of Crete, about 750, as proving the Apostleship of Titus.

brother? Professor Robinson renders it,* "*an associate, or colleague in office or dignity.*" In either case, Timothy must have had an office similar to that of St. Paul.

Epaphroditus is also called the Apostle of the Philippians. (Phil. ii. 25.) The verse, according to the English version, reads thus: "Epaphroditus, my brother and companion in labor, and fellow-soldier, but your messenger." The word rendered *messenger* is, in the Greek, *apostolon*, (αποστολον,) usually rendered *Apostle*, and the fact of the Apostleship depends upon the question of what is the true rendering of the word in this place. To enable our readers to form their own opinion upon this point, we give the following summary of the arguments by which the question must be decided.

The Greek word *Apostolos*, from αποστελλω, *to send away, send off, send forth, send out*, signifies, *one sent, a messenger, ambassador.*† In this, and in a higher sense also, it is applied to the twelve, chosen to be *messengers of Christ, ambassadors of the Gospel*, and *Apostles*, as being the founders and governors of the Churches. It is so used in the singular number, in a great variety of places.‡

3. It is once used in a similar sense, and applied to CHRIST himself. (Heb. iii. 1.) 4. In three other places, the word in

---

* Rob. 26.

† Synonymous with this word, or nearly so, is the word *Angel*, employed in the first and second chapters of Revelation. "Αγγελος, a messenger, one sent," &c., (Rob. 6,) from "αγγελλω, to bring tidings, or a message, to do the office of an envoy or messenger."

‡ Rom. i. 1; xi. 13. 1 Cor. i. 1; ix. 12; xv. 9. 2 Cor. i. 1; xii. 12. Gal. i. 1. Eph. i. 1. Col. i. 1. 1 Tim. i. 1; ii. 7. 2 Tim. i. 1, 11. Tit. i. 1; and in the same sense in the plural, in Matt. x. 2. Mark vi. 3. Luke vi. 13; ix. 10; xi. 49; xvii. 5; xxii. 14; xxiv. 10. Acts i. 26; ii. 43; iv. 35; v. 18; viii. 1. Rom. xvi. 7. 1 Cor. iv. 9; xii. 28, 29; xv. 9. 2 Cor. xi. 5, 13; xii. 11. Gal. i. 17, 19. Eph. iii. 5; iv. 11. 1 Thess. ii. 6. 2 Pet. iii. 2. Jude 17. Rev. ii. 2; xviii. 20.

the common English version is rendered differently. John xiii. 16—The servant is not greater than his Lord, neither *he that is sent,* greater than he that sent him. 2 Cor. viii. 23—Our brethren, the *messengers* of the Churches. Phil. ii. 25—But your *messenger.**

The *authority* of the English version, as far as any argument can be drawn from the use of the word in the New Testament, is in favor of our conclusion. The word *Apostolos,* we have seen, is used in *fifty-four* places, and in *fifty-one* of them, is rendered Apostle. In order, therefore, to justify a different translation, it must clearly appear from the *sense,* that an Apostle, in his *official character,* could not have been meant. That Epaphroditus was a *messenger* and *ambassador* from the Church of Philippi, the narrative deter-

* On the origin and authority of the English version, the following remarks may be made:—The passage in John (xiii. 16) was rendered by Tyndal, and the Bishop's Bible, "neither the *messenger* greater than he that sent him;" by Coverdale, "neither the *Apostle,*" &c.; by the Genevan translators, "neither the *ambassador,*" &c. But the translators, in the time of King James, differed from all, and substituted, "neither *he that is sent,*" &c. The verse in 2 Corinthians, (viii. 23,) was rendered by Tyndal, the Bishop's Bible, and the Genevan translators, "the *messengers* of the congregations;" but Coverdale rendered it, "the *Apostles,*" &c. In Philippians, (ii. 25,) Tyndal, Coverdale, and the Bishop's Bible, rendered *Apostolos,* by *Apostle;* while the translation made at Geneva, under the eye of Calvin, substituted "your *messenger,*" and in this they were followed by King James' translators. As far, therefore, as an argument can be founded on the agreement of the English versions, it is in favor of the Apostleship of Epaphroditus. We see, also, that the present rendering had *its origin* among the Genevans, whose system of Church government it would contradict, if not destroy, if otherwise translated. We may also add, that Luther translated this word *Apostle,* in all three places, and that there is not a single version of the Scriptures, to our knowledge, that does not render the word *Apostle,* in Philippians, (ii. 25,) except those that have followed the Genevan.

mines. Was he any thing more? By an examination of the narrative, we shall find the following circumstances in favor of the Apostleship of Epaphroditus:—

(1.) Notwithstanding the eminence of St. Paul, and the near relation he bore to the Church at Philippi, he supposed it more necessary to send Epaphroditus to them, than to send his tried and beloved son Timothy, or more necessary, even, than to go himself. "I trust in the LORD JESUS, to send Timotheus shortly unto you; yea, that I shall myself come shortly unto you. Yet I supposed *it necessary** to send you Epaphroditus, my brother and companion in labor, and fellow-soldier, BUT YOUR APOSTLE, and the *minister to my wants*."† The relation which Epaphroditus bore towards the Apostle, was that of a "brother and companion in labor, and fellow-soldier;" *but, on the contrary*,‡ to the Philippians he was an *Apostle*.

(2.) If Epaphroditus were merely a delegate or messenger of the Church in Philippi, it is not easy to conceive why his presence was more necessary in that Church, than that of Paul or Timothy. History gives no account of any pre-eminence of this man, that will account for the application of this language to him, unless he was, in an official sense, *their Apostle*, the highest officer and ruler of the Church in Philippi.

(3.) The anxiety experienced by Epaphroditus while sick, is such as supposes the existence of ties of no ordinary kind, binding him to that place. "He longed after you all," that is, *he earnestly desired to see you all*.§ It will be difficult to imagine any motive which could operate thus strongly upon his mind, if he were merely a messenger of the Church; but if he were their Apostle, how intense must have been his

* Rob. 45.
† Phil. ii. 19, 24, 25. Rob. 478.
‡ Rob 169.
§ Rob. 313.

anxiety for them. And how appropriate the language of the Apostle. In sending Epaphroditus "*the more speedily*,"* St. Paul was, therefore, consulting the good of the Church at Philippi, and the pleasure and gratification of its members.

(4.) That Epaphroditus was more than simply a member of the Church in Philippi, before he went to bear their alms to Paul, seems probable from the active part he took in procuring them. "He spared not his own life, to supply me with that service which was lacking on your part," is the strong language of St. Paul. The whole tenor of this account, is, therefore, in exact accordance with the character of an Apostle, having the care, supervision, and government of the Church, while the language can not be applied to the character of a mere delegate, without doing violence to its natural import.

(5.) The language of the Apostle describes an office similar to that which he held himself, calling him "my brother and companion in labor, my fellow-soldier," (Phil. ii. 25,) and "a true yoke-fellow," (Phil. iv. 3,) epithets which could not, with any propriety, be applied to a person not *associated in office* with the Apostle.

(6.) Another argument in favor of this view of the subject, may be derived from the admitted uniformity of the Apostolic Churches. As we have proved the existence of this class of officers at Ephesus, Crete, and other places, it follows that there must have been such an officer at Philippi also; and as the language applied to Epaphroditus is in exact accordance with that supposition, and there being no contradictory evidence, we need not hesitate to say, that he filled that office, and that there was in the Church at Philippi, *one* Apostle, having under him *many* Presbyter-bishops and Deacons.

---

* Rob. 766.

This conclusion is also favored by the practice of the Primitive Church, in sending their most eminent ministers, as messengers, to such as were in affliction, and hence, perhaps, they received the name of Angels. Thus when Ignatius was on his way to Rome to be offered, the "Churches came to meet him by their governors;"* among whom were Onesimus, Bishop of Ephesus;† Damas, Bishop of the Church in Magnesia;‡ Polybius, Bishop of the Trallians;§ and others whose names are not mentioned. Bishops who went on these errands of mercy and love, might with propriety be called Apostles and Angels, both in the sense of an Apostolic-bishop, and as messengers of the Churches. And that this was the capacity in which Epaphroditus visited St. Paul, there can be no reasonable doubt.||

To these considerations may be added the testimony of antiquity, as all who speak of Epaphroditus, call him the Apostle of the Church in Philippi. Thus Jerome says: "In process of time, *others were ordained Apostles*, by those whom our Lord had chosen, as that passage in Philippians shows, 'I supposed it necessary to send unto you Epaphroditus, your Apostle.'"¶ And Theodoret says: "Epaphroditus is called the Apostle of the Philippians, because he was their Bishop."**

We see, therefore, that the Scriptural use of the word Apostle; the language of the narrative; and the testimony of the Fathers sustains the Apostleship of Epaphroditus.

There is no reasonable doubt, therefore, that Timothy, Titus, and Epaphroditus, are called Apostles in the New

---

* Martyr. Ign. c. 4. † Ign. Ep. Eph. c. 1.

‡ Ep. Mag. c. 2. § Ep. Trall. c. 1.

|| See on this practice, Col. iv. 12, 13; 2 Tim. i. 15, 16, 17, and Hug's Intd. N. T. Par. ii. c. 2, § 129.

¶ Com. Gal. i. 19. ** Com. Phil. ii. 25.

Testament. But it is sometimes answered to this,* that "The DISTINCTIVE CHARACTERISTIC of the Apostleship was *to go forth and testify* AS *eye witnesses*, among all nations, to the great facts connected with the history of JESUS CHRIST, especially to the fact of his resurrection from the dead. *They must have seen him alive after his crucifixion.* A small number of competent witnesses, originally twelve, were appointed for this purpose."

Hence it is said, there could be no Apostles but the twelve. This argument is based upon the language of CHRIST, (Luke xxiv. 48,) "Ye are *witnesses* of these things;" the language of Peter, (Acts ii. 32; v. 22,) "We are *witnesses*;" (x. 40, 41,) "Was showed openly to chosen *witnesses*;" and on the language made use of at the election of Matthias, and the account given by Paul of his conversion. (Acts xxii. 14, 15; xxvi. 16; 1 Cor. ix. 12; xv. 8.) From this it has been inferred by some, that, "*to have seen* the LORD JESUS," was an indispensable requisite of the Apostleship. Each of these passages we shall examine by itself.

The first passage usually cited in support of the preceding supposition, is Luke xxiv. 48: "*Ye* are *witnesses* of these things." The "things" of which the persons to whom this language was addressed, were to be *witnesses*, is agreed to have been "the death and resurrection of CHRIST," and this, it is said, "was the object of the *special* appointment" of the twelve. Now the whole force of this argument depends upon the truth of two *assumed* facts; (1,) that this language was addressed directly to the eleven, and to them *only*, for *if* it was addressed to others than the eleven, then they too were

* This point was discussed at length by Bishop H. U. Onderdonk, of Pennsylvania, and Rev. Albert Barnes, of Philadelphia, and the language of "the objector" under this head, is copied from Mr. Barnes.

to be "witnesses" of the same *things;* and *if* others beside the eleven were to be "witnesses," then the *witnessing* was not a "*peculiarity* of the Apostolic office;" and, (2,) it is assumed that this was a peculiarity of the office, for it would by no means follow, that this was a characteristic of that office, if there were no other witnesses. We are surprised that no attempt has been made to prove the truth of that most material point—the first of the above positions, and more surprised, that no one has even averred its truth.

But though no one has attempted to show that this language was *not* spoken to others beside the eleven, we will show that it *was* spoken to others; and hence, that this point was not "a peculiarity of the Apostolic office," or that there were more than eleven Apostles. "And they [the two disciples which had been to Emmaus] rose up the same hour, and returned to Jerusalem, and found the eleven and they that were with them, gathered together, saying, . . . And as they spake, Jesus himself stood in the midst of them, and said unto them— . . . It behooved CHRIST to suffer, and to rise again the third day; and that repentance and remission of sins should be preached in his name, beginning at Jerusalem. And *ye* are witnesses of these things." (Luke xxiv. 33–48.)

The whole of this transaction, according to St. Luke, took place at the same time; and hence, *all* to whom this language was spoken, were *equally* witnesses of the same things. Now the persons present were, the two disciples who returned from Emmaus, and who could not have been of the eleven, as "they found the *eleven* gathered together, with those [persons] who were *with* [that is, who consorted or associated with] the Apostles." This assembly was therefore composed of the *brethren* generally, and the declaration, "ye are witnesses," is applied equally to all; hence, all the brethren present were made *Apostles*, or, the *witnessing* was not "a peculiarity of the Apostolic office."*

The next passage cited is Acts i. 21, 22, which gives an account of the election of Matthias, when Peter said, "One must be ordained to be a witness with us of his resurrection." On this we need only remark, that as there is nothing here which declares this to be the *only* object of the election of Matthias, the conclusion attempted to be drawn, does not follow. Besides, St. Luke, who wrote this account, can not be understood as saying that none but the Apostles were to be witnesses, as we have seen the last chapter of his own gospel informs us that the fact was not so.

The next passage cited, is Acts ii. 32: "This JESUS hath GOD raised up, whereof *we are all* witnesses." Now it is important for those who set up the claim we are considering, to show who were intended by "we all," as it is essential to their argument that it should include the *twelve*, and no more

---

* WE can not but express our surprise that men of intelligence should insist upon such a supposition as this, which the reading of ten verses in connection would have overthrown; and not only this, but that they should entirely overlook things so vitally important to the truth of their conclusions; and also at the very strange, if not absurd position, in which this hypothesis places the sacred historians—since all of the Evangelists have given us an account of several things contained in the Apostolic commission, which the objectors consider of minor importance; while Luke, who was not one of the twelve, is the only one who has taken the least notice of that which our opponents profess to consider the only essential thing in that commission. It is indeed passing strange, if the hypothesis under consideration be the true one, that neither Matthew nor John, who were of the twelve, have alluded to that which is said to be the main object and design of their appointment. Surely they must have known the facts, and it is fair to presume, that if they had considered this point of as much consequence as some moderns would be glad to make it, they would at least have mentioned it.

and no less. But this they can not do, as will be seen from the following considerations. It is said, Acts ii. 1, that "they [the Christians] were *all* with one accord, in one place." And after the news of the miracle which had been wrought had gone abroad, a multitude of people came together, and when they had thus assembled, "Peter stood up with the eleven, and said," (ii. 14.) Now if Peter, when thus situated, had said, as is represented, "*We* are witnesses," and said nothing more, it would only include *the eleven*, and hence Matthias would not be included, as it is not said that he was there; but when he uses the strong language, "We are *all* witnesses," it is evident that he intended to include all "the brethren" present.

Next, Acts v. 32: "And we are his witnesses." If Peter, when saying that the Apostles were "his witnesses," had intended to say that they were "his *only* witnesses," it is matter of surprise that he did not give some intimation of the kind.

Again, Acts x. 39–41: "And *we* are witnesses of all things which JESUS did, both in the land of the Jews, and in Jerusalem, whom they slew and hanged on a tree; Him GOD raised up and showed openly; not to all the people, but unto witnesses chosen before of GOD—to us who did eat and drink with him after he rose from the dead." In regard to this passage, two things deserve consideration. First, who was intended by "we" and "us"? The narrative gives no account of any one being present who had seen the LORD, save Peter himself; and hence, the words refer simply to the speaker himself. The second point is, who were the "chosen witnesses" to whom CHRIST was shown? The Apostle tells us that "GOD showed him not openly *to all the people, but* to witnesses *chosen before of God*." Every person, therefore, to whom CHRIST was shown after his resurrection, was a "chosen witness" to his resurrection, "chosen of GOD" for this very purpose. It will, therefore, be incumbent on the objector to prove, *either* that CHRIST was seen only by the twelve,* or that St. Peter was mistaken; or else give up this hypothesis in regard to the peculiarity of the Apostolic commission; or else allow that there were more than twelve Apostles. But this can not be done; for, if the fact of having seen the Saviour after his resurrection constituted an Apostle, the election of Matthias was unnecessary; as upon the principles in question, he was as much an Apostle before, as after his election, as he had witnessed things from the beginning. (Acts i. 19–22.)

The foregoing passages, it is claimed by the objector, contain "*all* that is said in the New Testament of the original design of the appointment of the Apostolic office." And surely, our readers will agree with us, that if this be "*all* of the peculiarity of the Apostolic office," then there was no peculiarity of that office; at least, none which can affect the *government* of the Church.

All the other passages referred to, relate to the conversion of Paul, and the language relied upon is, he was "called to be a minister and witness of the things he had seen and heard." (Acts xxii. 14, 15; xxiii. 11; xxvi. 16. 1 Cor. ix. 1, 2; xv. 8.) Now the question whether the "*witnessing*" was the peculiarity of this Apostle's commission, depends mainly upon the fact, whether that was the distinguishing feature of the Apostolic office, which we have seen was *not* the case. Hence, this could not be the material point in the commission of St. Paul.

That the Apostles appointed successors to themselves, in all Churches, is proved by the unanimous voice of all antiquity. Thus, Clement of Rome, the disciple and associate

---

* But he was seen "by above *five hundred* brethren at once." 1 Cor. xv. 6.

of St. Paul, expressly says,* that "they appointed persons [to the ministerial office] and then gave direction in what manner, when these should die, other approved men should succeed in the ministry." And in another place,† he says, "GOD hath himself ordained by his supreme will, both where and by what persons [our offerings and services] are to be performed." The same thing is testified to, by Irenæus, the disciple of Polycarp,‡ and by Tertullian, in the same age.§

Many of the names of the persons so appointed, have been preserved to the present day. Thus, Hegesippus, who wrote about 150 or 160, says, that "JAMES received the government of the Church at Jerusalem, from the Apostles."‖ And Clement of Alexandria, bears witness to the same fact.¶ PHILIP is also said to have been first Bishop of Hierapolis;** THOMAS, first Bishop of Parthia;†† ANDREW, first Bishop of Scythia.‡‡ So TIMOTHY was ordained by St. Paul, first Bishop of Ephesus;§§ TITUS, ordained by St. Paul, first Bishop of Crete;‖‖ POLYCARP, ordained by St. John, second Bishop of Smyrna;¶¶ EVODIUS, ordained by St. Peter, first Bishop of Antioch,*** and IGNATIUS, the second Bishop, by St. Paul;††† LINUS, ordained by St. Paul,

* Ep. Cor. c. 44.

† Ep. Cor. c. 40.

‡ Adv. Hær. iii. 3.

§ Præs. Adv. Hær. c. 32.

‖ Com. L. v. in Euseb. Ecc. Hist. ii. 23.

¶ Inst. L. vi. in Euseb. Ecc. Hist. ii. 1.

** Ep. Polycr. in Euseb. v. 24.

†† Euseb. iii. 1.

‡‡ Euseb. iii. 1.

§§ Euseb. iii. 4. Phot. Bib No. 254. Apos. Cons. vii. 46. Chrys. Hom. 1 Tim. iii. 1, 5. Theod. Com. 1 Tim. iii. 1.

‖‖ Euseb. iii. 4. Chrys. Hom. Tit. i. 1. Theod. Argum. Tit. Jerome. Cat. Ecc. Scrip. Apos. Cons. vii. 46.

¶¶ Iren. Adv. Hær. iii. 3. Apos. Cons. vii. 46

*** Euseb. iii. 22. Apos. Cons. vii. 46.

††† Apos. Cons. vii. 46.

first Bishop of Rome,* but CLEMENT, the third Bishop, by St. Peter;† ANNIANUS, ordained by St. Mark, first Bishop of Alexandria;‡ DIONYSIUS, ordained by the Apostles, first Bishop of Athens.§

In the age of Irenæus and Tertullian, this fact was appealed to, as a test of orthodoxy, and as one unfailing *Note* of a true Church. Thus Tertullian addresses the Heretics,‖ "If any dare mingle themselves with the Apostolic age, that thus they may appear to be handed down from the Apostles, because they were under the Apostles, we may say: Let them show the beginnings of their Churches; let them declare the series of their Bishops, so running down from the beginning by successions, that the first Bishop may have been one of the Apostles, or Apostolic men who yet continued with the Apostles, for their author and predecessor. For in this manner the Apostolical Churches trace their origin."

And Irenæus also says,¶ "It is easy, therefore, for all in the whole Church, if they desire to know what is truth, to ascertain it, the tradition of the Apostles having been manifested to the whole world. And we are able to enumerate those who were appointed by the Apostles, Bishops in the Churches, and their successors, in a continued course to us, who have taught nothing of this, neither have they known (any thing) of what is idly talked of by them, (i. e. heretics.) For if the Apostles had known hidden mysteries, which they taught secretly to the perfect, separate from the rest, they would most assuredly have taught it to those to whom they also committed the Churches. For they desired those to be

* Iren. Adv. Hær. iii. 3. Euseb. iii. 2. Apos. Cons. vii. 46.

† Apos. Cons. vii. 46.

‡ Euseb. ii. 24.

§ Ep. Dion. Bp. Cor. in Euseb. iv. 23.

‖ Præs. Adv. Hær. c. 32.

¶ Adv. Hær. iii. 3.

very highly perfect and irreproachable in all things, whom they left their successors—giving (to them) their own office of governing; as great usefulness would result from their acting correctly, but the greatest evils from their falling."

2. To the Apostles, and those to whom they had committed Apostolic authority, belonged the exclusive right of appointing or ordaining Presbyters and Deacons. It is sufficient proof of this, that there is no mention of an appointment or ordination to such an office, by any one but an Apostle; for it is agreed that the Apostolic history and epistles contain allusions to the organization of the Apostolic Church, sufficiently distinct to enable us to determine what it was. We are not permitted, therefore, to infer or presume any thing in regard to the organization of that Church, except from statements made concerning it, or references to it, contained in the Apostolic writings. Hence, to assume that the exclusive right of ordaining Presbyters and Deacons was not vested in the Apostles, *because* it is not *expressly* alleged in Scripture to be so, is to give up every principle of argument upon which these inquiries must proceed. If, then, the Apostles did ordain, *they* had a right to ordain; and, if no one else ordained, then no one else had a right to ordain. To take any other ground, is to deny that we can ascertain the organization of the Apostolic Church from the Bible—is to say there is no use in inquiring about it. If, then, we can prove that the Apostles, and those upon whom they had conferred Apostolic authority, did ordain, we are authorized to say, that they only had the right to ordain; unless it can be clearly shown that others also ordained.

That the Apostles did ordain, is conceded by all, and testified to by the whole body of ancient writers in the Primitive Church. Thus we have the record of numerous ordinations by the Apostles, in particular Churches, which will be considered elsewhere, to which we add a quotation from Clement of Alexandria, A. D. 175. He says, after the death of the Roman Emperor, the Apostle St. John returned "from the isle of Patmos to Ephesus. He went also to the neighboring regions of the Gentiles; in some to appoint Bishops, in some to institute entire new Churches, and in others to appoint to the ministry those that were pointed out by the HOLY GHOST."*

In order, however, to place the subject beyond doubt, we shall briefly consider the various instances in the New Testament, where an ordination or appointment to such an office is spoken of. The first account of this kind is that of the seven Deacons, (Acts vi.,) which has been claimed by those who deny the *official* character of the Apostles, as an election by the people, instead of an Apostolic ordination. But we have before shown, that the act of the Church was not an election or an appointment to office, but a testimony to the character of those the Apostles were to appoint;† and, in this case, we know the Apostles were the ordainers. The next case relates to the "ordination of Presbyters in every Church," (Acts xiv. 23;) which has also been claimed by the same class of persons, as an election to office by the votes of the members of the Church; but which we have shown could not have been the fact, and that the concurrence of the brethren, if any, consisted only in bearing testimony to the unblemished and Christian character of those the Apostles were about to ordain.‡

The next case claimed as an ordination by others than Apostles, is that of Timothy; and the proof cited is the language of Paul, (1 Tim. iv. 14,) "Neglect not *the gift* which was given thee by prophecy, *with the laying on of the hands of the Presbytery.*" In connection with this, however, we

---

* Quis Dives Salv. in Euseb. iii. 23. † Ante. p. 142

‡ Ante. p. 155.

must consider what the same Apostle says to the same person, (2 Tim. i. 6:) "Wherefore I put thee in remembrance, that thou stir up *the gift of God* which is in thee, *by the putting on of* MY *hands*." Now these are distinct, independent statements of a matter of fact, and are both universally admitted to have reference to an ordination. Hence, then, either Timothy was ordained, first, by the Presbytery, and *subsequently* by an Apostle; or else both refer to the same ordination. But the most strenuous opponents of the exclusive right of the Apostles to ordain, do not contend for two ordinations, but agree in referring both to the same transaction. To refer this to two transactions, would be to suppose two ordinations; one by the Presbytery, and a subsequent one by St. Paul, which would lead us to suspect the first insufficient. We must, therefore, put such a construction on both accounts, as will harmonize them. Putting the independent parts of the two passages together, and it will read thus: "Neglect not the gift of God which is in thee, BY *the putting on* of my hands, WITH *the laying on of* the hands of the Presbytery." Nothing can be plainer than this. The ordination was BY an Apostle, *with* the concurrence of the Presbytery. And yet, plain as it appears, a thousand shifts have been made, a thousand subterfuges laid hold of, in order to evade the force of this evident conclusion. This fact must be our apology for devoting more time to a consideration of these passages, than otherwise would be necessary.

In 2 Timothy, (i. 6,) the gift is said to have been given *by* (δια) the putting on of my hands; and in 1 Timothy, (iv. 14,) *with* (μετα) the laying on of the hands of the Presbytery. The force of the language here used, depends upon the signification of *by* and *with*, and much time and labor has been expended to show that both were the same thing; that the Apostle merely used *by*, for the sake of euphony. This notion, however, is as fallacious as it is contrary to the evident language of Scripture.

Dia, says Prof. Robinson,* "is a preposition with the primary signification, *through, throughout*, governing the genitive and accusative; with the genitive (as in this case) *through*. When the instrument or immediate cause, that which intervenes between the act of the will and the effect, *through* which the effect proceeds, is spoken of, *through, by means of;* and when applied to persons through whose hands any thing, as it were, passes *through*, or by whose agency or ministry an effect takes place or is produced, denotes *the efficient cause*." "*By* the laying on of Paul's hands," denotes, therefore, that "the gift of God," as it were, passed *through* Paul, and was conveyed to Timothy, *by* the imposition of the Apostle's hands, *he* being "the efficient cause, *by* whose agency the effect was produced."

"*Meta*," says Prof. Robinson,† "is a preposition governing the genitive and accusative; in poets also the dative, with the primary signification, *mid, amid*, i. e. *in the midst, with, among*, implying accompaniment, and thus differing from *sun*, which expresses conjunction, union. With the genitive (as in this case) implies, companionship, fellowship; signifying *with*, i. e. *together with*, and with the genitive of a thing designates the state or emotion of mind which accompanies the doing of any thing, *with* which one acts; or, (as here,) designates an external action, circumstance, or condition *with* which another action or event is accompanied." The ordination of Timothy was, therefore, *by* Paul, *with* the concurrence of the Presbytery. And this concurrence was, no doubt, manifested in the same manner as the concurrence of the people, in the selection of Deacons. Such a concurrence could not have been necessary for the Apostle, and conse-

---

* P. 178. † P. 509.

quently must have been designed as a *precedent* to guide the Church in after ages.*

We have pursued this question thus far, as though the meaning of Presbytery had been settled, and that it signified a council composed solely of the order of ministers in the Apostolic Church, called Presbyters. This however has not been shown, nor can it be proved. The word Πρεσβυτεροι, (Presbytery,) is used in Luke, (xxii. 66,) to denote *the elders of the people*, or council before which JESUS was arraigned, and in Acts, (xxii. 5,) to signify *the estate of the elders*, or the council before which Paul was arraigned, and in 1 Tim., (iv. 14,) to signify the body, (if any,) that concurred with Paul in the ordination of Timothy. Now as *Presbytery* literally signifies *a council of elders*,† and a name does not determine the nature of an office in the Church, and as this is the only place in the New Testament where this word is used in this sense, we are not authorized to infer the nature of this body from the name by which it is called. There are various ways in which this body might have been made up, entirely consistent with the meaning of the word, whether it is determined by Scripture or other authority. (1,) It might have been composed of Apostles alone; (2,) of Presbyters alone; (3,) of Apostles and Presbyters together; or (4) of Apostles, Presbyters, and people. Amid such uncertainty, it is altogether illogical, as well as unauthorized, to assume that the second of these meanings is the true one, and to make that the foundation of an argument, whereon to rest the authority of the ministry in any Church, as those who assert the authority of ordination by Presbyters are obliged to do.

---

* It was decreed by the 4th Council of Carthage, A. D. 399, that at the ordination of a *Presbyter*, all the Presbyters present should lay their hands upon the head of the candidate, along with the Bishop.

† Rob. 697.

But further, if *Presbytery* here denotes an ecclesiastical council, the admitted uniformity of the Apostolic Churches compels us to suppose that it was composed of the same class of persons who made up the other councils in the Apostolic Church, that is, of Apostles and Presbyters, as in Acts xv.

Again, it is not certain that *Presbytery* denotes a council, and it has been held by some strong advocates of ordination by Presbyters, to denote the office to which Timothy was appointed, and not the means by which he was appointed to it. Such was the opinion of John Calvin, as expressed in his Institutes.*

Another case sometimes quoted as an instance of ordination by Presbyters, is that of Paul and Barnabas. (Acts xiii. 1–3.) To this it is sufficient to reply, that Paul and Barnabas were both in the ministry *before* this time; and that St. Paul had been a preacher, at least several. Consequently, this act could not have been an ordination to the priesthood. If, then, it was an ordination at all, it must have been to the Apostleship. But this is rendered altogether improbable by St. Paul's own account of the matter. He assures the Galatians, (c. i. 1,) that he was "an Apostle, not of (απο) men, neither by (δια) man, but by Jesus Christ, and God the Father." This language, according to Professor Robinson, signifies, "an Apostle, not from, or of men, nor *by the agency or ministry of* men, but *by the agency and ministry of* Jesus Christ, and God the Father."† If, then, St. Paul did not receive his Apostleship from man, nor by the agency or ministry of men, this transaction could not have been an ordination to the Apostleship.

The passages we have examined are the only ones which

* L. iv. c. 3, as quoted by Abp. Potter on Church Gov. p. 267.

† Rob. 179. So in Rom. i. 3–5: "Jesus Christ our Lord . . . by whom we have received Apostleship."

can be urged in favor of Presbyter-ordination, and as they do not authorize it, the inference is inevitable, that the Apostles, and those to whom they had committed Apostolic authority, had the sole and exclusive power of ordaining Presbyters and Deacons in the Apostolic Church.

If we turn to the Fathers, we shall find the evidence entirely conclusive, that the Bishops, who were considered the successors of the Apostles, and they alone, had the exclusive power to ordain. The *Apostolical Canons*, which describe the customs of the Greek and Oriental Churches in the second century,* give directions concerning the ordination of the several orders of the clergy. The first canon enacts, that "A Bishop must be ordained by two or three Bishops. A Presbyter or Deacon, by one Bishop."

And the whole current of ancient authorities are all so uniformly to the same purpose, that no one has pretended to find a single opposing authority, until more than *two hundred and fifty* years after the death of St. John, A. D. 100; that is, not before A. D. 350. Such a person can not be authority, (1,) because he did not live at the time; and (2) because he is directly contradicted by earlier authorities. Yet as much stress is laid upon an author of this period, we shall quote all he says, entire.

That the opinion of Jerome concerning the distinction between Bishops and Presbyters, was different from that of his predecessors, those acquainted with ecclesiastical history are well aware. Hence, he has become the favorite author of two classes of opponents of Apostolic organization: those who would subvert it, by teaching the original equality of all the clergy, and those who would subvert the independency of it, by teaching that all Bishops are mere delegates of a chief Bishop; and both classes of opponents use much the

* Murdock's Mosheim, vol. 1, p. 224.

same arguments, to gain their respective ends. But though it is generally known that the opinions of Jerome on this subject were different from those of his predecessors, it does not seem to be generally known, what his opinions were. Now it matters not what they were, *so far as the authority of Apostolical organization is concerned*, since he lived and wrote about 250 years after the death of all the Apostles, and could not, therefore, know any thing on the subject, except from history. And we have numerous earlier authors, who contradict the usual interpretation put upon his writings; yet for the better understanding of the subject, we shall quote all the passages at length, usually cited from Jerome against the Apostolic practice. In this way, our readers will be able to see how far anti-Apostolic Jerome was, and of course, how much his pretended followers of the present day, can make out of his testimony. The three passages relied upon, are, his *Epistle to Oceanum*,* his *Epistle to Evangelum*,† and his *Comment on Titus* i. 7.

In his *Epistle to Oceanum*, Jerome is commenting on the language of St. Paul, in his *Epistles to Timothy and Titus*, when he says: "In both Epistles, whether Bishops or Presbyters, (although *among the ancients, the same who were Bishops, were also Presbyters*,) they were commanded to be chosen into the clergy, who had but one wife."

The *Epistle to Evangelum*, (*if it be genuine*,) was written on hearing that some one had given *Deacons* preference to *Presbyters*, as though they were of a superior order. Upon this, he says: "I hear that one was so impudent as to rank Deacons before Presbyters, that is, Bishops. Now the Apostle plainly declares *the same to be Presbyters, who also are Bishops*." And after mentioning some of the duties of Dea-

* 82, or 83.

† Old Editions, *Evagrius*, 101, or 85.

cons and Presbyters, he proceeds to quote Phil. i. 1; Acts xx. 17, 18; Tit. i. 5, 7; 1 Tim. iii. 8, in proof of the position he had before laid down, when he adds:

"Who are significantly called in the Greek, *episcopountes*, from whence the name of *Episcopi* (Bishops) is derived." He then quotes from one Caius, a Presbyter, who says:—"In the See of Alexandria, from St. Mark, the Evangelist, to Heraclas and Dionysius, Bishops, the Presbyters always elected one from among themselves, and raising him to a higher rank, they called him Bishop; much as an army chooses an Emperor, or as Deacons elect one from among themselves, and call him Arch-deacon. Indeed, *what can a Bishop do, that a Presbyter may not do, except* ORDINATION?" Then, after saying that the same practice existed in all places, he adds: "*Wherever the Bishop be*, whether at Rome, or Eugubium, or Constantinople, or Rhegium, or Alexandria, or Tanais, *he is of the same degree, and of the same Priesthood;* FOR ALL ARE SUCCESSORS OF THE APOSTLES."* And after some remarks concerning the Roman custom, he adds: "Let them know wherefore Deacons were established; let them read the Acts of the Apostles, and remember their condition. Presbyter is a title of age; Bishop of office. *Wherefore,* [in the Epistles,] to Timothy and Titus, *is mention made of the ordination of Bishops and Deacons, but not of Presbyters?* BECAUSE IN THE BISHOP THE PRESBYTER IS CONTAINED. We are advanced from the less to the greater; if, therefore, the Deacon is ordained from among Presbyters, then is the Presbyter the least; but if the Presbyter is ordained from among Deacons, then is the Presbyter of a higher order of the Priesthood. *And we know from Apostoli-*

* In his 54th Ep. he condemns the Montanists, for denying that the Bishops are the Apostles' successors, and the first order of the clergy.

cal tradition, taken from the Old Testament, that what Aaron and his sons and the Levites have been in the Temple, the same the Bishops, and the Presbyters, and the Deacons may claim as their own in the Church."*

The other passage from Jerome, on which reliance is placed by the objector, is from his *Comment on Titus* i. 7, where, after some remarks on the necessary qualifications of a Bishop, he applies the same to Presbyters, and goes on to say:—"*The same, therefore, is a Presbyter, who also is a Bishop;* for before, by the instigation of the devil, parties were formed in religion, and it was said by the people, I am of Paul, and I of Apollos, and I of Cephas, the Churches were governed by the Council of Presbyters. But after some began to consider those which he had baptized to be his own, not CHRIST'S, it was decreed throughout the whole world, that one be elected, who should be put over the rest of the Presbyters, to whom the care of all the Church should pertain; and thus the seeds of schism were taken away. If any one esteems it not of Scripture, but to be our opinion, that Bishops and Presbyters are one; this being a title of age, that of office; he is referred to the language of the Apostle to the Philippians." Here follow the same passages quoted in the *Epistle to Evangelum*, referred to above, when he goes on to say:—"This much, therefore, that we might show *the same to have been Presbyters among the ancients, who also were Bishops;* but by degrees, that every sprout of dissension might be rooted out, all the authority was conferred upon one alone. As, therefore, they know the Presbyter himself to be in subjection, by the usage of the Church, who of himself may have been chief, so the Bishops themselves, more by the introduction of a new custom, than by virtue of the

* The same idea is brought out in another Epistle, Ad. Nepot.

Lord's direction, are greater than the Presbyters, who have the right to rule the Church in common."

On these passages, the following remarks should be made: (1.) Jerome does not say that *the office* of Presbyter is the same as that of Bishop; but he expressly asserts, that the name Presbyter did not originally signify *office*, but *age*. (2.) He does not deny the existence of the second grade of the ministry, now called Presbyter, at the time the Apostle wrote the Epistles above referred to; but indirectly admits their existence, by giving as a reason why this rank is not mentioned, that *the Presbyter is included in the Bishop*. (3.) He does not say, that the office of Presbyter was ever the same as that of Bishop. (4.) And though he did not consider the *office* of Presbyter as ancient as that of Bishop, he considered it Apostolic. (5.) He expressly says, the power of ordination, even at Alexandria, was never vested in the Presbyter. (6.) He plainly declares, that the offices of Bishop, Presbyter, and Deacon, in the Christian Church, are as distinct, and are related to each other, as were those of High Priest, Priest, and Levite, in the Jewish Church. (7.) And finally, he tells us, that all, who in his day held the office of Bishop, *were successors of the Apostles*, that is, in the government of the Churches.

We have given the above quotations, that our readers may see what were the real sentiments of Jerome on the subject of Apostolic Order. That he differed from those of his own time, he himself admits; and we know this to be a fact, because it is admitted by *all* who have examined the subject, that, "*No Church without a Bishop*, has been a fact as well as a maxim, since the days of Irenæus and Tertullian," A. D. 175.* After allowing all the weight to the testimony

* Gib. Dec. and Fall, vol. I. p. 272, n. 111.

of Jerome which can be claimed for it, it still remains true, that according to his own account of the matter, the sole and exclusive power of ordination belonged to the Apostles and their successors, in accordance with the testimony of the Primitive Fathers.

But there is another objection to the testimony of Jerome; we know the facts were not as stated by Caius, in regard to the practice in Alexandria. This will appear from the ancient historians, especially from the testimony of the great ecclesiastical historian of the Copts, Severus, Bishop of Ashmonia, whose station in the Church gave him access to all its records, and who expressly states that he had consulted the Greek and Coptic Monuments, which in his time were preserved in the monastery of St. Macarius.

The statement of Caius is, that "in Alexandria, from St. Mark to Heraclas, *the Presbyters chose one from among themselves,*" *and ordained him.* Now this statement is not true, as a matter of history. We give the list of the Patriarchs of Alexandria, down to the time of the Council of Nice, A. D. 325, with the length of their episcopates, and the time of their death, as they stood in the *Oriental Chronicle*, in order to show the minute accuracy with which the records of the Alexandrine Church had been kept. The reader may easily reduce the dates to our computation, from the table already given.*

* Those marked with a *star*, are taken from the *Senkesar*, or *Calendar of the Ethiopian Christian Church.* (Harris's Ethiopia, App. viii.) The Ethiopians commemorate the memory of twelve of these twenty, viz.; 1st, 2d, 4th, 8th, 9th, 10th, 11th, 12th, 13th, 16th, 19th, and 20th; and with a single exception, on the days above mentioned. Two translations of the *Oriental Chronicle* are given in the *Byzantine Historians*, vol. xvii., one by Ecchellensis, the other by Assemani. The last is best, and the *dissertations* are valuable.

		Y.	Day.		Died.	A. D.
1	St. Mark,	7				
2	Ananias,	18	216,	Sunday,	Athor 20th,	86
3	Melianus,	12	286,	Monday,	Thoth 1st,	99
4	Cerdon,	10	280,	Saturday,	Paoni 11th,	109
5	Primus,	12	52,	Sunday,	Mesori 3d,	124
6	Justus,	10	315,	Saturday,	Paoni 22d,	135
7	Eumenius,	10	122,	Sunday,	Paophi 10th,	146
8	Marcianus,	9	86,	Sunday,	Tobi 6th,	155
9	Claudianus,	14	183,	Thursday,	Epiphi 9th,	169
10	Agrippinus,	11	211,	Friday,	Mechir 5th,	181
11	Julianus,	10	33,	—	[Phamenoth 8th,*]	191
12	Demetrius,	32	219,	—	[Phamenoth 12th,*]	224
13	Heraclas,	16	56,	Monday,	Choiak 8th,	240
14	Dionysius,	19	281,	—	—	261
15	Maximus,	12	211,	Sunday,	Pharmuthi 14th	273
16	Theonas,	9	263,	Wednesday,	Tobi 8th,	284
17	Peter-martyr,	10	333,	Friday,	Athor 29th,	295
18	Archelaus,	0	200,	Tuesday,	Paoni 19th,	295
19	Alexander,	22	308,	Monday,	Pharmuthi 22d,	318
20	Athanasius,	46	15,	Thursday,	Pachon 7th,	364

Concerning some of these, we make the following extracts from Severus.* The numbers refer to the preceding list.

(2.) ANIANUS, or Hanânias, (called by Eusebius, Ananius.) "When St. Mark received information of their design, [viz. the design of the Heathens to put him to death,] he constituted Anianus Bishop of Alexandria, and likewise three Presbyters and seven Deacons; which eleven persons he instituted for the service and confirmation of the faithful brethren. He himself departing thence, went to the Pentapolis, and remained there two years, preaching and ordaining, or constituting Bishops, Presbyters, and Deacons, in all the provinces thereof."

(4.) CERDON. "The Priests and Bishops who had been

* See also *Oriental Chronicle*, by Assemani, Byz. Hist., and Hist. Pat. Alex. by Renaudot.

before him in that region, having notice that the Patriarch was dead, assembled with grief in the city of Alexandria, and having consulted with its orthodox inhabitants, cast lots to decide who should be worthy to hold the See of St. Mark the Evangelist, after Melianus. And by the aid of our LORD JESUS CHRIST, their minds were agreed upon a chosen man, who feared GOD, and whose name was Cerdon."

(9.) CLAUDIANUS, (called in the Coptic catalogues *Kelasdianos*, and by Eusebius, Celadion.) "There was in those days a man among the people [i. e. a layman] who loved GOD, and whose name was Claudianus. Him the orthodox people, assembling with the Bishops who were in those days in Alexandria, took and constituted, or ordained, Patriarch, and placed him in the Evangelical See, and he was beloved by all the people." Several instances are recorded of laymen thus chosen. Thus Primus and Demetrius, (5, 12,) were also elected from among the laity.

(11.) JULIANUS. "There was a certain Presbyter, a wise man, who had studied the Holy Scriptures with great diligence, whose name was Julianus, and who walked in the way of continence, religion, and meekness. The Bishops, therefore, being assembled in council, and at the same time the orthodox people in the city of Alexandria, and making diligent inquiry among the whole people, they found no man like this Presbyter. Wherefore hands being laid upon him, they constituted him Patriarch."*

---

* In Egypt the custom anciently was, and now is, to have a threefold imposition of hands in the creation of Bishops. The votes of the people were given and numbered by lifting up of hands, and confirmed by the laying on of hands of the principal laity. The Presbyters laid their hands twice on the head of the person elected, first in giving their votes, and afterwards their solemn approbation of his admission to the Episcopate. The Bishops also twice laid on their hands, first to confirm the suffrage, and finally at his consecration. The following is the

There are a few other places occasionally referred to, as authority for ordination by Presbyters. Thus it is sometimes said, that "Hermas uses the terms Bishop and Pres-

order prescribed in the ancient constitutions of the Church in Alexandria. "Let the Bishop be constituted on the first day of the week, all giving their consent for his promotion, and the people and the Priests attesting for him. Let the Bishops, who are present to lay their hands on him, wash their hands that they may then consecrate him, the people standing by with silent reverence; and let them raise their hands over him, saying, We lay our hands upon this chosen servant of God, in the name of the Father, and of the Son, and of the Holy Ghost, to constitute him into a good and stable order of the one unspotted Church of the living invisible God." It then goes on to speak of the final act of consecration, in the following words: "After these things, let the presiding Bishop (primus Episcopus ex illis) lay his hands upon him, and pronounce the formula of consecration or ordination; and let all the people say, Amen. Then let all the Bishops give him the kiss, and let all the Priests and people say, Worthy, worthy, worthy; and let them all give him the kiss, and pray that he may have peace and health."

This also furnishes an answer to another argument sometimes urged against this conclusion. During the troubles in the reign of Charles I. an attempt was made to prove that the Church of Alexandria, founded by St. Mark, was originally Presbyterian.* An extract from the Annals of Eutychius, who succeeded Christodulus, A. D. 933, as the Melchite Patriarch of Alexandria, was employed for this purpose. Selden, who made this discovery, had not a profound knowledge of Arabic, nor was he well versed in ecclesiastical history. His translation, therefore, was inaccurate in several points which vitally affected his argument; and he seems not to have been aware, that the ancient records of the Egyptian Church were inaccessible to Eutychius, and that his testimony is of no value, excepting with regard to the history of the Melchites. These facts show most conclusively, that both Caius and Eutychius were mistaken, and that at Alexandria, as elsewhere, none but Bishops ordained. This Jerome himself allows, in opposition to the authority he had quoted, if indeed it is quoted correctly. S. F. J.

* Eutych. p. xxix. ed. Seld. in Geis. E. H. § 32. The translation of Selden has been controverted by Morinus, Pearson, Le Quieu, Renaudot, Petavius, Ecchellensis, *etc.*

byter promiscuously, and speaks of Presbyters as *presiding over* the Church at Rome."* This is a mistake, as Hermas, who wrote in Latin, says nothing of Presbyters, and seldom speaks of Bishops.

Also that "Clement, of Alexandria, sometimes speaks of Bishop and Presbyter as the same."† Never having been able to find the place where Clement says this, we apprehend this is also an error.

Also, that "Eusebius affirms that in *his* day, Evangelists sometimes ordained Pastors."‡ The facts related by Eusebius in the chapter referred to, took place in the days of Quadratus, who lived, *not* in the time of Eusebius, that is, in the beginning of the fourth century, as is affirmed, but in the beginning of the second century, 200 years *before;* and the "Evangelists" were those "who," according to Eusebius, "held the *first rank* in the Apostolic succession,"§ that is, in the language of Eusebius, who were Bishops.

3. To the Apostles belonged the sole power of administering Confirmation. By *Confirmation*, we mean a rite which existed in the Apostolic Church, and which consisted in the laying on of an Apostle's hands, upon those who had received the ordinance of baptism. This is implied in Hebrews vi. 2: "The doctrine of *baptism*, and of *the laying on of hands*, and of the resurrection of the dead, and of eternal judgment." There can be no doubt, that baptism and the "laying on of hands" spoken of in this passage, are entirely distinct; as much so as the resurrection and eternal judgment. The order in which the things are mentioned, also compels us to believe, that as the judgment follows the resurrection, so "*the laying on of hands*" *succeeds to baptism.*

---

* Prof. Pond, of Bangor, in *The Church*, p. 62. † Ib. 65.

‡ Ib. 66, and Euseb. iii. c. 37 § H. iii. 37.

But this text furnishes no evidence as to who performed the rite; and we must, therefore, have recourse to other portions of Scripture to determine the question.

When Philip went down to Samaria and preached the gospel, many believed and were baptized. As soon as intelligence of this event reached Jerusalem, two Apostles, Peter and John, were sent down to Samaria, "for as yet the HOLY GHOST had fallen upon none of the Samaritans, only *they had been baptized.*" (Acts viii. 16.) These Apostles, therefore, "prayed *and laid their hands on those who had been baptized, and they received the* HOLY GHOST." (viii. 15, 17.) So also at Ephesus, when Paul "*laid his hands on those who had been baptized, they received the* HOLY GHOST." (xix. 6.) Here, then, is the doctrine or fact of *the laying on of hands subsequent to baptism,* existing at Samaria and Ephesus; and, as it is agreed that the Apostles had an uniform system of organization, we are compelled to believe the same practice existed in the other Apostolic Churches, although there is no account of it in Scripture. There is, however, mention of something which appears to be equivalent to, or identical with it.

After Paul and Barnabas had preached the gospel in several cities of Asia, they returned "to Lystra and Iconium, and Antioch, *confirming* the souls of the disciples, [that is, those who had before been made such by baptism,] *exhorting* them to continue in the faith; *ordaining* Presbyters for them in every Church, *with prayer and fasting.*" (Acts xiv. 22, 23.) This *confirmation,* therefore, in whatever it consisted, was something distinct from, and in addition to, preaching, praying, and the ordinary means of edifying the Church. Some time subsequent, and after the great dissension at Antioch relative to the rite of circumcision, Paul and Barnabas returned again to Antioch, in company with Judas and Silas, and after much exhortation "confirmed." (Acts xv. 32.)* It is worthy of remark, that "*and confirmed*" (και επιστεριξαν) is an independent sentence, the narrative not informing us by whom the *Confirmation* was performed, or by whom received; and it should also be borne in mind, that Antioch is the only place where we have any account of Confirmation being performed a second time; and that the foregoing is the only place in the Scriptures where such a sentence occurs. We are led, therefore, to infer that this Confirmation was limited, for on no other hypothesis can we account for the change of language in this place. And if limited, then only such were now *confirmed*, as had not received the rite when administered by Paul and Barnabas some time previous.

Leaving Antioch, Paul passed "through Syria and Cilicia, *confirming* the Churches," (xv. 41;) and still later, passed through the "country in Galatia and Phrygia, in order, *confirming all the disciples.*" (xviii. 23.) That the *Confirmation* here mentioned does not signify any act of the mind, an addition to, or strengthening of the faith, but some outward and external rite, is evident, both from the meaning of the word, and from its use by the sacred historians.†

---

* The Old Syriac version of the New Testament furnishes presumptive evidence of the correctness of this conclusion. In that language, the word denoting Baptism, is from a root which signifies *to stand, to cause to stand,* and hence *to establish,* (ante, p. 84;) that signifying Ordination, is also from a root signifying *to stand, to cause to stand, to raise up,* and hence *to constitute,* (ante, p. 156;) and the word signifying Confirmation, or whatever else is referred to in these passages, is from the same root, ܩܘܡ, (*kom.*)

† The word επιστοριζω signifies literally *to fix firmly in* or *on* some place, and hence *to lean upon* or *to be supported on,* and is only used in this latter sense in the Greek version of the Old Testament, (2 Sam. i. 6; Is. xxxvi. 6,) and is not used in the New, except in the passages quoted in the text.

St. Paul evidently contrasts this *Confirmation* with mental strengthening, or addition to the faith, and reckons this as one means of obtaining it. After he left Antioch in company with Silas, (Acts xv. 40, 41,) he passed through various cities, "*confirming* [the members of] the Churches," delivering "to them the decrees of the Apostles and Presbyters to keep." And so "were the Churches *established in the faith*," (xvi. 5,) that is, by the praying, preaching, exhortation, and Confirmation of the Apostles, of which the historian had just given an account. We have, therefore, *the laying on of an Apostle's hands on those who had received baptism* in the Churches of Samaria and Ephesus, and something called *Confirmat'on, which was administered to them who had been baptized* in the Churches of Derbe, Lystra, Iconium, Antioch, Syria, Cilicia, Galatia, and Phrygia. Now, as the Apostolic system was uniform, both of these must have existed in all the Churches; and hence, either the same rite is intended in both cases, or else there were two distinct rites performed upon all persons in the Apostolic Church, who had received the sacrament of baptism. The first conclusion is the most probable, and is strengthened by the consideration, that both were administered only by an Apostle, upon only such as had been baptized, and there is no intimation that both were ever administered in the same Church. It is, therefore, certain, that if they were not like each other, they were unlike every thing else.

The same inference must also be drawn from the parallel language in Acts, (xv. and xvi.) 2 Corinthians, (i. 21, 22,) and Ephesians, (i. 13, 14; iv. 30.) Thus in Acts, the historian, after giving an account of the acts and labors of the Apostles, adds, "so were the Churches established in the faith." (xvi. 5.) And Paul to the Corinthians says, (2 Ep. i. 21,) "he which *stablisheth* us with you in CHRIST, and hath *anointed* us, (χριω, '*hath consecrated or set us apart to the ser-*

vice and ministry of CHRIST *and his gospel,'*)* is GOD, who hath also *sealed* us, (σφραγιζω, '*hath set his seal or mark upon us, in token of our being genuine and approved'*) [*Christians ;*]† and given the *earnest* (αρραβων, '*the pledge,* scil. *something given to ratify a contract'*)‡ of the Spirit in our hearts." This passage evidently contains a reference to the performance of some external rite, by which the recipient *was consecrated* or set apart to the worship of GOD through CHRIST, which was to them, not the *evidence* of their Christian character, but a *token* of it, and not the Spirit, but a *pledge* of it in the heart.

Of the same purport is the language in Ephesians, (i. 13, 14,) "*after ye believed in* CHRIST, *ye were sealed* with the HOLY SPIRIT of promise; which is the *pledge* of our inheritance, until the redemption of the purchased possession;" where *believing* and *being sealed* are so removed from each other, as evidently to be distinct things. It is needless for us to dwell upon the coincidence of thought in these various passages. The reference is so direct, the allusion so distinct, as to be apparent even to the casual reader. Here, then, are several presumptions, arising from different sources, tending to the same point, uncontradicted by any evidence whatever, all coinciding to prove the existence of a rite called Confirmation in the Apostolic Church, which was performed by the imposition of the hands of an Apostle, on those recently baptized; and according to the rules of evidence by which we are guided in these inquiries, we may say the existence of the rite is proved.

The language made use of by Paul in his Epistle to the Corinthians, was used in the Church immediately after the age of the Apostles, to signify Confirmation. Thus Clement,

* Rob. 900, and comp. χρισμας, p. 899.

† Rob. 800.

‡ Rob. 100

of Alexandria, in the second century, in a work entitled, "*What rich man shall be saved?*" gives an account of a young man who was first baptized and then "*sealed with the Lord's seal as a perfect safeguard.*"* Tertullian also, employs similar language. "That faith [of the Christian,] she [the Church] sealeth with water [in baptism,] clotheth with the Holy Spirit [in Confirmation,] feedeth with the Eucharist."† We add a single quotation from the epistle of Cornelius, Bishop of Rome, about A. D. 250, to Fabius, concerning the heretic Novatian. According to the account there given, Novatian was baptized in sick-bed, but, when he recovered, "*neglected to be sealed by the Bishop.*"‡. The rite of Confirmation, however, is more accurately described by Cyprian in the same century. He says: "those who have been baptized in the Church, are brought to the President of the Church, that by our prayer and imposition of hands, they may receive the HOLY GHOST, and be consummated with the Lord's seal."§ But we learn from Tertullian, in the second century, who was the instructor of Cyprian, the nature of this rite, with equal certainty. He informs us that "hands were imposed upon those who had been baptized, with prayer and invocation of the HOLY GHOST."‖ This describes the rite so accurately, as to leave no doubt of its existence.

4. The Apostles, and those to whom the Apostles had committed Apostolic authority, had the rule over Presbyter-bishops and Deacons. St. Paul exhorts the Hebrews, to "obey them that have rule over them." (Heb. xiii. 17.) And Timothy was besought to abide at Ephesus, "that he might charge, or *command*¶ that none teach other doctrines,"

---

* Euseb. iii. 23.
† De Præscrip. c. 37.
‡ Euseb. Ecc. Hist. v. 43.
§ Ep. 73.
‖ De Bap. c. 8, comp. also De Resur. Car. c. 8.
¶ Rob. 615.

(1 Tim. i. 3,) than those he was to "command and teach." So also, he was to allow no man to despise him, (iv. 11, 12;) and Titus was to exhort "and rebuke with all authority." (Titus ii. 15.) Timothy too was to "count the Presbyters that ruled well, worthy of double honor," (1 Tim. v. 17,) and he was "not to receive an accusation, i. e. *a judicial complaint,** against a Presbyter, *except in the presence of*† two or three witnesses," (1 Tim. v. 19;) which is proof that he had authority over Presbyters, and must therefore, from the nature of the case, have been superior to them. Indeed, the whole tenor of the language in the Epistle to Timothy and Titus so evidently authorizes them to speak in a tone of authority, that nothing can make it plainer than it now is. The terms "*command,*" (1 Tim. i. 3; ii. 11; iv. 17; 2 Tim. ii. 14,) "*rebuke,*" (1 Tim. v. 20; 2 Tim. iv. 2,) "*with all authority,*" (Titus ii. 15,) "*and sharply,*" imply rule, power, and authority, and demand a corresponding submission, subjection, and obedience in the persons over whom these were to be exercised.

Obedience to the Bishops, as the successors of the Apostles, is one of the leading topics in the epistles of Ignatius. The times in which he lived, were full of disquiet. Heresy had begun to show itself, and schism had become rampant in many places. It required, therefore, a strong and steady hand to preserve the Church in quiet. And such a man was Ignatius; who, for active zeal and ardent piety, was early called to a martyr's grave. On his way to his death, with the evils of the times full in view, he wrote seven epistles to six different Churches. In all, a prominent topic is, *obedience to the Bishops.* Nor does he advise it simply as a matter of expediency, but urges it as a matter of divine appointment.

---

* Rob. 436. † Rob. 257, 299.

And he must have known whether it was so, as he was the disciple and pupil of St. John.*

To the *Ephesians*, he says:† "Wherefore it becomes you to run together, according to the will of your Bishop, even as also ye do."

To the *Magnesians*, he says:‡ "It is your duty also, not to despise the youth of your Bishop, but to yield all reverence to him, according to the power of GOD the Father. As, also, I perceive your holy Presbyters do. . . . . It is, therefore, fitting that we should not only be called Christians, but be so; as some call a Bishop by the name, but do all things without him."

To the *Trallians*,§ "It is, therefore, necessary that ye do nothing without your Bishop, even as ye are wont. . . . He that is within the altar, is pure. But he is not, that doeth any thing without the Bishop, Presbyters, and Deacons."

To the *Philadelphians*,‖ "For as many as are of CHRIST, are with their Bishop. . . . . . I cried whilst I was among you, I spake with a loud voice. Give ear to the Bishop, and to the Presbyters, and to the Deacons. . . . . . See that ye follow your Bishop, as JESUS CHRIST, the Father; and the Presbytery, as the Apostles; and reverence the Deacons, as the command of GOD."

To the *Smyrneans*,¶ "He that honors the Bishop, shall be honored of GOD."

And to *Polycarp*, he says:** "Hearken unto the Bishop, that GOD may hearken unto you. My soul be security for those who submit to their Bishop, Presbyters, and Deacons."

The same thing is also clearly apparent from other primi-

---

* Martyr. Ign. c. 3. The reasons why some of our quotations from Ignatius are different from the ordinary translations, may be seen in the *Appendix*.

† Ep. c. 4. ‡ Cc. 3, 4. § Cc. 2, 7.

‖ Cc. 3, 7, 8, 9. ¶ C. 9. ** C. 6

tive writers. Thus it is said in the account given of the martyrdom of Ignatius, A. D. 109 or 116, that "he *governed* the Church of Antioch with all care."* So it is said by Hegesippus,† that James "received the *government* of the Church at Jerusalem, from the Apostles." And Irenæus‡ says, that the Apostles "delivered their own place of *government* to their successors." And Tertullian§ tells us, that neither Presbyters nor Deacons might baptize, "without the Bishop's consent." Towards the close of this century, or as early as A. D. 200, it was directed,|| that "A Presbyter who, disregarding the Bishop, should form a separate congregation, and build a separate altar, should be deposed. And that the laymen who followed him should be excommunicated."

5. To the Apostles, and those to whom they had committed Apostolic authority, belonged the exclusive right of disciplining the Church. We have already shown that the Apostles had rule over, and of course, the power of disciplining the inferior orders of ministers, and also, that these inferior orders had the oversight and inspection of the laity, or the members of the Church. Hence, it would follow, that the Apostles had the ultimate authority over the people, if there were no other evidence on the subject. But this is not all.

The language of Paul to Timothy, is still more emphatic. Speaking of Hymeneus and Alexander, he says, "*I have delivered them unto Satan,* that they may learn not to blaspheme." (1 Tim. i. 20.) And to Titus, he says, "A man that is an heretic, after the first and second admonition, reject," (iii. 10,) which being spoken only of those who were in the Church, necessarily implies, that they were to be cast out of the Church. The whole tenor of the epistle sustains this opinion. The Romans were directed to avoid all who

* Martyr. Ign. c. 1. † Com. v. in Euseb. ii. 22.
‡ Adv. Hær. iii. 3. § De Bap. c. 17. || Apos. Can. 24.

brought in dissensions and contrary doctrines, (xvi. 17,) and the Thessalonians were commanded to withdraw themselves from every one that walked disorderly, and to have no company with them. (2 Thess. iii. 6, 14.) John also commands those to whom his epistle was addressed, not to receive those into their houses who brought not the doctrine he taught, nor to bid them GOD speed. (2 John 10, 11.)

The language of Paul to the Corinthians, is still more authoritative. "Shall I come to you with *a rod of scourging*,* or in love?" (1 Cor. iv. 21.) "The LORD hath given *our authority* for edification, and not for your destruction." (2 Cor. x. 8.) And "I write to them that heretofore have sinned, and to all others, that if I come again, *I will not spare*." (2 Cor. xiii. 2.) If Paul did not possess the power of disciplining the Churches, this must be the language of vain declamation, or bold usurpation. We are authorized, therefore, to say, that he did possess it, and hence, that to the Apostles belonged the exclusive right of disciplining the Church.

6. It was the right and duty of the Apostles, and those on whom they had conferred Apostolic authority, to preside in all councils, and to declare the sentiments of the council. The account in the fifteenth chapter of Acts is proof of this point. The decrees of that council were "the decrees of Apostles and Presbyters," (xvi. 4,) though James alone "gave sentence." (xv. 19.) James, therefore, was only the organ of the council, in declaring their opinion, and it would be strange if that should be done by any other than the *presiding* officer; and though this is the only instance of the kind recorded in Scripture, it is conclusive evidence of the Apostolic practice. In addition to this, it should be remembered, that all antiquity declares St. James to have been the first Bishop of Jerusalem.†

---

* Rob. 734.

† Ante, p. 185.

7. In every Apostolic Church, there was one Apostle, or person endued with Apostolic powers, having under him a plurality of Presbyter-bishops and Deacons. This, as we have already remarked, is an important and fundamental question touching the Constitution of the Apostolic Church. It is therefore necessary that we examine it somewhat in detail.

(1.) In the Church at Jerusalem, we have seen there was one Apostle, St. James, and the narrative shows that there were many Presbyters and Deacons in that Church. And this is said to have been the model Church, after which all others were formed.* In the language of Irenæus, Jerusalem was the Metropolitan city of the New Testament, and from that Church, all other Churches had their beginning.† If, then, other Churches were modeled after this, there must have been one Apostle, or person clothed with Apostolic powers, in every Church, having under him a plurality of Presbyter-bishops and Deacons. Besides, when we have proved the existence of these in one Church, the admitted uniformity of the Apostolic Church requires us to suppose they existed in all. But we are not permitted to rest here, as there is much more evidence to be examined.

(2.) Titus, whom Paul calls an Apostle, (2 Cor. viii. 23,) was possessed of Apostolic authority in Crete. He alone was "to ordain Presbyters in every city," (Tit. i. 5,) and the better to prepare him for that business, Paul gives him directions concerning the qualifications and character of the persons he should ordain. But the power of ordaining was not the only power conferred upon this Apostle. He was to "exhort and rebuke with all authority," (ii. 15,) and if ne-

* Gies. Ecc. Hist. Div. 1, § 28: comp. Synod. Ep. Conc. Const. in Theod. Ecc. Hist. v. 9, Jerome, in Is. ii.

† Adv. Hær. iii. 12.

cessary to do it, " sharply, yea, to stop their mouths, i. e. *to put them to silence;*"* by which we understand, that he was to deprive them of "the authority or license to preach," which they obtained at their ordination. He alone was to reject heretics, (iii. 10,) and was to suffer no man to despise him, (ii. 15.) We see then, that in Crete, there was one Apostle or person endowed with Apostolic powers, with authority to ordain and depose Presbyter-bishops, and therefore Deacons, and with all disciplinary powers over the whole Church.†

(3.) At Ephesus we find Timothy, who was also an Apostle, possessed of Apostolic powers, quite as extensive as those of Titus, in Crete. To Timothy, who was a young man, (1 Tim. iv. 12,) very particular directions were given concerning the qualifications of Presbyter-bishops and Deacons, and various other topics, "that he might know how he ought *to conduct himself in the Church of God.*"‡ But after all, he was "to lay hands suddenly on no man," (1 Tim. v. 22,) was not to ordain without due consideration. His authority also included the supervision, trial, and judging of inferior orders of the ministry. He was "to charge some, that they teach no other doctrine," (1 Tim. i. 3;) he was to count the Pres byters "who ruled well, worthy of double honor," (1 Tim. v. 17;) and "not to receive an accusation against a Presbyter, except in the presence of two or three witnesses." (1 Tim. v. 19.)§

It has been objected, that Timothy had no regular charge at Ephesus, that he was left there only for a short period, and that his residence there was temporary. But were this objection sound, it would not affect the question of his *superiority* over Presbyter-bishops and Deacons. It should, however, be borne in mind, that there is no evidence whatever,

---

* Tit. i. 10, 13. Rob. 316.

† See ante, pp. 173, 187–194

‡ 1 Tim. iii. 15. Rob. 54.

§ See ante, pp. 173–5.

that Timothy ever exerted the least authority in any other place than Ephesus, nor any evidence, that he ever *resided* anywhere else after he was intrusted with authority there. If, then, it could be shown, that he was often away from that city, it would not affect the question in the least.

From these considerations it appears, that Timothy and Titus were *officers* and ministers in the Churches at Ephesus and Crete, with official jurisdiction over those places; and that by their offices they were entitled to the sole power of ordaining, supervising, and ruling Presbyters and Deacons. They had also various other rights, and performed many other duties; but as they were all incident to the Apostolic office, it is not necessary to examine them further at this time.

(4.) Epaphroditus was the Apostle of the Church at Philippi, having under him Presbyter-bishops and Deacons. The Epistle to the Philippians is directed to the "Bishops, Deacons, and Saints at Philippi," and seems to have been sent to them by Epaphroditus, whom Paul calls "their Apostle." (Phil. ii. 25.) As we have already alluded to the Apostleship of Epaphroditus, and enumerated some of the *circumstances* which lead us to infer that he was the Apostle of that Church, it can not be necessary for us to consider it further.*

(5.) The case of the seven Churches of Asia, also tends to prove the existence of an office higher than that of Presbyter-bishop, in the Apostolic Church. From the first three chapters of the Revelation of St. John, we learn, that in each of the seven Churches, there was *an Angel*, who is addressed as if responsible for the conduct and character of the Churches in which he was placed. The word *Angel*, like that of *Apostle*, signifies literally, one sent, that is, a *messenger*, and hence

---

* Ante. pp. 175–180.

we might infer the identity of their office. But as *a name* of itself determines nothing, we must look to *acts*. We read, then, that one of the complaints against the Angel of the Church of Pergamos was, that he suffered the Nicolaitans and those that taught the doctrine of Balaam, to remain in the Church. (Rev. ii. 14, 15.) So against the Angel of the Church in Thyatira, it is said that he suffered the false prophetess Jezebel, to continue in the Church. (Rev. ii. 20.)* If then it was wrong for the *Angel* to permit these things, it follows from the very nature of the case, that he had power to prevent them, and consequently, that he exercised some power and authority in the Church, and, therefore, must have been an officer in the same. Now we have shown, that in the Church of Ephesus, one of the seven Churches, there was an Apostle, possessing authority to rule and govern the Church, and, therefore, should very properly be held in some degree answerable for the character of the Church over which he presided. Indeed, the language in this very place supposes such authority. The "seven stars," which were "the Angels of the seven Churches," (Rev. i. 16, 20,) were *in the hand*, and consequently the executioners of the will of the Son of Man. We are, therefore, led to conclude, that there was in the Church at Ephesus, and hence in all others, an Apostle and an Angel, or else that both of these words denote the same officer, as their primary signification would lead us to conclude. The last conclusion is the most rea-

* Instead of "that *woman* Jezebel," as our English Bible reads, most of the ancient versions, and many excellent manuscripts have, "thy *wife* Jezebel," and this reading has been adopted by Griesbach. Tertullian, however, in the second century, reads as the present English. (De Pudicit. c. 19.) And so does the Vulgate, which dates from about the same period. This alteration, however, proves two things; (1,) that the Angels of the Churches were then regarded as *individual persons*, and (2) that at that period the Bishops were permitted to marry.

sonable, and is much strengthened by the fact, that the capacity in which both appear to have acted was the same, while there is no intimation in Scripture that two offices of that kind existed in any one Church. In addition to this, it should be borne in mind, that in the Church at Ephesus, we know there was a *plurality* of Presbyter-bishops, (Acts xx. 17, 28,) and if the Angel was an officer answerable for the conduct of the whole Church, these were included, and hence he must have been superior to them. We conclude, then, that the Apostles and Angels of the Churches were the same, and have proved, therefore, *the existence of Apostles* in Jerusalem, Ephesus, Crete, Philippi, Smyrna, Pergamos, Thyatira, Sardis, Philadelphia, and Laodicea, and consequently, in all the Apostolic Churches, *having under them a plurality of Presbyter-bishops and Deacons.*

(6.) To the foregoing, we must add the Church at Colosse, in which Epaphras appears to have been the Apostolic Bishop. The epistle is addressed to "the saints and faithful brethren at Colosse," (i. 2,) and in it Epaphras is described by the Apostle as "our dear fellow-servant, *who is for you a faithful minister of Christ;* who also declared unto us your love," (i. 7, 8,) and though in bonds, (Philemon 23,) is spoken of as "always laboring fervently for you in prayers, that ye may stand perfect and complete in all the will of God." (iv. 12.)

(7.) So also, Archippus appears to have been the Apostolic Bishop, probably in the Church of Laodicea.* To the Colossians, the Apostle says: "And when this epistle is read among you, cause that it be read also in the Church of the Laodiceans; and that ye likewise read that from Laodicea. And say to Archippus, Take heed to the ministry which thou hast received in the Lord, that thou fulfill it." (iv. 16.)

* The Apostolical Constitutions say, "of Laodicea, in Phrygia." (B. vii. c. 46.)

From this, it seems evident, that Archippus did not belong to the number of brethren at Colosse, as in that case St. Paul would have addressed him, and not directed others to do it. That he was the head of a Church, is clear from what is said in the epistle to Philemon: "To Archippus, our fellow-soldier, and to the Church in thy house." (ver. 2.) This evidently implies that Archippus was over this Church, wherever it might have been.

(8.) We have just spoken of "Archippus, and the Church in his house." To this we must add, that we find the Apostle making mention of "Nymphas, and the Church in his house," (Col. iv. 15,) and of "Aquila and Priscilla, and the Church in their house." (Rom. xvi. 5; 1 Cor. xvi. 19.) By the phrase, "the Church in their house," is frequently, if not generally understood, "a body of Christians accustomed to meet in the private houses of these particular individuals."

If the signification be thus limited, then we must render these phrases, not as signifying those Christians which *assembled* in his house, but those which *dwelt* in his house; the words "that is," in Romans xvi. 5, and 1 Corinthians xvi. 19, not being in the original. Hence, it must be translated, "the Church within thy house," that is, those belonging to it, and consequently, of his *household;* in which case, the word *Church* is used figuratively, to denote *the Christians of his household.*

The existence of Apostles or Angels in these and other Churches, is also attested by early history, and we know the names of many of them. Among those *in the first century,* we can enumerate the following, who occupied the seat of the Apostles, or who succeeded to the Apostles in the government of the Churches. James, the first Bishop of *Jerusalem;** Anianus, ordained by St. Mark, the first Bishop of

* Euseb. Ecc. Hist. iii. 5.

Alexandria;* Philip, one of the twelve, Bishop of *Hierapolis*;† Thomas, one of the twelve, Bishop of *Parthia*;‡ Andrew, one of the twelve, Bishop of *Scythia*;§ Timothy, the first Bishop of *Ephesus*;|| Titus, the first Bishop of *Crete*;¶ Polycarp, ordained by St. John, the first Bishop of *Smyrna*;** Linus, ordained by St. Paul, the first Bishop of *Rome*;†† Dionysius, ordained by St. Paul, the first Bishop of *Athens*;‡‡ and Evodius, ordained by St. Peter, the first Bishop of *Antioch*.§§ Inasmuch, then, as all the Churches of which we possess any account, did, in the first century, have a Bishop, and only *one* Bishop; and as all had under them a plurality of Presbyters, or, as we have called them, Presbyter-bishops and Deacons; the inference is irresistible, that these officers existed in all the other Churches: for, if they did not exist in all the Churches, the organization was not uniform, and our inquiries are fruitless. And if they did exist, then the *Angels* of the Churches in Asia Minor must have belonged to the first class or order of ministers; that is, must have been Bishops who succeeded to the Apostles, in their places as governors of the Churches.

That there could be *only one* Bishop in a city, is evident from what Ignatius says in his Epistles. But there is still stronger evidence of this fact, in St. Cyprian's *Treatise on the Unity of the Church*;|||| where he expressly declares, that "the Episcopate is one and indivisible." And Cornelius, Bishop of Rome, in an epistle to Fabius, Bishop of Antioch, A. D. 252, speaks of the rule of "the Catholic (or-

---

* Euseb. ii. 1, 23; iii. 5. Clem. Inst. 6.
† Ep. Polycr. Euseb. v. 24.
‡ Euseb. iii. 1.
§ Euseb. iii. 1.
|| Ante, p. 173.
¶ Ante, p. 173.
** Euseb. Ign. and Iren.
†† Iren. Adv. Hær. iii. 3. Apos. Cons. vii. 46.
‡‡ Euseb. iii. 4; iv. 23. Apos. Cons. vii. 46.
§§ Euseb. iii. 22. Apos. Cons. vii. 46.
|||| C. 4.

thodox) Church," that there should be "but one Bishop in a Church."*

It has been objected to this conclusion, by those who deny the original superiority of Bishops, that inasmuch as there is no mention made of Timothy, nor of any other Apostolic Bishop at Ephesus, in the Epistle to that Church, there could have been no such officer there at that time. But it will be seen upon consideration, that this inference by no means follows. The admitted uniformity of the Apostolic Churches, enables us to infer the existence of a particular office in one Church, from its known existence in another Church. But, on the other hand, the omission to mention a particular office, in a *general* epistle on another subject, does not even raise a *presumption* against its existence. Now it was evidently no part of St. Paul's design in his Epistle to the Ephesians, to say any thing of the ministry of the Church, except in so far as it tended *immediately* to spiritual edification. Consequently, he has scarcely any thing on the subject in this Epistle. Now, if the omission to mention Timothy's residence there, and authority in that Church, proves that *he* was not an officer in that Church; the omission to mention either Bishops or Deacons would also prove that none of these existed there, and that there were no officers at all in that Church.

But the assumption that there is no mention of any Apostle as existing in the Church at Ephesus, is opposed to the fact. In chapter second, St. Paul assures the Ephesians that Christ had broken down the wall of partition which had before his death separated the Gentiles from the Church of God, and that then the Gentiles also were fellow-citizens with the children of Israel, in the *Christian Church*, which, he assures them, is "built upon the Apostles and Prophets,

* Euseb. iii. 43.

JESUS CHRIST himself being the chief corner-stone." (Eph. ii. 20.) Here, then, is an express recognition of the two superior orders mentioned in 1 Corinthians, (xii. 28,) accompanied by an unequivocal declaration, that *these* are the *frame-work* of that Church, which, resting upon the divine authority of CHRIST himself, for its sure foundation-stone, contains and supports "the Church of the living GOD." Now it would be marvellous indeed, if St. Paul should thus publicly and solemnly assure the Ephesian Christians, that "the Apostles and Prophets" were the very frame-work of the Church, when at the same time there was no such thing as an Apostle in the Church he was addressing. Such a conclusion can not be admitted without strong proof.

It may, however, be said, as it has been before, that by "Prophets" in this place, the Apostle meant the *Prophets* of the Old Testament; but this can not be allowed, since it would overturn the whole of the Apostle's argument concerning the Christian faith. For, (1,) the *Prophets* are placed posterior and inferior to Apostles, which would not have been done, had men of previous times been referred to. (2.) Because in no sense can it be said that the Prophets of the Old Testament are the frame-work, or foundation of the Christian Church, unless we suppose that, by a figure of speech, the Apostle put *the men for the doctrine.* But if we assume that by *Prophets,* is meant the *doctrine* of the Prophets, consistency requires us to construe the *Apostles,* to signify the doctrine of the Apostles; and JESUS CHRIST, to signify the doctrine of JESUS CHRIST; making, therefore, as the Socinians do, the Church to rest for its foundation, NOT *on the atonement and mediatorial sacrifice of* CHRIST, but merely on the *doctrine* he preached. And (3,) it is clear, that by *Prophets* St. Paul did not mean the Prophets of the Old Testament, from what he has said in the same Epistle. Thus he tells us, (Eph. iii. 5,) that "the mystery of the

Christian dispensation, ... *was not in other ages*, made known to the sons of men, *as it is now* revealed unto his holy Apostles and *Prophets* by the Spirit." The Prophets here spoken of, must be the same mentioned only seven verses before, and which, with the Apostles, compose the frame-work of the Church; and these Prophets were living when St. Paul was writing. If any doubts remained concerning the persons designated by "Prophets," they would be removed by chapter iv. 11, 12, where it is said that these very "Apostles and Prophets" were created "for the perfecting of the Saints, *for the work of the ministry*, for the edifying of the body of CHRIST—the Church." So far, therefore, from there being any thing in the Epistle to the Ephesians *opposed* to the idea that Timothy was the Apostle of that Church, we are *obliged* to infer, that if *he* was not, somebody else was.

But there is another consideration, connected with this Epistle, deserving of notice. It is allowed by all, that the superintendence of the inspiring Spirit over the Apostles, is a safeguard against their committing any error relative to the gospel or the Church; and that, whatever was *necessary* to be done, they *did*, and what they did, it was their *duty* to do. Hence, we may not suppose, that any thing was omitted by the Apostles in any Church, necessary to its existence or well-being. Consequently, when we find the Apostle assuring a Church in any place, that the Church is "built on the Apostles and Prophets," we are compelled to conclude, that both Apostles and Prophets *must* have existed in all those Churches to which such an Epistle was sent.

Now it will be no news to many of our readers, that the Epistle to the Ephesians is believed by many learned men,*

---

* As Archbishop Usher; and after him, Michaelis, Haenlein, Bengel, *etc.* Horne, Intd., P. VI. c. 3.

to have been an *Encyclical* or *Circular Epistle* to the Churches of Asia Minor, and was entitled, "to the Ephesians," on account of the priority or pre-eminence of that city. The reasons for this opinion are, briefly: (1.) The words "at Ephesus" (c. i. ver. 1) are wanting in some of the best manuscripts. (2.) The same words appear to have been wanting in the manuscript copies of this Epistle, used by the commentators of the Primitive Church.* (3.) Some of the persons to whom this Epistle was addressed, had never seen Paul, as is evident from what he says, (c. iii. 1, 2, 3; iv. 20, 21,) although he had resided at Ephesus two years before he wrote this Epistle. (Acts xix. 10.) (4.) Paul wrote an Epistle, which was sent to the Church at Laodicea, and from thence to the Church at Colosse, (Col. iv. 16,) which is lost, if this be not the very same, as many learned men have supposed.† (5.) This is rendered probable, also, by the fact, that the Epistle to the Ephesians seems to have been written at the same time, and we know it was sent by the same person, as that to the Colossians. (Eph. vi. 21; Col. iv. 7.) And (6) this is still further evident, from the identity of thought and expression, occurring in both; especially in Ephesians v. 19–vi. 9, compared with Colossians iii. 16–24.‡ The most reasonable conclusion, therefore, is, that the Epistle to the Ephesians was originally an *Encyclical Letter,* addressed to all the Churches of Asia Minor, and if so, it proves the existence of Apostles and Prophets in all the Churches within that territory.§

---

* Basil, Adv. Eunonium.

† Hug. Intr. N. T., Par. ii. § 121–126.

‡ See Paley's Horæ Paulinæ, cc. 6, 8.

§ Another view is, that Timothy was not simply Bishop of Ephesus, but Metropolitan Bishop of Asia Minor, and hence the reason why he is not mentioned in the Epistle. (Usher Codex. Can. c. v. Bev. Cod. Can. L. c. 5. Ham. Præf. Com. Ep. Titus.)

It has also been objected to our conclusion, that the Epistle to the Galatians is addressed to the "Churches of Galatia." (Gal. i. 2.) It is sufficient, in reply, to mention that Galatia was a *country*, not a *city;* that it comprised two civil provinces; and, at the time of the Council of Nice, had ten Dioceses, and of course ten distinct Churches. According to the plan pursued by the Apostles, there must have been at least two distinct Churches, or Dioceses, in this country when that Epistle was written; and hence the reason why it was addressed to them in the plural number.*

It has also been asked, in answer to our conclusion, "Who was Bishop of Philippi, when Polycarp wrote his Epistle to that Church?" And because it does not clearly appear from the Epistle itself, that there was then a Bishop in that city, it has been inferred that there were no Bishops in the Primitive Church. Now, if we were to admit that the fact was as is alleged in regard to Philippi, the inference would by no means follow, as it might have been without a Bishop at that juncture, or be subject to the provisional supervision of some other Bishop, as among us. It does not follow, that because a Church is without a Bishop *at a particular time*, that it is not Episcopal. In regard to the Church at Philippi, when Polycarp wrote his Epistle, the fact seems to have been, that it had no Bishop at that time, and that it was subject to the temporary supervision of Polycarp, until it had elected a Bishop.

This opinion is fairly inferred from the language of Polycarp himself. His epistle is addressed, "POLYCARP, *and the Presbyters* who are with him, to the Church of GOD at Philippi," &c. In this address two things are to be noted: (1,) the language is such that Polycarp could not have been one

* Bing. ix. c. 23, § 5. An. Univ. Hist. XII. 349, XVIII. 351. Liv. xxxviii. cc. 12–28.

of the Presbyters; (2,) the Epistle was *to* the Church of Philippi, but not *from* the Church of Smyrna, over which Polycarp was Bishop, *but* from Polycarp himself. Indeed, it does not appear from the Epistle, that the Church of Smyrna had any knowledge of its existence, as they are not, as was usual, even joined in the closing salutation. The act was, therefore, the *personal* act of Polycarp, done *with the consent* "of the Presbyters who were with him," but in which the Church in Smyrna took no part. That Polycarp had such a *supervision*, seems to be expressly asserted in the beginning of chapter third. "These things, brethren, I write to you concerning justice, not because I would arrogate to myself power, but because ye yourselves *have* before *called upon me for aid.*"

There will be no doubt on the part of any one concerning the correctness of this translation, unless it be in regard to the word we translate, *to call upon for aid*. That this is the proper meaning of the word, is evident, both from its popular use among the Greeks,* and from the connection in which it stands. The Philippians had called upon Polycarp for something; but clearly not to write to them on these subjects, for in that case he would not have disclaimed all "arrogance," but rather have said, "in compliance with your request I write," &c. In fact, he uses such language as this in reference to another subject, about which they had written to him.† Now as the fact is universally admitted, that in the primitive Church, the Bishops of one Church were not allowed to exercise any function of the ministry within the limits of another Bishop, without his permission, or, in case of his death, without the consent of those who had the oversight of the Church,‡ any exercise of Episcopal functions within the

* Rob. 309. † C. 13.

‡ Apos. Can. 28. Nice, Can. 15. Antioch, Can. 13. 3 Constantinople, Can. 1. 1 Carthage, Can. 5, 10. 3 Carthage, Can. 20.

limits of the Church in Philippi, by Polycarp, must have been performed at the request of the Church, or its Bishop. The most obvious inference, therefore, is, that Polycarp had been requested by the Church in Philippi to exercise Episcopal jurisdiction over that Church. Upon this supposition a good and sufficient reason is afforded, why Polycarp should write to the Church at Philippi, and to that Church alone; and hence, also, the reason of his peculiar phraseology, which is to the following effect: "I write these things, brethren, not because I would arrogate power to myself, but because ye have desired me to exercise a provisional supervision over you." Nothing can be plainer, nothing more probable, nothing more consistent. And having thus prepared the way, he proceeds to exhort and admonish "every class of persons among them; Presbyters and Deacons, young men and maidens, old men and widows, husbands and their wives;" directing them in what manner they ought to behave themselves, and that too, in a tone of authority which even the much abused Ignatius did not assume.* This conclusion is also supported by what is said in chapter thirteen. "Both ye and Ignatius wrote to me, that if any one went hence into Syria, he should also bring back your letters with him; *which also I will do*, if I have a convenient opportunity, *either by myself*, or by the Legate† *I shall send on your account.*"

From this it is evident, that Polycarp must either soon visit Philippi in person, or "send a legate on their account;" and that this "legate" was not to be a mere Presbyter, or inferior member of the Church, appears from the next chapter, where it is said that this same epistle was sent to Philippi by Crescens, who seems to have been a Presbyter, originally at Smyrna, and afterwards at Philippi, and whom (if a conjec-

* Comp. cc. 3–11.

† Ancient. Ver. legatus, Greek of Nicophorus, (πρεσβουσοντα,) iii. 19.

ture might be allowed) Polycarp thought worthy of being elected Bishop of that Church. "These things I have written unto you by *Crescens,* whom by this present epistle I have recommended to you, and do now again commend. For he hath had his conversation without blame among us, and I trust in like manner also with you."* One other fact which goes to strengthen this conclusion, should also be mentioned in this place. Ignatius, in his Epistle to Polycarp, requests him to take the oversight of the Church at Antioch, until all things should be again quietly settled there.† Upon a review of all the evidence, there is every presumption in favor of supposing that, *at the time Polycarp wrote his Epistle to the Church at Philippi, that Church was without a Bishop, and that Polycarp was exercising a temporary supervision over it, at their own request.*

There are also two passages quoted from the fathers, one from Clement of Rome, and the other from Irenæus, which are claimed to be opposed to our conclusions. Clement of Rome, according to the common translation, says:‡ "The Apostles thus preaching through countries and cities, they appointed the first fruits of their conversions to be *Episcopous* (επισκοπους) and *Diaconous,* (διακανους,) over such as should afterwards believe, having first proved them by the Spirit. Nor was this any new thing; seeing that long before it was written concerning *Episcopon* (επισκοπον) and *Diaconon,* (διακονον,) as saith the Scripture in a certain place, 'I will appoint their *Episcopous* in righteousness, and their *Diaconous* in faith.'"

The argument of the objector is based upon the assumption, that *Episcopous* and *Diaconous* are to be interpreted in an *official,* and not in a general sense. But to this we object, (1,) that there is no evidence that Clement ever uses these

* C. 14. † Ep. Pol. cc. 7, 8. Euseb. iii. 36. ‡ Ep. Cor. c. 42.

words in an official sense; (2,) that in another place,* he describes the *three orders* by other names; (3,) that to sustain the interpretation given to this text, we are obliged to suppose that Clement understood the text quoted from Isaiah, (lx. 17,) as describing the *names of the offices* of the Christian ministry. But this is absurd, for in the Greek of the Old Testament, which was his own language, the words are *rulers* (αρχοντας) and *overseers*, (επισκοπος.) If then, he quoted this passage for the purpose alledged by the objector, he was guilty of *forging* Scripture to suit his purpose, and that too, when he could have no possible motive for doing it. (4.) And it is evident from the whole tenor of the chapter from which this quotation is made, as well as from the one following, that he intended to apply the language to a single office. Hence the words should be rendered *overseers* and *ministers*, throughout the passage.

The other passage is from Irenæus.† "Such Presbyters the Church nourisheth, and of such the Prophet saith, 'I will give them *rulers* (αρχοντας) in peace, and *overseers* (επισκοπος) in justice.'" The objector, here, also, makes Irenæus guilty of the absurdity of supposing that this passage describes the *name of an office* in the Christian ministry; than which nothing could have been further from his mind.

8. To each Apostle, there seems to have been allotted a particular portion of country, in which he preached the gospel, and over which he exercised jurisdiction. Thus St. Peter addresses those to whom he preached the gospel, "scattered throughout Pontus, Galatia, Cappadocia, Asia, and Bithynia."‡ (1 Pet. i. 1.) That he had authority in

---

* C. 40. † Adv. Hær. iv. 44.

‡ It is worthy of observation, that Paul and Silas "were forbidden by the Holy Ghost to preach the word in Asia," where Peter was to preach; and that when they "assayed to go into Bithynia, [which was

all these Churches, is evident from what he says in the same epistle: "The Presbyters which are among you, I, who am a co-Presbyter, exhort."* Hence it follows, that Peter not only had *general* authority over *all* these Churches, but also, that he had authority in each *particular* Church; and consequently, was entitled to exercise jurisdiction in them. For if he had no authority in particular Churches, he could not have been a co-Presbyter.

But this point is more fully illustrated in the history of St. Paul. To the Romans, he writes, (Rom. xvi. 19, 20,) "For I will not presume to speak of those things which CHRIST hath not wrought by me, to make the Gentiles obedient by word and deed, through mighty signs and wonders, by the power of the Spirit of GOD, so that from Jerusalem, and round about Illyricum, I have fully preached the gospel of CHRIST. Yea, so have I strived to preach the gospel, *not where* CHRIST *was named*, lest I should build on another man's foundation." These verses, in the language of Mr. Locke's paraphrase, read: "For I shall not venture to trouble you with any thing concerning myself, but only what CHRIST hath wrought by me, for the bringing of the Gentiles to Christianity, both by profession and practice, through mighty signs and wonders, by the power of the HOLY GHOST, so that from Jerusalem and the neighboring countries, all along, quite to Illyricum, I have effectually preached the gospel of CHRIST; but so as studiously to avoid the carrying of it to those places where it was

in Peter's region,] the Spirit suffered them not." (Acts xvi. 6, 7.) And there is no intimation that Peter and Paul ever proclaimed the gospel in the same portion of country, unless it were in "the regions of Galatia." These facts afford an *intimation*, at least, that the Apostles were to confine their labors to districts not yet Christianized.

* 1 Ep. v. 1. Rob. 783, and Geis. Ecc. Hist. p. 59. The Bishops in later times called themselves *co-Presbyters*. Dion. Alex. in Euseb. vii. 20. And the *Address* in the Epistle of Polycarp is to the same effect.

already planted, and where the people were already Christians, lest I should build on another man's foundation." This principle is still more fully illustrated in his second Epistle to the Corinthians. As the figurative language of the original, the imagery of which was borrowed from the technical language of the Grecian games,* prevents the mere English reader from obtaining the full import of the language, we shall give, on the authority of Professor Robinson, a modified translation, to which will be subjoined Mr. Locke's paraphrase. From these, we trust every reader may obtain a very distinct idea of the meaning of the passage. "We will not boast of things *without our allotment*,† but according to *the limit of the allotment* which God hath distributed to us, *an allotment* to reach even unto you. But we stretch not ourselves beyond *our limit*, as though we reached not unto you; for we are come as far as to you also, in the gospel of Christ; not boasting of things *beyond our limit*, that is, of other men's labors; but having hope, when your faith is increased, that we shall be enlarged by you according *to our limit*, abundantly, to preach the gospel in the regions beyond you, but not to boast of things made ready to our hands, *in another man's limit*."‡ In the paraphrase of Mr. Locke, the same passage reads, "But I, for my part, will not boast of myself in what has not been measured out, or allotted to me; i. e. I will not go out of my own province to seek matter of commendation; but proceeding orderly in the province which God hath measured out and allotted to me, I have reached even unto you; i. e. I have preached the gospel in every country, as I went, till I came as far as you. For I do not

* Adam Clark, *in loco*.

† Rob. pp. 415, 515, on μετρον, and κανον, and Locke on αμετρα, and note on the passage

‡ 2 Cor. x. 13–16.

extend myself further than I should, as if I had skipped over other countries in my way, without proceeding gradually to you; no, for I have reached even unto you, in preaching the gospel in all countries as I passed along; not extending my boasting beyond my own bounds, into provinces not allotted to me, nor vaunting myself in any thing I have done in another man's labors; i. e. in a Church planted by another man's pains; but having hope, that your faith increasing, my province will be enlarged by you yet further; so that I may preach the gospel to the yet unconverted countries beyond you, and not take glory to myself from another man's province, where all things are made ready to my hand." In this language of the Apostle, the principle is most fully recognized, that to him a particular portion of country was allotted or assigned; that his labors were mainly confined to this territory; and if we take the trouble to examine the various epistles of St. Paul, we shall see that all of them are directed to some Church within this territory; except that to the Hebrews, which is general in its direction. This construction makes the meaning of the Apostle's language evident; while on no other hypothesis can it be made intelligible. To this we may add the express declaration of this Apostle, that upon him came "the care of all the Churches," (2 Cor. ii. 28;) that is, as the Corinthians would understand him, "of all the Churches within his *limit*," and to which he had preached the gospel.

In accordance with this conclusion, is the testimony of the primitive historians, who uniformly assign the several Apostles to different countries. Thus Origen tells us, "That according to tradition, Thomas received Parthia as his allotted region; Andrew received Scythia; John, Asia."* Other historians inform us to what places others of the twelve were

---

* Expos. Gen. L. III. in Euseb. iii. 1.

sent. From these facts, and from the admitted uniformity of the Apostolic Churches, we are authorized to infer, that *to each Apostle a particular portion of country was assigned, in which he preached the gospel, and over which he exercised jurisdiction.*

9. The country thus allotted to the Apostles was divided into several districts, and Apostolic authority committed to particular individuals in each of those districts. In order fully to appreciate the evidence on this point, it is necessary to bear in mind, that the Apostles were not permanently located in any particular place; that they went to one place, gathered a Church, appointed officers, and established laws for its government, and then proceeded to still other places. Indeed, their character seems to have been almost precisely like that of our present Missionary Bishops. It is not probable, however, that every Church was completely organized at once. Suitable persons might not have been procured, or the Churches might at first have been so small that no Bishop was appointed.

Among these smaller districts, we have already enumerated the following places, where we have proved the existence of an Apostolic Bishop: (1,) Jerusalem; (2,) Corinth; (3,) Ephesus; (4,) Philippi; (5,) Crete; (6,) Rome; (7,) Smyrna; (8,) Pergamos; (9,) Thyatira; (10,) Sardis; (11,) Philadelphia; (12,) Laodicea; (13,) Antioch; (14,) Alexandria; (15,) Magnesia; (16,) Trallia; (17,) Colosse; (18,) Hierapolis; (19,) Parthia; (20,) Scythia, and other places. It devolves, therefore, on those who deny these conclusions, to prove, either that we have entirely mistaken the nature of the evidence, or, that the Churches in other places were differently organized. And if they can not do either, our conclusions must stand.

CHAPTER XVI.

THE ORGANIZATION OF THE APOSTOLIC CHURCH DESIGNED TO BE PERMANENT.

HAVING ascertained what was the organization of the Apostolic Church, we are led to inquire, whether it was designed to be permanent or temporary? It is admitted by all, that Christianity was designed to be permanent, and that its requirements are of perpetual obligation. The natural and obvious inference, therefore, is, that those institutions which were formed for propagating and preserving it, should have the same perpetuity. In the absence of opposing evidence, we must believe such an inference the true one. This follows from the principles on which we have shown all argument in this case proceeds; and which, for the purpose of illustration, we shall here repeat. Thus, in the case we then supposed, the bare mention of a custom, regulation, or practice of the American army, in one of the *letters* before described, without any intimation of its being either unusual or extraordinary, would be conclusive evidence of its forming a customary regulation. Now every *customary* regulation forms a part of the practice or discipline of the army; and hence, unless countermanded, continues while the army exists. The same reasoning applies to the organization of the Apostolic Church, or it is fruitless to inquire concerning that organization. The fact, therefore, that numerous things are mentioned in the letters of St. Paul to *his* friends, concerning the practice and discipline of the Church, without any intimation of their being unusual, extraordinary, or temporary, makes this case parallel to the one supposed; and hence, what would be conclusive in that, must be final in this. Whatsoever things, therefore, we find existing in the Apostolic Church, unaccompanied by any intimation that they were *temporary*, we must reckon among the customary regulations of that Church. And these, of course, must continue while the Church continues, unless countermanded by some authority equal to that by which they were established. Upon every principle of sound reasoning, therefore, it is not necessary there should be an express command to render the Apostolic practice binding upon succeeding generations. On the contrary, there should be an *express permission* to authorize a deviation from it.

Yet the truth of this reasonable inference is sometimes denied, and it is claimed, that, as the Apostles did not *command* that the ecclesiastical organization which they had adopted should be continued in the Church, it is not obligatory upon us, and we are at liberty to follow it or not, as we choose. But if we examine the principle from which this conclusion is drawn, we shall find it so broad, as to be of dangerous tendency; for if one man may fairly urge that the Apostolic form of the Church is not binding on *us*, because there is no command requiring *our* obedience to it, another may urge, upon the same principles, that the doctrines which they preached are not obligatory upon us, as there is no command requiring *us* to obey them. Some persons, however, have obtained the belief, that the doctrines of the gospel are of divine authority and of perpetual obligation, because delivered under the influence and guidance of the Holy Spirit; while the form of the Apostolic Church they suppose not to be of divine authority, and, therefore, not of perpetual obligation; because, as they imagine, the Apostles, in establishing it, were not guided by inspiration, but left to consult their own views of expediency. If such persons would endeavor to look up some authority for this opinion, they would find it not only destitute of any Scriptural foundation, but in direct opposition to the whole tenor of it.*

When speaking of the *orders* of the ministry, St. Paul is unusually explicit as to their divine original. In order, however, to see the full force of the language where he enumerates them, we must bear in mind, that the first Epistle to the Corinthians was written in *answer* to one they had previously written to him. Thus, St. Paul says to them: "*Now* concerning the things *whereof ye wrote*," (vii. 1;) that is, having finished that part of his Epistle which related to things not spoken of in their letter, he recurs to it and says: "*Now* concerning *the things* whereof ye wrote;" continuing to reply to their inquiries to the end of the Epistle. One of these inquiries related to "spiritual gifts," (xii. 1,) and especially to the degree of precedence, which should be observed among those who were endowed with such gifts. It would seem, also, from the tenor of his argument, that they had inquired "whether those who wrought miracles and spoke with tongues, were not entitled to the highest places or rank in the Church, even above the permanent officers thereof?" In reply to this, St. Paul says, (xii. 28:) "GOD *hath set in the Church, first,* (πρωτον,) that is, *first of all,* or *before all,*† APOSTLES; *secondarily,* PROPHETS; *thirdly,* TEACHERS; *afterwards,* (επειτα,) *miracles, gifts of healing,*" &c. Now *epeita*, according to Buttman,‡ often expresses "censure and reproach, the cause of the indignation or surprise being first stated," which is precisely the usage in this place;

* Unless they take that ground of Dr. Whately, that the Apostles were *supernaturally withheld from recording these things*, in order to allow us to deviate from their forms, if we please; a position which seems to us absurd, and the arguments urged in its support, sophistical. See *King. Christ.*

† Comp. Matt. xxiii. 26. Acts xiii. 46. Rom. i. 8. 1 Cor. xi. 18.

‡ Gr. Gram. § 149, p. 429.

and, consequently, the Apostle expresses his surprise that they should have thought of asking such a question; and censures them for so far forgetting *the order* of God's Church as to ask it. The question of the Corinthians was a plain one, and the answer of the Apostle, strikingly explicit. This answer asserts, (1,) that the ministry is of *divine appointment;* (2,) that it *consists of three orders*, called Apostles, Prophets, and Teachers; and (3) that the power of working miracles, and the gift of tongues, form no necessary part of the ministerial office, and is, in fact, to be regarded as inferior to it. The *orders of ministers* in the Apostolic Church, were, therefore, the suggestions of divine wisdom, equally with the doctrine contained in the gospel; and hence, *the Apostles* had no more right to change them, than they had to vary the doctrines they had received from Christ. And if the inspired Apostles did not possess such authority, surely it would seem that their uninspired successors could not be endowed with it.

We have proceeded thus far, as though the Scriptures gave no intimation concerning the perpetuity of the Apostolic Church, and that, therefore, the whole was to be made out by inference; but we shall now show, that this is not the fact. We have already seen, that the Great Head of the Church, in the commission he granted to his Apostles, expressly promised, "to be with them always, *even unto the end of the world.*" But as this could not be fulfilled in their own persons, it requires us to suppose *a perpetual succession.* It would not be enough to suppose perpetuity without succession, for in that case, the language could not apply to the Apostles. The language, "I will be with you always, even unto the end of the world," is equivalent to the phrase, I will be with you and your successors, to the end of the world. This conclusion is in exact accordance with the every-day practice of mankind, and is sanctioned by the plainest dictates of common sense. If a body of men were made a perpetual corporation, with power to fill all vacancies which should happen in their numbers, either by death or removal, no one would hesitate to say, that a grant to such corporation *forever*, was for the benefit of the present members and *their successors*, though the latter were not mentioned.* So in the case under consideration, Christianity is made permanent and perpetual, and the Church which was founded to preserve and propagate it, must, therefore, be alike durable; and as we have shown that the Apostles were officers in the same, having authority to add to their numbers, it follows that a grant or promise to them *forever*, must inure to their successors, though they are not named.

The command of Paul to Timothy is decisive of the continuance of the office which Timothy held, which we have already shown was that of an Apostle. "The things that thou hast heard of me, the same *commit thou* (i. e. *give in charge, or intrust*)† to faithful men, who shall be able to teach others also." (2 Tim. ii. 2.) The same inference flows from the language of Paul to the Ephesians, where it is said *the ministry* which CHRIST established, will continue "until we come unto a perfect man, unto the measure of the stature of the fulness of CHRIST," (Eph. iv. 13;) or, "until the Church of GOD shall have obtained a state of perfection in a future world."‡ The language of St. John, in the *Revelation*, is to the same effect. To the Angel or Apostle of the Church of Ephesus, he says: "Repent, or I will come unto thee quickly, and will remove thy candlestick out of its

* This is the *common law*, (which is said to be "the perfection of common sense,") on this subject, so that a grant of lands to a corporation aggregate, passes a fee simple, without the word *successors*. (Coke on Littleton, L. ii. § 133, fol. 94, b, and Hargrave's Note, No. 4.)

† Rob. 624.

‡ Storr and Flatt, Elem. Bib. Theol. B. 4, Sec. 102, Ill. 6.

place," or, destroy the Church, (Rev. ii. 5; and comp. i. 20;) which threat would be idle and unmeaning, unless the Church and the office of Apostle were designed to be permanent.

The argument made use of by Paul, in his Epistle to the Hebrews, leads to the same conclusion. Thus he tells us, that "perfection came not by the Levitical Priesthood," therefore "the Priesthood *was changed*, and has now become an *unchangeable* Priesthood." (Heb. vii. 11, 12, 24.)

From this, we are led to infer, that the Apostolic Church, with its three orders of ministerial officers, viz., Apostles, Presbyter-bishops, and Deacons, was designed to be a permanent and perpetual institution—a conclusion sustained by every presumption of Scripture. We are led to believe, therefore, that this conclusion is just; and, therefore, binding on all succeeding ages.

CHAPTER XVII.

THE MINISTRY OF DIVINE APPOINTMENT.

HAVING seen that the Scriptural evidence compels to the conclusion, that the ministry *was of divine appointment*, and was designed to be permanent, and is of universal and perpetual obligation, we might rest our inquiry. But to render assurance doubly sure, to do away all possible ground of cavil, and to examine all the evidence that can be produced on the subject, we shall proceed to inquire how the Primitive Christians understood this matter. But first, we must ascertain when a thing can properly be said to be of divine appointment or authority.

In reply to such an inquiry, we answer, *whatever is done*

by the command of God, is of divine authority. If, then, the Church was instituted by the command of God, then the Church is of divine authority. Or if any part of its organization was directed by God, then that also, is of divine authority. And if the Church, or any part of its organization, is of divine appointment, then that may not be changed or modified, except by divine authority. Now we have seen that the Apostle makes *the ministry of the Church of divine appointment,* (1 Cor. xii. 28; Eph. iv. 11, 12;) and consequently, it may not be changed or modified, but by the same authority. We shall now proceed to show how this thing was understood by the immediate disciples of the Apostles.

Clement of Rome, A. D. 87, says: "We ought to take heed, that looking into the depths of divine knowledge, we do all things *in order,** whatsoever our Lord hath commanded us to do: that we perform the [eucharistic offering] and public worship to God, at their appointed seasons; for these he hath commanded to be done, not rashly and disorderly, but at certain determinate times and hours. He hath himself ordained by his supreme will, both when and by whom they are to be performed."† And in another place: "The Apostles have preached to us from our Lord Jesus Christ; Jesus Christ from God. Christ, therefore, was sent by God; and the Apostles by Christ. Thus both were orderly sent, according to the will of God.‡ For having received their command, . . . they went forth proclaiming that the kingdom

---

* Comp. 1 Cor. xiv. 40.

† C. 40. The usual mode of evading the force of this language, is, to say that Clement spoke *of* the Jewish dispensation, and uses language applicable to that. But this interpretation requires us to suppose, that the Christian Churches had nothing in common with the Temple, and that Clement was guilty of the absurdity of talking *of* the Jews when speaking *to* Christians, as though they were one and the same.

‡ Tert. Præs. Hær. c. 2, holds the same language.

of God was at hand. And thus preaching through countries and cities, they appointed the first-fruits of their conversions to be *overseers* and *ministers* over such as should afterwards believe."* In the opinion of Clement, therefore, the ministry was *of divine appointment*. Ignatius entertained the same opinion. But we shall understand his language better by considering that of Clement of Alexandria first.

Clement of Alexandria says:† "In the Church, the celestial is the image of the terrestrial." And in another place he adds:‡ "I take the progressions of Bishops, Presbyters, and Deacons, to be imitations of the Angelic glory." The point here brought out, is, that the Church Militant is a type of the Church Triumphant. This seems evidently to have been the opinion of Ignatius, and explains language which on any other hypothesis it is not easy to understand. We quote a few sentences, inserting in brackets what the language evidently implies, according to this figurative, or typical character of the Church, which both he and his readers would take for granted.

To the Magnesians, he says:§ "I exhort you that ye study to do all things in a divine concord, your Bishop presiding [in the Church Militant, as] in the place of God [in the Church Triumphant;] and your Presbyters [filling in the Church Militant,] the place of the council of the Apostles [in the Church in heaven."]

To the Trallians:|| "Let all reverence the Deacons as [the visible ministers of the invisible minister,] Jesus Christ; and the Bishop, as [the representative in the visible Church of] the Father [in the invisible;] and the Presbyters, as [the visible representatives in the Church on Earth of] the council of God and assembly of the Apostles [in the Church above."]

---

* C. 42. † Strom. iv. p. 500. ‡ Strom. vi. p. 667.
§ C. 6. || C. 3.

This interpretation gives a common sense meaning to language, which otherwise does not seem to have any meaning at all, or at least a very extravagant or strange one. And if this be the meaning, there can be no doubt Ignatius considered the ministry of divine appointment. In another place,* he speaks without figure. "The Bishops, Presbyters, and Deacons, appointed according to the will of JESUS CHRIST."

We see, therefore, that Clement, of Rome, A. D. 87, Ignatius, A. D. 107, or 116, and Clement, of Alexandria, A. D. 175, all held the Church to be divine, and its ministry of *divine appointment.* To which we may add Irenæus† and Tertullian,‡ about the same age. But we need not enlarge upon this point, as all the evidence tends to prove that this was the universal opinion in that time.

There is another consideration deserving of notice here, which goes to sustain this conclusion, as also to prove the original Apostolic institution of Episcopacy. That the organization of the Church was uniform so early as about A. D. 200, no thorough scholar, however strongly he may be opposed to Episcopacy, pretends to deny. And that that organ ization was Episcopal, every one allows. It is also conceded by all, that whatever changes might have occurred between the Apostolic age and that, there is no intimation of any change, in any of the writers that have been preserved. Now this Episcopal organization had existed from the beginning, or had been introduced within less than a century and a half, and so introduced, as to be adopted by every one. Now upon the supposition, that there was no particular form of Church government prescribed by the Apostles, as many pretend to believe, and that each Church was left to devise such system as might seem best adapted to their particular wants, is it credible, from what are known of men, and the

* Intd. Ep. Phil. † Adv. Hær. iii. 3. ‡ De Præs. Hær. cc. 21, 37

principles of human action, that in the midst of despotisms, and monarchies, and republics, and democracies, the same form of Church government should have grown up, or have been adopted? If the several Churches had been left to plan the model of their Ecclesiastical organization, can we believe they would have been uninfluenced by the forms of governments around them? Would the democratic Greek, and the republican Roman, and the Theocratic Jew, and the despotic Persian, be likely to agree on this point, when they differed upon every other? Besides, we know that the various Churches did differ about matters of much smaller moment, and that each adhered most pertinaciously to its own customs. Would they be unlike themselves, in regard to this one? Every presumption, arising from our knowledge of *men*, and of the men of that age in particular, leads us to the conclusion. that this perfect uniformity, at that early period, in the organization of all Churches, could not have been secured by any thing short of a firm belief in its divine original. Since, then, there is in history, no intimation of any change, and as every presumption is against it, we must conclude, not only that the government of Bishops was primitive, but also, that it has always been held to be of divine institution.

In addition to this, it should be mentioned, that the testimony of the council of Nice, 325, was as full and explicit to the universality and apostolicity of Episcopal government, as to the canon of Scripture, or the faith of the Church.

CHAPTER XVIII.

BISHOPS SUCCESSORS OF THE APOSTLES.

THE next point to which our attention is naturally turned, is, *were the Bishops of the second century considered successors* *of the Apostles in governing the Churches?* That they were so, is evident from all the Fathers who have written on the subject. Thus Clement, of Rome, A. D. 87, says: "Our Apostles knew by our LORD JESUS CHRIST, that contentions would arise concerning the *authority of* (ονομα) the Bishop. And, therefore, having a perfect foreknowledge of this, they appointed persons, as we have before said, and then gave direction in what manner, when they should die, other approved men should *succeed in their ministry.*"* Here then is the doctrine of a future succession, taught so explicitly that it can not be misapprehended. The Church of Ephesus was commended A. D. 107, as one who had "always agreed with the Apostles,"† and the Trallians for "continuing in the Apostolic character."‡ So Ignatius is said by those who witnessed his martyrdom, to be "a man in all things like unto the Apostles who governed the Church at Antioch with care;"§ and the Church at Smyrna describes Polycarp as "a truly Apostolical and prophetical teacher and Bishop of the Church at Smyrna."|| The whole tenor of the language at this period denotes that those Churches were considered the most eminent, and their opinions entitled to the most weight, who had an Apostolic man for a Bishop, and had ever maintained their Apostolic character.

In the latter part of this century, however, when all the

---

* Ep. Cor. c. 44. The general signification of ονομα, "name," does not answer the argument of Clement. The word *office*, perhaps, would express his idea best, and is not without sanction. But *authority* is more in accordance with Scripture usage. See Mark xvi. 17; Luke xxiv. 47; John v. 43; Acts iii. 6, iv. 7; 1 Cor. v. 4, and 2 Thess. iii. 6, where it has the sense of *authority*. Also, Acts i. 15; Rev. iii. 4, and xi. 13, where *onoma* is put for person, or thing. Comp. also, Tert. Apol c. 2, Apos. Cons. v. 7, for similar usages.

† Ign. Ep. c. 11. ‡ Trall. Introd.

§ Martyr. Ign. c. 1. || Martyr. Pol. c. 16.

Bishops ordained by the Apostles were dead, another mode of reasoning became necessary, and gave rise to another mode of proving the Apostolic character. This consisted in appealing to *the succession of Bishops*, and that Church which could not trace its succession, so that its first Bishop should have been ordained by an Apostle, or one commissioned by an Apostle, was considered as wanting in one of the essential characteristics of a Church. And the minister who could not trace his succession in the registers of the office, was left out of the priesthood, as was done in the days of Nehemiah.* Thus Tertullian, in reply to the Heretics, A. D. 190, says: "If any dare to mingle themselves with *the Apostolic age*, so that they may appear to be handed down from the Apostles, because they were under the Apostles, we are able to say, let them produce the origin of their Churches, let them set forth the series of their Bishops, *so running down from the beginning by successions,*† *that the first Bishop may have some of the Apostles, or Apostolic men who continued with the Apostles, for their author or predecessor.* For in this manner the Apostolical Churches trace their origin, as the Church of Smyrna, having Polycarp, relates that he was placed there by St. John. In like manner also, the rest of them show that they have grafts of the Apostolic seed, who were appointed to the Episcopate by the Apostles. Let the heretics do any thing like this."‡ Had it not been, in the days of Tertullian, a well-known fact, that all the Apostolic or orthodox Churches were able to trace the succession of their Bishops *as such*, to the days of the Apostles, and to show that the first Bishop had

---

* Neh. vii. 61.

† One of the first signs or Notes of a Church, according to Irenæus, (Adv. Hær. iv. 63,) is the "succession of Bishops."

‡ De Præ. Hær. c. 32. This argument is employed by Irenæus. Adv. Hær. iii. 1, 2, 3; iv. 26, Orig. de Princ. Pref. 2, *etc.*

been ordained by an Apostle, or some one authorized by an Apostle, this public challenge to the heretics would never have been made, as it would have recoiled upon himself.

Irenæus, also, who lived and wrote about the same time, and who had himself been a pupil of Polycarp, says: "We can enumerate those who were appointed by the Apostles, Bishops in the Churches, *and their successors*, even unto us." And again, "The Apostles wished those to be very perfect and irreprehensible, in all things, whom they left *their successors*, delivering to them their own place of government." But because it would be tedious to enumerate *the succession* in all the Churches, he gave only that of Rome, when he adds: "By this *ordination and succession*,* the tradition which is from the Apostles, and the doctrine of the truth hath come even to us."† We have, therefore, the positive testimony of Irenæus and Tertullian, that all the Orthodox Churches of their day, that is, from A. D. 150 to A. D. 200, were able to trace the succession of their Bishops back to those who were appointed Bishops by the Apostles, and to whom the Apostles delivered their own place of government in the Churches. There is, therefore, no room for doubt, that the Bishops of the second century were believed to be the successors of the Apostles in governing the Churches. Indeed, the primitive writers of the Church seem not to have entertained a thought of the possibility of any other lawful organization. They believed that all legitimate authority must come from the Apostles; and, consequently, that all lawful rulers in the Church must have derived their authority from the Apostles, or some of the Apostolic men. They knew of no other foundation of Christian communities, than the institution of CHRIST, or his Apostles, and they knew no other mode of transmitting it, than that of regular succession, in the way pointed out, or

---

* Cyprian (Ep. 75) holds similar language.

† Adv. Hær. iii. 3.

sanctioned by the founders of the Churches.* Those, therefore, who would seek authority for other organizations, and for other modes of transmitting authority, must seek elsewhere than in the practice or principles of the primitive Church.

CHAPTER XIX.

HISTORICAL CHARACTERISTICS OF THE FIRST AND SECOND CENTURIES.

HAVING seen that the Primitive Christians, in the first and second centuries, regarded the Church as a divine institution, and its ministry as of divine appointment, and of perpetual obligation, and the Bishops as the successors of the Apostles in the government of the Churches, we shall consider several other questions immediately connected therewith. But before we do this, we ought to remark, that writers on this subject have too generally regarded the whole period as one, not attending to the different circumstances which have characterized different periods, and not sufficiently discriminating between the statements of early and later writers. There have been great and striking differences at different times, producing an almost entire change of phraseology, in reference to ecclesiastical organization. What the most important of these differences were, and the influences they have exerted on the history of the Church, within the first and second centuries, it is our design briefly to point out.

---

* Tert. De Præscrip. c. 21. "If the LORD JESUS CHRIST sent the Apostles to preach, no others ought to be received as preachers than those whom CHRIST appointed."

The history of the Church in this period may be divided into four divisions, each characterized by something which, in reference to the account given of its organization, was peculiar to that time, and which ought to be regarded when considering the history of that period. The first of these periods may be considered as reaching from the crucifixion to the death of St. Paul, A. D. 67, being thirty-three years,—emphatically the *Apostolic period;* the second, as extending from the death of St. Paul to the death of St. John, A. D. 100, being thirty-three years, including the period when the government of the Church was passing from the hands of the Apostles into those of their successors, and may be called the *transition period;* the third, as reaching from A. D. 100 to 150; and the fourth, from A. D. 150 to 200—each of which we propose to examine by itself.

1. The peculiar characteristic of the first period, was the general superintendency of the Churches by the Apostles in person, having Presbyters and Deacons under them, as ministers and rulers in the Church. Out of this relation grew *three orders of ministers* in the Church, called at this time, Apostles,* Presbyters or Bishops, and Deacons. But with the death of St. Paul, *as far as history informs us*, ended this relation, and, of consequence, this phraseology. After his death, therefore, we hear little of the existence of Apostles in the Church, in any capacity, although St. John remained thirty-three years longer.

2. The second, or *transition period,* was characterized by a peculiarly unsettled state of ecclesiastical phraseology, consequent on the unsettled state of things in the Church itself. This was the time when the government of the Churches

---

* During this period, all the governors of the Churches were called Apostles. (Theod. Com. Phil. i. 1; ii. 25. 1 Tim. iii. 1. Ambrose, Com. Eph. 4. Gal. i. 1. Bing. B. ii. c. 2, § 1.)

was passing from the Apostles, into the hands of their successors—when the spirit of pride and insubordination, which even the authority of the Apostles had not been able wholly to restrain, would be likely to break out with violence, and rage with fury. Besides, though the power and duty of the officers of the Church may have been well defined, and generally understood, there was a difficulty not easily surmounted. Most of the Apostles had gone to their rest, but some remained, and of course the name was still in existence and use. To such, therefore, all appeals must be made, and heresy and schism would rear itself under the pretence of Apostolic sanction. This state of things was peculiar to this period, and ended at the death of St. John, A. D. 100.

While this state of things continued, the three orders of ministers were designated by names different from those used in the preceding period. The first and highest was called by St. John, the Angel of the Church; while Clement, Bishop of Rome, the only writer of this period whose works have been preserved, calls him the High Priest, and the other orders, Priests and Levites. The people or members of the Church were, for the first time, denominated by him *laymen;* a name by which they have ever since been known. The language of Clement is clear to this point. "*God hath himself ordained by his supreme will,* both where and *by what persons* we should perform our service and offerings unto him. They, therefore, who make their oblations at the appointed seasons, are accepted and happy; for they sin not, inasmuch as they obey the commandments of the Lord. For to the Chief Priest, (Bishop,) his peculiar offices are given; and to the Priests, (Presbyters,) their own place is appointed; and to the Levites, (Deacons,) appertain their proper ministries; and the layman is confined within the bounds of what is commanded to laymen."* It will be evident to every one who examines the epistle of Clement with attention, that he not only considered the ministry of the Church as divinely instituted, but that it was also made by the same authority to consist of three orders.

Similar language is occasionally used by still later writers. Thus Tertullian speaks of the "High Priest, who is the Bishop."† And Jerome tells us, that the Bishops, Priests, and Deacons, hold the same place in the Christian Church, that the High Priest, Priests, and Levites did, in the Jewish Church.‡ This language also occurs at a still later period. Thus, in the Liturgy of St. Basil,§ "Grant, therefore, that we, thy servants, my *Fathers* and Brethren, the *Priests* and *Levites*, and all thy faithful people, may all be freed," etc. The Bishop is also called the "High Priest," and his office the "High Priesthood," in the Apostolical Constitutions, in the third or fourth century;|| in the ancient Ordinal of the Greek Church, for consecrating a Bishop;¶ also, in the Ordinals of the Gothic Churches, before A. D. 550;** in the Pontifical of Egbert, Archbishop of York, A. D. 800;†† and occasionally by other writers.

3. The peculiar characteristic of the third period, consisted in ascertaining the extent of authority appertaining to the clerical office, and in settling the meaning of ecclesiastical phraseology as it remains to the present day. Thus, within seven years after the death of St. John, we find that

---

* Ep. Cor. c. 40. Those who deny our conclusions, apply this language to the Jewish Church; but this is unauthorized and improbable. It is incredible that Clement should make an exhortation to the Jews, when writing to Greek Christians.

† De Bap. c. 17.

‡ Ep. Evang.

§ Brett. p. 79.

|| B. viii. 4, 5.

¶ Goar. Ritual. Græc. pp. 302–4.

** Murator. vol. II. p. 670.

†† Martene Ant. Ecc. Rit. L. i. c. 8, Art. 11, Ord. 2.

the three orders of ministers were denominated Bishop, Presbyter, and Deacon, and to each was assigned the same office, with nearly or quite the same power and duty, as appertains to them at the present day. This distinction of name and office was made by Ignatius, Bishop of Antioch,* and by Polycarp, Bishop of Smyrna, A. D. 107;† by the account given of the martyrdom of Ignatius, by eye-witnesses of the event, about A. D. 108 or 109;‡ by the Church at Smyrna, in the Circular Epistle which they addressed to the other Churches, on the martyrdom of Polycarp,§ about 167 or 168, which properly belongs to this period, though written a little later.

A good and sufficient reason for the strong language of Ignatius, in reference to the orders of ministers, and the obligation of obedience to them, may be found in the peculiar evils of those times. The presence, and of course, much of the influence of the Apostles, was withdrawn; the enemies of the Church were untiring in their opposition; heresies, foul and dark, sprung up in the hearts, and were manifested in the lives of hypocritical friends and misguided devotees, while schisms and discords‖ were originated by the envy of

* Ep. Eph. cc. 2, 4, 5, 20. Mag. cc. 2, 3, 4, 6, 7, 13. Trall. cc. 2, 3, 7, 12. Phil. Intd. cc. 4, 7, 10. Smyr. cc. 8, 12. Pol. c. 6.

† Ep. Phil. cc. 5, 6, 13. Comp. with Intd. and Martyr. Ign. c. 3, and Martyr. Pol. c. 16.

‡ Martyr. Ign. cc. 1, 3.

§ Martyr. Pol. c. 16.

‖ The first attempt to corrupt the faith of the Church in Jerusalem, was by Thebuthis, who was disappointed in not having been elected Bishop, in place of Simeon, the second Bishop of that city. (Heg Com. in Euseb. iv. 22.) One of the earliest heresies in the Roman Church, the Novatian, arose A. D. 252, from a similar cause. (Euseb. vi. 43.) Many similar cases are mentioned in the early history of the Church, fully verifying the prediction of the Apostles, that dissension should arise on account of the ministry. (Clem. Rom. Ep. Cor. c. 44.)

disappointed ambition, or the cunning of false professors.* At such a time, deep, heartfelt, pervading piety, united to the highest degree of wisdom and skill, accompanied by bold, decisive, and energetic action, were indispensable requisites in the character of those who were to be the defenders of the Church—who were to bear the ark of God with safety through the difficulties and dangers which so thickly beset it on every side. And such was the character of Ignatius, as every one can see, who reads his epistles; and such, save the boldness and energy of character, was Polycarp, whose praise is in all the Churches; and such, no doubt, were many others, whose names are only recorded in the Lamb's book of life.

We shall make a few extracts, that our readers may see in what light these things were viewed by the Christians of this period. The Church at Philadelphia is saluted by Ignatius: "Especially if at unity with the Bishop, and the Presbyters, and Deacons with him, appointed according to the will of Jesus Christ, whom he hath settled according to his own will, in all firmness by the Holy Spirit."† From the Epistle to the Ephesians, we learn that Onesimus was Bishop of the Church in that city,‡ having under him Pres-

* The following remarkable passage on this subject from Hegesippus, A. D. 150, is copied from Eusebius, Ecc. Hist. iii. 32. "The Church had continued until then, [the time of Simeon,] as a pure and uncorrupt virgin; whilst if there were any at all that attempted to pervert the sound doctrine of the saving gospel, they were yet skulking in dark retreats. But when the sacred choir of the Apostles became extinct, and the generation of those that had been privileged to hear their inspired wisdom had passed away, then also the combinations of impious error arose, by the fraud and delusion of false teachers. These also, as there were none of the Apostles left, henceforth attempted, without shame, to preach their false doctrines against the gospel."

† Intd. Ep. Phil.

‡ Ep. Eph. c. 1.

byters and Deacons,* and that that Church "had always agreed with the Apostles."† At the same time, Damas was Bishop of the Church at Magnesia,‡ having Presbyters and Deacons under him.§ We learn from the same source, that Polybius was Bishop of the Church at Tralles,|| and that there were many Presbyters and Deacons in that Church at the same time.¶ At this time, also, Polycarp was Bishop of the Church at Smyrna,** having many Presbyters and Deacons subject to him.†† And to the Philadelphians, Ignatius says: "Give ear to the Bishop, and to the Presbytery, and to the Deacons."‡‡ To the Trallians: "He that doeth any thing without the Bishop and Presbyters, and Deacons, is not pure in his conscience;"§§ and in another place he says: "without these, there is no Church."|||| It is certain, therefore, that at this time there were three orders of ministers in the Church; and that the distinction between Bishop and Presbyter was well understood.

But we are not obliged to rely on the authority of Ignatius alone, for evidence that this distinction was well understood when he wrote. The account given of the martyrdom of Ignatius,¶¶ and the epistle written by the Church of Smyrna on the martyrdom of Polycarp,*** as well as Irenæus, who was the disciple of Polycarp,††† all agree in calling Polycarp *Bishop of Smyrna*. This Polycarp, in the epistle he

---

* Cc. 2, 4, 20.
† C. 10.
‡ Ign. Ep. Mag. c. 2.
§ Cc. 2, 3, 6, 7, 13.
|| Ign. Ep. Trall. c. 1.
¶ Cc. 2, 3, 7, 12, 13.
** Ign. Ep. Pol. Intd. Ep. Mag. c. 15. Martyr. Ign. c. 3. Martyr. Pol. c. 16.
†† Ign. Ep. Smyr. cc. 8, 12. Ep. Pol. 6. Pol. Ep. Phil. Intd. cc. 5, 6, 11.
‡‡ Ep. Phil. c. 7.
§§ Ep. Trall. c. 8.
|||| Ib. c. 3.
¶¶ C. 3.
*** C. 16.
††† Ep. Ad. Flor. Euseb. iv. 14, v. 19.

wrote to the Church at Philippi, says: "The epistles which Ignatius wrote to us, (i. e. that to Polycarp, and that to the Church of Smyrna,) and others, as many as we have we send to you, according to your order;" when he adds, "they treat of faith and of patience, *and of all things pertaining to edification in the Lord.*"* Now we have seen that Polycarp was expressly called Bishop in one of these same epistles, and that the distinction between Bishop and Presbyter was made in the other; and hence, as he has *endorsed* these same epistles without exception, he has *adopted* the distinction in question. The testimony of Polycarp on this subject is, therefore, precisely that of Ignatius.

4. The peculiar characteristic of the fourth period, was the introduction of technical terms of ecclesiastical jurisprudence and theological science, from the Greek into the Latin tongue, accompanied by an enlargement of the ecclesiastical phraseology, both in the Greek and Latin Churches. Thus, we find almost at the commencement of it, Hegesippus in Palestine, A. D. 160,† and Dionysius, Bishop of Corinth,‡ speaking of the office of Bishop as "the Episcopate and the Episcopal seat." The same language was also used by the Churches of Lyons and Vienne, about the middle of this period, in a Circular Epistle which they addressed to the other Churches,§ immediately after the martyrdom of their Bishop, Pothinus; and from this time to the year 200, it is of frequent occurrence. But what proves more conclusively than any thing else the general use of such words, is the fact, that they had, before the middle of this period, become technical terms in ecclesiastical history, and though Greek words, were in common use among those who spoke the Latin language, and are used by the Latin writers without any inti-

* C. 13.

† Euseb. ii. 23, iv. 22.

‡ Euseb. iv. 23.

§ Euseb. v. 1.

mation of their having been borrowed from another tongue, which would not have been done, had they not been common words. This usage is frequent in Tertullian, the oldest of the Latin Fathers, who writes the Greek Episcopos, "Bishop," Presbuteros, "Presbyter," and Diaconos, "Deacon," with Roman letters, only changing their terminations to accommodate them to the genius of that language, as *Episcopus, Presbyter*, and *Diaconus*. So also he copied the word *Eucharistia*, "the LORD'S Supper,"* *Ecclesia*, "the Church," *Exomologesis*, "confession,"† *baptisma*, "baptism," and some other words.‡ This fact alone is proof, that before the days of Tertullian the distinction between Bishop and Presbyter was well understood and definitely settled, as also, Episcopate and Episcopal seat, which are frequent in his writings; that they had become, as it were, naturalized in that language, and must, therefore, have been familiar to Christians of different nations.

The leading characteristics of these different periods in reference to the organization of the Church, were; in the *first*, three orders of ministers, called Apostles, Presbyters, and Deacons; in the *second*, three orders of ministers, called High-Priests, Priests, and Levites, and the word layman was introduced to designate, as it has ever since, the members of the Church; in the *third*, three orders, denominated Bishop, Presbyter, and Deacon; and in the *fourth*, an enlargement of ecclesiastical phraseology in the Greek, and its transplantation into the Latin tongue,§ each of which should be borne in mind when consulting the writings of the primitive Christians, in reference to the organization of the Church.

---

* De Orat. c. 14. De Cor. c. 3. De Præscr. Hær. c. 36, 37, etc.

† De Pœnit. c. 9.

‡ See, Diabolus, Holocaustama, Idoleum, Idolicus, Monogamia, Neophytos, Patriarcha, Prophetis, Propheticus, Sabbatizo, Satan, Schisma, *etc.*

§ Some terms of ecclesiastical technology were also made in the Latin

CHAPTER XX.

ONE BISHOP IN A CHURCH, BUT MANY INFERIOR CLERGY.

THAT there was to be one, and only one Bishop in a Church, may be inferred from what we have already proved; for if in every Apostolic Church there was one Apostle or Apostolic Bishop, having under him a plurality of Presbyter-bishops and Deacons, it is reasonable to conclude, that there was but one Apostle, or Apostolic Bishop in a Church. That this was the case at Jerusalem, Crete, Ephesus, Philippi, Smyrna, Pergamos, Thyatira, Sardis, Philadelphia, Laodicea, Rome, Athens, Antioch, Alexandria, Magnesia, Trallia, Colosse, and elsewhere, we have already shown; and the admitted uniformity of the Apostolic Churches authorizes us to infer a similar organization in all other Churches. But this is not the whole amount of the evidence we have on the subject. The language of Ignatius is clearly to the same purpose.

Thus he says to the Smyrneans:* "Let no one do any thing which belongs to the Church, separately from the Bishop. Let that Eucharist be looked upon as well established, which is either offered by the Bishop or one whom the Bishop has approved." And to the Magnesians he says:† "Wherefore, come ye all together as unto one temple of GOD, as unto *one altar*, as unto one JESUS CHRIST." So also the Apostolical Canons‡ go upon the supposition, that all exercise of ecclesiastical authority within certain limits was committed

---

language. Thus Tertullian seems to have made, from the adjective *Justificus*, the verb *justifico*, from whence our verb *to justify*, and its derivatives. At least, he is the earliest author that used the word.

* C. 8. † C. 7. ‡ Can. 28, 29, 31, 33, 34, 66.

solely in one Bishop. And so rigidly was this rule enforced, that any Bishop who should presume to perform ordination, or any other Episcopal function, in any place not within his jurisdiction, without the consent of the Bishop, or if no Bishop, of those who had the direction of ecclesiastical matters, he was to be deposed.* And this rule was subsequently recognized and adopted by several general Councils.† That this principle was a law of the Church before 250, is evident from the epistle of Cornelius, Bishop of Rome, addressed to Fabius, Bishop of Antioch, concerning Novatian and his schism,‡ and also from the Epistle of Cyprian to Cornelius.§

There is, however, one exception to this, that of assistant Bishops. The first instance on record of the *translation* of a Bishop, was about A. D. 250, when Alexander, a Bishop of Cappadocia, was elected *assistant* to Narcissus, Bishop of Jerusalem. This is also the first recorded instance of an assistant Bishop.‖ There is also another instance in early times of two Bishops in one city, that of Novatian, who procured himself to be ordained Bishop of Rome, while Cornelius held the Episcopate, for which he was condemned by a large council, and excommunicated as a schismatic.¶

But though there was never but one Bishop in a Church, there were, when the Church was completely organized, many Presbyters and Deacons. We have already seen that in the Apostolic Church, there was a plurality of Presbyters and Deacons under every Apostle, or Apostolic Bishop. This arrangement also continued in the succeeding age. That there were a number of Presbyters in the Church of Corinth,

* Can. 28.

† Nice, Can. 15. Antioch, Can. 13. 3 Constantinople, Can. 1. 1 Carthage, Can. 5, 10. 3 Carthage, Can. 20, and in England, Coun. Hereford, A. D. 673, Can. 2, 6, 8.

‡ Ep. Cor. ad Fab. in Euseb. vi. 43.

§ Ep. 45.

‖ Euseb. vi. 11.

¶ Euseb. v. 43.

when Clement wrote his Epistle to the Corinthians, is evident from his language, for he speaks of "Presbyters that have been driven out of the ministry;"* of "a sedition against the Presbyters,"† and exhorts them to be "at peace with the Presbyters."‡ There were too a number of Presbyters and Deacons in the Church in Smyrna when Polycarp wrote his Epistle to the Philippians, A. D. 107;§ a number of both in the Church at Philippi;|| as also at the same time in the Church in Ephesus;¶ in Magnesia;** in Trallia;†† and in Philadelphia.‡‡ So A. D. 176, there were many Presbyters in the Church at Lyons.§§ And at A. D. 252, there were no less than *forty-six* Presbyters and *seven* Deacons in the Church in Rome.|||| The number of Presbyters and Deacons would of course depend upon the number of Christians.

CHAPTER XXI.

INDEPENDENCE OF THE BISHOPS.

THE original independence of each Bishop may be inferred, (1,) from the nature of the constitution of the Church, for we have seen that the language of the Apostle, giving to every Church *a head*, negatives the idea of a head over other heads; (2) from the nature of the Apostolic commission, which confers equal authority upon all; and (3) from the fact, that in every Apostolic Church there was one and only one Apostle or Apostolic Bishop, having under him a plurality of Presbyter-

* C. 44. † C. 47. ‡ Cc. 54, 57.
§ Intd. Ign. Ep. Smyr. c. 8. Ep. Pol. c. 6. || Cc. 5, 6, 11.
¶ Ign. Ep. Eph. cc. 2, 4, 20. ** Ign. Ep. Mag. cc. 2, 6, 7, 13.
†† Ign. Ep. Tral. cc. 2, 3, 7. ‡‡ Ign. Ep. Phil. cc. 4, 7, 10.
§§ Ep. Ecc. Lug. in Euseb. v. 4. |||| Ep. Corn. ad Fab. Euseb. vi. 43

bishops and Deacons. The same inference might also be drawn from the fact, that the earliest Fathers make no mention of any superiority of one Bishop over another. This conclusion is also sustained by the course pursued by the Eastern and Western Bishops, relative to the time of keeping Easter. In the Eastern Churches it was customary to commemorate the death of CHRIST on the day in which the Jews prepared to eat the passover,—that is, the fourteenth day of the first new moon after the vernal equinox, being the fourteenth of the Hebrew month Nisan; while in the Western Churches the Friday following that day of the moon was observed for this purpose. This difference of practice gave rise to much discussion and controversy; and Polycarp, Bishop of Smyrna, and Anicetus, Bishop of Rome, about A. D. 166, held a conference on the subject. About A. D. 200, several Councils were held, one at Cæsarea, at which Theophilus, Bishop of that Church, presided; one at Jerusalem, at which Narcissus presided; one in Pontus, at which Palmas presided; and another in Gaul, at which Irenæus presided; all of which recommended the practice of the Western Churches.* Another Council of Asiatic Bishops was convened at Ephesus, at which Polycrates, Bishop of that city, presided, which adhered to the custom of the Eastern Churches, defending it by reference to the practice of the Apostle St. John.† At the same time Victor, Bishop of Rome, interposed his influence, first to persuade, and second, to compel the Bishops of Asia to come into the practice of the Western Churches, but without effect. To all this Polycrates replied in an epistle, from which we make the following extract.

"I, therefore, brethren, am *sixty-five years* in the LORD, [i. e. having been a Christian sixty-five years,] who having

* Euseb. vi. 23. † Euseb. iii. c. 31. Ep. Polycr. Euseb vi. c. 24.

conferred with the brethren throughout the world, and having studied the whole sacred Scriptures, am not at all alarmed at those things with which I am threatened to intimidate me."* The language of St. Cyprian is equally pertinent and decisive. "Our LORD gives to all the Apostles an equal power, and says: 'As my Father sent me, even so send I you; receive ye the HOLY GHOST; whosesoever sins ye remit, they shall be remitted to him, and whosesoever sins ye retain, they shall be retained.' . . . Certainly the other Apostles also were what Peter was, endowed with an equal fellowship of honor and power."† And in his Epistle to Jubianus, he says, "No one ought to make himself Bishop of Bishops, or pretend to awe his brethren, for every Bishop is at liberty to do as he pleases."

A custom, however, was early introduced into the Church, of holding Synods in the principal or Metropolitan cities, at which the Bishops of those cities presided. In this way the Bishops of such cities came to be considered as presiding Bishops, and hence were called Metropolitans, and sometimes Primates. This arrangement was in existence as early as the second century, and the Apostolical Canons‡ directed that two such Synods should be held each year, at which the Bishops were to examine each other concerning their faith, to settle all ecclesiastical difficulties, and to confer with each other on subjects of importance. They also directed that no Bishop should undertake any thing of *general* interest, without consent of his Metropolitan. Nor might the Metropolitan himself undertake any thing of *general* interest, without the consent of the Synod.§ But each Bishop was permitted to do whatever pertained to his own Diocese, without consulting any other Bishop.‖ The existence of Metropolitans or Pri-

* Apud Euseb. vi. 24. † Unity Church, c. 3. ‡ Can. 30.
§ Can. 27. ‖ Can. 27.

mates, about A. D. 250, is testified to by Cyprian,* and their authority and precedence was regulated by the Council of Antioch, A. D. 341.† There is abundant evidence that the independence of every Bishop continued many years later, and in many places continues to the present day. We are authorized, therefore, to assert the original independence of each Bishop, of every other Bishop.

Such an independence is also necessarily supposed, by the very *theory* of the Apostolical system. The primitive Christians, as we have seen, regarded the Church as *one*, with a *visible* organization, typical of the *invisible* and spiritual kingdom, in which CHRIST is the Great and only Head. Since, then, there is but one *invisible* Bishop, so, *theoretically*, there is but one visible Bishop. Consequently, every Bishop at the time of his consecration, becomes, by virtue of that consecration, a Bishop, not of any particular Church, but of the whole Church Catholic. Each Bishop is, therefore, strictly speaking, Bishop of the Universal Church. But since it is impossible that any one man should perform all the duties devolving upon a Bishop, the Church within a particular region is regarded, for certain purposes, *as the Church*, and its Bishop is limited in the exercise of his power to that particular territory. But, his power extending originally to the whole Church, he may still perform the functions of his office, in places not within his territory, when properly called upon to do so. It follows from this, that every Bishop in the Church Militant, is a type of the Head of the Church Triumphant, so that each individual Bishop is but a reiteration of the same type, *the Episcopate itself being but one.*‡ The language of St. Cyprian upon this point is striking and pertinent: "The

* Ep. 45.

† Can. 9.

‡ See on this subject, Thornton's note to Cyprian, De Unit. Ecc. in Cyp. Treat. 8vo. Oxford, 1839, p. 150.

Episcopate is one; it is a whole, in which each enjoys a full possession."* If, then, the Episcopate be one, "in which each enjoys a full possession," it is impossible there should be any Bishop on earth over other Bishops.

CHAPTER XXII.

CUSTOMS OF THE CHURCH.

HAVING considered the most important points touching the order and organization of the Primitive Church, we shall glance at some customs and practices prevailing in the Church at the close of the second century. References are occasionally made to later authorities, as showing the continuance of the same regulations.

BISHOPS.—To the powers and duties elsewhere enumerated, as pertaining to the Bishop, we may add the following. They were to superintend and take care of the property belonging to the Church,† but were not permitted to apply any of it to their own use, nor to the use of their friends, except to supply their necessities, or to assist needy and travelling brethren; and they were forbid to engage in secular pursuits, or to receive usury.‡ Bishops were to be deposed, who separated themselves from their wives, under pretext of devotion; who refused to receive the Eucharist; or who communicated with persons who had been excommunicated; or who had been guilty of fornication, or perjury, or theft, or drunkenness, or playing at dice, or any other unlawful

---

* De Unit. Ecc. c. 4. † Apos. Can. 31, 33, 34.

‡ Apos. Can. 31, 33, 34, 36. Elvira, Can. 18, 20. Arles, Can. 12. Nice, Can. 17.

act.* So were those who procured their places by money, or made use of civil rulers to procure the office. So also were those who re-baptized a person who had been sufficiently baptized; or submitted to a re-ordination; or performed ordination out of their own jurisdiction, without the consent of the ecclesiastical rulers there; or abstained from matrimony, meat, or wine, from pretended religious abhorrence; or were found eating at a public house, unless when travelling.† And so were those who neglected the clergy or people of their charge; or refused to supply the wants of needy clergymen, when able to do so; or held communion with heretics; or read spurious books in Church; or denied their office; or celebrated the festivals either of the Jews or heathen; or, having been ordained, refused to enter upon the duties of their office.‡

Bishops accused of any crime, were to be tried at a Synod of Bishops, of which two were held annually.§ Though each Bishop in the Primitive Church was held to be independent, the right of the brethren to call them to account for crimes, or heresy, was distinctly asserted in the second century.|| No person who had married a widow, or one that had been a mistress or an actress, or two sisters, or his

---

* Apos. Can. 3, 6, 8, 9, 18, 21, 35. Laod. Can. 33. Elvira, 19, 79. Antioch, Can. 4.

† Apos. Can. 22, 23, 28, 39, 43, 45, 46, 60. Carthage, A. D. 252. Arles, Can. 8. 1 Carth. Can. 1, 5, 10. Nice, Can. 15. Antioch, Can. 3. 3 Const. Can. 3 Carth. Can. 20, 27. Alex. Can. 1. Ancyra, Can. 14. Gangra, Can. 9, 10, 14, 24. Laod. Can. 55.

‡ Apos. Can. 29, 37, 50, 51, 52, 57, 63. 4 Carth. Can. 50. Laod. Can. 59. Elvira, Can. 50. Ancyra, Can. 18. Antioch, Can. 17.

§ Apos. Can. 30, 66. 3 Carth. Can. 7. Nice, Can. 5. Antioch, Can. 20.

|| Cyp. Ep. 67, 68. Dup. Hist. Ecc. Writ. Cent. iii. p. 130.

niece, could become a Bishop.* Nor one who had been guilty of adultery, fornication, or other forbidden act, after his baptism; or had made a eunuch of himself; or was insane; nor one recently converted; nor slaves, without the consent of their masters.† And no stranger was to be received to the communion of the Church, without letters of commendation.‡

Presbyters and Deacons.—All that has been said of Bishops, in regard to qualification and character, is equally applicable to Presbyters and Deacons. To these, the following must be added. They were not permitted to baptize, without the Bishop's consent; nor Presbyters to administer the communion without the same consent.§ They were not to leave their parishes without the Bishop's consent, and if, when they had done so, they refused to return when requested by their Bishop, were to be deposed.‖ And so were those who formed separate congregations, without the consent of the Bishop.¶ In short, they were not permitted to do any thing relative to the Church, without the consent of the Bishop.**

Laymen.—The same moral character was required of laymen, in the Primitive Church, as of clergymen; but some regulations in regard to marriage did not include them, and

* Apos. Can. 14, 15. Elvira, Can. 61, 62. Neo-Ceas. Can. 2. Gangra, Can. 4.

† Apos. Can. 17, 33, 70, 71, 72. Tert. De Pudic. c. 12. Cyp. Ep. 52. Nice, Can. 1. Alex. A. D. 235. Elvira, Can. 80. Gangra, Can. 2. 5 Carth. Can. 8, 82.

‡ Apos. Can. 26. Elvira, Can. 25, 28. Laod. Can. 41, 42. Antioch, Can. 6. 1 Carth. Can. 7. 2 Carth. Can. 7. Saragossa, Can. 5.

§ Ign. Ep. Smyr. c. 8. Tert. De Bap. c. 17.

‖ Apos. Can. 12. Ant. Can. 3. Sardica, Can. 20.

¶ Apos. Can. 24. Ign. Ep. Mag. c. 7. Antioch, Can. 5. Gangra, Can. 5. Laod. Can. 34. 2 Carth. Can. 8.

** Apos. Can. 32.

some acts which did not exclude them from communion, debarred from entering the ministry. No effort was spared which would enable them to draw a broad line of distinction between Christians and the Jewish and Gentile world. Hence the rule of the Primitive Church, that Christians who frequented the synagogues of the Jews, or the temples of the heathens, or who celebrated their festivals and fasts, were to be excommunicated.* Christianity could be propagated, only by requiring those who professed it, to come out and be separate from the world; and they shrunk from no privation, and from no duty which the cause of CHRIST and his Church demanded at their hands. Indeed, no one can attentively read the history of those early times, or the productions of the eminent saints whose works have survived the ravages of time, without being convinced that, for pureness of character, for rigidness of morality, for heavenly-mindedness for holiness, and for disinterested devotion of life, the Christians of the first and second centuries stand pre-eminent above all succeeding times.

FASTS.—Besides the things we have already mentioned, the Primitive Christians made use of various other expedients to quicken their devotion, and to keep alive a remembrance of their duty. Among these, fasting held a prominent place. Fasts were of two kinds, weekly and annual.

1. WEEKLY FASTS.—Fasting was common, even under the former dispensation, and was adopted by the Apostles under the Christian, (1 Cor. vii. 5,) though the Apostle would have it done voluntarily.† The days made choice of for this purpose, were Wednesdays and Fridays;‡ at which time, it

---

* Apos. Can. 62, 63.

† Col. ii. 16, 18, 23. Study of Celtic Lang. p 13, on *ethelo-threskeia.*

‡ Comp. Herm. Sim. iii. c. 5, and Fabric. Cod. Vet. Test. iii. p. 928. Clem. Alex. Strom. vii. p. 744. Tert. De Jejune, c. 14.

was customary "to lay aside the expense which would have been made on other days, and give it to the widow, the fatherless, and the poor."* Towards the close of the second century, fasts were prescribed in some places for one or both of these days.† It was also customary to fast for some time preceding baptism,‡ and on other important occasions.§

2. ANNUAL FAST.—The only annual fast observed in the Primitive Church, was on the day preceding our LORD's crucifixion, now called Lent, and Passion Week. This fast has been observed from the days of the Apostles. The Western Church, from the earliest ages, observed it as we now do, on the Friday following the Paschal full moon, but the Eastern Christians observed it on the particular day of the moon in which our Saviour suffered, without any reference to the day of the week. This difference of practice gave rise to a controversy on the subject, as early as A. D. 150. About 166, Polycarp, Bishop of Smyrna, visited Rome, and held a conference on the subject, with Anicetus, the tenth Bishop of that city.‖ But nothing was effected, and things remained as they were before. In the days of Victor, the thirteenth Bishop of Rome, several councils were held on this subject, and there is extant part of an epistle written by Polycrates, Bishop of Ephesus, in which he appeals to the practice of the Apostle John, as authority for their usage.¶ The extent of this was various, in various places. Some fasted but a single day, (Good Friday ;) others, two or more, up to forty.

FESTIVALS.—The evidence on the subject of the festivals of the Church, is less full than on that of fasts, but is still sufficient to enable us to tell what were the principal ones.

1. THE RESURRECTION, now called *Easter Sunday ;* that

---

* Herm. Sim. iii. c. 5.
† Apos. Can. 61.
‡ Just. Mar. Apol. i. c. 79.
§ Tert. De Jejune, cc. 13, 14.
‖ Iren. Ep. Victor. in Euseb. v. 25.
¶ Euseb. v. 24.

is, the day of the resurrection.—Bede says: "So called from the Goddess *Eostre*, whose festivities were in April."* But we conjecture, that it is from the same root as *East*, which denotes *rising*; hence *East*, "the place of rising;" *Easter*, "the resurrection." This festival is and ever has been kept by all who observe a fast in commemoration of the Crucifixion, and is acknowledged by all to have been universal.†

2. PENTECOST, now called *Whit-Sun-tide*, or *Whitsunday*.—This day seems to have been observed as a festival by the Apostles themselves. Thus, on one occasion, St. Paul "hasted if it were possible for him to be at Jerusalem the day of Pentecost." (Acts xx. 16.) And on another occasion, when about to visit the Corinthians, he tells them that he shall "tarry at Ephesus until Pentecost." (1 Cor. xvi. 8.) This festival is mentioned by Tertullian, A. D. 180,‡ and the Apostolical Canons, A. D. 200,§ and was then made to include the whole fifty days from Easter to Pentecost. This period was, even in the second century, one of the set times for baptism.||

3. ASCENSION DAY.—Those who made the feast of Pentecost continue for fifty days, necessarily observed this day also. In the fourth century, it was kept as a separate festival, and St. Austin says, that it was so ancient in his day, A. D. 390, that its origin could not be traced; and he very justly concludes, that those things which, not being commanded in Scripture, are nevertheless received throughout the world, as coming down from Apostolic times, must have taken their rise in the days of the Apostles.¶

* Bd., de Temp. Rat. Works, ii. 81.
† Bing. xx. 5. Mosh. B. I. Cent. I. Par. ii. c. 4.
‡ De Idol. c. 14. De Bap. c. 13.
§ Can. 30.
|| Tert. De Bap. c. 13.
¶ Aug. Ep. 118, Ad. Januarium.

4. The Nativity, now called *Christmas.*—The direct evidence of the observance of this festival in the first century, is less than that of many others. Still, there is every reason to believe that it is primitive, if not Apostolic, and that, with a few exceptions, it has always been observed on the twenty-fifth of December.* Chrysostom, about 390, says, that this

---

* There is a passage in Clement of Alexandria, which has been supposed to refer the birth of Christ to another season of the year. He says, (Strom. i. p. 340,) that "some curious persons assign, not only the year, but also the day of our Saviour's nativity, which they say was in the 28th of Augustus, on the 25th of [the Egyptian month] Pachon . . . but some say he was born the 24th or 25th of [the month] Pharmuthi." Pamelius, in his notes on Tertullian, (Contr. Jud. c. 8,) says Pachon answered to *December*, but Bingham says it was *May*. (Ant. xx. c. 4. § 1.) Which of these months was meant, if either, is uncertain, as the Egyptians at that time employed two kinds of years, one *fixed*, consisting of 365¼ days, and the other *variable*, or revolving, of 365 days,—each consisting of 12 months and certain intercalary days called *Epagomanæ*. The two kinds of years commenced on the same day, only once in 1460 years, when both began August 29th. The calendar of the *fixed year* has been given on page 114, which corresponds with the account of Bingham. But the other kind of year remained in common use much later than the time of Clement, and he furnishes no clue to the kind of year he employed himself, nor, as to that employed by those to whom he referred. Consequently, no inference can be drawn from this language.

But there is another consideration, which goes to show that the inference drawn from the language of Clement, is far from being sustained. In the Ethiopian Liturgy, which was copied from the Alexandrian, about A. D. 330, the birth of Christ, like several other important festivals, is celebrated on the 29th of every month of the year, corresponding to Dec. 25, Jan. 24, Feb. 23, March 25, April 24, May 24, June 23, July 23, Aug. 22, Sept. 26, Oct. 26, and Nov. 25, while the "feast of Gena," or of the *vigil of the birth*, (Christmas-eve,) is only celebrated on the 24th of December. As far, therefore, as any inference can be drawn from these calendars, it is in favor of December 25th being the true day. Rev. Glid. Egpt. in Bib. Rep. [N. S.] x. 146, Harris' Ethiopia, App. No. VIII.

festival was "one of great antiquity and long continuance, the most venerable and tremendous of all festivals, being famous and renowned in the Church from the beginning, far and wide, from Thrace to the Gaddes, in Spain."* Augustin, about 390, speaks of "the ancient and universal tradition concerning the observance of this festival;"† and Jerome, twenty years before, speaks to the same effect.‡ For some years, the Greek Church observed the Epiphany and Christmas on the same day, January sixth, but Chrysostom, about 390, says, that that Church then began to celebrate this festival on the twenty-fifth of December.§ What the precise evidence was, by which the day was determined, we do not know. But that it was of a convincing nature, is evident from the fact that it induced the Eastern Christians to change the day from January *sixth* to December *twenty-fifth*.|| And there was certainly no place where the true date could be so well ascertained at that time, as at Rome, as all the records of the Empire were there, and every means of fixing the time of all the occurrences alluded to in the Gospels was then at hand.

It has been objected, that Christmas was copied from a heathen festival—the Roman Saturnalia. But *ancient* authors say, the Saturnalia was at first celebrated only on the seventeenth of December.¶ Other days were subsequently added, until the number became three, and by order of Caligula were extended to five.** Two other days, called

---

* Hom. 31, De Bap. Ch. Bing. Antiq. L. xx. c. 4.

† De Trin. L. iv. c. 5.

‡ Com. Ezek. c. 1. Bing. Antiq. L. xx. c. 4.

§ Orat. 31, De Nat. Ch. Bing. Antiq. xx. c. 5.

|| One of the greatest obstacles in the way of determining the precise day on which any event happened, in ancient times, is the diversity of reckoning time which prevailed in those days.

¶ Liv. L. xxii. c. 1. Univ. An. Hist. vol. XI. p. 311. B. iii. c. 2.

** Adams, ubi sup.

Sigilaria, were subsequently added ;* but even then, the festival ended on the twenty-fourth of December.

The authority for this assertion, in regard to the festival of Christmas, appears to be Gibbon, who says: "The Romans, as ignorant as their brethren of the real date of the birth of CHRIST, fixed this solemn festival to the twenty-fifth of December, the *Brumalia,* or winter solstice, when the Pagans annually celebrate the birth of the Sun."† But Bingham, whom Gibbon professes to rely upon as authority, by no means supports his conclusion. Bingham's language is, "*Some* [i. e. objectors] *say* that the design of appointing the feast of CHRIST'S *Nativity and the Epiphany* at this season of the year, was to oppose the vanity and excess of the heathen, in the Saturnalia and Kalends of January, at this very time of the year." But he had before shown, that this opinion was without foundation.

Nor does Beausobre say, as Gibbon would have his readers infer, but, that this feast was instituted to oppose the heresy of the Manicheans, who denied the reality of the birth of CHRIST, and of his death and resurrection. The Manichees, therefore, with Cerdon, and the Priscillianists, who disbelieved the birth of the Saviour, very naturally refused to keep a festival in commemoration of an event which they said had never occurred.‡

There is still another hypothesis of the objector, as to the origin of this festival, and instead of deriving it from the Roman Saturnalia, they imagine that it was copied from the Yule of the Northmen; an opinion so improbable and absurd, and so destitute of all historical probability, as not to require an answer.

---

* Menol. Satur. L. i. c. x.

† Dec. and Fall Rom. Emp. c. xxii. n. 22, referring to Bing. Antiq. xx. c. 4, and Beaus. Hist. Crit. Man. tom. 2, 690—700.

‡ Comp. Bing. xx. c. 4. Beaus. ubi sup.

The weight of evidence points to an early origin of the festival of the nativity of CHRIST, probably within the first, at any rate within the second century; and so soon as Christians were permitted to build houses of worship, the celebration of this festival became notorious; it occupied a share in public attention, filled a larger space in the histories of the day, and the errors of the heretics and the vices of the pagans gave it still more celebrity. It was celebrated, too, as we now celebrate it, by the same or similar worship.*

5. EPIPHANY, or the *manifestation to the Gentiles.*—All the Churches at all times have agreed in celebrating the *Epiphany* or *Theophani* on the 6th of January, on which day, for some time, the Greek Church also kept Christmas. But as early as 390 the Greek Church, in consequence of the facts brought forward in proof that the twenty-fifth of December was the real day of CHRIST's nativity, acknowledged her error and altered her practice.†

SAINTS' DAYS.—Another custom of the Primitive Church, was that of celebrating the anniversaries of the martyrdom of eminent Saints, and other important occurrences. Thus the martyrdom of Ignatius was celebrated by the Church of Antioch.‡ And the martyrdom of Polycarp was celebrated by the Church at Smyrna.§ These days were called the birth-days of the martyrs, as being the day of their entrance into the world of bliss. Thus it is said by Tertullian:‖ "We make anniversary oblations for the dead on their birth-days." And Cyprian says:¶ "We continually offer oblations for them as often as we celebrate the passions and days of the

---

* Apos. Cons. v. 13, 14, viii. 33.

† Greg. Naz. Orat. Nat. Christ, 38; Chrys. Hom. 31, de Bap. Ch. Orig. Hom. 8. de dio; St. Aug. de Trin. L. iv. c. 5; St. Basil Serm. Nat. Ch.; Bing. Antiq. Church, xx. c. 4.

‡ Martyr. Ign. c. 7.

§ Martyr. Pol. c. 18.

‖ De Coron. Mil. c. 3.

¶ Ep. 39.

martyrs in our annual commemorations." And Peter Chrysologus, in his *Sermon on the martyrdom of Cyprian*, addresses his hearers thus: "When ye hear of a *birth-day* of Saints do not imagine that that is spoken of, in which they are born on earth of the flesh, but that in which they are born from earth into heaven, from labor to rest, from temptation to repose, from torments to delights, not fluctuating, but strong, stable and eternal, from the derision of the world to a crown of glory. Such are the *birth-days* of the martyrs that we celebrate."

STATED HOURS OF PRAYER.—The practice of observing stated hours of prayer is probably as old as Christianity itself. Thus, "Peter and John went up to the temple at the hour of prayer, being the ninth hour." (Acts iii. 1.) The expression here made use of is a distinct recognition of an existing custom observed by the Apostles. So also it is said of Cornelius, that he fasted, and "at the ninth hour he prayed." (Acts x. 30.) Hence it is evident that the ninth hour was observed as a stated time of prayer. Again, it is said, that "Peter went up upon the house-top to pray about the sixth hour." (Acts x. 9.) Whence it is probable that the sixth hour was also a stated time of prayer. So on the day of Pentecost, the disciples "were all with one accord in one place," (Acts ii. 1,) and probably in the temple, "at the third hour of the day," (Acts ii. 15.) From this we may reasonably infer, that this also was a stated hour for prayer. And again it is said, that "at midnight Paul and Silas prayed." (Acts xvi. 25.)

Here then we have a distinct statement, that prayers were offered at certain specified times, and in one case it is expressly said to be "the hour of prayer." Consequently, we may infer from the nature of the evidence, by which these questions are to be decided, that in all cases where the precise time of offering prayer is mentioned, it was a stated time. This conclusion is sustained by the language of Clement, of Rome, for he tells us* that we ought to perform our public worship of God, "at the appointed seasons, for this he hath commanded to be done, not rashly and disorderly, but at certain determinate times and hours." And we learn from Clement, of Alexandria,† Tertullian,‡ Origen,§ and Cyprian,‖ that these appointed seasons were at sunrise, the third, sixth, and ninth hours of the day, and at sunset. And we know that these hours were observed by all the Churches in the centuries following. In the time of Tertullian, it was not regarded as a "prescribed" rule, to observe these "stated hours," though the practice of the ancients was supposed to bind them to "three times a day."¶

Vestments.—The whole controversy concerning vestments in the Primitive Church, with the reasons for their use, may be classified under the following heads:—

1. White garments have always been esteemed as emblems of purity. We learn from the inspired Apostle, that the seven angels, commissioned from heaven to inflict the last plagues upon man, were to appear "clothed in pure and white linen," (Rev. xv. 6,) that all "the armies in heaven are clothed in fine linen, *white* and clean." (Rev. xix. 14.) The saints, too, "those who had not defiled their garments," (Rev. iii. 4,) "those who had been slain for the word of God," (vi. 9,) "with the four and twenty elders that surrounded the throne of the Most High," (iv. 4,) and the "mighty multitude, which no man can number, from all nations, kindred, people, and tongues, who had in much tribulation washed their robes in the blood of the Lamb," (vii. 9, 14,) were dressed in "*white* raiment, having *white* robes upon them." So, too, the bride and spouse of the Lamb, when decked in her bridal

---

* Ep. Cor. c. 40.
† Strom. vii.
‡ De Jejune, c. 10. De Orat. c. 25.
§ De Orat. c. 12.
‖ De Orat. Domin. c. 22.
¶ Tert. Orat. cc. 24, 25.

garments, was "to be arrayed in fine linen, clean and *white*, for the *white* linen is [emblematic of] the righteousness of the Saints." (Rev. xix. 8.) The same may be proved by numerous passages in the Old Testament.* And the heathen nations used garments of the same color, with the same design.†

2. White garments were prescribed for the Jewish priests, and from them copied by the heathen nations. The linen ephod was prescribed for the Jewish priests by Moses,‡ which we know, from the meaning of the original term, was white; so that the use of white garments has been practised ever since the establishment of the Jewish Theocracy, about 1650 years before the Christian era. Now since the Pagans are unable to prove their use of these within a thousand years as early as we know they were used by the Jews, the presumption is, that they were copied. But though the Pagan priests sometimes wore white garments, it was not the only, if their usual color.§

3. That for a similar reason, white garments were used by the Primitive Christians, in the rite of baptism. Among many ancient nations, persons who died were first washed, then anointed and clothed in white garments, as emblematic of the purity required of those who were about to enter into

---

* Comp. Ps. li. 7; Isa. i. 18; Ezek. xvi. 9–13; xliv. 16, 17; Lev. xix. 19; Deut. xxii., xi.

† Archæ. Græc. Robinson, v. 3, p. 419. Potter's Gr. Antiq. iv. c. 3. Univ. Hist. vol. XI. 239.

‡ Robinson's Calmet, in loco. Josephus' Antiq. Jud. iii. 7. Judges viii. 27; xvii. 5; xviii. 14. 1 Sam. ii. 18; xxviii. 14, 15; xxiii. 6, &c.

§ Anarcharsis, the Younger, in his Grecian travels, says: "The Priests officiated in rich vestments, having upon them the names of their particular Deities to which the temple was consecrated, in letters of gold." (Vol. II. p. 415.) These garments point to the magnificent ephod of the Jewish High Priest, (Exod. xxviii. and xxix.,) as the original from whence they were derived.

another world.* The renovation of Israel is described by the Prophet under the similitude of a wretched infant, who was taken in its distresses, "washed in water, anointed in oil, and decked in fine white linen." (Ezek. xvi. 9–13.) So in the Primitive Church, those who, being buried to the world in baptism, died unto sin, and rose to life in CHRIST, "were washed in the laver of regeneration," anointed with oil, and clothed with white garments, in token that they had renounced "the devil and all his works, the vain pomp and glory of the world, with all covetous desires of the same, and the sinful desires of the flesh; that hereafter they should not be ashamed to confess the faith of CHRIST crucified, and manfully to fight under his banner against sin, the world, and the devil; and to continue CHRIST's faithful soldier and servant unto their life's end."†

4. White garments were used as priestly vestments in the Christian Church, before the commencement of the third century. The Apostolic Constitutions make mention of the "splendidam vestem;" that is, the bright, clear, or pure garments, so called from their *white* color, worn by the Priests when ministering at the altar.‡ Eusebius notices the "sacred gown and sacerdotal garments worn by the Bishops and Priests."§ So also he speaks of the *petalon*,‖ which Professor Cruse renders "sacerdotal plate," but which seems rather to denote some kind of garment worn as a badge, and probably made of linen. Jerome, also, speaks of the *white*

* Rob. Archæl. Græcæ. v. c. 3, p. 410. Jahn, Bib. Arch. p. I. c. 13, sect. 204. Univ. An. Hist. vol. I. p. 490.

† Tertullian, in his treatise on baptism, speaks of the "unctione de pristina disciplina," (c. 7, p. 226.) See also Apos. Cons. iii. 15, 16, 17, 22, p. 368; Recog. Clem. iii. 67; Cyril Hieros. Cat. Mystag. 2; Chrys. Orat. 6, sub finem; Ep. ad Coloss. Dionys. 2; Aug. Serm. de illitu Neophy.; and Serm. de Mys. Bap. Ambrose de Sacra, i. 2.

‡ B. viii. 12. § Euseb. x. 4. ‖ B. v. 24.

garment worn by the Bishop and Priest at the communion.* And Gregory Nazianzen alludes to the use of similar garments.† Pontius, in his account of the martyrdom of St. Cyprian, prefixed to the works of that Bishop, calls "white linen an ensign of Episcopal honor;"‡ and Bede makes mention of Episcopal garments worn in his time.

Celibacy.—The early Church, relying on the language of St. Paul to the Corinthians, (1 Cor. vii. 1–11,) very soon came to place a high estimate upon the practice of virginity. Thus Ignatius, A. D. 107, says: "If any one be able to remain in chastity, to the honor of the Lord of all flesh, let him do so without boasting. If he boast he is undone. If he desire to be esteemed above his Bishop, he is corrupt."§ So Justin Martyr, A. D. 150, writes: "Many, both men and women, of the age of sixty or seventy years, who have been disciples of Christ from their youth, continue in immaculate virginity."|| Towards the close of the second century, the ardent but unstable Tertullian, though himself a married man, was loud in his praises of virginity, in which he was followed, to a considerable extent, by Cyprian.

But virgins had not been formed into separate communities, even in the third century, as appears from Cyprian's Treatises.¶ And it was one ground of complaint with him, that they sought to attract attention by their dress,** attended marriage parties,†† public exhibitions,‡‡ as other women, thereby endangering themselves, and becoming snares to others. Nor was the vow of virginity then considered per-

* Adv. Pelag. i. 9, tom. 2d, p. 565. The 4th Council of Carthage, A. D. 398, Canon 41, directed the Priest to wear the surplice at the communion.

† Orat. 31, tom. 1, p. 504.

‡ Op. Cyp. Pont. Diac. Vita. S. Cyp. p. 9, Ox. 1682.

§ Ep. Pol. c. 5.

|| Apol. i. c. 18.

¶ De Habitu Virginum.

** Cc. 5, 7.

†† C. 10.

‡‡ C. 11

petual, for even Cyprian says of the virgins, "If they can not, or will not remain virgins, let them marry."*

Nor was celibacy at this period required even in the clergy. Eusebius, A. D. 325, collected and published what he could find relative to the marriage of the Apostles, and he tells us, on the authority of Clement of Alexandria, that Peter and Paul were married, that Philip was married, had children, and gave his daughters in marriage.† This is also corroborated by Polycrates, Bishop of Ephesus, A. D. 195, who adds, that two of the daughters of Philip were never married.‡ So he tells us that Domnus, the 16th Bishop of Antioch, was son of Demetrianus, the 14th Bishop of that city.§ Indeed, the evidence is abundant, that for ages after celibacy was recommended, it was not required. Even so late as 530, Felix IV., the 54th Bishop of Rome, was the son of a priest.|| So Silverius, the 58th Bishop of Rome, 536, was the son of Hormisdas, the 52d Bishop of Rome; Theodore I., the 73d Bishop of Rome, 642, was the son of the Patriarch of Jerusalem; and John XI., 126th Bishop of Rome, 931, was son of Sergius III., 120th Bishop of Rome.¶

CHAPTER XXIII.

SUCCESSION OF BISHOPS.

HAVING seen that in every Church there was one Apostle, or Apostolic Bishop, who alone possessed the power of ordi

---

* Ep. Pomp. 4, or 62. † Hist. iii. 30.

‡ Ep. Pol. in Euseb. v. 24.

§ Circ. Ep. Coun. Antioch, in Euseb. vii. 30.

|| Walsh, Hist. Popes, p. 73. ¶ Ib. 75, 93, 125

nation, and having seen that this arrangement was designed to be permanent, it follows necessarily, that there ought to be an *uninterrupted succession* of such Bishops. It is important, therefore, for us to inquire whether there is sufficient proof that such a succession has been kept up; and if so, where it is to be found, and what is the evidence of its existence. This will require us to dwell a moment upon the early practices of the Church in this particular.

The first Apostolical Canon, which is acknowledged by all historians to describe the "customs of the Church in the East, in the second and third centuries,"* directs that "a Bishop should always be ordained by two or three Bishops."† And it was ordained at the Council of Arles, 314, that at the ordination of a Bishop, there should never be less than three Bishops, and that seven should be present, if they could be procured. And the Council of Nice, the first general council, all the Bishops of the Roman empire having been summoned, decreed, A. D. 325, that the ordination of Bishops should be done by all the Bishops of the Province, if they could be convened; but that no ordination should be performed by less than three Bishops. This canon has ever since been regarded as the law of the Church, so that a consecration, or ordination of a Bishop by a less number than three Bishops, though it might be valid, would be uncanonical and irregular, if not schismatical.

If, now, we turn over the pages of the historian, we shall find the practice of the Church has been in accordance with these principles. References to some of the earliest records are given. It was not customary in the Primitive Church to record the name of the consecrators of the Bishops, nor the day of their consecration, but only the year thereof.

---

* Mosh. B. I. Cent. II. Par. ii. c. 2, and Dr. Murdock's note.

† SS. Patr. Apos. II. 437.

The Episcopate being regarded as one, of which each enjoyed a full possession,* it was considered immaterial from what source it was derived, if so be it could be traced back to one of the Apostles or Apostolic men.† Still, the consecrating Bishop in any particular region, was, in ordinary cases, the metropolitan Bishop.‡ The names of the consecrators, or the persons consecrating, were, however, sometimes incidentally mentioned; and, from these incidental notices, we gather the following names of consecrators.

A. D.

35. JAMES *the Just*, ordained by St. Peter, St. James, and St. John, first Bishop of Jerusalem.§

54. EVODIUS, ordained by St. Peter, first Bishop of Antioch.||

56. TITUS, ordained by St. Paul, first Bishop of Crete.¶

59. TIMOTHY, ordained by St. Paul, first Bishop of Ephesus.**

61. ANNIANUS, ordained by St. Mark, first Bishop of Alexandria, in Egypt.††

63. LINUS, ordained by St. Paul, first Bishop of Rome.‡‡

68. IGNATIUS, ordained by St. Peter, second Bishop of Antioch.§§

68. SIMEON, ordained by Peter and the other Apostles, second Bishop of Jerusalem.||||

---

* Cyp. Unit. Ecc. c. 4.

† Tert. De Præ. Hær. c. 32.

‡ Apos. Can. 27. Coun. Nice, Can. 6. Antioch, Can. 9. Laod. Can. 12. 2 Arles, Can. 5, 6.

§ Clem. Alex. Inst. vi. in Euseb. ii. 1.

|| Euseb. iii. 22. Apos. Cons. vii. 36.

¶ Euseb. iii. 4. Apos. Cons. vii. 46. Chrys. Hom. Tit. 1. Theod. Arg. Tit.

** Euseb. iii. 4. Life of Tim. in Phot. Bib. n. 254. Apos. Cons. vii. 46. Chrys. Hom. 1 Tim. iii. 1, 5, 9. Theod. Com. 1 Tim. iii. 1.

†† Euseb. ii. 24.

‡‡ Iren. Adv. Hær. iii. 3. Euseb. iii. 2. Apos. Cons. vii. 46.

§§ Apos. Cons. vii. 46

|||| Euseb. iii. 11; iv. 22.

A. D.

79. Cletus, ordained by Linus, first Bishop of Rome, to be his successor.*

85. Polycarp, ordained by St. John, second Bishop of Smyrna.†

91. Clement, ordained by St. Peter, about A. D. 64,‡ succeeded Anacletus as Bishop of Rome, about A. D. 90.§

97. John, ordained by St. John, second Bishop of Ephesus.‖

98. Cerdon, fourth Bishop of Alexandria, ordained by the Bishops of the neighboring Churches.¶

100. Evaristus, fourth Bishop of Rome, ordained by St. Clement to be his successor.**

107. Heros, third Bishop of Antioch, appears to have been consecrated at a council called by Polycarp, at the suggestion of Ignatius.††

109. Primus, fifth Bishop of Alexandria, elected from among the laity, and consecrated by the Bishops of the neighboring provinces.‡‡

121. Justus, sixth Bishop of Alexandria, ordained by the Bishops of the neighboring Churches.§§

132. Eumenius, seventh Bishop of Alexandria, ordained by the Bishops of the neighboring Churches.‖‖

---

* Euseb. iii. 13.

† Iren. Adv. Hær. iii. 3. Tert. De Præs. Hær. 32. Euseb. iii. 36; iv. 14. Niceph. Ecc. Hist. iii. 34.

‡ Apos. Cons. vii. 46. Epiph. Hær. xxvii. Bd. iii. 4. Tert. Præs. Hær. 32. Chrys. Hom. John xxi. Clem. Ep. Cor. c. 54; and Le Clerc's note.

§ Euseb. iii. 15.

‖ Apos. Cons. vii. 46.

¶ Sev. Ash. Ann. 98.

** Euseb. iii. 34.

†† Ign. Ep. Pol. c. 7. Ads. Ep. Mar. 5, and Ush. n. Euseb. iii. 36.

‡‡ Sev. Ash. Ann. 109. Orient. Chron. 74.

§§ Sev. Ash. Ann. 121. Orient. Chron. 75.

‖‖ Sev. Ash. Ann. 132. Orient. Chron. 75.

A. D.

152. Celadion, ninth Bishop of Alexandria, ordained by the neighboring Bishops.*

178. Julianus, eleventh Bishop of the same place, consecrated at a council called for that purpose.†

187. Elvanus, second Archbishop of London, consecrated by Eleutherus, twelfth Bishop of Rome.‡

199. Dius, thirty-first Bishop of Jerusalem, consecrated by the neighboring Bishops, upon the abdication of Narcissus.§

236. Fabian, nineteenth Bishop of Rome, ordained by a large number of Bishops, assembled in council for that purpose.‖

237. Alexander, Bishop of Cappadocia, translated to Jerusalem, after the restoration and death of Narcissus, and became the thirty-fourth Bishop of that city.¶

240. Gregory *Thaumaturgus*, ordained Bishop of Neo-Cesarea, by Phædmius, Bishop of Amasea.**

248. Cyprian, ordained Bishop of Carthage, "by a great number of Bishops."††

250. Cornelius, twentieth Bishop of Rome, ordained by sixteen Bishops, of whom two were from Africa.‡‡

252. Novatian, surreptitiously ordained Bishop at Rome by three Italian Bishops, upon whom he had imposed.§§

256. Felix and Sabinus, ordained at a council of Spanish Bishops, over the Dioceses of Leon and Astorga.‖‖

---

* Sev. Ash. Ann. 152. † Ib. Ann. 178.

‡ Reg. Lland. in Mona. Ang. III. 186. § Euseb. vi. 10.

‖ Ib. vi. 29. ¶ Ib. iv. 1.

** Dup. Ecc. Writ. Cent. iii. p. 147.

†† Cyp. Ep. Ad Corn. Dup. Ecc. Writ. Cent. iii. p. 117.

‡‡ Cyp. 55. Dup. Ecc. Writ. Cent. iii. p. 118. Walsh, Lives of the Popes, p. 35.

§§ Ep. Corn. in Euseb. v. 43. ‖‖ Cyp. Ep. 67.

A. D.

267. ANATOLIUS, Bishop of Laodicea, ordained by Theotecnus, Bishop of Cesarea, and other Bishops.*

269. DOMNUS, son of Demetrianus, the fourteenth Bishop of Antioch, was ordained the sixteenth Bishop of Antioch, at a large council of Bishops, at which Paul of Samosata was deposed.†

To prevent schismatical ordinations, and mistakes in regard to the succession, consecrations were generally performed at a Synod of Bishops, of which two were held annually in the Primitive Church.‡ The continuance of this practice was enjoined by Cyprian, A. D. 252; by a council of Eastern Bishops, held at Antioch, 341;§ and by the Bishops of England, at the Council of Hereford, 673.|| At these, the Bishop of the principal city, or the one oldest in office, called Patriarch, Metropolitan, or Primate, presided; and was generally the consecrating Bishop.¶ The number of such Sees in the third and fourth centuries, mentioned by historians, were four: Rome, Alexandria, and Antioch, for their size, and being civil Metropoles; and Jerusalem for its antiquity and honor.

There is, however, still another important question. Allowing that there has been this care in regard to the succession, has the record of it been preserved? And is there proof now existing, worthy of confidence, sufficient to establish it? On this point there can be no doubt. Thus Irenæus, the disciple of Polycarp, who was the disciple of St. John, as we have already seen, assures us, that in his day, A. D. 175, "they could enumerate those appointed Bishops by the Apostles and their successors, even to his day."¶

---

* Euseb. vii. 32. † Euseb. vii. 30. ‡ Apos. Can. 30.

§ Ep. 67. Can. 19, 20. || Can. 7.

¶ Coun. Nice, Can. 6. Antioch, Can. 9. Laod. Can. 12. 2 Arles, Can. 5, 6, etc. ¶ Adv. Hær. iii. c. 3.

And Tertullian, about 200, says, that all orthodox Churches in his day, "could show the series of their Bishops, so running down from the beginning by successions from the first Bishop, as to be able to show that he was one of the Apostles, or Apostolic men."* And both writers appeal to this fact, as evidence that they were in possession of the truth. The great ecclesiastical historian of the Primitive Church, Eusebius Pamphilius, Bishop of Cesarea, gives the "successions of the Apostles," as he found them recorded in the archives of the Churches.† We give the successions of the four Patriarchal Sees—of Rome, Alexandria, Jerusalem, and Antioch—as given by Eusebius, who copied them from the records of the Church and authors extant in his time.‡ To these Churches it was common to appeal in controversies with the heretics.§ The list comes down to 305, when his history closes.

	ROME.	ALEXANDRIA.	JERUSALEM.	ANTIOCH.
1.	Linus,	Annianus,	James,	Evodius,
2.	Cletus,	Avilius,	Simeon,	Ignatius,
3.	Clement,	Cerdon,	Justus,	Heros,
4.	Evaristus,	Primus,	Zaccheus,	Cornelius,
5.	Alexander,	Justus,	Tobias,	Eros,
6.	Sixtus,	Eumenius,	Benjamin,	Theophilus,

* Præs. Adv. Hær. c. 32. † Hist. B. iii. c. 3, 37. Int. B. viii.

‡ Very many of these records, though now lost, were preserved in his day, in the library at Jerusalem, founded by Alexander, Bishop of that city, about A. D. 250, to which Eusebius had access, and from which he drew many of the materials for his history. (B. v. 20. See also i. 1, Intd. ii. iii. 3, 4, 37.) And he tells us expressly that he had drawn all the names of those who held places "in the first rank of the Apostolic succession," from "accounts delivered in the various comments on Apostolical doctrine." (H. iii. 37.) He had also the large library of Pamphilius, in which were preserved all the ancient historians, from which to draw materials. (Euseb. vi. 32.)

§ Iren. Adv. Hær. iii. 3. Tert. De Præsc. cc. 30–36.

	Rome.	Alexandria.	Jerusalem.	Antioch.
7.	Telesphorus,	Marcus,	John,	Maximus,
8.	Hyginus,	Celadion,	Matthew,	Serapion,
9.	Pius,	Agrippinus,	Philip,	Asclepiades,
10.	Anicetus,	Julius,	Seneca,	Philetus,
11.	Soter,	Demetrius,	Justus,	Zebinus,
12.	Eleutherus,	Heraclas,	Levi,	Babylus,
13.	Victor,	Dionysius,	Ephrem,	Fabius,
14.	Zephrynus,	Maximus,	Joseph,	Demetrianus,
15.	Calixtus,	Theonus,	Judas,	Paul,
16.	Urban,	Peter,	Marcus,	Domnus,
17.	Pontianus,	A. D. 302.	Cassianus,	Timæus,
18.	Anteros,		Publius,	Cyrillus,
19.	Fabian,		Maximus,	Tyrannus,
20.	Cornelius,		Julian,	A. D. 302.
21.	Lucius,		Caius,	
22.	Stephen,		Symmachus,	
23.	Sixtus,		Caius,	
24.	Dionysius,		Julian,	
25.	Felix,		Maximus,	
26.	Eutychianus,		Antonius,	
27.	Caius,		Capito,	
28.	Marcellinus,		Valens,	
29.	A. D. 296.		Dolchianus,	
30.			Narcissus,	
31.			Dius,	
32.			Germanio,	
33.			Gordius,	
			[Narcissus,]	
34.			Alexander,	
35.			Mazabanes,	
36.			Hymenæus,	
37.			Zambdas,	
38.			Hermon,—A. D. 300.	

This brings us down within twenty years of the great Council of Nice, and is sufficient to demonstrate, that both the succession and the record of it were carefully preserved, and that both were undoubted at the time of the Council of Nice, A. D. 325. The lists of these Bishops are also given by several other early writers, of different countries, so as to render the facts indisputable.* We shall consider, in the next chapter, the nature of the Apostolic Succession, and the fact of its continuance to the present day.

CHAPTER XXIV.

SUCCESSION OF THE CHURCH IN ENGLAND.

We propose in this chapter, to consider two points connected with the succession of Bishops in the English Church, which are often confounded. Bishops are said to succeed each other, when they follow in the same See, or Diocese. Consequently, the succession of Bishops in a particular Diocese, is the list of Bishops who have governed that Diocese, and may be called a succession of Episcopal governors. But this is a very different thing from the Apostolic succession, on which all Episcopal power depends. The difference may be briefly explained thus: When one Bishop ordains another Bishop, he commits to the person ordained, the same Episcopal powers which he himself possesses. Every Bish-

* That of *Rome* is given by Irenæus, to the middle of the second century; by the Pontifical of Bucherius, to the third; by Jerome, to the fourth, *etc.* That of Alexandria, by the ancient *Oriental Chronicle*, preserved among the Byzantine historians; by Severus, Bishop of Ashmonia; by Le Quien and Assemani, from Coptic MSS., *etc.* That of Antioch, by Assemani, from Oriental writers and MSS., *etc.*

op, therefore, receives his authority to minister as a Bishop in the Church of CHRIST, at the time of his ordination, or consecration; and he receives it through him who ordained, or consecrated. Hence, if we wish to trace back the authority of the present Bishops, we must go, not in the line of Bishops occupying a particular See, but in the line of their consecrators. The one we call the *Succession of Episcopal Governors;* the other, the *Apostolic Succession.* Our meaning may be explained by an example. All the colonies were originally attached to the jurisdiction of the Bishop of London, and hence each of the Dioceses in this country, where there was an Episcopal Church before the Revolution, would trace the succession of Episcopal Governors back to the Bishops of London. But the Apostolic succession is traced back through the Archbishops of Canterbury, the first Bishops of this country having been consecrated by the Archbishop of Canterbury. Or we may trace it through the Archbishops of York, as the Archbishop of York assisted at the consecration of our first Bishops.

But we may also trace our Apostolic succession back to the Church of Scotland; for one lawful Bishop is sufficient to confer the Apostolic succession;* and as there are at least three Bishops ordinarily engaged in the consecration of a

* Doubts have been raised by some Theologians, whether ordinations of Bishops, by *one* Bishop are valid; but, as seems to us, without sufficient reason. They would be *uncanonical,* and therefore *irregular,* but still valid. So held Beveridge, Mason, Hallier, Paludanus, Sylvester, and others. (Pal. Church, P. vi. c. 5.) Others have held the contrary opinion; but this has been practised by the Romish Bishops in Ireland, Scotland, and America. Even Archbishop Carroll, the fountain of Romish Orders in this country, was ordained by one Bishop only, and that one a mere titular Bishop. (Pal. Church, P. vi. c. 11.) And Bishop Cheverus was ordained by Archbishop Carroll *alone.* That these things occurred in the Primitive Church, and were held valid, see Bing. ii. 11, 5

Bishop, we may trace the Apostolic succession through any of the ordaining Bishops. Now Bishop Seabury was consecrated by Robert Kilgour, Arthur Petrie, and John Skinner, Scottish Bishops, November 14, 1784. From him we have received the Apostolic succession, thus:

Samuel Seabury assisted in the consecration of Thomas John Claggett, September 17, 1792.

Thomas John Claggett assisted in the consecration of Edward Bass, May 7, 1797.

Edward Bass assisted in the consecration of Abraham Jarvis, October 18, 1797.

Abraham Jarvis assisted in the consecration of John Henry Hobart and Alexander Viets Griswold, May 29, 1811.

John Henry Hobart and Alexander Viets Griswold assisted in the consecration of Thomas Church Brownell, October 27, 1819.

The *Succession of Episcopal Governors* in Connecticut, is, therefore,—

Bishops of London, till	1784.
Samuel Seabury,	1784—1796.
Vacancy a year and a half.	
Abraham Jarvis,	1797—1813.
Vacancy six and a half years.	
Thomas Church Brownell,	1819— —

During a part of the six and a half years' vacancy, this Diocese was under the provisional supervision of Bishop Hobart, of New York.

The *Apostolic Succession* is,—

1. Samuel Seabury.	4. Abraham Jarvis.
2. Thomas John Claggett.	5. John Henry Hobart.
3. Edward Bass.	6. Thomas Church Brownell.

There are now (1842) in the United States, twenty Bishops of the Episcopal Church. They trace their succession to the Archbishops of Canterbury and York, as follows:—

To BISHOP WHITE,

Who was consecrated by the Archbishops of Canterbury and York, Feb. 4, 1787—

Rt. Rev. Alexander Viets Griswold, of Massachusetts, May 29, 1811.

Rt. Rev. Philander Chase, Illinois, Feb. 11, 1819.

Rt. Rev. Thomas Church Brownell, Connecticut, Oct. 29, 1819.

Rt. Rev. Henry Ustick Onderdonk, Pennsylvania, Oct. 25, 1827.

Rt. Rev. William Meade, Virginia, Aug. 19, 1829.

Rt. Rev. Benjamin Tredwell Onderdonk, New York, Nov. 26, 1830.

Rt. Rev. Levi Silliman Ives, North Carolina, Sept. 22, 1831.

Rt. Rev. John Henry Hopkins, Vermont, Oct. 31, 1832.

Rt. Rev. Benjamin Bosworth Smith, Kentucky, Oct. 31, 1832.

Rt. Rev. Charles Petit McIlvaine, Ohio, Oct. 31, 1832.

Rt. Rev. George Washington Doane, New Jersey, Oct. 31, 1832.

Rt. Rev. James Hervey Otey, Tennessee, Jan. 14, 1834.

Rt. Rev. Jackson Kemper, Missouri, Sept. 25, 1835.

To BISHOP GRISWOLD,

Who stands in the preceding list—

Rt. Rev. William Heathcote Delancey, Western New York, May 9, 1839.

Rt. Rev. Christopher Edwards Gadsden, South Carolina, June 21, 1840.

Rt. Rev. William Rollinson Whittingham, Maryland, Sept. 17, 1840.

Rt. Rev. Alfred Lee, Delaware, Oct. 12, 1841.

To BISHOP H. U. ONDERDONK,

Who also stands in the same list—

Rt. Rev. Samuel Allen McCoskry, Michigan, July 7, 1836.

To BISHOP MEADE,

Who also stands in the same list—

Rt. Rev. Leonidas Polk, Arkansas, Dec. 9, 1838.

Rt. Rev. Stephen Elliott, Georgia, Feb. 28, 1841.

Now as we have shown before, how Bishop Griswold traces his succession to Scotland, it follows, that all those whom he has consecrated, or has assisted in consecrating, can trace their succession to Scotland also. Those who trace it in this way, are—

Bp. Brownell,	Bp. Meade,	Bp. Hopkins,
" McIlvaine,	" Delancey,	" Gadsden.
" Whittingham,	" Lee,	

We have also seen how Bishop Hobart traced his succession to Scotland. Those who trace it through him, are,—

Bishop Chase, Bishop H. U. Onderdonk.

Those who trace it through Bishop Hobart and Bishop H. U. Onderdonk, are,—

Bp. B. T. Onderdonk,	Bp. Smith,	Bp. Kemper,
" Ives,	" Otey,	" McCoskry.

The other Bishops trace their succession to Scotland, thus:

Bishop Doane, through Bishops B. T. Onderdonk, H. U. Onderdonk, Hobart, and then as before.

Bishop Polk and Elliott, through Bishops Smith, H. U. Onderdonk, and then as before.

Again; the Archbishops of Canterbury and York were assisted in the consecration of Bishops White and Provoost, by the Bishops of Peterborough, and of Bath and Wells. Consequently, if either of these four Bishops had received a valid consecration, the consecration of Bishops White and

Provoost must also be valid. And as every Bishop now living, or that ever has lived in this country, can trace his succession to all these Bishops, all may trace their succession through which line they please.

Again; the Archbishop of Canterbury was assisted in the consecration of Bishop Madison, by the Bishops of London and Rochester. And since all the Bishops now living, or that ever have lived in this country, can trace their succession, through Bishop Madison, to either of these Bishops, it follows, that if either of these had received a valid consecration, our Bishops have been validly consecrated. We see, therefore, that if either the Archbishops of Canterbury or York, or the Bishops of London, or of Bath and Wells, or of Peterborough, or of Rochester, or of Ross and Murray, or of Aberdeen, had had a valid consecration, our Bishops have all been validly consecrated, and the succession has been preserved unbroken.

We have detailed these facts more at large than we should have done, had we not designed to have used them to illustrate an important point in this inquiry, which seems not to be well understood. We know, that from the second century to the present time, at least three Bishops have been required in the consecration of another Bishop, when they could be procured. Now, if it should ever happen, that either one, or even two, of the three ordaining Bishops, should prove not to be lawful Bishops, the one remaining lawful Bishop would be sufficient to transmit the Episcopal authority. We see, therefore, if Bishops White, Provoost, and Madison, who were consecrated by the Archbishop of Canterbury, had never been consecrated at all, but had assumed to themselves the Episcopal office, without any authority, still all the Bishops in our Church would now be lawful Bishops, as all can trace their succession to Bishop Seabury. And yet Bishop Seabury never assisted in the consecration of but a single Bishop!

And what may seem more singular still, is, that there never has been a Bishop consecrated in the Episcopal Church in this country, that could not trace his succession to Bishop Seabury. This will enable the reader to see that the evidence in favor of the Apostolic succession, is of that high degree of probability, not to say certainty, that the supposition of a break in it is one of the most improbable ideas that could ever enter one's head, and that it is next to impossible that it should ever occur. It will be seen from this, also, that there may have been ever so many vacancies in the line of Episcopal Governors, without affecting in the least the Apostolic succession. A particular See may often have been vacant, and remained vacant for a great number of years. During this interval, all acts peculiarly pertaining to the Apostolic office, must be performed by the Bishop of some other See. This is so obvious to one at all acquainted with the subject, that it would seem unnecessary to mention it, if such vacancies had not been spoken of by the opponents of Episcopacy, as breaking the line of succession. But men, wise in other matters, are not aware of the fallacy, because they confound Episcopal government with Apostolic succession. We shall give the English succession in several different ways.

I. SUCCESSION FROM EPHESUS.

The Archbishops of Canterbury, through whom the succession of the English Bishops is usually traced, received their succession, not, as is often said, from Rome, but from Arles, Augustine, the first Saxon Bishop, as well as the first Archbishop of Canterbury, having been consecrated at Arles, by Virgilius, the twenty-fourth Archbishop of Arles, Ætherius, the thirty-first Bishop of Lyons, and probably other Bishops of that province.* The reason why Augustine was

* Bede, Hist. i. 27. Gallia Christiana, vol. I., pp. 519–540. Vol. IV. pp. 4–10. Dupin, Hist. Ecc. Writr. vol. V. p. 90.

consecrated at Arles, was, that from the time of the Emperor Honorius, Arles, which received its Episcopate from Lyons and Vienne, had been the metropolitan city of Gaul.* At a still earlier period, as appears from the ancient Notitia, it belonged to the Arch-Diocese of Vienne,† while at a still earlier period the whole province was reckoned as the Arch-Diocese of Lyons,‡ a name it still retains. Arles and Lyons, therefore, derived its Episcopate from the same source, and the succession of Bishops has continued in the same line, as the Bishop of one city was the consecrating Bishop, at the ordination of a Bishop for the other. Hence it is proper to give both lines, and, providentially, the Bishops of both cities assisted in the consecration of Augustine.

The source from whence the Gallic Churches derived their Episcopate and ecclesiastical rites, has been somewhat disputed, but without sufficient reason. The ancients themselves traced it back to St. John.§ Pothinus, the first Bishop of Lyons, was a Greek,|| and died at the advanced age of ninety, A. D. 176.¶ Pothinus, therefore, was fourteen years old when St. John died, and eighty years when Polycarp died.** Irenæus, the successor of Pothinus, was also a Greek, and was the disciple of Polycarp,†† Polycarp himself having been ordained Bishop of Smyrna, by St. John.‡‡ And the associates with Irenæus, in the ministerial office, were also Greeks.§§ So, too, when the Churches of Gaul were suffering violent persecution, they wrote a circular epistle to the Asiatic Churches, which was addressed: "The servants of

* Gall. Chris. I. 2. Bede, i. 27.
† Gall. Chris. I. 1.
‡ Euseb. v. cc. 1, 23.
§ Gallia Christ. I. 5–12. Spel. Coun. i. 176. Bd. v. 25.
|| Greg. Tour. i. 28, 29.
¶ Euseb. v. 1.
** Ep. Church, Smyr. Mart. Pol.
†† Iren. Adv. Hær. iii. 3. Ep. Flor. Euseb. v. 23, 24.
‡‡ Iren. Adv. Hær. iii. 3.
§§ Ruin. Acta. Martyr. 80.

CHRIST dwelling at Lyons and Vienne, in Gaul, to the brethren in Asia and Phrygia."* Now Ephesus was the residence of St. John, after his return from Patmos until his death,† though he went from city to city constituting Churches, and ordaining Bishops.‡ After his death Polycarp exercised a kind of supervision over the vacant Churches, as we read was the case in Philippi,§ Antioch,|| and probably elsewhere.¶ So also, the Churches of Gaul, as we have already seen, received their ecclesiastical rites, and even the technical phraseology of their ecclesiastical customs, from Asia. An ancient Irish historian of the sixth or seventh century, says, that "the Gallican course (i. e. Liturgy) was first chanted by St. John, the Evangelist, then by the blessed Polycarp, the disciple of St. John, then by Irenæus, Bishop of Lyons, in Gaul."** In the famous controversy between Wilfrid, Archbishop of York, and Coleman, Bishop of Durham, on the subject of keeping Easter, the latter appealed to the universally received opinion, that they derived their ecclesiastical usages from St. John,†† in which the Church of Gaul differed from Rome, even in the second century,‡‡ but corresponded with that of the Asiatic Churches.§§ That the Gallican Liturgy was derived from the Ephesian, or that of St. John, has been satisfactorily shown.|||| So also much of their ecclesiastical language was copied from the Greek, as we have already seen was the case in regard to the word *Church*,¶¶ which was never used at Rome, the Latins having

---

* Euseb. v. 1. † Ep. Polycr. Bp. Ephesus, Euseb. iii. 23, v. 24.

‡ Clem. Alex. Quis. Dios. Salv.? Euseb. iii. 23.

§ Ep. Pol. Phil. cc. 3, 13. || Ign. Ep. Pol. cc. 7, 8.

¶ Ante, p. 226. ** Spel. Coun. i. 176.

†† Bd. iii. 25 ‡‡ Euseb. v. 23.

§§ Euseb. v. 23, 24.

|||| Pal. Orig. Liturgy, i. pp. 143–189, and Ante, pp. 118, 119.

¶¶ Ante, p. 118.

adopted the word *Ecclesia*. All those Churches, therefore, which adopted the word *Church*, from the Greek *Curiacon*, could not have derived the *rites* of their Church from a people that never used the word. We also know that the old Gothic version of the Bible, was made by a Gothic Bishop, Ulfilas, from the Greek,* and from a manuscript of Eastern origin.† These facts leave no doubt that the Gallic Churches received their Episcopate, along with their ecclesiastical customs and usuages, from Asia, in accordance with the testimony of ancient historians.

Here we are not able to consult the original records, as they have been kept in a different country, and are at present imperfect, many of the early ones having been destroyed when the South of Europe was overrun by the Northern barbarians. Since the fourth century, however, we are able to give the dates of the several successions, and enough has been preserved to give us the order of the succession up to the most primitive times. We copy from the great work of the Benedictines, entitled *Gallia Christiana*, in eleven folio volumes, and which was above forty-five years going through the press. The year standing against the names, is either the time of accession, or the period that individual is known from history to have flourished.

St. JOHN.
1, Polycarp, Bp. of Smyrna.

	Bishops of Lyons.‡	*Bishops of Arles.*§
2,	(1,) Pothinus, 177,	
3,	(2,) Irenæus, 177—202,	
4,	(3,) Zacharias,	
5,	(4,) Elias,	(1,) Trophimus,
6,	(5,) Faustinus,	(2,) Regulus,

* Hug. Intd. N. T. Par. i. § 139.
† Ib. § 140.
‡ Gall. Chris. vol. I. pp. 519–540.
§ Gall. Chris. vol. IV. pp. 5–40.

Bishops of Lyons.

7, (6,) Verus,
8, (7,) Julius,
9, (8,) Ptolomy,
10, (9,) Vocius,
11, (10,) Maximus,
12, (11,) Tetradus,
13, (12,) Verissimus,
14, (13,) Justus, 374,
15, (14,) Albinus,
16, (15,) Martin,
17, (16,) Antiochus,
18, (17,) Elpidius,
19, (18,) Sicarius,
20, (19,) Eucherius I., 427,
21, (20,) Patiens, 451,
22, (21,) Lupicinus,
23, (22,) Rusticus, 494,
24, (23,) Stephanus, 499,
25, (24,) Viventiolus, 515,
26, (25,) Eucherius II., 524,
27, (26,) Lupus, 538,
28, (27,) Licontius, 542,
29, (28,) Sacerdos, 549,
30, (29,) Nicetus, 552,
31, (30,) Priscus, 573,
32, (31,) ÆTHERIUS, 589.

Bishops of Arles.

(3,) Martin I., 254,
(4,) Victor, 266,
(5,) Marinus, 313,
(6,) Martin II.
(7,) Valentine, 346,
(8,) Saturnius, 353,
(9,) Artemius,
(10,) Concerdius, 374,
(11,) Heros,
(12,) Patroclus, 412,
(13,) Honoratus, 426,
(14,) Hilary, 433,
(15,) Ravenus, 449,
(16,) Augustalis, 455,
(17,) Leontius, 462,
(18,) Æonius, 492,
(19,) Cæserius, 506,
(20,) Ananius, 543,
(21,) Aurelian, 546,
(22,) Sapandus, 557,
(23,) Licerius, 586,
(24,) VIRGILIUS, 588.

ARCHBISHOPS OF CANTERBURY.

The principal authorities for the succession of the Archbishops of Canterbury, to the time of the Reformation, are the following :—

A. D.

596—737. BEDE's *Eccles. History of the English Nation, to the year* 737. The authorities on which this author relied, were the *Records of the Church of Canterbury*, and the histories of earlier writers, especially, as it regards the Province of Canterbury, of Albinus, a pupil of Abp. Theodore, who wrote about A. D. 670.*

596–1152. THE SAXON CHRONICLE, which is a collection of *Annals*, written by various authors, viz. :—

596–891. By Phlegmund, Archbishop of Canterbury, in the time of Alfred the Great, who wrote up, or caused to be written, the *Annals* to his own times, and are quoted under the title of *Archbishop Phlegmund's Annals*.†

891–959. By Dunstan, Archbishop of Canterbury, who continued the *Annals* to his time, quoted by the name of *Archbishop Dunstan's Annals*.‡

959–1038. By Elfric, Archbishop of Canterbury, who continued the *Annals* to his time, quoted by the name of *Archbishop Elfric's Annals*.§

1038–1052. By Archbishop Stigand, who continued the *Annals* to his time, quoted by the name of *Archbishop Stigand's Annals*.‖

1052–1087. By Wulstan, a monk of Peterborough, who wrote a continuation of the *Annals*,

* Ess. Dedic. to King Ceowulph.

† Pref. Ingraham's Sax. Chron.

‡ Ib.

§ Dis. Sax. Chron. pp. 50–136, 271–291. The account given of Elfric by the Romish historians, cannot be relied upon. His writings were strongly opposed to transubstantiation, and there seems to have been a design to destroy his authority.

‖ Dis. Sax. Chr. pp. 419–436.

A. D.

quoted by the name of *Wulstan's Annals*.*

1087–1121. By Nicholas, a prior of Worcester, who wrote a continuation of the *Annals* to his time, quoted by the name of *Nicholas' Annals*.†

1121–1132. By Remaldus, a monk of Peterborough, who wrote a continuation of the *Annals*, which are quoted by the name of *Remaldus' Continuation of the Saxon Chronicle*.‡

664–1051. INGULPH'S *History of the Monastery of Croyland.*

596–1114. WILLIAM, a monk of Malmsbury, in two works, entitled; *The Acts of the Kings of England*, and *The Acts of English Pontiffs.*

596–1138. HENRY, Archdeacon of Huntingdon, *History of England, in eight books.*

596–1203. ROGER, of Hoveden, *Annals, in two parts.*

1067–1259. MATTHEW PARIS, a monk of St. Albans, *History of England.*

1260–1272. WILLIAM RISHANGER, a monk of St. Albans, continuation of the same.

1278–1361. Various authors, who wrote at or near the time.

1361–1503. The original *Registers of the Archbishops* in part, and cotemporary authors in part.

1503–1790. *Registers of the Archbishops.* These have been continued down, but as the American succession begins at that date, it was not deemed expedient to enlarge the list.

From this account, it will be seen that we rely entirely upon what may be considered cotemporaneous authorities, and that these have been preserved to us in so many

* Dis. Sax. Chron. pp. 295–359.

† Ib. pp. 79–135, 363–397.

‡ Ib. pp. 399–409.

ways, and by such widely different means, that there is, humanly speaking, no possibility of mistake. It will also be seen, that it is an easy matter to trace the consecrations of the consecrators, through nearly the whole line of Archbishops.

The Canons of the Church of England, from the earliest ages to the present time, have required *three Bishops* to be present at the consecration of another Bishop; and the consecrator was to be the Metropolitan of the Province, or some Bishop designated by him, or, in case of a vacancy, designated by the King. Consequently, when consecrations have been made by the Archbishop of Canterbury, it has not been generally customary to name him; whereas, when others have been the consecrators, they have generally been mentioned. A single instance, out of many, will serve as an example. Thus *Hovedon*, speaking of the consecrations of *Wakelin* of Winchester, and *Stigand* of Sussex, says: "The Archbishop of Canterbury having been deposed, and the Archbishop of York being dead, they were consecrated by Armenfrid, Bishop of Seduni," &c.

33, (1,) AUGUSTINE, consecrated by Virgilius, twenty-fourth
596. Bishop of Arles, assisted by Ætherius, thirty-first Bishop of Lyons, A. D. 596; died May 26, 605.*

34, (2,) LAWRENCE, consecrated by Augustine to be his suc-
605. cessor, Mellitus and Justus being the assisting Bishops; died Feb. 2, 619.†

35, (3,) MELLITUS, consecrated Bishop of London by Augus-

* Bd. i. 27, 28. Hen. Hunt. iii. 184. Wend. i. 45. Gall. Chris. i 540; iv. 35. Malms. i. 111.

† Bd. ii. 4. Ann. Phleg. 26. Hen. Hunt. iii. 187. Wend. i. 109. Malms. i. 111.

619. tine, 604; translated to Canterbury, Feb. 619; died April 25, 624.*

36, (4,) 624. Justus, consecrated Bishop of Rochester by Augustine, 604; translated to Canterbury, April, 624; died Nov. 10, 633.†

37, (5,) 634. Honorius, consecrated by Paulinus, Archbishop of York, 634, (Paulinus having been consecrated by Justus, July 21, 625;‡) died Sept. 30, 653.§

Vacancy eighteen months.||

38, (6,) 654. Adeodatus, or Deusdedit, consecrated by Ithamar, Bishop of Rochester, March 26, 654, (Ithamar having been consecrated by Honorius, 644;¶) died July 14, 664.**

Vacancy three years, eight months, and fifteen days, —during which time Wilfrid of York exercised a provisional oversight.††

39, (7,) 668. Theodore, of Tarsus, in Cilicia, consecrated by Vitalian, seventy-sixth Bishop of Rome, March 26, 668; died Sept. 16, 690.‡‡

40, (8,) 693. Birthwald, elected July 1, 692; consecrated June 29, 693, by Godwin, forty-second Bishop of Lyons, then Metropolitan of Gaul; died January 8, 731.§§

---

* Bd. ii. 3, 7. Ann. Phleg. 24, 26. Hen. Hunt. iii. 187 Wend. i. 120. Malms. i. 111.

† Bd. iii. 8. Ann. Phleg. 24. Hen. Hunt. iii. 187. Wend. i. 104. Malms. i. 111.

‡ Bd. ii. 3, 8. Paulinus died Oct. 10, 644. Bd. iii. 14.

§ Bd. ii. 9. Ann. Phleg. 27, 28. Hen. Hunt. iii. 189. Wend. i. 149. Malms. i. 111.

|| God. Præs. Ang. 40.

¶ Bd. iii. 14.

** Bd. iii. 20. Ann. Phleg. 33. Malms. i. 111, 132. Wend. i. 149.

†† Bd. iii. 28; iv. 2; v. 19.

‡‡ Bd. iv. 1; v. 8. Ann. Phleg. 40. Malms. i. 111. Wend. i. 160.

§§ Bd. v. 8. Ann. Phleg. 47. Malms. i. 112. Wend. i. 185–188 Some MSS. read *Walliarum*, (*Wales*,) instead of *Galliarem*, (*Gaul*,) but the latter, we think, is the true reading. See Gall. Chris. iv. 50.

41, (9,) TATWINE, consecrated June 10, 731, by Daniel,
731. Bishop of Winchester; Ingauld, Bishop of London; Aldwin, Bishop of Lichfield and Coventry; and Aldwulf, Bishop of Rochester—all of whom had been consecrated by Birthwald and his suffragans; died January 31, 734.*

42, (10,) NOTHELM, consecrated, 735, by the Bishops of the
735. Province of Canterbury—then being Aldwulf of Rochester, Ingauld of London, Aldwin of Lichfield, and Daniel of Winchester, who had been consecrated by Birthwald and his suffragans; and Sigifrid of Seolsy, (Chichester,) and Alwich of Sidnacester, (Lincoln,) who had been consecrated by Tatwin and his suffragans.†

43, (11,) CUTHBERT, consecrated by Nothelm and his suffra-
742. gans, Bishop of Hereford, 736; translated to Canterbury, 742; died 760.‡

44, (12,) BREGWIN, consecrated on the feast of St. Michael's,
760. Sept. 29, 760, by the Bishops of the Province of Canterbury—then being Aldwulf of Sidnacester, (Lincoln,) Hemel of Lichfield, Tidfrid of Dunwich, (Norwich,) Totta of Dorchester, (Lincoln,) and Werebert of Leicester; he died 762.§

45, (13,) LAMBERT, or, as other manuscripts read, Jambert,
763. or Anbriht, consecrated by Paul, ninety-fourth Bishop of Rome, 763; died 790.‖

* Bd. v. 18, 23. Ann. Phleg. 50–53. Malms. i. 112, 132; ii. 136. Hen. Hunt. iv. 194. Wend. i. 219. Hov. i. 230. Ingulph. 485.

† Bd. v. 23. Ann. Phleg. 54. Hen. Hunt. iv. 198. Malms. i. 112. Hov. i. 230. Wend. i. 225.

‡ Ann. Phleg. 55. Malms. i. 112. Hen. Hunt. iv. 196. Hov. i. 236. Wend. i. 227.

§ Ann. Phleg. 59. Malms. i. 113. Hov. i. 231. Wend. i. 236.

‖ Ann. Phleg. 60. Malms. i. 113. Hov. i. 231. Wend. i. 236.

46, (14,) ÆTHELRED I., consecrated by Lambert and his
793. suffragans, Bishop of Winchester, 780; translated to Canterbury, July 21, 793; died 803.*

47, (15,) WULFRED, consecrated by Leo III., ninety-seventh
803. Bishop of Rome, 803; died 830.†

48, (16,) THEOGILD, or Feogild, elected May 7; consecrated
830. June 9, 830, by the Bishops of the Province of Canterbury—then being Osmund of London, Herewin of Lichfield, Cedd of Hereford, Adelstan of Schirebourne, (Salisbury,) Humbert of Elmham, (Norwich,) Godwin of Rochester; all of whom had been consecrated by Wulfred and his suffragans. He died Aug. 30. 830.‡

49, (17,) CEOLNOTH, consecrated by the same Bishops, Sept.
830. 830; died 870.§

50, (18,) ÆTHELRED II., consecrated by Ceolnoth and his
871. suffragans, Bishop of Winchester, 862; translated to Canterbury, 871; died June 30, 889.||

51, (19,) PHLEGMUND, "chosen of GOD, and by all his holy
891. people, Archbishop of Canterbury," consecrated by Formosus, Bishop of Oporto, one hundred and twelfth Bishop of Rome, 891; died 923.¶

52, (20,) ATHELM, or Adelm, consecrated by Phlegmund

---

* Ann. Phleg. 65. Malms. i. 113. Hen. Hunt. iv. 197. Ingulph. 486. Wend. i. 236.

† Ann. Phleg. 69. Malms. i. 113. Hov. i. 236. Ingulph. 486 Wend. i. 251.

‡ Ann. Phleg. 72.

§ Ann. Phleg. 73. Malms. i. 113. Hen. Hunt. iv. 198. Hov. i. 198 Ingulph. 488–492. Wend. i. 277.

|| Ann. Phleg. 80. Malms. i. 113; ii. 137. Wend. i. 312. Hov. i. 239. Erroneously printed, 233, in Ed. 1594.

¶ Ann. Phleg. 90. Malms. i. 113. Hen Hunt. v. 201. Hov. i. 241 Wend. i. 354.

915. and his suffragans, Bishop of Wells, 905; six other Bishops being consecrated at the same time, —Frithstan, to Winchester; Adelstan, to Wilton, (Salisbury;) Werstan, to Sherbourne, (Salisbury;) Edulf, to Devon, (Exeter;) Bernegus, to Seolsy, (Chichester;) Kenulf, to Dorchester, (Lincoln.) He died 924.*

53, (21,) WULFELM, consecrated by Athelm and his suffra-
924. gans, Bishop of Wells, 915; translated to Canterbury, 924; died 934.†

54, (22,) ODO SEVERUS, consecrated by Athelm and his suf-
941. fragans, Bishop of Wilton, 920; translated to Canterbury, 934; died July 4, 958.‡

55, (23,) DUNSTAN, consecrated by Odo and his suffragans,
959. Bishop of Worcester, 957; translated to London, 958, and thence to Canterbury, 959; died May 19, 988.§

56, (24,) ÆTHALGAR, consecrated by Dunstan and his suffra-
988. gans, Bishop of Seolsy, (Chichester,) May 6, 980; translated to Canterbury, 988; died 989.||

57, (25,) SIRICUS, consecrated by Dunstan and his suffra-
989. gans, Bishop of Wiltshire, 986; translated to Canterbury, 989; died Oct. 28, 995.¶

* Malms. i. 113; ii. 144. De Gest. Reg. ii. 26. Hov. i. 242. Ingulph. 494. Wend. i. 372.

† Ann. Dunst. 114. Malms. i. 113; ii. 144. Wend. i. 380.

Malms. i. 114; ii. 141. Hov. i. 142. Ingulph. 499. Wend. i. 383, 391.

§ Ann. Dunst. 114. Malms. i. 114; ii. 141. Hov. i. 244. Ingulph. 501, 502. Wend. i. 408, 425.

|| Dis. Sax. Chr. 271. Malms. i. 115; ii. 146. Hen. Hunt. v. 205. Hov. i. 245. Wend. i. 426.

¶ Ann. Elf. 271. Malms. i. 115; ii. 142. Hen. Hunt. v. 205 Hov. i. 245. Wend. i. 426

58, (26,) 996. ALURICUS, or Alfric, consecrated by Siricus and his suffragans, Bishop of Wiltshire, 990; translated to Canterbury, 996; died 1005.*

59, (27,) 1005. ELPHEGE, consecrated by Dunstan, Bishop of Winchester, Nov. 14, 983; translated to Canterbury, 1005; murdered April 19, 1012.†

60, (28,) 1013. LIVING, or Leoning Elskan, consecrated by Alfric and his suffragans, Bishop of Wells, about 1001; translated to Canterbury, 1013; died 1020.‡

61, (29,) 1020. AGELNOTH, or Æthelnot, consecrated Nov. 13, 1020, by Wulstan, Archbishop of York, assisted by the Bishops of the Province of Canterbury—then being Ethelric of Chichester, Alfsius of Winchester, Birthwold of Salisbury, Etheric of Lichfield, all consecrated by the Archbishops of Canterbury; and several others, the precise date of whose consecration is not known. He died Oct. 30, 1038.§

62, (30,) 1038. ELFRIC, or, as it is usually written, Edsin, Edsius, and Elsin, consecrated by Living and his suffragans, Bishop of Winchester, 1015; translated to Canterbury, 1038; died Oct. 28, 1050.||

63, (31,) 1050. ROBERT Gemeticensis, or Robert Norman, consecrated by Elfric and his suffragans, Bishop of Lon-

---

* Ann. Elf. 273. Malms. i. 115; ii. 142. Hen. Hunt. v. 205. Hov i. 246. Wend. i. 426.

† Ann. Elf. 277. Malms. i. 115. Hen. Hunt. vi. 207. Hov. i. 246, 247. Wend. i. 437, 440.

‡ Ann. Elf. 284. Malms. i. 116; ii. 144. Hen. Hunt. vi 207. Hov. i. 248. Wend. i. 463.

§ Ann. Elf. 421. Ann. Stig. 450. Malms. i. 116. Hen. Hunt. vi. 208. Hov. i. 205. Ingulph. 508. Wend. i. 463.

|| Ann. Stig. 423. Malms. i. 116; ii. 140. Hen. Hunt. vi. 209. Hov. i. 251. Wend. i. 476.

don, 1044; translated to Canterbury, 1050; expelled from his See, 1052.*

64, (32,) 1052. STIGAND, consecrated by Elfric and his suffragans, Bishop of Helmsham, 1040; translated to Winchester, 1045, and to Canterbury, 1052, Robert being still living; suspended, 1062; deposed 1070.†

65, (33,) 1070. LANFRANC, consecrated August 29, 1070, by William of London, Siward of Rochester, Wakelin of Winchester, Herfast of Norwich, Walter of Hereford, Giso of Bath and Wells, Herman of Salisbury, and Stigand of Chichester; those absent consecrating by their legates. Of these, *William* had been consecrated by Robert and his suffragans; *Wakelin* and *Stigand*, by Armenfrid, Bishop of Seduni, in Gaul, assisted by the Bishops of the Province of Canterbury; *Walter* and *Giso*, by Nicholas II., Bishop of Florence, and 153d Bishop of Rome; *Herman*, by Siward, assistant to Elfric and consecrated by him; *Siward*, by Stigand, and Herfast, by some of the Bishops of the Province of Canterbury, after the suspension of Stigand. He died May 28, 1089.‡

66, (34,) 1093. ANSELM, consecrated December 4, 1093, by Thomas of York, assisted by the Bishops of the Province of Canterbury—Wakelin of Winchester, Wulstan of Worcester, Maurice of London, Robert of Chester, Gundulph of Rochester, Robert of Lich-

* Ann. Wuls. 306. Malms. i. 116; ii. 135. Hen. Hunt. vi. 209. Hov. i. 252. Wend. i. 486.

† Ann. Wuls. 319. Ann. Stig. 430. Malms. i. 116; ii. 136, 140. Hen. Hunt. vi. 209. Hov. i. 255. Wend. i. 483.

‡ Ann. Wuls. 324. Ann. Osb. 446. Malms. i. 117; ii. 136, 140 Hen. Hunt. vi. 209. Hov. i. 255. Wend. ii. 8, 36. Mat. Par. 7.

field, Osmund of Salisbury, Godfrey of Chichester, and John of Bath and Wells;—Wakelin having been consecrated as above stated; Wulstan, by Aldred of York, who was consecrated by Robert of Canterbury, and the others by Lanfranc. He died March 22, 1109.*

67, (35,) RODULPH, or Ralph, consecrated Bishop of Roches-
1114. ter, August 11, 1108, elected Archbishop April 26, 1114, installed July 27, 1115; died Oct. 20, 1122. He was consecrated by Anselm, assisted by William of Winchester, Radulph of Chichester, and Richard of London; all of whom had been consecrated by Anselm and his suffragans.†

68, (36,) WILLIAM *Corbell*, nominated by the King Feb. 2,
1123. 1123, consecrated March 19, 1123; died November, 1136; the consecration being by William of Winchester, Ernulf of Rochester, Bernard of Wales, (St. David's,) and Roger of Salisbury:—William and Roger having been consecrated by Anselm, assisted by Gerard of York, Robert of Lincoln, John of Bath, Herbert of Norwich, Robert of Chester, Ralph of Chichester, and Ranulf of Durham;—Gerard, both Roberts, John and Herbert, having been consecrated by Anselm and his suffragans; and Ranulf, by Thomas of York, who was consecrated by Lanfranc and his suffragans,—*Ernulf* and *Bernard*, by Rodulph and his suffragans.‡

69, (37,) THEOBALD, elected by the Bishops of England, as-

---

* Ann. Nich. 371, 390. Malms. i. 124. Hen. Hunt. 213. Hov. i. 266. Wend. i. 44, 185. Mat. Par. 18.

† Ann. Nich. 392. Malms. i. 131, 133, 146. Hen. Hunt. vii. 217. Hov. 270. Wend. ii. 184, 192. Mat. Par. 63, 65.

‡ Ann. Remald. 414. Hen. Hunt. vii. 219. Hov. i. 271 273. Wend. ii. 193, 194. Mat. Par. 63, 66, 69.

1138. sembled in Council, in the city of London, at Christmas, 1138, consecrated at the same time by Albert, Bishop of Ostia, assisted by the Bishops present at the Council; died April 18, 1161;—the Bishops then being, Turstan of York, consecrated by Calixtus II., Bishop of Vienne, and 160th Bishop of Rome; Roger of Salisbury, Henry of Winchester, Nigel of Ely, Roger of Coventry, Simon of Worcester, Robert of Hereford, Sifrid of Chichester, and Gunfrid of Durham, who were consecrated by William Corbell and his suffragans, and Alexander of Lincoln, who had been consecrated by Anselm and his suffragans.*

70, (38,) THOMAS *à Becket*, elected by the clergy and people
1162. of the Province of Canterbury, consecrated Trinity Sunday, 1162, by Henry of Winchester, who had been consecrated by William and his suffragans, assisted by the other Bishops of the Province of Canterbury,—then being, Walter of Rochester, Gilbert of Hereford, Geoffry of St. Asaph's, Jocelin of Salisbury, William of Norwich, who had been consecrated by Theobold and his suffragans; Hugo of Durham, consecrated by Anastasius IV., Bishop of Sabina, and 166th Bishop of Rome; Bartholomew of Exeter, consecrated by Walter of Rochester, assisted by other Bishops; and Hilary of Chichester, the date of whose consecration is unknown.†

71, (39,) RICHARD, elected by the Bishops of the Province

* Ann. Remuld. 414. Hen. Hunt. 223. Hov. i. 271–277. Wend. ii. 203–225. Mat. Par. 60–77.

† Hov. 281, 282. Wend. ii. 225–292. Mat. Par. 76–98. Chron. Lich. Whar. i. 110.

1174. of Canterbury, July 6, 1174; consecrated by Alexander III., 168th Bishop of Rome, 1174; died Feb. 16, 1184.*

72, (40,) 1184. BALDWIN *Fordensis*, consecrated by Richard and his suffragans, Bishop of Worcester, August 10, 1180; translated to Canterbury, December 2, 1184; died 1190.†

73, (41,) 1191. REGINALD *Fitz-Joceline*, consecrated by Richard at Rome, June 23, 1174, Bishop of Bath and Wells, the Archbishop of Tarentasia being present and assisting; elected to Canterbury, December 5, 1191, but died in a few days after his election.‡

74, (42,) 1193. HUBERT *Walter*, consecrated by Baldwin and his suffragans, Bishop of Salisbury, November 1, 1189; translated to Canterbury, May 30, 1193; died 1205.§

75, (43,) 1207. STEPHEN *Langton*, consecrated by Innocent III., 174th Bishop of Rome, June 27, 1207; died July 9, 1228.||

76, (44,) 1229. RICHARD *Wethersfield*, consecrated June 5, 1229, by Henry of Rochester, assisted by the other Bishops of the Province of Canterbury—then being Hugh of Lincoln, Hugh of Hereford, Geoffry of Ely, Thomas of Norwich, William of Exeter, and Ralph of Chichester, who had been consecrated by Stephen and his suffragans; Peter of Winchester, who had been consecrated by the

---

* Hov. ii. 307, 308. Wend. ii. 370–411. Mat. Par. 127, 129. Chron. Lich. Whar. i. 111.

† Hov. ii. 355. Wend. ii. 409; iii. 34. Mat. Par. 140–142.

‡ Hov. 307, 308, 405. Wend. ii. 370; iii. 54. Mat. Par. 127, 167. God. 369.

§ Hov. ii. 377, 415. Wend. iii. 13, 183. Mat. Par. 154, 160.

|| Wend. iii. 212; iv. 170. Mat. Par. 222. Can. Lich. Whar. i. 115.

Bishop at Rome; Alexander of Lichfield and Coventry, consecrated by Honorius III., 175th Bishop of Rome; Joceline of Bath and Wells, consecrated by William of London, (who had been consecrated by Hubert;) Robert of Salisbury, consecrated by Alexander of Lichfield and Coventry; and William of Worcester, (the date of whose consecration is unknown.)*

77, (45,) 1234. EDMUND, consecrated April 2, 1234, by Roger Niger of London, assisted by Henry of Norwich, Hugh of Lincoln, Hugh of Hereford, Thomas of Norwich, William of Exeter, Ralph of Chichester, Peter of Winchester, Alexander of Lichfield and Coventry, Joceline of Bath and Wells, Robert of Salisbury, and William of Worcester, above named; and Hugh of Ely, who, with Roger of London, were consecrated at the same time, and by the same persons, as Richard of Canterbury. He died 1240.†

78, (46,) 1245. BONIFACE, elected 1242; consecrated by Innocent IV., 178th Bishop of Rome, at a council held at Lyons, 1245. He died August 10, 1275.‡

79, (47,) 1272. ROBERT *Kirlwarby*, consecrated February 26, 1272, by William Britton, or Button, Bishop of Bath and Wells, assisted by the Bishops of the Province of Canterbury—*William* having been consecrated by Celestine V., Bishop of Sabina, and 178th Bishop of Rome;—the other Bishops then being Lawrence of Rochester, Roger of Lichfield and

* Wend. iv. 185–226. Mat. Par. 197–363. Chron. Lich. Whar. i. 115. Ann. Ecc. Rof. Whar. i. 347.

† Wend. iv. 267. Mat. Par. 363–545. Chron. Lich. Whar. i. 115.

‡ Mat. Par. 850–960. Chron. Lich. Whar. i. 115. Guth. i. 816, 852

Coventry, Walter of Exeter, Richard Benedict of Lincoln, Nicholas of Ely, Robert of Salisbury, who had been consecrated by Boniface and his suffragans; John of Hereford, and Roger of Norwich, the date of whose consecration is not certainly known;—Hugh of Ely, Richard of St. David's, and Henry of London, who were canonically incompetent to join in the consecration, having been suspended by Boniface, and not yet restored—being also present. He was made Cardinal of Oporto, and resigned his Archbishopric, 1277.*

80, (48,) John *Peckham*, consecrated by Nicholas III., 186th
1278. Bishop of Rome, 1278; died 1294.†

81, (49,) Robert *Winchelsey*, consecrated by Suabino, a
1294. Cardinal Bishop, September 12, 1294; died 1313.‡

82, (50,) Walter *Reynold*, consecrated by Robert and his
1313. suffragans, Bishop of Worcester, October 13, 1308; translated to Canterbury, October 24, 1313; died 1328.§

83, (51,) Simon *Mepham*, consecrated by John XXII. Bishop
1328. of Oporto, 194th Bishop of Rome, September 26, 1328; died October 14, 1332.||

84, (52,) John *Stratford*, consecrated Bishop of Winchester,
1333. by Cardinal Vitali, Archbishop of Albanense, June

---

* Mat. Par. 1008. Guth. i. 259, 291. Rapin, i. 354.

† Ann. Wav. 232, in Guth. ii. 261, 264. Stowe, Chron. 200. God. 100.

‡ Chron. Lich. Whar. i. 117. Guth. ii. 264, 268. Ush. MSS.

§ God. 103, 105, 462. Stowe, 229. Guth. ii. 269, 273. Rym. iii. 439, 454.

|| Can. Lich. Whar. i. 118. God. 105. Stowe, 231. Guth. ii. 273, 4. Hard. vii. 1857.

26, 1323; translated to Canterbury, December 6, 1333; died 1348.*

85, (53,) 1349. THOMAS *Bradwardine*, consecrated by Bertrand, a Cardinal Bishop, July 19, 1349; died same year.†

86, (54,) 1349. SIMON *Islip*, consecrated January 13, 1349, by Rodolph Stratford, Bishop of London; William Edendon, Bishop of Winchester; and John Thorsby, Bishop of St. David's;—Rodolph having been consecrated March 12, 1339, William, May 14, 1346, and John, September 23, 1347, by John Stratford and his suffragans. He died 1366.‡

87, (55,) 1366. SIMON *Langham*, consecrated by Islip and his suffragans, Bishop of Ely, March 19, 1362; translated to Canterbury, November 4, 1366; made Bishop of Præneste, and died, 1367.§

88, (56,) 1368. WILLIAM *Wittlesey*, consecrated by Islip and his suffragans, Bishop of Rochester, Feb. 6, 1361; translated to Worcester, 1362, and to Canterbury, Oct. 5, 1368; died 1375.‖

89, (57,) 1375. SIMON *Sudbury*, consecrated by Islip and his suffragans, Bishop of London, March 30, 1362; translated to Canterbury, May 4, 1375; murdered 1381.¶

90, (58,) 1381. WILLIAM *Courtnay*, consecrated by Wittlesey and his suffragans, Bishop of Hereford, 1369; trans-

---

* Rym. iv. 583. God. 110. † God. 111. Stowe, 247.

‡ Chron. Lich. Whar. i. 119. God. 58, 113, 185, 265, 581. Stowe, 266. Guth. ii. 281, 284.

§ God. 115, 265. Guth. ii. 284, 5.

‖ Reg. Wit. 1. God. 532. Rym. vi. 596. Stowe, 270. Guth. ii. 286.

¶ Reg. Sud. 1. Hard. vii. 1887. Stowe, 287. Guth. 286, 311.

lated to London, 1370, and thence to Canterbury, 1381; died August 1, 1396.*

91, (59,) 1396. THOMAS *Arundel*, consecrated by Wittlesey, Bishop of Ely, April 6, 1375; translated to York, April 3, 1388, and thence to Canterbury, Oct. 13, 1396; died Feb. 20, 1414.†

92, (60,) 1414. HENRY *Chichely*, consecrated June 12, 1409, Bishop of St. David's, by Gregory XII., Bishop of Venice,—Patriarch of Jerusalem, and 203d Bishop of Rome; translated to Canterbury, May 5, 1414; died 1443.‡

93, (61,) 1443. JOHN *Stafford*, consecrated May 17, 1425, by Chichely and his suffragans, Bishop of Bath and Wells; translated to Canterbury, May 3, 1443; died 1452.§

94, (62,) 1452. JOHN *Kemp*, consecrated July 6, 1419, by Chichely and his suffragans, Bishop of Rochester; translated to Chichester, March 2, 1420, thence to York, April 8, 1421, and thence to Canterbury, Aug. 12, 1452; died 1454.||

95, (63,) 1454. THOMAS *Bourcher*, consecrated May 15, 1435, by Chichely and his suffragans, Bishop of Worcester; translated to Ely, Dec. 20, 1443, and thence to Canterbury, April 22, 1454; died 1486.¶

96, (64,) 1486. JOHN *Morton*, consecrated Jan. 31, 1478, by Bourcher and his suffragans, Bishop of Ely; translated to Canterbury, Oct. 6, 1486; died Oct., 1501.**

---

* Reg. Court. 324. Stowe, 294, 313. Guth. 648. Hard. vii. 1889.

† Can. Lich. Whar. i. 122. Rym. vii. 537. God. 266. Hard. vii. 1923. Stowe, 344. Guth. ii. 454.

‡ Reg. Chich. i. 2. Stowe, 344, 383.

§ Reg. Chich. i. 38. God. 127. Stowe, 383, 396.

|| Reg. Chich. ii. 23, 32. Reg. Kemp. 210. God. 692. Stowe, 396, 398.

¶ Reg. Chich. ii. 52. Reg. Staff. 13. God. 129. Stowe, 398, 471. Hard. ix. 1376.

** Hist. Ely in God. 131. Stowe, 471, 482. Hard. ix. 1517.

97, (65,) 1501. HENRY *Dean*, consecrated by Morton and his suffragans, Bishop of Bangor, 1496; translated to Salisbury, 1500, and thence to Canterbury, 1501; died Feb. 16, 1503.*

98, (66,) 1503. WILLIAM *Warham*, consecrated by Dean and his suffragans, Bishop of London, Sept. 30, or Oct. 1, 1502; translated to Canterbury, July 2, 1503; died August 23, 1532.†

This brings us down to the predecessor of Archbishop Cranmer. From that time to the present, we shall give the names of the consecrators of each consecrator, in order to give our readers the means of judging for themselves, how idle are the objections made to the succession, and how unfounded are all pretences of a break in it. We give immediately under the name of the Bishop, reference to the original Register where the consecration is recorded; and immediately under that, the various dioceses to which the several Bishops mentioned, have been translated. It will be seen from this list, that we do not trace our succession through Cranmer's successor, Cardinal Pole.‡ We give, therefore, his

* God. 132, 625. Stowe, 482, 484.

† Whar. i. 124. God. 132, 190. Hard. ix. 1918. Burn. i. 168.

‡ SUCCESSION OF ARCHBISHOP POLE.

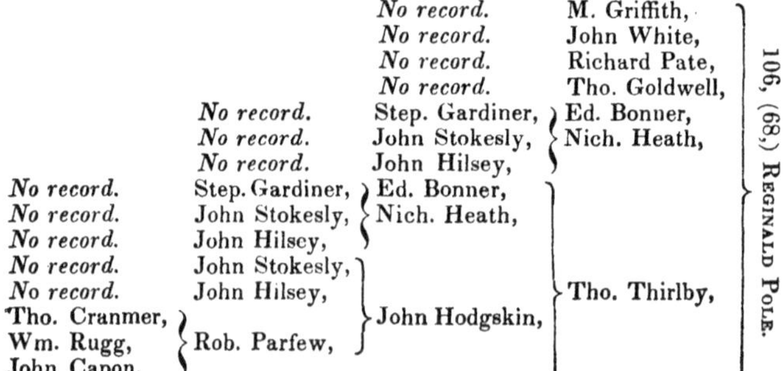

succession, so far as it can be traced, from which it appears, that the only one of his consecrators whose succession can be traced historically, traces it through Hodgskins, one of the consecrators of his successor, Matthew Parker. But inasmuch as only *three* Bishops are necessary to the regular consecration of a Bishop, and inasmuch as there have often been more than this number engaged in the consecration of the Bishops of England, we shall give the names of only three.

Among the persons mentioned as consecrators of English Bishops, consecrated previous to Standish, are Robert Sherbourne, consecrated Bishop of St. Davids, 1505; translated to Chichester, 1508;* John Fisher, (Cardinal,) consecrated Bishop of Rochester, 1504;† Cuthbert Tunstall, consecrated Bishop of Durham, 1530;‡ Nicholas West, consecrated Bishop of Ely, by Archbishop Warham, 1515.§

Name of Bishop.	*Diocese.*	*Consecrators.*
1, Henry Standish,	St. Asaph,	July 6, 1715.
War. Reg. 21.		WARHAM, Canterbury.
		Sherborn, Chichester.
		John Young, Tit. Bp.
2, John Voysey,	Exeter,	Nov. 6, 1715.
War. Reg. 22.		WARHAM.
		John Rochester.
		Thomas Leighlin.
3, John Longland,	Lincoln,	May 5, 1721.
War. Reg. 23.		WARHAM.
		Fisher, (Cardinal.)
		John Exeter, 2.

* Reg. War. 12.
† Rich. God. Roffen. *Ann.* 1504.
‡ Rich. God. Dunelm. *Ann.* 1530.
§ Reg War. 19.

Name of Bishop.	*Diocese.*	*Consecrators.*
4, THOMAS CRANMER, 99 from St. John, (67) Archbishop of Canterbury,	Canterbury,	March 30, 1533.
Cran. Reg. 4.		John Lincoln, 3.
		John Exeter, 2.
		Henry St. Asaph, 1.
5, John Capon,	Bangor,	April 19, 1534.
or Salcott,		Thomas Canterbury, 4.
Cran. Reg. 162.		John Lincoln, 3.
		Christopher Sidon.
6, Hugh Latimer,	Worcester,	1535.
Lam. Reg. 173.		*Names of Consecrators not given.*
7, William Rugg,	Norwich,	1536.
or Repps.		Ib.
Lam. Reg. 200, 212.		
8, Robert Parfew,	St. Asaph,	July 2, 1536.
or Wharton,		Thomas Canterbury, 4.
Cran. Reg. 197.		John Bangor, 5.
Hereford, 1554.		William Norwich, 7.
9, John Hilsey,	Rochester,	1536.
		Names consec. not given.
10, John Hodgskin,	Bedford,	Dec. 9, 1537.
Cran. Reg. 203, 204.		John (Stokely) London.
		John Rochester, 9.
		Robert St. Asaph, 8.
11, Henry Holbeach,	Bristol,	March 24, 1537.
Cran. Reg. 215.		John Rochester, 9.
Rochester, 1544.		Hugh Worcester, 6.
Lincoln, 1547.		Robert St. Asaph, 8.
12, Nicholas Ridley,	Rochester,	Sept. 5, 1547.
Cran. Reg. 321.		Henry Lincoln, 11.
London, 1550.		John Bedford, 10.
		Thomas Sidon.

Name of Bishop.	*Diocese.*	*Consecrators.*
13, Miles Coverdale,	Exeter,	Aug. 30, 1551.
Cran. Reg. 334.		Thomas Canterbury, 4.
		Nicholas London, 12.
		John Bedford, 10.
14, John Scory,	Rochester,	Aug. 30, 1551.
Cran. Reg. 333.		Thomas Canterbury, 4.
Chichester, 1551.		Nicholas London, 12.
Hereford, 1559.		John Bedford, 10.
REGINALD POLE, 100 from St. John, (68) Archbishop of Canterbury.		
15, MATTHEW PARKER, 101 from St. John, (69) Archbishop of Canterbury,	Canterbury,	Dec. 17, 1559.
Park. Reg. 10.		John Hereford, 14.
		John Bedford, 10.
		Miles Exeter, 13.
		William Barlow.*

* As the Jesuits endeavor to invalidate the consecration of Parker, because we are unable to trace historically the succession of Barlow, one of the consecrators, it will be well to state the facts in detail, in regard to him.

William Barlow, Doctor and Professor of Divinity, and Prior of the Canons regular of Bisham, was elected Bishop of St. Asaph, by royal license, dated January 7, 1525, 27th Henry VIII. The royal assent being given, February 22d, he was consecrated and confirmed in his See by the Archbishop, February 23d. Richard Rawlins, the eightieth Bishop of St. David's, having died on the eighteenth of February, 1535, Barlow was translated to that See in the month of April following, which, as the year began at the Vernal Equinox, was early in 1536. The Archbishop's act of consecration is dated April 21, 1536, 28th Henry VIII. William Knight, the forty-fifth Bishop of Bath and Wells, died Sept. 29, 1547, and Barlow was again translated by virtue of letters patent of Edward VI., dated Feb. 3, 1548. He continued Bishop of Bath and Wells till the accession of Mary, when he fled to Germany, and continued to live there in poverty and exile till he was recalled by Elizabeth. During the eighteen years of his Episcopate in the Sees of St.

Name of Bishop.	*Diocese.*	*Consecrators.*
16, EDMUND GRINDAL, of Canterbury,	102 from London,	St. John, (70) Archbishop Dec. 21, 1559.
Par. Reg. 18.		Matthew Canterbury, 15.
York, 1570.		John Hereford, 14.
Canterbury, 1573.		John Bedford, 10.
17, Edwin Sandes,	Worcester,	Dec. 21, 1559.
Par. Reg. 32.		Matthew Canterbury, 15.
London, 1570.		John Hereford, 14.
York, 1576.		John Bedford, 10.

David and Bath and Wells, he was present and assisting at the consecration of Arthur Bulkly, Bishop of Bangor, Feb. 19, 1541. John Christopherson, the forty-first Bishop of Chichester, died January 1st or 2d, 1557–8, and Barlow was elected his successor; but as Cardinal Pole died Nov. 17, 1558, the same day on which Queen Mary died, the See of Canterbury was vacant, and consequently there could be no confirmation of Barlow's election by the Metropolitan, as the law required. For this reason, in Elizabeth's commission to consecrate Parker, dated Dec. 6, 2d Eliz., (1559,) he is styled " William Barlow, sometime Lord Bishop of Bath and Wells, now elect of Chichester." The consecration of Parker took place Dec. 17, 1559. The royal assent was given to the election of Barlow, Dec. 18, 1559, and on the 20th of December, he received the confirmation of the Archbishop. The temporalities were restored to him on the 23d of March, following, or the beginning of the new year. He held the See of Chichester till his death, which took place August 13th, 1568. It may also be added, on the question of the canonicalness of Abp. Parker's consecration, that all the consecrations in the time of Mary were uncanonical, having been made by authority of the Bishop of Rome, whose authority had been renounced by the Synods of the Anglican Church. Consequently, these had no canonical right to consecrate any Bishop in England. The Bishops, therefore, who alone could canonically consecrate Parker, were Salisbury of Thetford, Barlow, late of Chichester, Hodgskins of Bedford, Bonner of London, Thirlby of Ely, Kitchen of Llandaff, Coverdale, late of Exeter, Scory, late of Bath and Wells. Of these, Bonner and Thirlby were incapacitated, having been concerned in the murder of their metropolitan, *Cranmer*. The remainder assented to the consecration, and four of them performed it.

Name of Bishop.	*Diocese.*	*Consecrators*
18, Thomas Young,	St. David's,	Jan. 21, 1560.
Par. Reg. 54.		Matthew Canterbury, 15.
York, 1560.		Edmund London, 16.
		John Bedford, 10.
19, Robert Horne,	Winchester,	Feb. 16, 1560.
Par. Reg. 88.		Matthew Canterbury, 15.
		Thomas St. David's, 18.
		Edmund London, 16.
20, John Piers,	Rochester,	April 15, 1575.
Grind. Reg. 17.		Edmund Canterbury, 16.
Salisbury, 1575.		Edwin London, 17.
York, 1588.		Robert Winchester, 19.
21, John Aylmer,	London,	March 24, 1576.
Grind. Reg. 27.		Edmund Canterbury, 16.
		Edwin York, 17.
		John Rochester, 20.
22, JOHN WHITGIFT, 103 from St. John, (71) Archbishop of Canterbury,	Worcester,	April 21, 1577.
Grind. Reg. 34.		Edmund Canterbury, 16.
Canterbury, 1583.		John London, 21.
		Robert Winchester, 19.
23, John Young,	Rochester,	March 16, 1577.
Grind. Reg. 43.		Edmund Canterbury, 16.
		John London, 21.
		John Salisbury, 20.
24, Richard Fletcher,	Bristol,	Dec. 14, 1589.
Whit. Reg. 62.		John Canterbury, 22.
Worcester, 1593.		John London, 21.
London, 1594.		John Rochester, 23.
25, Richard Vaughan,	Bangor,	June 25, 1595.
Whit. Reg. 71.		John Canterbury, 22.
Chester, 1597.		Richard London, 24.
London, 1604.		John Rochester, 23.

Name of Bishop.	*Diocese.*	*Consecrators.*
26, Anthony Watson,	Chichester,	Aug. 15, 1596.
Whit. Reg. 90.		John Canterbury, 22.
		John Rochester, 23.
		Richard Bangor, 25.
27, RICHARD BANCROFT, 104 from St. John, (72) Archbishop of Canterbury,	London,	May 8, 1597.
Whit. Reg. 82.		John Canterbury, 22.
Canterbury, 1604.		John Rochester, 23.
		Richard Bangor, 25.
28, William Barlow,	Rochester,	June 30, 1605.
Banc. Reg. 35.		Richard Canterbury, 27.
Lincoln, 1608.		Richard London, 25.
		Anthony Chichester, 26.
29, Launcelot Andrews,	Chichester,	Nov. 3, 1605.
Banc. Reg. 42.		Richard Canterbury, 27.
Ely, 1609.		Richard London, 25.
Winchester, 1618.		William Rochester, 28.
30, James Montague,	Bath and Wells,	April 17, 1608.
Banc. Reg. 68.		Richard Canterbury, 27.
		William Rochester, 28.
		Launcelot Chichester, 29.
31, Richard Neyle,	Rochester,	Oct. 9, 1609.
Banc. Reg. 83.		Richard Canterbury, 27.
Coventry, 1610.		Launcelot Chichester, 29.
Lincoln, 1613.		James Bath and Wells, 30.
Durham, 1617.		
Winchester, 1627.		
32, GEORGE ABBOTT, 105 from St. John, (73) Archbishop of Canterbury,	Lichfield,	Dec. 3, 1609.
Banc. Reg. 96.		Richard Canterbury, 27.
London, 1609.		Launcelot Ely, 29.
Canterbury, 1611.		Richard Rochester, 31.

Name of Bishop.	*Diocese*	*Consecrators.*
33, Samuel Harsnet,	Chichester,	Dec. 3, 1609.
Banc. Reg. 102.		Richard Canterbury, 27.
Norwich, 1619.		Launcelot Ely, 29.
York, 1628.		Richard Rochester, 31.
34, John Buckeridge,	Rochester,	June 9, 1611.
Abb. Reg. i. 26.		George Canterbury, 32.
Ely, 1628.		Launcelot Ely, 29.
		Richard Coventry, 31.
34*, John King,	London,	Sept. 8, 1611.
Abb. Reg. i. 28.		George Canterbury, 32.
		Richard Coventry, 31.
		John Rochester, 34.
35, Nicholas Felton,	Bristol,	Dec. 14, 1617.
Abb. Reg. i. 93.		George Canterbury, 32.
Ely, 1619.		John Rochester, 34.
		Launcelot Ely, 29.
		Mark, Archbishop Spalatro.
36, George Monteigne,	Lincoln,	Dec. 14, 1617.
Abb. Reg. i. 105.		George Canterbury, 32.
London, 1621.		John Rochester, 34.
		John London, 34*.
		Mark, Archbishop Spalatro.
37, John Howson,	Oxford,	May 9, 1619.
		George Canterbury, 32.
Durham, 1621.		John Rochester, 34.
		Nicholas Ely, 35.
38, John Williams,	Lincoln,	Nov. 11, 1621.
Abb. Reg. ii. 62.		George London, 36.
York, 1641.		Nicholas Ely, 35.
		John Oxford, 37.

Name of Bishop.	*Diocese.*	*Consecrators.*
39, William Laud, 106 from St. John, (74) Archbishop of Canterbury,	St. David's,	Nov. 18, 1621.
Abb. Reg. ii. 69.		George London, 36.
Bath and Wells, 1627.		Nicholas Ely, 35.
London, 1628.		John Oxford, 37.
Canterbury, 1633.		
40, Robert Wright,	Bristol,	March 23, 1622.
Abb. Reg. ii. 85.		George Canterbury, 32.
Coventry, 1632.		John Lincoln, 38.
		Launcelot Winchester, 29.
41, Joseph Hall,	Exeter,	Dec. 23, 1627.
Abb. Reg. ii. 114.		George London, 36.
		John Rochester, 34.
		Richard Durham, 31.
42, Walter Curl,	Rochester,	Sept. 7, 1628.
Abb. Reg. ii. 156.		George Canterbury, 32.
Bath and Wells, 1629.		Richard Winchester, 31.
Winchester, 1632.		John Ely, 34.
43, John Bowle,	Rochester,	Feb. 7, 1629.
Abb. Reg. iii. 17.		George Canterbury, 36.
		Samuel York, 33.
		Walter Bath and Wells, 42.
44, William Juxon, 107 from St. John, (75) Archbishop of Canterbury,	London,	Oct. 7, 1633.
Laud. Reg. i. 18.		William Canterbury, 39.
Canterbury, 1660.		Richard York, 31.
		John Rochester, 43.
45, Matthew Wren,	Hereford,	March 8, 1634.
Laud. Reg. i. 44.		William Canterbury, 39.
Norwich, 1635.		Walter Winchester, 42.
Ely, 1638.		Joseph Exeter, 41.

Name of Bishop.	*Diocese.*	*Consecrators.*
46, Robert Skinner,	Bristol,	Jan. 15, 1636.
Laud. Reg. i. 66.		William Canterbury, 39.
Oxford, 1640.		William London, 44.
Worcester, 1663.		Matthew Norwich, 45.
47, Brian Duppa,	Chichester,	June 17, 1638.
Laud. Reg. ii. 46.		William Canterbury, 39.
Salisbury, 1641.		Robert Coventry, 40.
Winchester, 1660.		Matthew Ely, 45.
48, Accepted Freewen,	Lichfield and Coventry,	April, 1643.
Wood Ath. Oxon. ii. 1147.		John York, 38.
York, 1660.		Robert Oxford, 46.
		Brian Salisbury, 47.

From the death of Charles I., in January, 1648–9, to the restoration of Charles II., in 1660, Sir Edward Hyde, afterwards Earl of Clarendon, was, under Providence, the prop and stay of the fallen Episcopacy. The last consecration in England, before the subversion of the monarchy, took place in 1643; and at the time of the King's execution there were but twenty Bishops living. Of these, eleven died before the restoration. With good reason, therefore, did Sir Edward express himself in the following manner, in his correspondence with Dr. John Barwick: "I will not mention the age of the consecrators, though it hath put me into many a fright. If I were a Presbyterian, I should hope to spin out the time till all the Bishops were dead. I do wish, in all events, that the succession were provided for. The conspiracies to destroy it are very evident, and if there can be no combination to preserve it, it must expire. I do assure you, the names of all the Bishops who are alive, and their several ages, are as well known at Rome as in England; and both the *Papist* and *Presbyterian* value themselves very much, upon computing in how few years the Church of England must expire. God knows it will be almost a miracle, if the winter doth not take away half the Bishops that are left alive," &c. &c. In consequence of these earnest expressions of alarm, authority was obtained in 1659, from Charles II., then at Brussels, nominating for consecration Dr. Hammond, Dr. Sheldon, Dr. Lany or Lancy, Dr. Ferne, and Dr. Walton. But the restoration of the King and the re-establishment of the Church rendered this measure unnecessary. Of the nine Bishops then restored, one died in 1662, one in 1663, one in 1664, one in 1665, one in 1666, one in 1667, one in 1669, and two in 1670.*

Name of Bishop.	*Diocese.*	*Consecrators.*
49, GILBERT SHELDON, 108 from of Canterbury,	London,	St. John, (76) Archbishop Oct. 18, 1660.
Jux. Reg. 208.		Brian Winchester, 47.
Canterbury, 1663.		Accepted York, 48.
		Matthew Ely, 45.
50, Humphrey Hinchman,	Salisbury,	Oct. 18, 1660.
Jux. Reg. 208.		Brian Winchester, 47.
London, 1663.		Accepted York, 48.
		Matthew Ely, 45.
51, George Morley,	Worcester,	Oct. 18, 1660.
Jux. Reg. 208.		Brian Winchester, 47.
Winchester, 1662.		Accepted York, 48.
		Matthew Ely, 45.
52, Seth Ward,	Exeter,	July 20, 1662.
Jux. Reg. 302.		Gilbert London, 49.
Salisbury, 1667.		George Winchester, 51.
		Humphrey Salisbury, 50.
53, John Dolben,	Rochester,	Nov. 25, 1666.
Shel. Reg. 6.		Gilbert Canterbury, 49.
York, 1683.		Humphrey London, 50.
		George Winchester, 51.

* Mason's Vinc. Trans. Pref. § 31. p. lxxi.

Name of Bishop.	*Diocese.*	*Consecrators.*
54, Peter Mewes,	Bath and Wells,	Feb. 9, 1672.
Shel. Reg. 108.		Gilbert Canterbury, 49.
Winchester, 1684.		Humphrey London, 50.
		John Rochester, 53.
55, Henry Compton,	Oxford,	Dec. 6, 1746.
Shel. Reg. 123.		Gilbert Canterbury, 49.
London, 1675.		Seth Salisbury, 52.
		John Rochester, 53.
56, William Sancroft, 109 from St. John, (77) Archbishop of Canterbury,	Canterbury,	Jan. 27, 1677.
Sanc. Reg. 7.		Henry London, 55.
		Seth Salisbury, 52.
		John Rochester, 53.
57, William Lloyd,	St. Asaph,	Oct. 3, 1680.
Sanc. Reg. 43.		William Canterbury, 56.
Coventry, 1692.		Henry London, 55.
Worcester, 1699.		John Rochester, 53.
58, Thomas Spratt,	Rochester,	Nov. 2, 1684.
Sanc. Reg. 102.		William Canterbury, 56.
		Henry London, 55.
		Seth Salisbury, 52.
59, Jonathan Trelawney,	Bristol,	Nov. 8, 1685.
Sanc. Reg. 142.		William Canterbury, 56.
Exeter, 1689.		Henry London, 55.
Winchester, 1707.		Peter Winchester, 54.
60, Gilbert Burnett,	Salisbury,	March 31, 1689.
Sanc. Reg. 190.		Henry London, 55.
		William St. Asaph, 57.
		Peter Winchester, 54.
61, John Hough,	Oxford,	May 11, 1690.
Reg. Dean and Chap. Cant. 25.		Henry London, 55.
Coventry, 1669.		William St. Asaph, 57.
Worcester, 1717.		Peter Winchester, 54.

Name of Bishop.	*Diocese.*	*Consecrators.*
62, JOHN TILLOTSON, Canterbury,	110 from St. John, (78) Archbishop of Canterbury,	May 21, 1691.
Till. Reg. 9.		Peter Winchester, 54. William St. Asaph, 57. Gilbert Salisbury, 60.
63, THOMAS TENISON, of Canterbury,	111 from St. John, (79) Archbishop Lincoln,	Jan. 10, 1691.
Till. Reg. 95. Canterbury, 1694.		John Canterbury, 62. Henry London, 55. Gilbert Salisbury, 60.
64, John Evans,	Bangor,	Jan. 4, 1701.
Ten. Reg. i. 58. Meath, 1715.		Thomas Canterbury, 63. Henry London, 55. Gilbert Salisbury, 60.
65, WILLIAM WAKE, Canterbury,	112 from St. John, (80) Archbishop of Lincoln,	Oct. 21, 1705.
Ten. Reg. i. 100. Canterbury, 1715.		Thomas Canterbury, 63. Henry London, 55. Gilbert Salisbury, 60.
66, Richard Willis,	Gloucester,	Jan. 16, 1714.
Ten. Reg. i. 146. Salisbury, 1721. Winchester, 1723.		Gilbert Salisbury, 60. John Coventry, 61. John Bangor, 64.
67, JOHN POTTER, Canterbury,	113 from St. John, (81) Archbishop of Oxford,	May 15, 1715.
Ten. Reg. i. 176. Canterbury, 1737.		Jonathan Winchester, 59. William Lincoln, 65. Richard Gloucester, 66.
68, Edmund Gibson,	Lincoln,	Feb. 12, 1715.
Wake Reg. i. 21. London, 1723.		William Canterbury, 65. Jonathan Winchester, 59. Richard Gloucester, 66.

Name of Bishop.	*Diocese*	*Consecrators.*
69, Joseph Wilcocks,	Gloucester,	Dec. 3, 1721.
Wake Reg. i. 113.		William Canterbury, 65.
Rochester, 1731.		Richard Salisbury, 66.
		Edmund Lincoln, 68.
70, Richard Reynolds,	Bangor,	Dec. 3, 1721.
Wake Reg. i. 104.		William Canterbury, 65.
Lincoln, 1723.		Richard Salisbury, 66.
		Edmund Lincoln, 68.
71, Thomas Tanner,	St. Asaph,	Jan. 23, 1731.
Wake Reg. ii. 92.		William Canterbury, 65.
		Edmund London, 68.
		Joseph Rochester, 69.
72, Nicholas Clagett,	St. David's,	Jan. 23, 1731.
Wake Reg. ii. 100.		William Canterbury, 65.
Exeter, 1743.		Edmund London, 68.
		Joseph Rochester, 69.
73, Martin Benson,	Gloucester,	Jan. 19, 1734.
Wake Reg. ii. 153.		Edmund London, 68.
		John Oxford, 67.
		Joseph Rochester, 69.
74, THOMAS SECKER, 116 from St. John, (84) Archbishop of Canterbury,	Bristol,	Jan. 19, 1734.
Wake Reg. ii. 163.		Edmund London, 68.
Oxford, 1737.		John Oxford, 67.
Canterbury, 1758.		Joseph Rochester, 69.
75, THOMAS HERRING, 114 from St. John, (82) Archbishop of Canterbury,	Bangor,	Jan. 15, 1737.
Pot. Reg. 41.		John Canterbury, 67.
York, 1743.		Nicholas St. David's, 72.
Canterbury, 1747.		Joseph Rochester, 69.

Name of Bishop.	*Diocese.*	*Consecrators.*
76, Joseph Butler,	Bristol,	Dec. 3, 1738.
Pot. Reg. 68.		John Canterbury, 67.
Durham, 1750.		Joseph Rochester, 69.
		Nicholas St. David's, 72.
77, Edward Willes,	St. David's,	Jan. 2, 1742.
Pot. Reg. 114.		John Canterbury, 67.
Bath and Wells, 1743.		Joseph Rochester, 69.
		Richard Lincoln, 70.
78, MATTHEW HUTTON, 115 from St. John, (83) Archbishop of Canterbury,	Bangor,	Nov. 13, 1743.
Pot. Reg. 146.		Joseph Rochester, 69.
York, 1747.		Nicholas Exeter, 72.
Canterbury, 1757.		Joseph Bristol, 76.
79, John Thomas,	Lincoln,	April 1, 1744.
Pot. Reg. 169.		John Canterbury, 67.
Salisbury, 1757.		Joseph Rochester, 69.
Winchester, 1757.		Martin Gloucester, 73.
80, Richard Trevor,	St. David's,	April 1, 1744.
Pot. Reg. 190.		John Canterbury, 67.
Durham, 1752.		Joseph Rochester, 69.
		Martin Gloucester, 73.
81, Zachary Pearce,	Bangor,	Feb. 2, 1747.
Herr. Reg. 38.		Thomas Canterbury, 75.
Rochester, 1756.		Joseph Rochester, 69.
		Martin Gloucester, 73.
82, Robert Hay Drummond,	St. Asaph,	April 24, 1748.
Her. Reg. 65.		Thomas Canterbury, 75.
Salisbury, 1761.		Joseph Rochester, 69.
York, 1761.		Martin Gloucester, 73.

Name of Bishop.	*Diocese.*	*Consecrators.*
83, FREDERICK CORNWALLIS, 117 from St. John, (85) Archbishop of Canterbury,	Lichfield and Coventry,	Feb. 18, 1749.
Her. Reg. 121.		Thomas Canterbury, 75.
Canterbury, 1768.		Joseph Rochester, 69.
		Martin Gloucester, 73.
84, James Johnson,	Gloucester,	Dec. 10, 1752.
Her. Reg. 171.		Thomas Canterbury, 75.
Worcester, 1759.		Joseph Rochester, 69.
		Zachary Bangor, 81.
85, Edmund Keene,	Chester,	March 22, 1752.
Her. Reg. 154.		Thomas Canterbury, 75.
Ely, 1771.		Joseph Durham, 76.
		Frederick Lichfield, 83.
86, John Hume,	Bristol,	July 4, 1756.
Her. Reg. 244.		Thomas Oxford, 74.
Oxford, 1758.		Zachary Rochester, 81.
Salisbury, 1766.		Edmund Chester, 85.
87, John Egerton,	Bangor,	July 4, 1756.
Her. Reg. 255.		Thomas Oxford, 74.
Coventry, 1768.		Zachary Rochester, 81.
Durham, 1771.		Edmund Chester, 85.
88, Richard Terrick,	Peterborough,	June 3, 1757.
Hutt. Reg. 42.		Matthew Canterbury, 78.
London, 1764.		Edmund Chester, 85.
		John Bristol, 86.
89, Philip Younge,	Bristol,	June 29, 1758.
Seck. Reg. 30.		Thomas Canterbury, 74.
Norwich, 1761.		Zachary Rochester, 81.
		John Oxford, 86.
90, Robert Lowth,	St. David's,	June 15, 1766.
Seck. Reg. 235.		Thomas Canterbury, 74.
Oxford, 1766.		Richard London, 88.
		Edw. Bath and Wells, 77.

Name of Bishop.	*Diocese.*	*Consecrators.*
91, Charles Moss,	St. David's,	Nov. 30, 1766.
Seck. Reg. 261.		Richard London, 88.
Bath and Wells, 1774.		John Winchester, 79.
		Edw. Bath and Wells, 77.
92, Shute Barrington,	Llandaff,	Oct. 1, 1769.
Corn. Reg. 82.		Frederick Canterbury, 83.
Durham, 1791.		Richard London, 88.
		Zachary Rochester, 81.
93, John Hinchcliffe,	Peterborough,	Dec. 17, 1769.
Corn. Reg. 93.		Frederick Canterbury, 83.
		Richard London, 88.
		John Winchester, 79.
94, William Markham,	Chester,	Feb. 17, 1771.
Corn. Reg. 113.		Robert York, 82.
York, 1777.		Richard Durham, 80.
		James Worcester, 84.
95, John Thomas,	Rochester,	Nov. 13, 1774.
Corn. Reg. 171.		Richard London, 88.
		Philip Norwich, 89.
		Shute Llandaff, 92.
96, John Moore, 118 from St. John, (86) Archbishop of Canterbury,	Bangor,	Feb. 12, 1775.
Corn. Reg. 204.		Frederick Canterbury, 83.
Canterbury, 1783.		Edmund Ely, 85.
		Robert Oxford, 90.
97, Beilby Porteus,	Chester,	Feb. 9, 1777.
Corn. Reg. 25.		William York, 94.
London, 1787.		John Durham, 87.
		Shute Llandaff, 92.

Name of Bishop.	*Diocese.*	*Consecrators.*
WILLIAM WHITE,	Pennsylvania,	Feb. 4, 1787.
Moore Reg. 33.		John Canterbury, 96.
		William York, 94.
		Chas. Bath and Wells, 91.
		John Peterborough, 93.
SAMUEL PROVOOST,	New York,	Feb. 4, 1787.
Moore Reg. 33.		John Canterbury, 96.
		William York, 94.
		Chas. Bath and Wells, 91.
		John Peterborough, 93.
JAMES MADISON,	Virginia,	Sept. 19, 1790.
Moore Reg. 192.		John Canterbury, 96.
		Beilby London, 97.
		John Rochester, 95.

We see from the facts already detailed, that Augustine traced his succession back through Irenæus to St. John, and consequently our succession properly comes from that source. But the succession of the later Bishops may be traced through the line of the Bishops of Rome, if desired. Thus Theodore, the seventh Archbishop of Canterbury, was consecrated by the Bishop of Rome, and filled the Arch-Episcopal chair, from 668 to 693, twenty-five years. Those Bishops, therefore, who were consecrated by him in England, could trace their succession, through him, back to St. Peter, and through those who assisted him in consecrating, back to St. John. Now in this time, *three* Bishops were consecrated in the Diocese of Lichfield and Coventry ; *two* in the Diocese of London ; *two* in the Diocese of Helham, now Norwich ; *four* in the Diocese of Rochester ; *two* in the Diocese of Winchester ; *three* in the Diocese of Worcester ; and perhaps others in other places. Consequently, all the ancient Dioceses of Canterbury must have been filled with Bishops who could trace their succession in both of these ways, and hence, all subsequent Bishops must be able to do the same.

The successor of Theodore,—Birthwald, was consecrated by Godwin, according to some manuscripts, Metropolitan Bishop of Walliarum, (*Wales*,)* but according to others of Galliarum, (*Gaul.*) The latter is generally supposed to be the most probable, as Godwin was at that time Archbishop of Lyons, to which the Archiepiscopate had been removed from Arles, which was the source from whence the Anglo-Saxon Bishops had originally derived their orders—Arles having received its Episcopate from Ephesus and St. John. But if Wales be the true reading, it will be seen that the Bishops of that country traced their succession to Jerusalem and St. John. Birthwald filled the Arch-Episcopal See thirty-nine years, from 693 to 732, in which time there were consecrated for the Diocese of Lincoln, *two* Bishops, *one* in Lichfield and Coventry; *one* in London; *one* in Rochester; *two* in Salisbury; *one* in Winchester; *one* in Worcester, and probably others. All the Bishops in the Province of Canterbury, subsequent to the time of Birthwald, must, therefore, have been able to trace their succession through him to Jerusalem and St. James, and through those who assisted him in consecrating, to St. John and to St. Peter.

Again, Theobald, the thirty-seventh Archbishop of Canterbury, was consecrated by Albert, Bishop of Ostia; and during his Episcopate there were consecrated *one* Bishop each, in the Dioceses of St. David's, Hereford, Lincoln, Norwich, Salisbury; *two* Bishops each in the Dioceses of Ely, Llandaff, London, Rochester, and Worcester. There have also been

---

* Odoceus, third Bishop of Llandaff, was consecrated by Theodore of Canterbury, the predecessor of Birthwald, and the successor of Odoceus was Ubilwin, which might have been mistaken for Godwin, by the copyists.

several other consecrations by foreign Bishops, as, Robert Winchelsy, forty-ninth Archbishop, by Suabino, John Stratford, fifty-second Archbishop, by Vitali, and Thomas Bradwardine, fifty-third Archbishop, by Bertrand, all Cardinal Bishops, so that the succession may be traced in a great variety of ways.

There is one other foreign Bishop that deserves notice. In 1617, MARK A. DE DOMINIS, the Archbishop of Spalatro, a Church in communion with the See of Rome, assisted in the consecration of Nicholas Felton and George Monteigne, and these assisted in the consecration of so many other Bishops, that since 1633, there has not been a Bishop consecrated in England that could not trace his succession to the Archbishops of Spalatro, and thence back to the Apostles. Consequently, if there had been any break in the succession before that time, we should now have a valid succession.

There was also a commingling of the Saxon and British lines, whether Birthwald was consecrated in France or Wales. Cead, the second Archbishop of York, and subsequently Bishop of the Mercians, was consecrated by Wine, Bishop of the West-Saxons, assisted by *two British Bishops*,—Wine himself having been consecrated in France. And Cead must have aided Theodore in the consecration of other Bishops, as the canonical number could not be made without him.

II. SUCCESSION FROM JERUSALEM.

At whatever age Christianity was first introduced into Britain, whether in the first century, as we shall see in the course of the work is probable, or, as others suppose, at a still later period, it was preached by Greek missionaries. This is evident from the fact, that the old Greek and British historians relate the same occurrences, in regard to that primitive period, so similarly, that both must have derived their knowledge from the same source, or from the records

28*

of contemporaneous historians. The British Liturgy was also of Eastern origin, and unlike that of Rome. Their ecclesiastical rites were also those of the East, and not of the West, notwithstanding there was frequent intercourse between the Churches of Rome and Britain. The conquest of the Britains by the Saxons, and their entire subjugation, has rendered it necessary for us to depend mostly upon foreign and Saxon writers for the history of the British Church. From these materials, Archbishop Usher,* and Bishop Stillingfleet,† have drawn the following facts.

In the year 624 or 626, February 20, Honorius, the seventieth Bishop of Rome, issued a Bull, in which it is stated as a well-known fact in history, that Lucius, a British King, in the second century, granted certain privileges to the University of Cambridge; and in the antiquities of Cambridge, in the somewhat doubtful Annals of Burton, A. D. 141, this is said to have been done for the reason that Christianity had been faithfully preached there. It is also said in the old Register of Llandaff, that Lucius sent an embassy to Rome, and that Elvanus was consecrated Bishop by Eleutherus, the twelfth Bishop of Rome."‡ The names of the earliest British Bishops have not generally been preserved, but the following Archbishops of London have come down to us, but whether they form the full line, is uncertain.

1. Theanus, who founded St. Peter's Church, Cornhill, died about 187.§

2. Elvanus, consecrated by Eleutherus, twelfth Bishop of Rome.||

3. Cadoc, or Cadar.

---

* Britann. Eccles. Antiq., quarto, Dublin, 1629. † Orig. Britann.

‡ Mon. Angl. vol. III. p. 188.

§ Joc. Furn. Lib. Epis. Brit. in Ush. Primor. p. 67.

|| Reg. Lland. in. Mon. Ang. vol. III. p. 186.

4. Obinus.
5. Conanus.
6. Palladius.
7. Stephanus, suffered martyrdom, Sept. 17, A. D. 303.
8. Iltutus, or Restitutus, one of the three British Bishops present at the Council of Arles, A. D. 312, or 314.
9. Theodwin, or Dedwin.
10. Theodred.
11. Hilary.
12. Guidelinus.
13. Vodin, slain by Hengist, the Dane.
14. Theonus, consecrated Bishop of Gloucester, translated to London, fled from the Saxons, A. D. 587, and with the great body of his clergy, accompanied by Thadioc, Archbishop of York, went and settled in Wales.*

Previous to this time, there had been three Archbishoprics in Britain—London, York, and Caerleon; the two first of which were destroyed by the Saxons, and the latter transferred to *Meneva*, now St. David's. Our knowledge of the Bishops of this See commences some time before this. As early as A. D. 448, Germanus and Severus, two Bishops of Gaul, visited Britain, at the request of the British clergy, and while there consecrated several Bishops, among whom was Dubritius, the first Archbishop of Llandaff, and Sampson, Archbishop of York. The Bishops of Llandaff, therefore, are properly the successors of Theonus and Thadioc.† Consequently, Dubritius could trace his succession through Germanus and the Gallican Bishops, to Ephesus, in the same manner as we have seen the Bishops of Lyons and Arles could trace their succession to the same source.

About the same time, David and Eliud, also called Teliaus, and Paternus, three Britons, visited Jerusalem, and David

* Mat. West. A. D. 587.

† Post, c. xxviii. Ann. 448.

was there consecrated Bishop of Meneva by the Patriarch of Jerusalem,* and A. D. 519 was made Archbishop of Wales, by vote of a Synod, at which all the British Bishops were present.† He died A. D. 544,‡ and was so famous as to be canonized even among the Saxon saints. David was succeeded by Eliud,§ and Eliud by Kenoc, or Kenev.||

Dubritius, Bishop of Llandaff, died December 18th, 522,¶ and was succeeded by Teliaus, who accompanied David to Jerusalem.** His successor was Odoceus, consecrated by Theodore, Archbishop of Canterbury.†† The Patriarchate, or Arch-diocese of Meneva, (St. David's,) contained seven Dioceses.‡‡ Six of these seven Dioceses, as they now stand, were formed between 450 and 600; (1,) St. David's, by David; (2,) Llandaff, by Dubritius; (3,) Bangor, by Daniel, the origin of whose succession will hereafter be shown; (4,) St. Asaph's, about A. D. 583, by Kentigern, before that time Bishop of Glasgow, from which he had been driven by war.§§ (5,) Hereford, by Putta, also Bishop of Rochester, 659, and translated to Hereford, 680.|||| The names of the two others are uncertain. The succession of the Bishops in this Archbishopric came through St. David from Jerusalem; through Dubritius from Gaul and Ephesus; and through Odoceus from Arles and Rome. And from them, these successions have been spread through the whole body of English Bishops.

---

* Vitâ à Giraldo Cambrensi, in Ussh. Prim. 474, 528.

† Vitâ David, John Tinm. in Ussh. Prim. 81. Still. Orig. 216. Girald. Camb. L. i. c. 5; L. ii. c. 1.

‡ Prim. Ecc. Brit. pp. 76, 82, 526.

§ Reg. Llandaff.

|| Giraldo Cambr. ii. 1.

¶ Ussh. Prim. 526, 527.

** Ib. 83, 84, 528.

†† Reg. Lland. and Rich. God. *in loco.*

‡‡ Bd. ii. 2. Hov. Ann. ii. 454, 5, and Walter Convent. A. D. 1199 Galf. Mon. i. 12. Prim. Brit. 88–92.

§§ John Tinm. Vitâ, Kentig. in Usshur.

|||| Bd. iv. 2.

We give the succession of Bishops of Jerusalem, through whom the consecrators of the several Bishops received their succession, from Graveson, *Historica Ecclesiastica*, Tome 9.

PATRIARCHS OF JERUSALEM.

	Name of Bishops.	*A. D.*
1,	JAMES ALPHEUS, one of the Apostles,	35.
2,	Simeon,	65.
3,	Justus I.,	107.
4,	Zacheus,	111.
5,	Tobias,	112.
6,	Benjamin,	117.
7,	John,	119.
8,	Matthew,	121.
9,	Philip,	122.
10,	Seneca,	126.
11,	Justus II.,	127.
12,	Levi,	128.
13,	Ephraim,	129.
14,	Joseph,	131.
15,	Judas, (last Jewish Bishop,)	132.
16,	Marcus, (first Gentile Bishop,)	134.
17,	Cassianus,	146.
18,	Publius,	154.
19,	Maximus I.,	159.
20,	Julian,	163.
21,	Caius I.,	165.
22,	Symmachus,	168.
23,	Caius II.,	170.
24,	Julian,	173.
25,	Maximus II.,	178.
26,	Antonius,	182.
27,	Capito,	186.
28,	Valens,	191.
29,	Dolchianus,	194.
30,	Narcissus, (resigned,)	196.
31,	Dius,	200.
32,	Germanio,	207.
33,	Gordius and Narcissus again,	211.
34,	Alexander,	237.
35,	Mazabanes,	251.
36,	Hymenæus,	265.
37,	Zambdas,	298.
38,	Herman,	300.
39,	Macarius I.,	310.
40,	Maximus III.,	315.
41,	Cyril, (expelled by Arians,)	330.
42,	Herenius,	350.
	Cyril, (restored, deposed again by Arians,)	361.
43,	Hilary, (an Arian,)	364.
	Cyril, (restored, and died,)	379.
44,	John II.,	386.
45,	Praglius,	416.

	Name of Bishops.	*A. D.*
46,	Juvenal,	424.
47,	Anastasius,	458.
48,	Martyrius,	478.
49,	Salutis,	486.
50,	Elias,	494.
51,	John III., who consecrated DAVID,	513.
52,	Peter Eleutheropolite,	524.
53,	Marcarius II.,	544.
54,	Eustachius,	552.
55,	John IV.,	572.
56,	Amos,	574–601.
57,	Isichius, or Isaacius,	601.
58,	Zacharius,	609.
59,	Modestus,	631.
60,	Sophronius,	633–637.

When Jerusalem was taken by the Saracens, and the Patriarchate broken up.

	Bishops of St. David's.	*A. D.*
52,	(1,) David, consecrated by 51st Patr. Jerusalem,	519.
53,	(2,) Eliud,	544.
54,	(3,) Keneva.	
55,	(4,) Morvael.	
56,	(5,) Haernurier.	
57,	(6,) Elvaeth.	
58,	(7,) Gurnel.	
59,	(8,) Lendywyth,	712.
60,	(9,) Gornwist.	
61,	(10,) Gorwan.	
62,	(11,) Cledanke.	
63,	(12,) Enyaen.	
64,	(13,) Eludgaeth.	
65,	(14,) Eldunen.	
66,	(15,) Elvaoth.	
67,	(16,) Maelscwyth.	
68,	(17,) Madenew.	
69,	(18,) Catulus,	841.
70,	(19,) Silvay,	850.

	Bishops of Llandaff.	*A. D.*
	(1,) Dubritius, consecrated by Germanus, of Auxerre, Lupus, of Tricasse, etc.	448.
	(2,) Teliaus.	
40,	(3,) Odoceus, consecrated by Theodore, of Canterbury.	
41,	(4,) Ubilwin.	
42,	(5,) Aidan,	720.
43,	(6,) Elgistil.	
44,	(7,) Lunapejus.	
45,	(8,) Cormergen.	
46,	(9,) Argwistil.	
47,	(10,) Gurvan.	
48,	(11,) Guodlin.	
49,	(12,) Edilbin.	
50,	(13,) Grecielus.	
51,	(14,) Berthygwyn.	
52,	(15,) Trychean.	
53,	(16,) Elvogus.	

Bishops of St. David's.	*A. D.*
71, (20,) Navnis,	873.
72, (21,) Sathveni.	
73, (22,) Diothwall.	
74, (23,) Asser,	906.
75, (24,) Athvael.	
76, (25,) Sampson, (last Archbishop,)	910.
77, (26,) Ruelin.	
78, (27,) Rodherch.	
79, (28,) Elguni.	
80, (29,) Llywarch.	
81, (30,) Nergu.	
82, (31,) Silhidw,	924.
83, (32,) Everu,	942.
84, (33,) Morgenai,	944.
85, (34,) Nathan.	
86, (35,) Roderick.	
87, (36,) Jevan.	
88, (37,) Argustel.	
89, (38,) Morgenneth,	1023.
90, (39,) Ervyn,	1039.
91, (40,) Tramerin,	1028.
92, (41,) Joseph,	1055.
93, (42,) Bleitherd,	1061.
94, (43,) Sulghein, resigned,	1070.
95, (44,) Abraham,	1076.
Sulghein again, resigned,	1076.
96, (45,) Rythmarch.	
97, (46,) Wilfrid.	1115.
98, (47,) Bernard, consecrated by Arch-	

Bishops of Llandaff.	*A. D.*
54, (17,) Catgwaret.	
55, (18,) Careuhir.	
56, (19,) Nobis.	
57, (20,) Guilfrid.	
58, (21,) Nudd.	
59, (22,) Cimelianc.	
60, (23,) Libian,	929
61, (24,) Marchluith.	
62, (25,) Paternus.	
63, (26,) Roderick.	
64, (27,) Gogwan,	982.
65, (28,) Bledri,	993.
66, (29,) Joseph,	1022.
67, (30,) Herewald,	1059.
Vacancy four years.	
68, (31,) Urban,	1108.
69, (32,) Uchtryd,	1139.
70, (33,) Galfrid,	1148.
71, (34,) Nich. ab Gwrgant.	
Vacancy ten years.	
72, (35,) W. de Saltmarsh.	
73, (36,) Henry,	1199.
74, (37,) William,	1219.
75, (38,) E. de Radnor,	1230.
Vacancy four years.	
76, (39,) W. de Burgh,	1244.
77, (40,) J. de la Ware,	1253.
78, (41,) W. de Radnor,	1256.
79, (42,) W. de Braos,	1266.
80, (43,) J. Monmouth,	1296.
81, (44,) J. Eaglescliff,	1323.
82, (45,) J. Paschall,	1347.

Bishops of St. David's.	*A. D.*
bishop of Canterbury.	
99, (48,) David Fitz-Gerald.	
100, (49,) Pet. de Leia.	
101, (50,) Galfrid,	1198.
102, (51,) Girald Camb.	1199.
103, (52,) Geofrey,	1203.
104, (53,) Jorweth,	1214.
105, (54,) Anselm,	1230.
106, (55,) T. Wallensis,	1248.
107, (56,) R. de Carreu,	1256.
108, (57,) T. Becke,	1280.
109, (58,) D. Martin,	1293.
110, (59,) H. Gower,	1328.
111, (60,) J. Thoresby,	1347.
112, (61,) R. Brian,	1349.
113, (62,) T. Falstaff,	1353.
114, (63,) A. Houghton,	1361.
115, (64,) J. Gilbert,	1389.
Vacancy four years.	
116, (65,) Guy de Mona,	1401.
117, (66,) H. Chichely,	1408.
118, (67,) J. Ketterich,	1414.
119, (68,) S. Patrington,	1415.
120, (69,) B. Nichols,	1418.
121, (70,) T. Radbone,	1433.
122, (71,) W. Linwood,	1442.
123, (72,) J. Langton,	1447.
124, (73,) J. Delabere,	1447.
125, (74,) R. Tully,	1460.
126, (75,) R. Martin,	1482.
127, (76,) T. Langton,	1483.

Bishops of Llandaff.	*A. D.*
83, (46,) R. Craddock,	1361.
84, (47,) T. Rushook,	1383.
85, (48,) W. Bottlesham,	1386.
86, (49,) E. Broomfield,	1389.
87, (50,) T. Winchcomb,	1393.
88, (51,) A. Barrett,	1395.
89, (52,) J. Burghill,	1396.
90, (53,) T. Peverell,	1398.
91, (54,) J. la Zouch,	1408.
92, (55,) John Wells,	1425.
93, (56,) N. Ashley,	1441.
94, (57,) J. Hunden,	1458.
95, (58,) John Smith,	1476.
96, (59,) J. Marshall,	1478.
97, (60,) J. Ingleby,	1496.
98, (61,) M. Salley,	1500.
99, (62,) G. de Athequa,	1516.
100, (63,) R. Holgate,	1537.
101, (64,) A. Kitchen,	1545.

Bishops of St. David's.	*A. D.*	*Bishops of Llandaff.*	*A. D.*
128, (77,) Hugh Parry,	1485.		
129, (78,) J. Morgan,	1496.		
130, (79,) R.Sherbourne,	1505.		
131, (80,) E. Vaughan,	1509.		
132, (81,) R. Rawlins,	1523.		
133, (82,) W. Barlow,	1536.		
134, (83,) R. Farrar,	1548.		
135, (84,) H. Morgan,	1553.		

This brings us down to the REFORMATION, since which time, the English succession comes through Matthew Parker and his associates.

We see, from the foregoing, how the Bishops in these several Dioceses traced their succession, and that they could trace it to Jerusalem, to Rome, and to Ephesus. Now the early Bishops of these Dioceses were instrumental to a very great extent in preaching Christianity to the Saxons, in the West and North of England. Thus the counties of Chester, Nottingham, Derby, Stafford, Salop, Northampton, Leicester, Lincoln, Huntingdon, Rutland, Warwick, Worcester, Oxford, Gloucester, Buckingham, Bedford, Hereford, and part of Hertford, were converted by Finnan, Diuma, Ceollach, and Trumhere, Irish and British Bishops.* York, Lancaster, and most of the northern parts of England, by Aidan, a Bishop from the Monastery of Columbkill, in the island of Hii, or Iona, originally, we believe, a part of the Diocese of Sodor and Mann ;† and Essex and Middlesex, by Cedd, another Irish or British Bishop.‡ These Bishops founded several Dioceses, which of course trace their original succession to British Bishops, and in most cases, to the Archbishops of St. David's and Armagh.

The Arch-Diocese of York originally included the Dio-

* Bd. Hist. ii. 19–21. † Bd. Hist. iii. 3–6, 17. ‡ Bd. iii. 22.

ceses of York, Lindisfarne, now Durham, Sodor and Mann, Hexham, now extinct, and all the Bishoprics of Scotland, until 1466.* The first Archbishop of the Saxons was Paulinus, consecrated by Augustine of Canterbury.† The second was Cedd, a British Bishop, for three years,‡ who resigned and was appointed Bishop of Lichfield and Coventry. He was succeeded by Wilfrid, who was consecrated by the Archbishop of Paris, eleven other Bishops assisting him.§ The Bishops who assisted in the consecration of Bishops in the Province of York, traced their succession to the British Bishops, as Aidan, Finnan, and Coleman, who were ordained by the Bishops in the island of Hii, or Scottish Bishops who received their succession from Palladius.‖ There is every reason to suppose, however, that those Bishops who were ordained by Palladius, could also trace their succession to the British Bishops, as they must have assisted in the consecration of the Scottish Bishops.

Archbishops of York.	*A. D.*	*Archbishops of York.*	*A. D.*
1, Paulinus,	625–644.	12, Wimundus,	830.
Vacancy twenty years.		13, Wilferus,	854.
2, Cead,	664.	14, Ethelbald,	865.
3, Wilfrid I.,	669.	15, Redwardus,	921.
4, Bosa,	677.	16, Wulstan I.,	941.
5, St. John, of Beverly,	692.	17, Oskitel,	955.
6, Wilfrid II.,	718.	18, Athelwold, resigned,	971.
7, Egbert,	730.	19, Oswald,	971.
8, Albert,	767.	20, Ethelred II.,	993.
9, Ethelred,	780.	21, Wulstan II.,	1002.
10, Eanbald,	797.	22, Alfric Puttock,	1023.
11, Wulsius,	812.	23, Kinsius,	1050.

* Patr. Brit. p. 82. † Bd. ii. 9.

‡ Bd. ii. 28. Dup. Hist. Ecc. Script. Cent. viii. p. 128.

§ Bd. iii. 28. Dup. Ecc. Script. Cent. viii. p. 128.

‖ Ussh. Primordia. c. 1

Archbishops of York.	A. D.
24, Aldred,	1061.
25, Thomas I.,	1070.
26, Gerard,	1100.
27, Thomas II.,	1109.
28, Thurstan,	1114.
29, William(deprived,)	1144.
30, Henry Murdac,	1147.
St. William, restored,	1153.
31, Roger,	1154.
Vacancy ten years.	
32, Geoffry Plantagenet,	1191.
Vacancy four years.	
33, Walter de Grey,	1216.
34, Sewall,	1255.
35, Geoffry de Ludham,	1258.
36, Walter Giffard,	1265.
37, Wm. Wickwane,	1279.
38, John Le Romaine,	1285.
39, Hen. de Newark,	1296.
40, Thos. Corbridge,	1299.
41, Wm. de Greenfield,	1303.
42, Wm. de Melton,	1316.
43, Wm. de Lazouch,	1340.
44, John Thoresby,	1354.
45, Alex. Neville,	1374.
46, Thos. Arundel,	1388.
47, Robert Waldby,	1397.
48, Rich. Scrope,	1398.
49, Henry Bowet,	1407.
50, John Kemp,	1426.
51, Wm. Boothe,	1452.
52, Geo. Neville,	1465.
53, Laurence Boothe,	1476.

Archbishops of York.	A. D.
54, Thos. de Rotheram, or Scott,	1480.
55, Thos. Savage,	1508.
56, Chris. Bainbridge,	1508.
57, Thomas Wolsey,	1514.
58, Edward Lee,	1531.
59, Robert Holgate,	1544.
60, Nicholas Heath,	1555.
61, Thomas Young,	1560.
62, Edmund Grindal,	1570.
63, Edwin Sandes,	1576.
64, John Piers,	1588.
65, Mat. Hutton,	1594.
66, Tobias Matthew,	1606.
67, Geo. Monteigne,	1618.
68, Sam. Harsnet,	1628.
69, Richard Neyle,	1632.
70, John Williams,	1641.
Cromwell, vacancy 10 years.	
71, Accepted Freewen,	1660.
72, Richard Sterne,	1664.
73, John Dolben,	1683.
74, Thos. Lamplugh,	1688.
75, John Sharp,	1691.
76, Sir Wm. Dawes, Bart.,	1714.
77, Laun. Blackburne,	1724.
78, Thomas Herring,	1745.
79, Mat. Hutton,	1747.
80, John Gilbert,	1757.
81, Rob. Drummond,	1761.
82, Wm. Markham,	1777.
83, Edward Harcourt,	1808.

CHAPTER XXV.

SUCCESSION OF THE SCOTTISH, AMERICAN, AND IRISH CHURCHES.

It has been remarked, that one line of the succession of the American Church came through that of Scotland. This was also derived from the English succession, December 15, 1661, when Gilbert Sheldon, Bishop of London, assisted by George Morley, Bishop of Worcester, Richard Sterne, Bishop of Carlisle, and Hugh Lloyd, Bishop of Llandaff, consecrated Andrew Fairfull, to the Diocese of Glasgow; John Sharpe, to the Diocese of St. Andrews; Robert Leighton, to the Diocese of Dumblane, (translated to Glasgow, 1671;) and James Hamilton, to the Diocese of Galloway.* These consecrated other Bishops, but the original records are either lost or destroyed, until 1705. Again, February 24, 1693, the deprived Bishops of Peterborough, Norwich, and Ely, consecrated George Hickes, a Bishop of Scotland.† The Scottish succession is as follows:—

* Jux. Reg. 237.

† It has been objected by some that the consecration of Hickes was uncanonical, if not schismatical, and consequently, of doubtful validity. The facts are simply these. The consecrators of Hickes had been duly consecrated to Sees in England, but on the accession of William and Mary, were deprived of their Sees for refusing to take the oath of allegiance to William and Mary, deeming themselves bound by their oath of fealty to James. But, though expelled from their Sees, no act was done depriving them of their Episcopal character. Subsequent to their expulsion from their Sees, they consecrated Hickes, a Bishop for Scotland. That the consecrators of Hickes had authority to confer orders, is not doubted; that there was an irregularity in their proceeding is also conceded. That the irregularity amounted to schism, can hardly be claimed. But even were it conceded, mere schism, unaccompanied by any errors of doctrine, or any ecclesiastical censure, would not vitiate his orders.—*Bing.* iv. 7. 7.

	Name of Bishops.	*Diocese.*	*Date.*
1,	James Sharpe,	St. Andrews,	Dec. 15, 1661.
2,	Andrew Fairfull,	Glasgow,	" "
3,	Robert Leighton,	Dumblane,	" "
	" "	Glasgow, 1671.	
4,	James Hamilton,	Galloway,	" "
5,	George Haliburton,	Dunkeld,	May 7, 1662.
6,	Murdoch McKenzie,	Moray,	" "
7,	David Strachan,	Brechin,	" "
8,	John Patterson,	Ross,	" "
9,	David Fletcher,	Argyle,	" "
10,	Robert Wallace,	The Isles,	" "
11,	George Wishart,	Edinburgh,	June 1, 1662.
12,	David Mitchel,	Aberdeen,	" "
13,	Patrick Forbes,	Caithness,	" "
14,	Alexander Burnet,	Aberdeen,	1663.
	" "	Glasgow, 1664.	
	" "	St. Andrews, 1679.	
15,	Patrick Scougal,	Aberdeen,	Easter, 1664.
16,	Andrew Honyman,	Orkney,	1664.
17,	Henry Guthrie,	Dunkeld,	1665.
18,	William Scrogie,	Argyle,	1666.
19,	Alexander Young,	Edinburgh,	1671.
	" "	Ross, 1679.	
20,	James Ramsey,	Dumblane,	1673.
	" "	Ross, 1684.	
21,	John Patterson,	Galloway,	1674.
	" "	Edinburgh, 1679.	
	" "	Glasgow, 1687.	
22,	Arthur Ross,	Argyle,	Apr. 28, 1675.
	" "	Galloway, 1679.	
	" "	Glasgow, 1679.	
	" "	St. Andrews, 1684.	
23,	Robert Laurie,	Brechin,	1676

	Name of Bishops.	*Diocese.*	*Date.*
24,	William Lindsay,	Dunkeld,	May 1, 1677.
25,	James Aitkins,	Moray,	1677.
	" "	Galloway, 1680.	
26,	Andrew Wood,	The Isles,	1678.
	" "	Caithness, 1680.	
27,	George Haliburton,	Brechin,	1678.
	" "	Aberdeen, 1682.	
28,	Andrew Bruce,	Dunkeld,	1679.
	" "	Orkney, 1688.	
29,	Colin Falconer,	Argyle,	Sept. 5, 1679.
	" "	Moray, 1680.	
30,	Hector McLean,	Argyle,	1680.
31,	Archibald Graham,	The Isles,	1680.
32,	Robert Douglas,	Brechin, 1682.	
	" "	Dumblane, 1684.	
33,	Alexander Cairncross,	Brechin,	1684.
	" "	Glasgow, 1684.	
34,	James Drummond,	Brechin,	Dec. 25, 1684.
35,	Alexander Rose,	Moray,	1686.
	" "	Edinburgh, 1687.	
36,	John Hamilton,	Dunkeld,	Oct. 19, 1688.
37,	William Hay,	Moray,	1687.
38,	John Gordon,	Galloway,	Sept. 4, 1688.

		Consecrators.
39,	John Fullarton,	Jan. 25, 1705.
40,	John Sage,	John Glasgow, 21.
		Alex. Edinburgh, 35.
		Robert Dumblane, 32.
41,	**John Falconer,**	April 28, 1709.
		Alex. Edinburgh, 35.
		Robert Dumblane, 32.
		John Sage, 40.

Name of Bishops.	*Diocese.*	*Consecrators.*
42, Archibald Campbell,		Aug. 24, 1711.
		Alex. Edinburgh, 35.
		Robert Dumblane, 32.
		John Falconer, 41.
43, James Gadderar,*		Feb. 24, 1712.
		George Hickes, p. 340.
		John Falconer, 41.
		Archibald Campbell, 42.
44, Arthur Millar,		Oct. 22, 1718.
45, William Irvine,		Alex. Edinburgh, 35.
		John Fullarton, 39.
		John Falconer, 41.
46, David Freebairn,		Oct. 17, 1722.
47, Andrew Cant,		John Falconer, 41.
		Arthur Millar, 44.
		William Irvine, 45.
48, Alexander Duncan,		1724.
		John Falconer, 41.
		William Irvine, 45.
		Arthur Millar, 44.
49, Thomas Rattray,†	Dunkeld,	June 4, 1727.
		James Gadderar, 43.
		Alexander Duncan, 48.
		Andrew Cant, 47.
50, William Dunbar,‡	Moray,	June 18, 1727. (and)

* Exceptions have also been taken to the consecration of Gadderar, because Hickes was the chief consecrator. But if Hickes' orders were valid, no objection can be made to those of Gadderar, as the other two consecrators belonged to the College of Scotch Bishops, against whom no objection lies.

† Similar objections have been made to the consecration of Rattray, and the same answer applies.

‡ The same objection has been made to the consecration of Dunbar

Name of Bishops.	*Diocese.*	*Consecrators.*
51, Robert Keith,	Caithness,	James Gadderar, 43.
		Arthur Millar, 44.
		Thomas Rattray, 49.
52, Robert White,	Dumblane,	June 24, 1735.
		Thomas Rattray, 49.
		Robert Keith, 51.
		William Dunbar, 50.
53, William Falconer,	Caithness,	Sept. 10, 1741.
		Thomas Rattray, 49.
		Robert Keith, 51.
		Robert White, 52.
54, James Rait,	Brechin,	Oct. 4, 1742.
		Thomas Rattray, 49.
		Robert Keith, 51.
		Robert White, 52.
55, John Alexander,	Dunkeld,	Aug. 9, 1743.
		Robert Keith, 51.
		Robert White, 52.
		William Falconer, 53.
		James Rait, 54.
56, Andrew Gerard,	Aberdeen,	July 17, 1747.
		Robert White, 52.
		William Falconer, 53.
		James Rait, 54.
		John Alexander, 55.

and Keith, to which it is also added, that Millar, who belonged to the old College of Scotch Bishops, and who assisted in their consecration, was suspended by the College of Scotch Bishops for this very act. But the suspension was *subsequent* to the consecration, and could not, therefore, affect that. Besides, if we allow, as was unquestionably done in the Primitive Church, that one Bishop could confer orders, though such ordinations were uncanonical, all these objections are set aside, as there was always one or more of the old Scotch Bishops concerned in the ordination.—See *Bing.* ii. 11. 5.

Name of Bishops.	*Diocese.*	*Consecrators.*
57, Robert Forbes,	Ross and Caithness,	June 24, 1762.
		William Falconer, 53.
		J. Alexander, 55.
		A. Gerard, 56.
58, Robert Kilgour,	Aberdeen,	Sept. 21, 1768.
		Wm. Falconer, 53.
		J. Rait, 54.
		R. Forbes, 57.
59, Charles Rose,	Dumblane,	Aug. 24, 1774.
		Wm. Falconer, 53.
		J. Rait, 54.
		R. Forbes, 57.
60, Arthur Petrie,	Moray,	June 27, 1777.
		Wm. Falconer, 53.
		J. Rait, 54.
		R. Kilgour, 58.
		C. Rose, 59.
61, John Skinner,	Aberdeen,	Sept. 25, 1782.
		R. Kilgour, 58.
		C. Rose, 59.
		A. Petrie, 60.
SAMUEL SEABURY,	Connecticut,	Nov. 14, 1784.
		Robert Kilgour, 58.
		Arthur Petrie, 60.
		John Skinner, 61.

SUCCESSION OF BISHOPS IN THE AMERICAN CHURCH.

1, Samuel Seabury,	Conn. and R. I.,	Nov. 14, 1784.
		Scottish Bishops.
		Robert Kilgour, 58.
		Arthur Petrie, 60.
		John Skinner, 61.

Name of Bishop.	Diocese.	Consecrators.
2, William White, 119 from St. John, (86) from Augustin.		
	Pennsylvania,	Feb. 4, 1787.
		English Bishops.
		John Moore, 96.
		William Markham, 94.
		Charles Moss, 91.
		John Hinchliffe, 93.
3, Samuel Provoost,	New York,	Feb. 4, 1787.
		John Moore, 96.
		William Markham, 94.
		Charles Moss, 91.
		John Hinchliffe, 93.
4, James Madison,	Virginia,	Sept. 19, 1790.
		John Moore, 96.
		Beilby Porteus, 97.
		John Thomas, 95.
5, Thomas J. Claggett,	Maryland,	Sept. 17, 1792.
		American Bishops.
		Samuel Provoost, 3.
		Samuel Seabury, 1.
		William White, 2.
		James Madison, 4.
6, Robert Smith,	South Carolina,	Sept. 13, 1795.
		William White, 2.
		Samuel Provoost, 3.
		James Madison, 4.
		Thomas J. Claggett, 5.
7, Edward Bass,	Massachusetts,	May 7, 1797.
		William White, 2.
		Samuel Provoost, 3.
		Thomas J. Claggett, 5.

	Name of Bishop.	*Diocese.*	*Consecrators*
8,	Abraham Jarvis,	Connecticut,	Oct. 18, 1797.
			William White, 2.
			Samuel Provoost, 3.
			Edward Bass, 7.
9,	Benjamin Moore,	New York,	Sept. 11, 1801.
			William White, 2.
			Thomas J. Claggett, 5.
			Abraham Jarvis, 8.
10,	Samuel Parker,	Massachusetts,	Sept. 14, 1804.
			William White, 2.
			Thomas J. Claggett, 5.
			Abraham Jarvis, 8.
			Benjamin Moore, 9.
11,	John H. Hobart,	New York,	May 29, 1811.
12,	Alex. V. Griswold,	Eastern Diocese,	May 29, 1811.
			William White, 2.
			Samuel Provoost, 3.
			Abraham Jarvis, 8.
13,	Theodore Dehon,	South Carolina,	Oct. 15, 1812.
			William White, 2.
			Abraham Jarvis, 8.
			John H. Hobart, 11.
14,	Richard C. Moore,	Virginia,	May 18, 1814.
			William White, 2.
			John H. Hobart, 11.
			Alex. V. Griswold, 12.
			Theodore Dehon, 13.
15,	James Kemp,	Maryland,	Sept. 1, 1814.
			William White, 2.
			John H. Hobart, 11.
			Richard C. Moore, 14.

Name of Bishop.	*Diocese.*	*Consecrators.*
16, John Croes,	New Jersey,	Nov. 19, 1815.
		William White, 2.
		John H. Hobart, 11.
		James Kemp, 15.
17, Nathaniel Bowen,	South Carolina,	Oct. 8, 1818.
		William White, 2.
		John H. Hobart, 11.
		James Kemp, 15.
		John Croes, 16.
18, Philander Chase,	Ohio,	Feb. 11, 1819.
	Illinois, 1831.	William White, 2.
		John H. Hobart, 11.
		James Kemp, 15.
		John Croes, 16.
19, Thomas C. Brownell,	Connecticut,	Oct. 27, 1819.
		William White, 2.
		John H. Hobart, 11.
		Alex. V. Griswold, 12.
20, John S. Ravenscroft,	North Carolina,	May 22, 1823.
		William White, 2.
		Alex. V. Griswold, 12.
		James Kemp, 15.
		John Croes, 16.
		Nathaniel Bowen, 17.
		Thomas C. Brownell, 19.
21, Henry U. Onderdonk,	Pennsylvania,	Oct. 25, 1827.
(Assistant.)		William White, 2.
		John H. Hobart, 11.
		James Kemp, 15.
		John Croes, 16.
		Nathaniel Bowen, 17.

	Name of Bishop.	*Diocese.*	*Consecrators.*
22,	William Meade,	Virginia,	August 19, 1829.
			William White, 2.
			John H. Hobart, 11.
			Alex. V. Griswold, 12.
			Richard C. Moore, 14.
			John Croes, 16.
			Thomas C. Brownell, 19.
			Henry U. Onderdonk, 21.
23.	William M. Stone,	Maryland,	Oct. 21, 1830.
			William White, 2.
			Richard C. Moore, 14.
			Henry U. Onderdonk, 21.
			William Meade, 22.
24,	Benj. T. Onderdonk,	New York,	Nov. 26, 1830.
			William White, 2.
			Thomas C. Brownell, 19.
			Henry U. Onderdonk, 21.
25,	Levi S. Ives,	North Carolina,	Sept. 22, 1831.
			William White, 2.
			Henry U. Onderdonk, 21.
			Benj. T. Onderdonk, 24.
26,	John H. Hopkins,	Vermont,	Oct. 31, 1832.
			William White, 2.
			Alex. V. Griswold, 12.
			Nathaniel Bowen, 17.
27,	Benjamin B. Smith,	Kentucky,	Oct. 31, 1832.
			William White, 2.
			Thomas C. Brownell, 19.
			Henry U. Onderdonk, 21.
28,	Charles P. M'Ilvaine,	Ohio,	Oct. 31, 1832.
			William White, 2.
			Alex. V. Griswold, 12.
			William Meade, 22.

Name of Bishop.	*Diocese.*	*Consecrators.*
29, George W. Doane,	New Jersey,	Oct. 31, 1832.
		William White, 2.
		Benj. T. Onderdonk, 24.
		Levi S. Ives, 25.
30, James H. Otey,	Tennessee,	Jan. 14, 1834.
		William White, 2.
		Henry U. Onderdonk, 21.
		Benj. T. Onderdonk, 24.
		George W. Doane, 29.
31, Jackson Kemper,	Missouri and Ind.	Sept. 25, 1835.
		William White, 2.
		Richard C. Moore, 14.
		Philander Chase, 18.
		Henry U. Onderdonk, 21.
		Benj. T. Onderdonk, 24.
		Benjamin B. Smith, 27.
		George W. Doane, 29.
32, Samuel A. M'Coskry,	Michigan,	July 7, 1836.
		Henry U. Onderdonk, 21.
		George W. Doane, 29.
		Jackson Kemper, 31.
33, Leonidas Polk,	Arkansas,	Dec. 9, 1838.
Louisiana, 1841.		William Meade, 22.
		Benjamin B. Smith, 27.
		Charles P. M'Ilvaine, 28.
		James H. Otey, 30.
34, Wm. H. De Lancey,	Western New York,	May 9, 1839.
		Alex. V. Griswold, 12.
		Henry U. Onderdonk, 21.
		Benj. T. Onderdonk, 24.
		George W. Doane, 29.

Name of Bishop.	*Diocese.*	*Consecrators.*
35, Chris. E. Gadsden,	South Carolina,	June 21, 1840.
		Alex. V. Griswold, 12.
		George W. Doane, 29.
		Samuel A. M'Coskry, 32.
36, Wm. R. Whittingham,	Maryland,	Sept. 17, 1840.
		Alex. V. Griswold, 12.
		Richard C. Moore, 14.
		Benj. T. Onderdonk, 24.
		George W. Doane, 29.
37, Stephen Elliott,	Georgia,	Feb. 28, 1841.
		William Meade, 22.
		Levi S. Ives, 25.
		Chris. E. Gadsden, 35.
38, Alfred Lee,	Delaware,	Oct. 12, 1841.
		Alex. V. Griswold, 12.
		Richard C. Moore, 14.
		Philander Chase, 18.
		Thomas C. Brownell, 19.
		Henry U. Onderdonk, 21.
39, John Johns,	Virginia,	Oct. 13, 1842.
(Assistant.)		Alex. V. Griswold, 12.
		L. S. Ives, 25.
		Wm. Meade, 22.
		W. R. Whittingham, 36.
40, **Manton Eastburn,**	Massachusetts,	Dec. 29, 1842.
		Alex. V. Griswold, 12.
		T. C. Brownell, 19.
		B. T. Onderdonk, 24.
		Wm. H. De Lancey, 34.

	Name of Bishop.	*Diocese.*	*Consecrators.*
41	John P. K. Henshaw,	Rhode Island,	Aug. 11, 1843.
			T. C. Brownell, 19.
			G. W. Doane, 29.
			J. H. Hopkins, 26.
			W. R. Whittingham, 36.
			J. Johns, 39.
42,	Carlton Chase,	New Hampshire,	Oct. 12, 1844.
			P. Chase, 18.
			T. C. Brownell, 19.
			B. T. Onderdonk, 24.
			L. S. Ives, 25.
			B. B. Smith, 27.
43,	Nicholas Cobbs,	Alabama,	Oct. 12, 1844.
			P. Chase, 18.
			W. Meade, 22.
			C. P. M'Ilvaine, 28.
			G. W. Doane, 29.
44,	Cicero S. Hawks,	Missouri,	Oct. 12, 1844.
			P. Chase, 18.
			J. Kemper, 31.
			S. A. M'Coskry, 32.
			L. Polk, 33.
			W. H. De Lancey, 34.
45,	William J. Boone,	China,	Oct. 26, 1844.
			P. Chase, 18.
			G. W. Doane, 29.
			J. H. Otey, 30.
46,	Horatio Southgate,	Turkey,	Oct. 26, 1844.
			P. Chase, 18.
			S. Elliott, 37.
			J. P. K. Henshaw, 41.

Name of Bishop.	*Diocese.*	*Consecrators.*
47, G. W. Freeman,	Arkansas and Texas, Oct. 26, 1844.	P. Chase, 18. Jackson Kemper, 31. L. Polk, 33. A. Lee, 38.

We have explained in the preceding chapters, the nature of the Apostolic succession, as held by the Episcopal Church in England and America, and shown from what sources it has been derived; and having carefully traced it back to the Apostles, through all those times of peril when it was in danger, we might leave the subject. But, as mention has been made of Irish and Romish Bishops, we shall show from whence the Irish derived their succession, and how both can trace it. In the earliest ages of Christianity, Ireland had its Bishops from England or Scotland; but about 433, Patrick was consecrated Archbishop of Armagh, by the Bishop of Rome.* He established several Sees, and with the assistance of others consecrated Bishops for them; as, Erc, Bishop of Slane;† Senach, Bishop of Uamali;‡ Bron, Bishop of Sligo, 441;§ Mochthe, Bishop of Louth, 443, if he was not a Bishop before, which seems probable.|| He also founded the See of Clogher, the same year, and governed it awhile himself, but subsequently conferred it upon M'Martin.¶ In the year 445, he founded the Archiepiscopal See of Armagh, and governed it till 455, when he promoted Benignus to the Episcopate, who resigned it, and was succeeded by Jarlath, 465.** A. D. 447 he consecrated Germanus, Bishop of So-

* Life of Pat. p. 67. Usher, Prim. Brit. c. 18. Opusc. Patri. by James Ware, Lond. 1656.

† Life, p. 73. ‡ P. 78. § P. 79.

|| P. 81. ¶ P. 81. ** P. 82.

dor and Mann,* and in 454 he consecrated Mael, Bishop of Ardagh.† From these, the subsequent Bishops of Ireland traced their succession through the Archbishops of Armagh. We give the list from Usher's *Primordia;* Glover's *Patriarchate of Britain*, London, 1839; and the *Chronological Table of the Archbishops of Armagh*, appended to the Life of St. Patrick.

ARCHBISHOPS OF ARMAGH.

Name of Bishops.	*A. D.*	*Name of Bishops.*	*A. D.*
1, Patrick, consecrated by Celestine, Bishop of Rome,	433.	21, Ferdachry,	758.
		22, Foendelach,	774.
		23, Dubdalethy I.,	778.
2, Benignus,	455.	24, Affiat,	793.
3, Jarlath,	465.	25, Cudiniscus,	794.
4, Cormac,	482.	26, Conmach,	798.
5, Dubtach I.,	497.	27, Torlach,	807.
6, Ailild I.,	513.	28, Nuadd,	808.
7, Ailild II.,	526.	29, Flangus M'Loingle,	812.
8, Dubtach II.,	536.	30, Artrigius,	823.
9, David M'Guire,	548.	31, Eugenius,	833.
10, Feidlimid,	551.	32, Faranan,	834.
11, Cairlan,	578.	33, Diermuid,	848.
12, Eochaid M'Dermod,	588.	34, Facthua,	852.
13, Senachus,	598.	35, Ainmire,	874.
14, Mac Laisir,	610.	36, Catasach I.,	875.
15, Thomian M'Ronan,	623.	37, Maelcob,	883.
16, Segene,	661.	38, Mael-Brigid,	885.
17, Flan-febla,	688.	39, Joseph,	927.
18, Suibhny,	715.	40, Mael-Patrick,	936.
19, Cognusa,	730.	41, Catasach II.,	937.
20, Cele-Peter,	750.	42, Muredach,	957.

* Life of Pat. p. 83. † P. 88.

Name of Bishops.	A. D.	Name of Bishops.	A. D.
43, Dubdalethy II.,	966.	75, John Colton,	1382.
44, Murechan,	998.	76, Nich. Fleming,	1404.
45, Maelmury,	1001.	77, John Swayne,	1417.
46, Amalgaid,	1021.	78, John Prene,	1439.
47, Dubdalethy III.,	1050.	79, John Mey,	1444.
48, Cumasach,	1065.	80, John Bole,	1457.
49, Melisa,	1065.	81, John Foxalls,	1475.
50, DonaldM'Amalgaid,	1092.	82, Edw. Connesburg,	1477.
51, Celsus M'Aid,	1106.	83, Octav. De Palatio,	1480.
52, Maurice,	1129.	84, John Kite,	1513.
53, Malachy O'Morgair,	1134.	85, George Cromer,	1522.
54, Gelasius,	1137.	86, George Dowdall,	1543.
55, Cornelius,	1174.	87, Hugh Goodacre,	1552.
56, Gilbert O'Caran,	1175.	88, Adam Loftus,	1562.
57, Melissa O'Carrol,	1184.	89, ThomasLancaster,	1568.
58, Amlave O'Murid,	1184.	90, John Long,	1584.
59, Tomas O'Connor,	1186.	91, John Garvey,	1585.
60, Eug. M'Gillivider,	1206.	92, Henry Ussher,	1595.
61, Luke Netterville,	1220.	93, Chris. Hampton,	1613.
62, Donat O'Fidabara,	1227.	94, James Ussher,	1624.
63, Albert De Cologne,	1239.	95, John Bramhall,	1660.
64, Reiner,	1247.	96, James Margetson,	1663.
65, Abm. O'Connelan,	1254.	97, Michael Boyle,	1678.
66, Pat. O'Scanlain,	1262.	98, Hugh Boulter,	1702.
67, Nich. M'Melissa,	1272.	99, Nar. Marsh,	1702.
68, John Taaf,	1301.	100, Thomas Lindsay,	1713.
69, Walter De Jorse,	1306.	101, John Hoadley,	1742.
70, Roland Jorse,	1311.	102, George Stone,	1747.
71, Stephen Segrave,	1332.	103, Rich. Robinson,	1765.
72, David O'Hiraghty,	1334.	104, Wm. Newcome,	1795.
73, Richard Fitzralph,	1347.	105, William Stuart,	1800.
74, Milo Sweetman,	1361.	106, John G. Beresford,	1822.

CHAPTER XXVI.

SUCCESSION OF THE CHURCH OF ROME.

Owing to the fact that Rome has been the Capital of an Empire, since the first preaching of Christianity, and also the seat of a vast body of learned men, the materials for tracing the succession of that Church are more full and ample than those of any other. Consequently, we can generally determine the exact length of the reign of each Bishop, and give some history of the individual filling the Chair. In the early periods of this Church, translations from one See to another were not allowed. The first case of a translation to the Episcopate of Rome, was that of Formosus, who had been Bishop of Porto, translated to Rome, May 4, 891. Previous to that time, all the Bishops, at the time of their election, were Priests, Deacons, or Laymen. Among them, Fabian, the 19th Bishop, and John XIX., are known to have been Laymen. *Eleven* were Deacons at the time of their election, and are marked with a star (*) in the following catalogue. *Fifty-one* others had been Bishops elsewhere, before their election to the Pontificate. These are marked with a dagger (†) in the following catalogue. These Bishops having been translated from nearly every part of Christendom, it may safely be assumed, that nearly all the successions in the world enter into, and assist in authenticating that of the Bishops of Rome. Consequently, if in one or two instances, as some historians pretend to believe, the succession of a Bishop can not be traced historically, it would not invalidate at all their succession.*

In the earliest ages of the Church, the names of the Con-

* From about A. D. 750, the Bishops of Rome were consecrated by

secrators were not generally recorded, nor the day of the consecration, the year only being given.* The dates of the first seventeen Bishops are given on the authority of Eusebius: the subsequent ones have been compiled from GRAVESONS, *Historica Ecclesiastica*, vols. I.–IX., third edition, folio; BARONIUS, *Annales Ecclesiastica*, twelve volumes, folio, Antwerp, 1610–1629; MURATORI, *Annali d'Italia*, twelve volumes, folio, Genoa, 1773–1778; *Lives of the Popes*, by C. W. F. Walch, D. D., Divinity Professor, Gottingen, 8vo. London, 1759; Bower's *Lives of the Popes*, four volumes, quarto, London.

Name.	*Consecrated.*	*Died.*
1, Linus,	A. D. 67,	A. D. 79.
2, Anacletus,	79,	91.
3, Clement,	91,	100.
4, Evaristus,	100,	108.
5, Alexander,	108,	118.
6, Sixtus,	118,	128.
7, Telesphorus,	128,	138.
8, Hyginus,	138,	141.
9, Pius,	141,	155.
10, Anicetus,	155,	166.
11, Soter,	166,	174.
12, Eleutherius,*	174,	187.
13, Victor,	187,	198.
14, Zephrynus,	198,	216.
15, Calixtus,	216,	221.
16, Urban,	221,	229.
17, Pontianus,	229,	Sept. 28, 235.
18, Anterus,	Nov. 21, 235,	Jan. 3, 236.

the Bishops of Ostia, Oporto, and Alba, and the Bishops of these places were consecrated by the Bishop of Rome. Walch, 111.

* Euseb. iv. 5.

Name.	*Consecrated.*	*Died.*
19, Fabian,	Jan. 11, 236,	Jan. 20, 250.
20, Cornelius,	May 24, 251,	Sept. 4, 252.
21, Lucius I.,	Sept. 25, 252,	March 4, 253.
22, Stephen I.,	May 10, 255,	Aug. 1, 257.
23, Sixtus II.,	Aug. 24, 257,	July 30, 258.
24, Dionysius,	July 22, 259,	Dec. 26, 269.
25, Felix I.,	Dec. 28, 269,	Dec. 22, 274.
26, Eutychianus,	Jan. 5, 275,	Dec. 7, 283.
27, Caius,	Dec. 15, 283,	April 22, 296.
28, Marcellinus,	June 30, 296,	Oct. 24, 304.
29, Marcellus I.,	May 19, 308,	Jan. 16, 310.
30, Eusebius,	Feb. 5, 310,	June 21, 310.
31, Miltiades,	July 2, 311,	Jan. 10, 314.
32, Sylvester I.,	Jan. 31, 314,	Dec. 31, 335.
33, Mark,	Jan. 18, 336,	Oct. 8, 336.
34, Julius I.,	Feb. 6, 337,	April 12, 352.
35, Liberius,	July 22, 352,	Sept. 23, 366.
36, Felix II., (Liberius living, but having been driven into exile.)		
37, Damasus I.,	Oct. 1, 366,	Dec. 10, 384.
38, Siricius,	385,	398.
39, Anastasius I.,	Dec. 5, 398,	Dec. 14, 401.
40, Innocent I.,	Dec. 21, 402,	Mar. 12, 417.
41, Zosimus,	Mar. 18, 417,	Dec. 26, 418.
42, Boniface I.,	Dec. 29, 418,	Sept. 4, 422.
43, Celestine I.,	Sept. 10, 422,	July 18, 432.
44, Sixtus III.,*	July 24, 432,	Aug. 11, 440.
45, Leo I.,	Sept. 22, 440,	Nov. 4, 461.
46, Hilary,	Nov. 12, 461,	Feb. 21, 468.
47, Simplicius,	Feb. 25, 468,	March 1, 483.
48, Felix III.,	March 6, 483,	Feb. 24, 492.
49, Gelasius I.,	March 1, 492,	Nov. 19, 496.
50, Anastasius II.,	Nov. 24, 496,	Nov. 17, 498.

Name.	*Consecrated.*	*Died.*
51, Symmachus,	Nov. 22, 498,	July 19, 514.
52, Hormisdas,	July 27, 514,	Aug. 6, 523.
53, John I.,	Aug. 13, 523,	May 18, 526.
54, Felix IV.,	July 12, 526,	Sept. 18, 530.
55, Boniface II.,	Sept. 21, 530,	Oct. 17, 532.
56, John II.,	Dec. 31, 532,	May 26, 535.
57, Agapetus I.,	June 3, 535,	April 22, 536.
58, Silverius,	June 8, 536,	June 20, 540.
59, Vigilius,	540,	554.
60, Pelagius I.,	April 11, 555,	March 1, 560.
61, John III.,	July 17, 560,	July 13, 573.
62, Benedict I.,	June 3, 574,	July 30, 578.
63, Pelagius II.,	Nov. 30, 578,	Feb. 8, 590.
64, Gregory I.,*	Sept. 3, 590,	Mar. 12, 604.
65, Sabinus,*	Sept. 13, 604,	Feb. 12, 606.
66, Boniface III.,*	Feb. 8, 606,	Nov. 10, 607.
67, Boniface IV.,	Aug. 21, 608,	May 7, 615.
68, Deusdedit,	Oct. 19, 615,	Nov. 8, 618.
69, Boniface V.,	Dec. 23, 619,	Oct. 22, 625.
70, Honorius I.,	Oct. 27, 625,	Oct. 12, 638.
71, Severinus,	May 28, 640,	Aug. 1, 640.
72, John IV.,	Dec. 24, 640,	Oct. 10, 642.
73, Theodore I.,	Nov. 24, 642,	May 13, 649.
74, Martin I.,	July 5, 649,	Sept. 16, 654.
75, Eugenius I.,	Sept. 8, 654,	June 1, 657.
76, Vitalian,	July 30, 657,	Jan. 27, 672.
77, Adeodatus,	April 22, 672,	June 25, 676.
78, Domnus,	Nov. 1, 676,	April 11, 678.
79, Agatho,	June 27, 678,	Jan. 10, 682.
80, Leo II.,	Aug. 17, 682,	July 3, 683.
81, Benedict II.,	June 26, 684,	May 7, 685.
82, John V.,	July 23, 685,	Aug. 2, 686.
83, Conon,	Oct. 21, 686,	Sept. 21, 687.

Name.	*Consecrated.*	*Died.*
84, Sergius I.,	Dec. 15, 687,	Sept. 7, 701.
85, John VI.,	Oct. 28, 701,	Jan. 9, 705.
86, John VII.,	March 1, 705,	Oct. 17, 707.
87, Sissinnus,	Jan. 18, 708,	Feb. 6, 708.
88, Constantine,	Mar. 24, 708,	April 8, 715.
89, Gregory II.,	May 20, 715,	Feb. 11, 731.
90, Gregory III.,	Mar. 18, 731,	Nov. 28, 741.
91, Zachary,	Nov. 30, 741,	March 4, 752.
92, Stephen II., died before consecrated.		
93, Stephen III.,	Mar. 26, 752,	April 24, 757.
94, Paul I.,*	May 30, 757,	June 28, 767.
95, Stephen IV.,	Aug. 7, 768,	Feb. 2, 772.
96, Adrian I.,	Feb. 9, 772,	Dec. 25, 795.
97, Leo III.,	Dec. 27, 795,	June 12, 816.
98, Stephen V.,	June 22, 816,	Jan. 24, 817.
99, Paschal I.,	Jan. 25, 817,	Feb. 10, 824.
100, Eugenius II.,	Feb. 14, 824,	Aug. 827.
101, Valentine,* died before consecrated.		
102, Gregory IV.,	827,	Jan. 25, 844.
103, Sergius II.,	Feb. 10, 844,	Jan. 27, 847.
104, Leo IV.,	April 11, 847,	July 17, 855.
105, Benedict III.,	Sept. 29, 855,	April 8, 858.
106, Nicholas I.,	April 24, 858,	Nov. 12, 867.
107, Adrian II.,	Dec. 14, 867,	872.
108, John VIII.,	Dec. 14, 872,	Dec. 15, 882.
109, Martin II.,	882,	May, 884.
110, Adrian III.,	May, 884,	885.
111, Stephen VI.,	885,	May, 891.
112, Formosus,†	May 4, 891,	April 4, 896.
Boniface VI., 15 days, not numbered in the list.		
113, Stephen VII.,†	896,	897.
114, Romanus, about 4 months,		898.
115, Theodore II., 20 days,		898.

Name.	*Consecrated.*		*Died.*	
116, John IX.,	July 15,	898,	Aug. 1,	900.
117, Benedict IV.,	Aug. 2,	900,	Oct. 3,	903.
118, Leo V.,		903,		903.
119, Christopher,		903,		903.
120, Sergius III.,		903,		910.
121, Anastasius III.,		910,		913.
122, Landon,	Oct. 16,	913,	Apr. 26,	914.
123, John X.,†	Apr. 27,	914,		929.
124, Leo VI.,	June 28,	928,	Feb. 3,	929.
125, Stephen VIII.,	Feb. 3,	929,	Mar. 5,	931.
126, John XI.,	Mar. 5,	931,	Jan. 5,	936.
127, Leo VII.,	Jan. 8,	936,	July 18,	939.
128, Stephen IX.,	July,	939,	Dec.	942.
129, Martin III.,	Jan.	943,	July,	946.
130, Agapetus II.,		946,		956.
131, John XII.,		956,		964.
132, Benedict V.		964,		965.
133, John XIII.,†	Oct. 3,	965,	Sept. 8,	972.
134, Benedict VI.,	Dec.	972,	March,	974.
135, Domnus II.,		974,		975.
136, Benedict VII.,†	Mar. 25,	975,	July 10,	984.
137, John XIV.,†		984,		985.
138, John XV.,	Dec.	985,		996.
139, Gregory V.,†		996,	Feb. 18,	999.
140, Sylvester II.,†	April 2,	999,	May 11,	1003.
141, John XVII.,	May 13,	1003,	Dec. 7,	1003.
142, John XVIII.,	Dec. 26,	1003,		1009.
143, Sergius IV.,†		1009,		1012.
144, Benedict VIII.,†		1012,		1024.
145, John XIX.,		1024,		1033.
146, Benedict IX.,		1034,		1044.
147, Gregory VI.,		1044,		1046.
148, Clement II.,†		1046,	Nov. 7,	1047.

Name.	*Consecrated.*	*Died*
149, Damasus II.,†	July 17, 1048,	Aug.10, 1048.
150, Leo IX.,†	Feb. 2, 1049,	April 9, 1054.
151, Victor II.,†	Apr. 12, 1054,	1057.
152, Stephen X.,	Aug. 2, 1057,	Mar. 29, 1058.
153, Nicholas II.,†	Dec. 28, 1058,	June 3, 1061.
154, Alexander II.,†	Sept. 21, 1062,	Apr. 12, 1073.
155, Gregory VII.,*	Apr. 27, 1073,	May 25, 1085.
156, Victor III.,	May 25, 1086,	Sept. 16, 1087.
157, Urban II.,†	1087,	1099.
158, Paschal II.,	1099,	Jan. 21, 1118.
159, Gelasius II.,	Jan. 25, 1118,	Jan. 29, 1119.
160, Calixtus II.,†	Feb. 1, 1119,	Dec. 13, 1124.
161, Honorius II.,†	Dec. 21, 1124,	Feb. 14, 1130.
162, Innocent II.,	Feb. 15, 1130,	Sept. 24, 1143.
163, Celestine II.,	Sept. 26, 1143,	Mar. 9, 1144.
164, Lucius II.,	1144,	Feb. 25, 1145.
165, Eugenius III.,	Feb. 27, 1145,	July 7, 1153.
166, Anastasius IV.,†	Aug. 26, 1153,	Dec. 2, 1154.
167, Adrian IV.,†	Feb. 1154,	Sept. 1159.
168, Alexander III.,	Sept. 20, 1159,	Aug. 30, 1181.
169, Lucius II.,†	Sept. 6, 1181,	Nov. 24, 1185.
170, Urban III.,†	Nov. 25, 1185,	Oct. 19, 1187.
171, Gregory VIII.,	Oct. 21, 1187,	Dec. 17, 1187.
172, Clement III.,†	Dec. 19, 1188,	Mar. 28, 1191.
173, Celestine III.,*	Mar. 30, 1191,	Jan. 8, 1198.
174, Innocent III.,	Jan. 8, 1199,	July 16, 1216.
175, Honorius III.,	July 17, 1216,	Mar. 18, 1227.
176, Gregory IX.,†	1227,	1241.
177, Celestine IV.,† died before consecration; vacancy twenty months and fifteen days.		
178, Innocent IV.,	June, 1244,	Dec. 7, 1254.
179, Alexander IV.,†	Dec. 1254,	June 7, 1261.
180, Urban IV.,†	Sept. 4, 1261,	Nov. 1264.

Name.	*Consecrated.*	*Died.*
181, Clement IV.,†	Feb. 1265,	Nov. 25, 1268.
182, Gregory X.,*	Dec. 30, 1271,	Jan. 10, 1276.
183, Innocent V.,†	1276,	June 22, 1276.
184, Adrian V., died before consecrated.		
185, John XXI.,†	1276,	May, 1277.
186, Nicholas III.,*	Nov. 1277,	Aug. 22, 1280.
187, Martin IV.,	Feb. 22, 1281,	Mar. 29, 1285.
188, Honorius IV.,*	April 2, 1285,	April 3, 1287.
189, Nicholas IV.,†	Feb. 22, 1288,	April 4, 1292.
190, Celestine V.,	July, 1294,	Dec. 3, 1294.
191, Boniface VIII.,	Dec. 24, 1294,	Oct. 1303.
192, Benedict XI.,†	Nov. 1303,	July 4, 1304.
193, Clement V.,†	June 5, 1305,	Apr. 20, 1314.
194, John XXII.,†	Dec. 1316,	Dec. 4, 1334.
195, Benedict XII.,	Dec. 20, 1334,	Apr. 25, 1342.
196, Clement VI.,	May 7, 1342,	Dec. 4, 1352.
197, Innocent, VI.,†	Dec. 18, 1352,	Sept. 12, 1362.
198, Urban V.,	Sept. 25, 1362,	Dec. 9, 1370.
199, Gregory XI.,	Jan. 5, 1371,	Mar. 17, 1378.
200, Urban VI.,†	April 8, 1378,	Oct. 15, 1389.
201, Boniface IX.,	Nov. 2, 1389,	Sept. 1404.
202, Innocent VII.,†	Oct. 17, 1404,	Nov. 4, 1406.
203, Gregory XII.,†	1406,	June 15, 1409.
204, Alexander V.,†	1409,	May 4, 1410.
205, John XXIII.,	1410,	May 29, 1415.
206, Martin V.,	Nov. 11, 1417,	Feb. 22, 1431.
207, Eugenius IV.,	Mar. 3, 1431,	Feb. 17, 1447.
208, Nicholas V.,†	1447,	Mar. 24, 1450.
209, Calixtus III.,†	April 8, 1450,	Aug. 8, 1458.
210, Pius II.,†	Aug. 19, 1458,	Aug. 14, 1464.
211, Paul II.,	1464,	July 16, 1471.
212, Sixtus IV.,	1471,	1484.
213, Innocent VIII.,	Aug. 28, 1484,	July 25, 1492.

Name.	Consecrated.	Died.
214, Alexander VI.,†	Aug. 18, 1492,	Aug. 18, 1503.
215, Pius III.,	Sept. 22, 1503,	Oct. 18, 1503.
216, Julius II.,	1503,	Feb. 21, 1513.
217, Leo X.,	Mar. 15, 1513,	Dec. 1, 1521.
218, Adrian VI.,	Jan. 9, 1522,	Sept. 14, 1523.
219, Clement VII.,	1523,	Sept. 25, 1534.
220, Paul III.,†	Oct. 3, 1534.	Nov. 10, 1549.
221, Julius III.,	Feb. 8, 1550,	Mar. 23, 1555.
222, Marcellus II.,	April 9, 1555,	Apr. 30, 1555.
223, Paul IV.,	May 22, 1555,	Aug. 18, 1559.
224, Pius IV.,	Dec. 23, 1559,	Dec. 9, 1565.
225, Pius V.,	Jan. 7, 1566,	May 9, 1572.
226, Gregory XIII.,	May 13, 1572,	Apr. 10, 1585.
227, Sixtus V.,	April 24, 1585,	Aug. 27, 1590.
228, Urban VII.,	Sept. 15, 1590,	Sept. 27, 1590.
229, Gregory XIV.,†	Dec. 5, 1590,	Oct. 15, 1591.
230, Innocent IX.,	Oct. 30, 1591,	Dec. 30, 1591.
231, Clement VIII.,	Jan. 30, 1592,	Mar. 3, 1605.
232, Leo XI.,	April 1, 1605,	Apr. 28, 1605.
233, Paul V.,	May 17, 1605,	Jan. 28, 1621.
234, Gregory XV.,†	Feb. 9, 1621,	July 8, 1623.
235, Urban VIII.,	Aug. 6, 1623,	July 29, 1644.
236, Innocent X.,	Sept. 15, 1644,	Jan. 7, 1655.
237, Alexander VII.,	April 7, 1655,	May 22, 1667.
238, Clement IX.,	June 20, 1667,	Dec. 9, 1669.
239, Clement X.,	April 29, 1670,	July 22, 1676.
240, Innocent XI.,	Sept. 21, 1676,	July 31, 1689.
241, Alexander VIII.,	Oct. 7, 1689,	Feb. 2, 1691.
242, Innocent XII.,†	July 12, 1691,	Sept. 28, 1700.
243, Clement XI.,	Nov. 23, 1700,	Mar. 18, 1721.
244, Innocent XIII.,	May 7, 1721,	Mar. 3, 1724.
245, Benedict XIII.,†	May 29, 1724,	Feb. 21, 1730.
246, Clement XII.,†	July 11, 1730,	Feb. 6, 1740.

Name.	Consecrated.	Died.
247, Benedict XIV.,†	Aug. 17, 1740.	May 8, 1758.
248, Clement XIII.,	July 10, 1758,	Feb. 2, 1769.
249, Clement XIV.,	May 19, 1769,	Sept. 22, 1774.
350, Pius VI.,	Feb. 15, 1775,	July 1, 1799.
251, Pius VII.,	Mar. 14, 1800,	Aug. 23, 1823.
252, Leo XII.,	Sept. 27, 1823,	Feb. 1829.
253, Pius VIII.,	Mar. 31, 1829,	Nov. 30, 1830.
254, Gregory XVI.,	Feb. 2, 1831.	

Of those in the preceding list, who had been Bishops elsewhere, Urban IV., the one hundred and eightieth, was Patriarch of Jerusalem, and Gregory XIII., the two hundred and third, was Patriarch of Constantinople, at the time of their election.

CHAPTER XXVII.

ALLEGED BREAKS IN THE SUCCESSION.

From the facts detailed in the preceding chapters, it will be seen, that the idea of a break in the Apostolic succession is absurd; and the occurrence of such an event next to an impossibility. But notwithstanding objections have often been urged by those unlearned in these matters, the principal of which we shall consider. The first to which we refer is stated thus: "It has been said that, 'in the year 668, the successors of Austin being almost entirely extinct, by far the greatest part of the Bishops were of Scottish ordination by Aidan and Finnan, who came out of the Culdee Monastery of Columbanus, and were no more than Presbyters.'" The original authority for this assertion, is said to be the Venerable Bede, whom we have so often quoted. But Bede expressly tells us that Aidan and Finnan were the Bishops of Lindisfarne, now Durham, in the Arch-diocese of York, that Oswald, king of Northumberland, A. D. 635, sent to the Scottish rulers, desiring them to send *Bishops*—that they sent Aidan—that the Bishop coming to the king, had his Episcopal seat in Lindisfarne—that Bishop Aidan had been a Monk in the Island of Hii. Chapter fifth of the same book is entitled, "Life of Bishop of Aidan;" and it is said, "from this Monastery [in the Island of Hii] Aidan was sent, having received the office of a Bishop."

It does not devolve upon us to show how such mistakes have originated, but as the reason is obvious, we shall explain how it probably happened. The Picts were converted to Christianity by the preaching of one Columb, "an Irish Presbyter, Abbot, and Monk," A. D. 565.* Among other persons converted by the preaching of Columb, was Bridius, the king of the Picts, and in return for his eminence, his piety, and his labors, Bridius gave to Columb the Island of Hii, or Iona, and conferred upon him the government of the Island. Bede's account of this Island is: "That Island hath for its ruler an Abbot who is only a Presbyter, to whose government all the provinces, and even the Bishops, (contrary to the usual custom,) are subject, after the example of their first Doctor, who was not a Bishop, but a Presbyter and a Monk."† Now because the Governor of this Island was always to be the Abbot of that Monastery, and that Abbot always to be a Presbyter, the Bishop in civil matters was subject to one, who in all Ecclesiastical functions was his inferior; therefore objectors have inferred, that the Bishops themselves were Presbyters.

Concerning Finnan, we need give only one extract from Bede. Under date 652, he says: "Finnan succeeded him

---

* Bd. iii. 4. † Bd. iii. 4.

[Aidan] in the Episcopate, being also sent from the Monastery of Hii, in the Scottish Island, and remained a long time in the Episcopate, (Episcopatu.")*

To show beyond all question, the ignorance which originated this objection, and the folly of urging it, we shall mention a few of the Bishops then living in England. The period in question extends from 635, when Aidan came into Northumberland, to the year 668, mentioned in the foregoing extract.

PROVINCE OF CANTERBURY.

Diocese of Canterbury.

Honorius, consecrated by Paulinus of York,† 634–654.
Adeodatus, consecrated by Ithamar, of Rochester,‡ 654–664.
[Wilfrid of York,] consecrated by Archbishop of Paris and eleven others,§ 664–668.
Theodore, consecrated by 76th Bishop of Rome,|| 668– —.

Dorchester.

Birinus, consecrated by Bishop of Genoa,¶ 634–650.
Agilbert, consecrated in Paris,** 650–660.
Wina, consecrated in Gaul,†† 660– —.

Lichfield and Coventry.

Diuma, consecrated by Finnan,‡‡ 656–658.
Ceollach, consecrated by Scottish Bishops,§§ 658–660.
Trumhere, consecrated by Scottish Bishops,|||| 660–663.

London.

Mellitus, consecrated by Augustine,¶¶ 604–658.
Cedd, consecrated by Finnan and two other Bps.,*** 658–664.

---

* Bd. iii. 6, 17.
† Bd. iii. 7. Wend. i. 128.
‡ Bd. iii. 7. Wend. i. 149.
§ Bd. iii. 28, v. 19. Wend. i. 159.
|| Bd. iv. 4. Wend. i. 160.
¶ Bd. iii. 7. Wend. i. 135.
** Bd. iii. 7. Wend. i. 144.
†† Bd. iii. 7. Wend. i. 157.
‡‡ Bd. iii. 21. Wend. i. 154.
§§ Ib.
|||| Ib.
¶¶ Bd. ii. 3. Wend. i. 105.
*** Bd. iii. 22. Wend. i. 159

Norwich.

Felix, consecrated in Burgundy,*	634–648.
Thomas, consecrated by Archbishop Honorius,†	648–652.
Bregils, consecrated by Archbishop Honorius,‡	652–665.

Rochester.

Romanus, consecrated by Archbishop Justus,§	624–633.
Paulinus, consecrated by Archbishop Justus,‖	633–644.
Ithamar, consecrated by Archbishop Honorius,¶	644–656.
Damian, consecrated by Ithamar of Rochester,**	656–669.

Winchester.

Birinius, consecrated by Bishop of Genoa,††	636–660.
Wini, consecrated in Gaul,‡‡	660–670.

PROVINCE OF YORK.

Diocese of York.

Paulinus, consecrated by Archbishop Justus,§§	625–644.
Cedd, consecrated by Finnan and two other Bps.,‖‖	666–669.
Wilfrid, consecrated by Archbishop Paris,¶¶	669–678.

Lindisfarne, or Durham.

Aidan, consecrated by Scottish Bishops,***	635–652.
Finnan, consecrated by Scottish Bishops,†††	652–661.
Coleman, consecrated by Scottish Bishops,‡‡‡	661–664.
Tuda, consecrated by Scottish Bishops,§§§	664–665.
Eata, consecrated by Theodore,‖‖‖	665–684.
Cuthbert, consecrated by Scottish Bishops,¶¶¶	684–687.

* Bd. ii. 15. Wend. i. 129.
† Bd. iii. 20. Wend. i. 144.
‡ Ib.
§ Bd. ii. 8. Wend. i. 121.
‖ Bd. ii. 9. Wend. i. 133.
¶ Bd. iii. 14. Wend. i. 142.
** Bd. iii. 20.
†† Bd. iii. 7. Wend. i. 135.
‡‡ Bd. iii. 7. Wend. i. 157.
§§ Bd. iii. 7. Wend. i. 124.
‖‖ Bd. iii. 22.
¶¶ Bd. iii. 28, v. 19. Wend. i. 159.
*** Bd. iii. 3. Wend. i. 134.
††† Bd. iii. 6, 17. Wend. i. 148.
‡‡‡ Bd. iii. 25. Wend. i. 159.
§§§ Bd. iii. 26. Wend. i. 159.
‖‖‖ Vitâ Cuth. cc. 6, 25. Wend. i. 168.
¶¶¶ Vitâ Cuth. c. 25. Wend. i. 176.

We see, therefore, that at the time Aidan was consecrated Bishop of Lindisfarne, (Durham,) there were certainly *seven* Bishops living in England, one of whom was the Metropolitan of his own province. The objection is, therefore, without any foundation. The true reason why Oswald sent to Scotland for Bishops, was not the scarcity of Bishops of England, but the different practices of the two Churches concerning keeping Easter. The Northumbrians retained many of the customs of the British Churches, and among others, that of keeping Easter with the Greek Church. This was for a long time a subject of controversy between the Saxon and British Churches; and the old practice continued in Northumberland till 664, when it was changed by the King.*

Besides, there is another objection to the hypothesis of our opponents. When Cedd was consecrated Archbishop of York, A. D. 666, by Finnan,† in the absence of Wilfrid, exceptions were taken to his consecration, which was clearly uncanonical, Wilfrid having been previously elected and consecrated to the same See. But no exceptions were taken to the sufficiency of the consecration itself, and though he was displaced from the See of York, he received that of Lichfield, without any new consecration, and was confirmed by Theodore, Archbishop of Canterbury, the Primate of the realm, A. D. 669.‡

Another objection, often urged against the succession of the English Church, is stated thus: "The Church of England descended from the Church of Rome, and derived her orders from that Church. Hence it is said, that inasmuch as the Church of England has been excommunicated by the Bishop of Rome, the succession has been destroyed." To this objection we reply :—

1. That the Church of England did not descend from the

---

* Bd. iii. 25, 26.

† Bd. iii. 22.

‡ Bd. iv. 2. Wend. i. 159.

Church of Rome, as has been fully shown in the preceding chapters.

2. That each Bishop, having been originally, as we have shown, independent of every other Bishop, no Bishop could have power to depose or excommunicate other Bishops, unless that power had been subsequently granted to him by some sufficient authority. Now there is no authority that could grant this, unless a General Council; and no General Council ever has granted the Bishop of Rome this authority over the Bishops of England. On the contrary, it was expressly enacted by the sixth canon of the Council of Nice, A. D. 325, that the ancient customs and rights of the Churches should not be changed; and it is a matter of fact, which no one pretends to question, that the Bishops of England were then subject to the Metropolitan of Caerleon.

3. That whatever authority the Bishop of Rome may have over other Bishops, he has none over those of England, inasmuch as they have ever been legally and canonically independent of him. This will appear more plainly from a consideration of the original and continued independence of the British Churches, which will be given in the succeeding chapter.

CHAPTER XXVIII.

INDEPENDENCE OF THE BRITISH CHURCHES.

In treating of this subject, we shall first consider the state of things in Britain at the time Augustine arrived there, in order to gain a distinct idea of the situation of things in the British Church at that time. Augustine was consecrated at Arles, 596. In 598, he wrote to Gregory, Bishop of Rome, for advice touching certain points of inquiry. One of the questions was, In what manner he ought to deal with the Bishops of Gaul and Britain? Another, What course he ought to pursue in reference to the Gallic Liturgy, which, though different from the Romish Liturgy, was in use in the British and Gallic Churches? In answer, Gregory tells him, that he has nothing to do with the Bishops of Gaul, who were subject to the Bishop of Arles as their Metropolitan; that he ought to have authority over the British Bishops; and that in reference to the Liturgy, he ought to adopt that which would be most acceptable to the Saxon Church.* Here are three facts conclusively established: (1,) that there were canonical and lawful Bishops in Britain before Augustine went there. Consequently, he owed submission to the Metropolitan of Britain, according to the then existing canons of the Church. (2,) That the Liturgy used in Gaul was not the same as the Roman Liturgy; (3,) that this Liturgy was used in Britain. And this Liturgy, as we have already seen, was the Ephesian.

That these Bishops owed no subjection to the Bishop of Rome, is clear from the history of those times. Thus in the year 603, Augustine held a conference with the British clergy. At this conference, Bede informs us,† there were "seven British Bishops, and many learned men." In order to induce them to acknowledge his authority, Augustine promised them, if they would keep Easter on the same day as the Romish Church, would baptize according to the rites and ceremonies of that Church, and would preach the gospel to the Saxons, they should be allowed to enjoy all their other customs; to which the British Bishops replied, *we will neither do these things, nor submit to you as Archbishops over us.* Very little of what passed at that time has been preserved; but from that little it appears that the subject was strongly de-

* Bd. i. 27

† Bd. ii. 2.

bated.* Among the speakers was Dinoth, Abbot of the Monastery of Bangor. His answer has been preserved, and it goes the whole length of sustaining the entire independence of the British clergy, of the Pope of Rome. He said to Augustine:

"Be it certainly known unto you, that we all, every one of us, are obedient and subject to the Church of GOD, to the Pope of Rome, and to every pious Christian, to the loving of every one in his station, with perfect charity, and to the helping of every one of them by word and deed, to become the sons of GOD. And I know not of any other obedience than this, due to him you call Pope, or which may be claimed or demanded by the Father of Fathers. And this obedience we are ready to give; and to pay to him, and to every other Christian continually. Besides, we are under the government of the Bishop of Caerleon upon Uiske, who, under GOD, is to oversee over us, to cause us to walk in the way of life."†

---

* Bd. ii. 2.

† This important passage was first published by Sir H. Spelman, (*Concilia*, I. p. 108,) from an old MS. purporting to have been copied from one still more ancient, and is re-printed in Wilkin's, (*Concil.* and Smith's Bd. App. x. p. 716, and Fuller's Ch. Hist. in *anno* 601.) The genuineness of this answer has been assailed by the Romish writers, (Tuber. Man. p. 406. Ling. Hist. A. S. Church, p. 42,) but on insufficient grounds. It was defended by Stillingfleet (Orig. Brit. c. v. p. 224) and Bingham, (Antq. Ecc. ii. 9.) The first objection, that "the language is modern," is without foundation. The second, that the Metropolitan See was not then in Caer-leon, is also without foundation. The conference between Augustine and Dinoth, took place about A. D. 603, (Bd. ii. 2,) whereas the Archbishops of London and York had gone into Wales as early as 597, (Fur. Libro. Epis. Brit. in Ussh. Prim 67. Wm. Malms., De Gest. Reg. i. 6. Mat. West. An. 586,) and had fixed their seat at "Kaerllion ar Uyc," "*Caer-leon upon Uiske*," (O'Brien's Focal. Gaoidh. Intd. xvii., xix.)

These facts prove, beyond all cavil, that before Augustine came to England, there was a Church established there, duly organized, upon Apostolical principles, having the same officers or ministers as other Churches, with a Liturgy different from that of Rome, and with Bishops, owning and acknowledging no subjection to the Pope. The number of Bishops in England at that time we do not know. Bede says there were *seven* present at the conference with Augustine.* A very ancient author† reckons the number at *twenty-five* Bishops, and *three* Archbishops. And this is rendered probable by the fact, that the subscriptions of *three* Bishops are found in the ancient councils, as to that of Arles, 314.

We shall now go back and give a few brief historical notices of the British Church, anterior to the time of Augustine, showing that there had been a Church in England from the very time of the Apostles. The earliest history of the British Church has been involved in much obscurity, by the destruction of the records of that Church ; and much doubt and uncertainty has been thrown over it, by the manner in which it has been treated by the later Monkish historians, to whom we are indebted for very much of the history of those times.

A. D. 58. From those valuable historical documents, the Welsh Triads,‡ it appears that Caradog was betrayed and

* Hist. ii. 2.

† Galfrid. Mon. Hist. Brit. ii. 1. Asser. iv. 19, Ed. Heidelburg. See also Hen. Hunt. i. 170. Smith's Bd. App. iii., Ussh. Prim. 59.

‡ A couple of passages are of sufficient interest to be transcribed

"The three holy families of the isle of Britain :

"The first, the family of Bran the Blessed, son of Llyr Llediaith : that Bran brought the faith in Christ first into this island from Rome, where he had been in prison through the treachery of Aregwedd Foeddawg, daughter of Avarwy, son of Lludo.

"The second was the family of Amedda Wledig, who first gave land and privileges to God and his saints in the isle of Britain.

delivered up by Aregwedd Foedawg, about A. D. 51 or 52, who, with Bran, (Brennus,) his father, Cyllin, (Linus,) his son, and Eigan, his daughter, were carried prisoners to Rome, and remained in bondage seven years. While here, Bran, probably Caradog, certainly his son and daughter, became converts to Christianity. At the end of seven years, when Bran was set at liberty, he returned to Britain, taking with him three other converts to Christianity. Of these, one was Ilid, a converted Jew, another Cyndav, and the third Arwystli Hen, who appears to have been the person called Aristobulus,* whose "household" was saluted by Paul in his Epistle to the Romans, at the end of the same year, (A. D. 58,) or the beginning of the succeeding. This conclusion is strengthened by the fact, that Nicephorus, a Greek historian, and another Greek author, which goes under the name of Dorotheus, both record that Aristobulus went into Britain, and was ordained by St. Paul one of the first Bishops of that Church; that he

---

"The third was Brychan Brycheiniog, who gave his children a liberal education, that they might be able to teach the faith in Christ to the nation of the Cymry, when they were unbelievers."—*Triad* 18.

"The three sovereigns of the isle of Britain who conferred blessings:—

"Bran the Blessed, [A. D. 63,] son of Llyr Llediaith, who first brought the faith in Christ to the nation of the Cymry from Rome, where he had been seven years a hostage for his son Caradog, whom the Romans had taken captive after he was betrayed by treachery, and an ambush laid for him by Aregwedd Foeddawg.

"The second, Lleirwg, [A. D. 179,] the son of Coel, surnamed Llenfer Mawr, who made the first Church [building] at Llandaff, and that was the first in the isle of Britain, and who bestowed the privilege of country, and nation, and judgment, and validity of oath, upon those who should be of the faith of Christ.

"The third, Cadwalladr the Blessed, who granted the privilege of his land and all his property to the faithful, who fled from the infidel Saxons, and the unbrotherly ones who wished to slay them."—*Triad* 35.

* Taylor's Cal. by Rob. in Aristob.

made many converts, ordained Bishops, Priests, and Deacons, and died there.*

This account of the introduction of Christianity into Britain, from the Triads, is supported by Gildas, a British historian, who wrote about 560, who affirms, out of ancient records, that Christianity was introduced into Britain about the time of the revolt and overthrow of Boadice, A. D. 60 or 61.† So Tertullian, A. D. 190, says: "There are places in Britain inaccessible to the Roman arms, which were subdued to Christ."‡ And Origen, A. D. 230, says: "The power of God our Saviour is ever with them in Britain, who are divided from our world."§

63. About four years after this, A. D. 63, St. Paul is supposed by many to have visited Britain. That he had time, has been shown by Bishop Stillingfleet and others,‖ and that he had inducements to do it, there can be no doubt. There were many persons at Rome who would desire it. Thus Linus, who was a particular friend of St. Paul, mentioned by him in his second Epistle to Timothy, (iv. 21,) and ordained by Paul, first Bishop of Rome,¶ appears to have been a native Briton, the grandson of Bran, the British king. There were also many other Britons at Rome.** That St. Paul visited England, the early historians of the Church render altogether probable. Clement, of Rome, a disciple of Paul, (Phil. iv. 3,) and mentioned with commendation by him in his Epistle to the Philippians, about A. D. 87, or twenty

---

* These authorities are quoted at length in Ussher, *Primordia*, pp. 9, 744, 745, and several others added. Aristobulus is also described in the Greek *Martyrology*, and in the "Genealogy of Saints," originally written in the ancient British language, as the first Bishop of the Britons.

† Ep. 1. § 6, 8.

‡ Adv. Jud. c. 7.

§ Luke c. 1. Hom. 6.

‖ Orig. Brit. Clem. Rom. Ep. Cor. c. 5, and n. in SS. Pat.

¶ Apos. Cons. vii. 46.

** Still. Orig. Brit. c. 1.

years after the death of St. Paul, says, that in preaching the gospel, St. Paul "went to the utmost bounds of the west,"* which not only includes the island of Britain, but is the epithet by which that island was then known. Eusebius, A. D. 325, says that one of the Apostles "visited the British isles,"† and Theodoret, about a century later, A. D. 415, mentions Britain as one place where St. Paul labored.‡ There is, therefore, little doubt, that Christianity was preached, and a Church established, in England, as early as A. D. 63, and that there has been on that island at all times since, a Church of the living GOD. Aristobulus, being a Greek, and the disciple of St. Paul, when he went into Britain, would, of course, carry with him the ecclesiastical rites of the Eastern Churches, and this accounts for the correspondence of the Greek and British rites.

167. The Saxon historians, in speaking of this period, give account of Lucius, a King of the Britons, and tell us, that this King sent an embassy to Eleutherius, Bishop of Rome, requesting him to send ministers to Britain to preach the Gospel there; and that ministers were sent, who converted Lucius and many of his followers, and thus laid the foundation of the British Church.§ This account was rejected by historians, until the publication of the Triads, from which it appears that Lleurwg, (Lucius,) the grandson of Cyllin, or Linus, first Bishop of Rome, was permitted by the Romans to reign over a part of Britain, and that he exerted himself to promote the interests of Christianity in Britain. It is, therefore, not unlikely that he sent an embassy to the Bishop who filled the See once occupied by his grandfather, and not unlikely that the Bishop of Rome sent clergymen to the assistance of Lleurwg, or Lucius, though it would seem

* Ep. Cor. c. 5.

† Demon. Evang. iii. 5.

‡ Tom. iv. Serm. 9, in Ps. cxvi.

§ Bd. i. 4.

from the account given in the *Old Book of Llandaff*, that no persons returned but those who went to Rome from England, one of whom was Elvanus, the second Archbishop of London.*

179. The old Saxon historians agree that St. Peter's Church, Cornhill, was founded about this time, and that it was afterwards the Cathedral Church of the Archbishop of London, of which Theonus was the first Archbishop.† The Archiepiscopal See of York is supposed to have been founded about the same time, and Fagan and Theodosius are said to have been the first Bishops.‡ So also the Archiepiscopal See of Caerleon is supposed to have been founded soon after —a See which continued long after the others had been destroyed by the Saxons.§

303. During the persecution this year, many suffered death in Britain, whose names have been preserved by Gildas and Bede.||

St. Alban, of Verolam, the first British martyr, suffered May 23.¶

Aaron and Julius, as Bede says, of the city of Legion, by which is meant Leon, or Caer-Leon, suffered July 1.**

Socrates and Stephen suffered, Sept. 17.††

During this persecution, the Churches were demolished, the holy vessels carried off, Christians were cruelly murdered, and every indignity offered to their persons.

314. This year a Council was summoned by the Emperor Constantine, at Arles, in France, consisting of the Bishops of

* Mon. Ang. vol. III. p. 188. John Furn. Libro. Ep. Brit. in Ussh. Prim. p. 67.

† Ralph. Bald. Chron. An. 179, in Ussh. Prim. 66. J. Furn. Libr. Episc. Brit. in Ib.

‡ Prim. Brit. 71, 72.

§ Prim. Brit. 71, 72, 87–98.

|| Ep. § 10. Ecc. Hist. i. 7.

¶ Bd., and all the British historians.

** Ib.

†† Petr. de Nat. xi. § 250, in Prim. 169.

the principal cities in the various provinces of Italy, Gaul, and Britain, with a few from Africa, to hear and judge in the case of the schismatic Numidians. Three British Bishops—Eborius of York, Restitutus of London, and Adulfius, whose Diocese has been the subject of dispute—attended. His subscription, as it now stands in the MS. copies of the doings of that Council, is, *Ex civitate Colonia Londinensium.* But this is a copy of the original subscription, which, as Bishop Stillingfleet has shown, was probably* *Ex Civit. Col. Leg.*, which the transcriber would naturally construe to mean, as it is now written. Archbishop Ussher supposes it denoted *Cair-Colun*,† which, according to Galfrid of Monmouth,‡ denotes the city of *Chester*. But Mr. Selden§ and Sir H. Spelman,|| suppose it to be the *Old Colony of Camalodunum.* We suspect, however, that the subscription was as Stillingfleet supposes, *Ex Civitate Col-Legion*, which is the mere Latinization of *Caur-Leon*, or *Ligion*. The British Bishops present at the Council of Arles, were, therefore: Eborius, Archbishop of York; Restitutus, Archbishop of London; Adulfius, Archbishop of Caerleon; with Sacerdos, a Presbyter, and Arminius, a Deacon of that Church.

402. Kiarna and Declan preached the gospel in Ireland, and converted many to the faith.¶

431. Palladius, ordained Bishop of the Scots, by Celestine, forty-third Bishop of Rome.**

448. A Synod was held at Munster this year, at which Ailbe, Declan, Kieran, and Ibar, opposed Patrick's Archiepiscopal authority, alleging that they had equal authority with him, that they had been Bishops longer than he had, and that no one could give him authority over them without

---

* Orig. Brit. 48. † Prim. 60, 195. ‡ Hist. Brit. v. c. 6.
§ In Eutch. 118. || Conc. I. p. 39.
¶ Ussh. Prim. 781, 2, 86. Life Pat. 88. ** Ib.

their consent; but they conceded to his merits and to his success, what they refused to yield when claimed *as a right.* Ailbe, or Albeus, was settled as Bishop of Emly, (*Imelacensis;*) Declan, as Bishop of Ardmore; Kieran, as Bishop of Sageir, but subsequently translated to Aghavoe, and thence to Kilkenny; and Ibar made Bishop of Beg-eri.* While in England, Germanus established several schools, of which those taught by Dubritius and Iltutus, at a place now called Boverton, were far the most celebrated.† The school, afterwards the monastery of Bangor, seems to have commenced about this time. According to the Welsh Triads, there were 2400 religious persons connected with this establishment, when Augustine came to England; and Bede informs us that the Saxon King, as other historians say, at the instigation of Augustine, fell upon and slew 1200 of them.‡ While in England, Germanus also consecrated several Bishops, among whom were Dubritius, Archbishop of Llandaff; Daniel, Bishop of Bangor; and Iltutus, Bishop of a place of the same name.§

493. This year the Britons, under their new King, gained a considerable victory over the Saxons at Badon Hill.|| The Churches were now rebuilt, and Sampson, one of the pupils of Iltutus, and a man of eminent piety, was consecrated Archbishop of York. The theological schools established by Germanus were at the height of their reputation during the reign of Arthur, and among the many eminent scholars,

* Life Patr. 88. Prim. Ecc. Hist. 801, 866, 7.

† Still. Orig. Brit. c. iv. p. 126.

‡ Dup. Ecc. Writ. Cent. vii. p. 52.

§ Old Chron. in Leland. Collect. vol. II. p. 42. Old Reg. Lland. in Mon. Ang. vol. III. p. 188. Hen. Hunt. ii. 178. Galfrid. Mon. Hist. ix. 1. Math. Wes. A. D. 490. Still. Orig. Brit. c. 4, p. 126. Ussher, Prim. pp. 80, 979.

|| Still. Orig. Brit. 129.

we find the name of St. David, whose piety, virtue, and influence, secured him a place even in the catalogue of Saxon Saints.*

587. The Saxons at this time gained possession of a much larger tract of country, whereupon Thomas, Archbishop of London, and Thadioc, Archbishop of York, with their clergy, retired into Wales;† so that, from that time there was but one British Arch-diocese—that of Caerleon.

This brings us to the close of the sixth century, at which time Augustine came to England, and with him other missionaries from Rome, and commenced preaching to the Saxons. Here we must pause a moment, and note the situation of the British Church at that time. We have seen then, that the following circumstances existed at that period.

1. That Christianity was preached in Britain and the neighboring islands at an early period, and that the Church there had its Bishops and Liturgy, like other orthodox Churches.

2. That these Bishops did not derive their power from, nor acknowledge the authority of the Pope, and that they had continued their succession down to the days of Augustine.

3. That the British Liturgy and ecclesiastical rites were different from those of Rome, but corresponded in many particulars with those of the Asiatic Churches.

4. That notwithstanding this, the British Church kept up a friendly intercourse with the neighboring Churches, and were acknowledged, even by the Bishops of Rome, to be sound and orthodox.

5. That there were at least one Archbishop and seven Bishops in England when Augustine landed there, belonging to the Archiepiscopate of Caerleon.

---

* Breviary, Salisbury.

† Math. Westmin. A. D. 586.

6. That the authority of the Bishop of Rome to rule over other Bishops, was denied from the very first, in Ireland; to which it may be added, that the Pope could not persuade the Archbishops of Armagh to receive the Pall from him, until the twelfth century, as is witnessed by Roger Hovedon,* and the Annals of Mailross, A. D. 1152,† which is also acknowledged by St. Bernard himself.‡ These facts demonstrate, as clearly as facts can do it, the original independence of the British Churches. And here we might leave the point; for, if the Bishop of Rome had no rightful authority in England, so late as A. D. 600, it is clear that he never could have any. But, inasmuch as the subsequent acts of the Saxon Church are appealed to by the abettors of Romanism, as proof of their subjection, we shall give a brief chronological notice of some leading events, which show that this claim is as groundless as the former.

661. This year a Council was held at Northumberland, at which the subjects of difference between the Saxon and British Churches, especially the time of keeping Easter, were debated before Oswin, King of Northumberland. Wilfrid was the principal speaker on behalf of the Saxon Churches, and Coleman, Bishop of Lindisfarne, for the British customs. The King was persuaded to approve of the Roman custom, but the Bishops and clergy refused to comply.§

666. This year the King nominated Wilfrid, Archbishop of York, who went to Paris, and was consecrated by the Archbishop of Paris and eleven other Bishops.‖ In his absence the King nominated Cedd, a Briton, to the same office, who was consecrated by Wina, Bishop of London, who had been consecrated in Gaul,¶ and two British Bishops, one of whom

---

* Hov. ii. 454. † In Life St. Patr. 89. ‡ Life St. Malachi.
§ Bd. iii. 25. ‖ Bd. iii. 28.
¶ Bd. iii. 7. Hen. Hunt. ii. 191. Sax. Chron. 39.

was Finnan.* Wina was made Bishop of Winchester, 660,† and Bishop of London, 666.‡ Wilfrid, upon his return, went into Lichfield, and finally to Canterbury, where he officiated as Archbishop until Theodore's arrival. A. D. 669, Cedd was translated from the See of York to Lichfield, and Wilfrid became his successor.

673. On the death of Adeodatus, Archbishop of Canterbury, in 668, Pope Vitalian succeeded in procuring the election of Theodore, an Italian Monk of good repute, to that See, who exerted all his influence to introduce the Roman rites. During his Episcopate, a Council was held at Hereford, A. D. 673, which was attended by the King in person, and at which Theodore presided. At this time it was decreed that whatever had been canonically determined by the Fathers, should be observed in England.

The Pope could gain nothing from what was done by this Council, save an indirect influence he might obtain under the provisions of the fourth canon, which made Monks independent of their Bishops; whereas, his authority was effectually cut off by the second, sixth, and eighth, by which no Bishop could execute any Episcopal function in another Diocese. Under these canons, *the Pope himself could not, canonically, perform one ministerial act in England, without the consent of the Bishop in whose Diocese it was to be performed.* Besides, the eighth canon contains what *we* should now regard as a pointed rebuke upon his pretended supremacy; for though it had no immediate application except to England, it is an unequivocal declaration of the Bishops composing that Council, that they knew of, and acknowledged no superiority among Bishops, but such as their age and the order of their consecration conferred. They distinctly recognised that princi-

* Bd. iii. 28. Sax. Chron. 40.

† Sax. Chron. 39. ‡ Patr. Brit. 67.

ple which has governed the Church from the beginning, and which is still in force in this country.

We have now shown conclusively, that the British Church was not originally a branch of the Romish Church; that the Anglo-Saxon portion of it, though converted by missionaries from Rome, practically denied from the very outset, the supremacy of the Pope, *as* it is now claimed, and hence it follows, that all authority which the Pope ever exercised over that Church, at any subsequent period, was *usurpation;* and also, that when the Church of England threw off the Papal yoke, she only did that which, upon every principle, she had a right to do—asserted her PRIMITIVE INDEPENDENCE.

678. This year Egfrid, King of Northumberland, divided the See of York into three Dioceses, and had three Bishops ordained for them,* without consulting Wilfrid; at which he was so much offended that he appealed to the Bishop of Rome, and procured a decree for his restoration. This was the first instance of a Saxon Bishop appealing to Rome, but the decree was so little regarded, that Wilfrid was deposed from his Bishopric by Theodore, Archbishop of Canterbury, (who, it will be remembered, was ordained by the Bishop of Rome,) and imprisoned by Egfrid, where he remained several years.†

704. This year a Synod was held upon the river Nid, in Northumberland, at which Birthwald, Archbishop of Canterbury, presided. Here the decrees of the Bishop of Rome were read, but their authority was denied by Bosa, Bishop of York, and John, Bishop of Hexham. The difficulty was finally compromised by making John Archbishop of York, and Wilfrid, Bishop of Hexham.‡ The appeal of Wilfrid

---

* Ang. Sac. i. 693.

† Dup. Ecc. Writ. c. viii. 128. Crabb, H. C. L. 20. Ling. H. S. C. 108.

‡ Hard. Conc. III. 1825. Ed. Vit. Wilf. cc. 44–58, in Ling. H. A. S. C

was the first appeal from England to Rome, and though it was disallowed at the time, laid the foundation of subsequent appeals.

709. This year a Synod was held, at which *sixty-five different tracts of country were ceded to the Pope forever.* Though the Monks had been made independent of the Bishops in 673, they were not independent of the King. To accomplish this, Egwin, Bishop of Worcester, who had espoused the cause of Monasticism, represented that he had seen a vision, in which the Virgin Mary appeared to him and directed the Kings of England to give certain lands to the Pope, to enable him to establish monasteries; whereupon Constantine, who filled the See of Rome, wrote to Birthwald, Archbishop of Canterbury, desiring him to use his influence to procure the grant of such lands from Kenred and Offa, Kings of England. Through the conjoined efforts of Egwin, Constantine, and Birthwald, *sixty-five different tracts of country were ceded to the Pope forever,* for the purpose of establishing monasteries, which grant was confirmed by a Synod held this year.* In this way, the Pope was enabled to introduce into the heart of England, an army of Monks, who were almost entirely independent of the civil and ecclesiastical authority of the realm; and thus was laid the foundation of much of the authority the Bishop of Rome afterwards obtained in England.

747.* By the third canon of the Council of Hereford, A. D. 673, the monasteries had been made independent of their Bishops, and A. D. 709, virtually independent of the King. In consequence of this, they had become the resort of many besides Monks, so that they were filled with poets, musicians, and buffoons; and so great had this evil become, that the second Council of Clofeshoch, held this year, found it neces-

---

* Hard. Con. III. p. 1827. Col. Conc. Brit. T. I. Con. 709.

sary to make them again subject to the inspection of the Bishops, whose duty it was to see that the monasteries were what their name imports, places of silence, peace, and repose, the abode of persons occupied by spiritual reading, singing, and praying.*

787. It was enacted by the Councils of Northumberland and Mercia, that the Monks should not choose an Abbot for their monastery, without the consent of the Bishop. At these last Councils, and probably at the preceding, the King and his nobles were present, and assented to the canons.† Subsequent to this time we hear less of the British clergy, as distinct from the Saxon-English; yet as late as A. D. 812, there were so many of them in Wales, Ireland, and Scotland, that it was thought necessary, by the Council of Celchith, held that year, to prohibit the British Bishops from performing any Episcopal acts within the Dioceses of the English Bishops, even with their consent.‡ Councils were subsequently held in the years 788, 800, 803, 822, 824, 903, 923, 928, 944, 971, 977, 988.§ Nothing was done in these Synods, recognizing the authority of the Pope, yet it is evident that he was gaining ground in England, and that many of his claims were acquiesced in, though not acknowledged. The great number of Monks who had established themselves in England, conduced very much to this end. But the Pope did not obtain a sure foot-hold in this country until the Norman conquest, A. D. 1066.

WILLIAM I., 1066–1095. Having shown that the Saxon Church was legally and canonically independent of the Church of Rome, up to the time of the conquest, we shall take a hasty glance at such acts of subsequent times, as

* Hard. Conc. III. 1953.

† Hard. Conc. III. 2072.

‡ Dup. Ecc. Writ. Cent. ix. p. 117.

§ Hard. Conc. IV. 823–1265, VI. 589–715.

manifest a similar state of things. It is necessary to remark, however, that the Gallic Church to which William belonged, had not remained as independent of the Church of Rome as the English; and one of the first acts of this King was, to request the Pope to send a legate to England, to assist in reforming the English Church; by which he meant, the expulsion of the English clergy, and the substitution of the Norman.* William immediately separated the civil and ecclesiastical departments of the State, thus strengthening the power of the Pope.† Appeals, however, were still made by the clergy to the King, and not to the Pope.‡

William II., 1095–1100. William II. found it impossible to control the clergy as he wished, and consequently he contrived to keep a number of Sees vacant. At the time of his death he had in his hands one Archbishopric, and four Bishoprics.§ Anselm was nominated to the See of Canterbury, by William. He acknowledged the authority of Pope Urban, before he had been acknowledged by the nation. For this, the whole body of Bishops, at Rockingham, renounced the allegiance of the Archbishop.‖ He was afterwards reconciled to the King, but was not permitted to convoke Synods, nor to fill up vacant Dioceses.

Henry I., 1100–1135. Henry restored the Saxon laws,¶ re-united the ecclesiastical and secular branches of the government, and required the Bishops to attend the Councils of the nation.** Appeals to the Pope, however, were allowed,†† but not without licence from the King.‡‡ He disputed, but relinquished the right of investing Bishops with the ring and

* Ling. Hist. Eng. vol. II. p. 23

† Char. Rolls. Ric. II. No. 5. Wilk. Leg. Sax. 292.

‡ Crabb, Hist. Eng. Com. Law, p. 49.

§ Ling. H. E. II. 76.

‖ Ead. Vit. Ansl. 27. Ling. II. 79.

¶ A. S. LL. 301.

** LL. Hen. I. c. 5. Wilk. 301.

†† LL. Hen. I. c. 5.

‡‡ Ead. 112–116.

crosier.* He denied the right of the Pope to appoint a legate in England, save the Archbishop of Canterbury, unless by request of the King,† and maintained his ground against all opposition.

STEPHEN, 1135–1154. Nothing important transpired in this reign, though the encroachments of the Pope were continued.

HENRY II., 1154–1189. The growing power of the Pope met with an effectual check in the reign of Henry II., who called a council at Clarendon, A. D. 1164, composed of Archbishops, Bishops, Abbots, Lords, Barons, &c., at which sixteen canons were enacted, which, if they had been strictly adhered to, would have put an end to the power of the Pope in England forever.‡

By these canons the clergy were forbidden to leave the realm without the consent of the King—were made amenable to the secular courts—were prohibited from making appeals to the Pope. It was also required of them, that the election of Bishops should not be made without the King's consent—that no freeholder should be laid under interdict, without an application to the King, or Chief Justice, with several other regulations of a similar kind.§ These canons were transmitted to Rome, when Pope Alexander, in full Council, passed a solemn condemnation and revocation of them; but notwithstanding this, they were confirmed by the King, Lords, and clergy, at a Council in Northampton, A. D. 1176, in presence of the Legate of the Pope; and during the reign of Henry all were strictly adhered to, except that which required the clergy to answer for their crimes in the civil courts.||

* Ead. 90. Ling. 95.
† Ead. 58, 118, 126. Ling. II. 113.
‡ Mat. Par. 100.
§ Wilk. LL. A. S. 321–324
|| Crabb, H. E. C. L. 113.

RICHARD I., 1189–1199, did nothing touching this point of our inquiry.

JOHN, 1199–1216. During the reign of this inconstant and imbecile Prince, Popery raised its head within the British dominions, by consent of the King. At first John made a stand against the encroachments of the Pope, and refused to receive Stephen Langton, who had been made Archbishop of Canterbury, against the will of the monarch, in opposition to the choice of the Bishops and clergy, and the election of the Monks.* The King, however, was compelled to submit, to swear fealty to the Pope, to pay annually a thousand marks to the Pope, and to guarantee the payment of Peter-pence, which then amounted to about £200.†

HENRY III., 1216–1272. During the long reign of this monarch, the power of the Pope was at its height in England, and the oppressions of the clergy almost past endurance. The King, warned by the fate of his predecessor, acquiesced in silence, and the Barons imitated his example. But the opposition of the great body of the clergy was aroused. They remonstrated with the Pope, they complained to the King, and finally drew up a list of their grievances, sent it to the Pope, and appealed from him to a General Council.‡

EDWARD I., 1272–1307. In the reign of this Prince was commenced a series of laws, which eventually overturned the whole power of the Pope in England. He would not allow the Bishops of England to attend a General Council, until they had solemnly promised not to receive the papal benediction, and in the thirty-fifth Edward I., A. D. 1306, the statute *de Asportatis Religiosorum*§ was enacted, which forbid the carrying of any ecclesiastical property out of the realm, under penalty of being grievously punished for such

* Mat. Par. 222–245. Ling. III. 23, 24.

† Ling. III. 32, 33.

‡ Ling. III. 86–89.

§ Stat. Westm. 2. c. 41.

ontempt of the King's injunction, and was intended to annihilate the custom introduced by Nicholas, in the preceding reign. The preamble describes the taxes as laid by the Abbots, but the statute is couched in such terms as to leave no room for the Pope to interfere.* Edward, like most sovereigns of those days, when he wanted money, compelled those who had it to contribute to his necessities, and he laid heavy burdens on the clergy. They appealed to the Pope, and he issued a Bull, A. D. 1296, forbidding the clergy to pay such taxes, and excommunicating those who should lay them.† But Edward had both the disposition and ability to enforce his will, and with the approbation of the lay peers, the whole body of clergy were outlawed, until they made amends to the King.‡

Edward II., 1307–1327. The long disputed boundary between the ecclesiastical and civil judicatories, had been settled during the reign of Edward I., and the privileges of the clergy in criminal trials confined within much narrower limits, which were still further confined by the statute *de Articuli Cleri*, enacted in the ninth Edward II., A. D. 1316, by which certain canons published by Boniface, Archbishop of Canterbury, in the reign of Henry III., were revoked.§ By this statute the King was invested with authority to reverse any sentence of excommunication, that would affect his own liberty or safety.

Edward III., 1327–1377. After the passage of the statute *de Asportatis Religiosorum*, in the reign of Edward I., it was usual for the Abbeys and Priories to receive provisions, which they disposed of to persons called provisors, when they sent the money annually to Rome. To put a stop to this, a statute was passed the twenty-fifth Edward III., A. D. 1351, which

---

* Stat. Realm, I. 151.

† Rym. Foed. II. 706.

‡ Ling. III. 202.

§ Stat. 9 Ed. II.

declared all persons who purchased such provisions, traitors and outlaws, which was also confirmed by statutes enacted in 1353 and 1364.* An ordinance was also passed the fortieth of Edward III., A. D. 1366, making it criminal to carry the contributions called "Peter-pence," out of the kingdom.† This year, it was also declared by the King, Lords, and Prelates, that the donation which John had pretended to make to the Pope, was illegal and void, and that every person appealing to the court of Rome, or citing another to appear there, should be held as a traitor and outlaw.‡ And the three estates bound themselves, if the Pope attempted to enforce payment of the sums due him for Peter-pence, that they would resist him to the utmost of their ability. It was also asserted in this reign, that the Pope could not invest the Bishops with their temporalities, and that these must be given by the King.§

RICHARD II., 1377–1399. These laws being found insufficient to prevent the transportation of ecclesiastical property to Rome, a law was passed the third Richard II., A. D. 1379, subjecting all persons guilty of making gifts of ecclesiastical property to the court of Rome, or of sueing out any process from it, to forfeiture of property, imprisonment, and sometimes death.‖ Before the passage of this last act, the Lords, Commons, and Prelates, had pledged themselves to stand by the laws of the country, against the Pope and his adherents, in the cases specified.¶

---

* Stat. 25 Ed. III. St. 5, c. 6, and St. 6, c. 2. 27 Ed. III. St. 1, c. 1. 38 Ed. III. St. 1, c. 4. St. 2, c. 1.

† Stowe, Chron. 461. Fab. 40 Ed. III.

‡ Rot. Parl. II. 289, 290.

§ Spelm. Conc. ii. 435. Rym. Foed. in various places.

‖ Stat. 3 R. II., c. 3; 7 R. II., c. 12; 12 R. II., c. 15; 13 R. II., c. 2; 16 R. II., c. 5.

¶ Ling. IV., 186.

Henry IV., 1399–1413. Papal interference was still further prohibited by statute, second Henry IV., A. D. 1400, which made all persons guilty of buying bulls of exemption from the Pope, or who brought them into the kingdom, liable to the same penalties which had been made against provisors.*

Henry V., 1413–1422. By statute passed 1st Henry V. A. D. 1413, aliens were prohibited from holding benefices in England, except in case of Priors, and they were required to obtain sureties for their obedience to the laws of the realm.†

Henry VI. 1422–1452. Edward IV., 1452–1483.

Richard III. 1483–1485. Henry VII., 1485–1509.

The laws that had been enacted under former sovereigns were sufficient, had they been put in force, but the civil discords and the wars abroad, which distracted the kingdom during the reigns of these princes, left them little time to look after the Church. Consequently, all the old abuses were revived, and perhaps the Pope had never greater influence in England, than at the accession of Henry VIII.

Henry VIII., 1509–1547. Upon Henry's accession to the throne of England, he manifested no disposition to interfere with the claims of the Pope, and it was not until the twenty-first year of his reign that he made war upon the papal usurpations. This year, a statute was enacted,‡ regulating the fees in the ecclesiastical courts, and abolishing pluralities. The carrying of property to Rome was prohibited by severer penalties.§ The statutes against foreign jurisdiction passed in the reigns of Edward I. and III., and of Richard II. and Henry IV., were re-enacted, enlarged, and enforced, by se-

* 2 H. IV., cc. 3, 4. Stat. Real. II. 121, 122.

† 1 H. V., c. 7, and 2 H. V., St. 1.

‡ Stat. 21 H. VIII., cc. 5, 6, 13.

§ Stat. 23 H. VIII., cc. 6, 20. 32 H. VIII., c. 45.

verer penalties.* The election of Bishops, the publication of new canons, and other similar matters, were also regulated,† until the power of the Pope in England was completely overturned and annihilated.

This brief view of the legislation of the Anglo-Norman Church and nation, proves most unanswerably, that there never was a time, even under the reign of the Norman princes, when the Pope could legally and canonically exercise the powers he claimed in England, and hence, though his exactions and usurpations were from time to time submitted to, and his alliance frequently courted, the nation was at liberty to throw off his allegiance at any moment it saw fit. It would also be easy to show, that during this whole period, there were leading men in the English Church who made bold stand not only against the usurpations, but also against the corruptions of that Church. Even Archbishop Dunstan, in many things subservient to the Pope, did not hesitate to set at defiance the papal mandate, when he deemed it unjust or improper, A. D. 961.‡ And Alfric Puttock, Archbishop of York, from 1023 to 1050, openly impugned the doctrine of transubstantiation. In his "Sermon to be spoken to the people at Easter, before they receive the holy housel," (communion,) he teaches doctrines that would now be considered orthodox by sound theologians.§ In the next century, Gilbert Foliat, consecrated Bishop of Hereford, 1148, translated to London, 1163, died 1187, set at defiance the papal authority, and though twice excommunicated by the Pope, paid no regard to the thunders of the Vatican.|| Contemporary with

* Stat. 24 H. VIII., c. 12. 25 H. VIII., c. 19, etc.

† Stat. 25 H. VIII., c. 19, etc.

‡ Ling. H. A. Sax. Ch. 240.

§ Elfric's Sermon, in Petheram's Hist. Sk. A. S. Lit. p. 33. See also, Ecc. Const. about 1050, Wilk. LL. A. S. p. 159. Disc. Sax. Chr. p 251.

|| Mat. Par. 99–145.

Foliat, was Ormin, the poet, whose works present us with the purest English, and the purest doctrines of that age.* The next century was rendered famous by Robert Grostete, or Greathead, Bishop of Lincoln, from 1234 to 1258. In 1247, a demand was made by the Pope for six thousand marks, (about £50,000,) and he had the courage to refuse to levy it until he had the sense of the nation upon it. He visited Rome, and protested against its corruptions, before the Pope and Cardinals. After his return, the Pope again tried his courage by collating an Italian youth to a vacant Canonry in the Cathedral of Lincoln. But Grostete was inflexible. He set at naught the Pope's commands, for which he was excommunicated. But the thunderbolt fell harmless at his feet, and he died in peaceful possession of his See.† Other examples of a similar nature occur, but these are amply sufficient to show that many of the clergy asserted that, in their writings, to which they assented in their legislative capacities. It remains now simply to show, that the clergy consented to the Reformation individually, as well as collectively, which will be done in the next chapter.

CHAPTER XXIX.

THE ENGLISH REFORMATION CANONICAL.

We have already seen, that every Church is, in fact, independent of every other Church, and that the Bishops of any province, are independent of those in every other province. Consequently, the Bishops and clergy of any one province,

---

* Ear. Eng. Poets, N. Y. R. IX., 392.

† Le Bas Life Wick. pp. 79–84. Mat. Par. pp. 400–918.

with the consent of the laity, have the right to make any regulations for the government of their own branch of the Church, not inconsistent with Apostolical organization and order. That this was done by the English Reformers, will be evident from a brief survey of the manner in which they conducted the Reformation.

In the reign of Henry VIII. very little opposition was made by any of the clergy, to an assertion of the *Church's independence*, which was all that was then proposed, and very few deprivations were made. Even under the reign of Edward VI., very few of the clergy made any objection to the reformation of *doctrine and discipline*, which was then brought about. A few Bishops, however, were deprived in the reign of Edward; as, Bonner, of London;* Gardiner of Winchester;† Heath, of Worcester; and Day, of Chichester;‡ for non-conformity to laws enacted by Parliament, touching the proposed reforms, and Tunstall, of Durham, on the alteration of his Diocese. These were all restored upon the accession of Mary.§ Those deprived by Mary, were, Cranmer and Holgate, Archbishops of Canterbury and York; and Bishops, Taylor, of Lincoln; Hooper, of Worcester; Harley, of Hereford; Ferrar, of St. David's; Bush, of Bristol; Bird, of Chester;|| Scorey, of Chichester; Coverdale, of Exeter; Ridley, of London; and Poynet, of Winchester.¶ That is, *five* were restored and *eleven* deprived, making *sixteen*, or a majority of the *twenty-six* Dioceses. All this was done by Mary, before she attempted to restore the Popish religion.

---

* Burnet, vol. II. Par. 1, p. 166. † Ib. p. 216. ‡ Ib. p. 266.

§ Burnet, II. Ann. 1553, vol. III., p. 314.

|| Lingard, Hist. of Eng., vol. VII., 143. Rym. Foed. xv. 370, 371. The successors of all these but Cranmer, were consecrated while the Protestant Bishops were in possession of their Sees, and hence, upon primitive principles, were uncanonical and schismatical. Ling. VII., 143.

¶ Ling. VII., 293.

Nor even then did she attempt to restore the Romish practices *by authority of the Church*, but merely *by vote of Parliament.* The Reformation in the time of Edward, was brought about by THE CLERGY, convened in Synod, and approved by the laity in Parliament. In the reign of Mary, it was arrested by an interference of *the State*, without convening a Synod or consulting the clergy. Consequently, when, in the reign of Elizabeth, this unlawful interference was withdrawn, the Church became at once, legally and canonically, what it was in the reign of Edward.

At the accession of Elizabeth, or immediately after,* nine Dioceses, viz., Canterbury, Norwich, Chichester, Hereford, Salisbury, Rochester, Gloucester, Oxford, and Bangor, were vacant, by the death of the incumbents. After the enactment of the act of *Uniformity*, in the first year of Elizabeth, Kitchen, Bishop of Llandaff, took the oath of supremacy and conformed. About the same time, the oath of supremacy was tendered to fifteen other Bishops, who refused to take it, and were therefore deprived of their Sees. Of these, *six*, Tunstall, of Durham; Morgan, of St. David's; Ogilthorp, of Carlisle; White, of Winchester; Baines, of Lichfield and Coventry; and Holyman, of Bristol, *died* before their places were filled; and *three*, Scot, of Chester; Goldwell, of St. Asaph's; and Pate, of Worcester, abandoned their Sees and left the kingdom. The remaining *seven*, Heath, of York; Bonner, of London; Thirlby, of Ely; Bourne, of Bath and Wells; Turberville, of Exeter; Watson, of Lincoln; and Pool, of Peterborough; lived and died in England, but never attempted to exercise any Episcopal functions. Of these seven, *four* held places from which Protestant Bishops had been illegally and uncanonically ejected by Mary; viz., Bonner, of London, from which Ridley had been deprived;

---

* Strype, Eliz. p. 154. Linds. Vind. p. xxvi.

Turberville, of Exeter, from which Coverdale had been deprived; Bourne, of Bath and Wells, from which Barlow had been deprived; and Heath, of York, from which Holgate had been deprived.*

We have, therefore, in the foregoing list, twenty-six Dioceses, *fifteen* of which, at the time of the Consecration of Protestant Bishops under Elizabeth, had become vacant by death. The incumbents of *three* had abandoned their Sees; the incumbents of *four* held places from which Protestant Bishops had been unlawfully and uncanonically deprived by Mary, either because "they were married," or "had been consecrated according to the Ordinal of Edward VI.;"† and *one*, Kitchen, of Llandaff, had conformed. In the *fifteen vacant Dioceses*, even the Romanist will not deny the right of Parker to ordain Protestant Bishops, and these, with Kitchen, constituted a large majority of the twenty-six Dioceses. Nor is it presumed they will deny the right to fill the Sees of those who had gone abroad. And if they assume that the restoration of the Bishops of Winchester, Durham, London, Worcester, and Chichester, by Mary, was lawful, (had it been done canonically,) because they had been deprived under Edward, then it was lawful for Elizabeth to deprive the Bishops of York, London, Exeter, and Bath and Wells, for the same reason. Hence, then, at least *twenty-five* of the *twenty-six* Bishoprics were legally, properly, and canonically filled in the first years of Elizabeth, with Protestant Bishops.

Among the minor clergy, the case was widely different; for, as appears by a calculation made at the time, out of nine thousand four hundred ecclesiastical persons in the land, only one hundred and seventy-seven left their places, and of these, only eighty were Rectors of Churches.‡ Hence it

---

* Lind. Vind. pp. xx–xxviii. † Lingard, VII., 143.

‡ Strype, Eliz. p. 73. Camden, 47. There were *six* Abbots and

follows, that an immense majority of the clergy of the English Church consented to the Reformation. And all the acts of the clergy in Synod, both in the reigns of Edward and Elizabeth, were submitted to, and approved by the King and Parliament, so that every act of Reformation was performed upon strictly canonical and legal principles. It may, therefore, be said, with great propriety, that the Reformed Church of England was not *another*, but the *same* Church; though reformed, its identity, as a Church, was not affected. The Reformed Church of England is, therefore, the Old Catholic Church of that country. Consequently, all those who, in England, refuse to unite with it, but go off and establish another altar, and build another Church, are, upon Apostolical and Primitive principles, *schismatics*. This conclusion is as applicable to the Romanist as to any other dissenter. Their plea of submission to the Pope can not save them from the dilemma, (1.) because he has no rightful jurisdiction in England, and (2) because it was not the original ground taken, being an after-thought put into their heads by the Pope and his emissaries. Elizabeth succeeded to the crown of England, Nov. 17, 1558. As early as 1562, the various Dioceses were filled with Protestant Bishops, and no Bishop was allowed to execute any function of his office within the realm, without first taking the oath of supremacy. Consequently, no *Romish* Bishop could execute the duties of his office within that kingdom. But notwithstanding this, Pope Pius IV. seems never to have abandoned the idea of regaining Elizabeth and the Church of England to the See of Rome;* but his successor, Pius V., considered the caution

Abbesses, *twelve* Deans, *twelve* Archdeacons, *fifteen* heads of Colleges, and *fifty* Prebendaries. In Ireland, a still smaller number left their places. Linds. Vindic. cxix.

* Lingard, VIII., 39.

of his predecessor as a dereliction of duty. "In the spring of 1569, he sent Dr. Nicholas Morton, who had been a prebendary of York, under Mary, into the northern counties of England, with the title of Apostolical Penitentiary. The object of his mission appears to have been to impart to the [Roman] Catholic Priests, as from the Pope, those faculties and that jurisdiction which they could no longer receive in a regular manner from their Bishops. Camden says, that he urged the northern men to rebellion. . . . . Of his activity in promoting the insurrection, there can be little doubt."* On the 25th of February, 1570, the Pope issued a bull of excommunication against Elizabeth, pretending to put her out of the pale of the Church, assuming to depose her from the crown, to absolve her subjects from all allegiance to her, and requiring all the faithful to withdraw from her, under pain of excommunication. A copy of this bull was affixed to the gates of the Bishop of London, on the 15th of May, 1570, and other copies were circulated through the kingdom. The more intelligent and liberal-minded of the Romanists regretted the act, and considered it as "an imprudent and cruel measure,"† but it evidently had its effect upon the common people, and necessarily *compelled* all Romanists *to separate* from the Church of England; and hence the *English* Romanists may properly be said *to have separated* from the Reformed Church in the twelfth of Elizabeth, and thus, at that time, to have formed a *sect*.

The other sectaries and schismatics in England separated from the Church at a much later period, and hence a consideration of their history does not fall in with the design of this work. But some of the arguments by which they attempt to justify their separation, deserve to be considered; since, if true, they prove that the English Church, at the

---

* Lingard, VIII., 40. † Lingard, VIII., 56.

time of the Reformation, abandoned the fundamental principles of Apostolic organization and order, and was not, therefore, legally and canonically reformed. The arguments are mainly two, each of which will be considered separately.

First, it is claimed that "the Church of England separated from the Church of Rome, and, therefore, others may separate from the Church of England." This assumption is false in two respects, for (1) it would not follow, *if the Church of England* separated from the Church of Rome, that *individuals* might separate from the Church of England. The two cases are utterly unlike, and we can not reason from one to the other. But (2) the Church of England did not separate from the Church of Rome. The Church of England did no more than assert her original and primitive independence—an independence that she had enjoyed for more than five centuries unmolested, and which for nine centuries more, she had continually attempted to defend. The Reformation in the Church of England was simply a return to primitive truth and order. She separated from no one. She excommunicated no one; and it was not until the twelfth of Elizabeth that the Bishop of Rome presumed to cut himself off from her communion, for that was all that his pretended bull of excommunication could effect.

But, *second*, it is said, that the Reformers of the Church of England, and the Church of England herself, gave up, at the time of her Reformation, one of the fundamental principles of Apostolic organization and order—the necessity of Bishops to the due organization of the Church. This objection, as generally presented, divides itself into two branches—that the English Reformers believed, and the Church of England taught, (1,) that Episcopacy did not exist by divine right, that is, they believed it to be a human institution; and, (2,) that Bishops and Priests are not different orders of clergy. Now if these charges are true, the English Reformers gave up one fundamental principle of primitive order, and were, in fact, *Presbyterian*. And if the Church of England is Presbyterian, then there can be no doubt that others have a right to separate from her; for those who have themselves separated from Apostolic order, can not complain if others follow their example. In proof of these positions, our opponents are wont to quote the opinions of Cranmer, and sundry others who were among the leading Reformers of the English Church, in which some of them say something to the purpose for which they are quoted. We shall, therefore, inquire under what circumstances, and for what purpose, the opinions which are quoted in support of the above positions, were expressed, and what and how much they prove.

It must be borne in mind, that *all* the Reformers of the English Church had been educated in the Romish faith. A complete change of sentiment could not be wrought in a day or a year. The change must be gradual; unless, as often happens, it goes from one extreme to the other. But such was not the case with the English Reformers, and evidence of their progress appears in the productions of the various epochs of the Reformation. From this it will be seen, that the *date* of a document cited as evidence on this head, is most material. If a given document contains the opinion of Cranmer and others, who were *afterwards* Reformers, while they were Romanists, then to quote *that* as evidence of what the *Reformers* thought, is gross misrepresentation.

To show how these various documents came to be produced, and that our readers may see how far they are pertinent to prove the opinions of the *Reformers*, we shall allude to the manner in which the English Church was reformed. The first distinguishing feature of the English Reformation is, that *it was the calm, dispassionate, and deliberate act of the most pious and learned among the clergy*, approved by the great body of the laity; while in other countries it was usually the act of some rash and head-strong individual, *opposed* to the body of the clergy. The second is the *mode* in which they conducted their efforts for reformation. This we can not better state, than in the language of an historian of former days. He says: "*First*, the whole business they were to consider, was divided into so many heads, which were proposed as queries, and these were given out to the Bishops and Divines; and at a prefixed time, every one brought in his opinion in writing, on all the questions."*

In this manner all questions relating either to faith or practice, were examined. When these opinions had been handed in, the authors met and conferred upon their points of difference, until they were able to agree upon something to be laid before the convocation, to be approved by that body.† One of the first of these conferences was held in 1537 or 1538, at which a number of papers were drawn up. Two of these papers have been preserved by Burnet.‡ One of them is entitled, "A Declaration made of the Functions and *Divine Institution* of Bishops and Priests." This paper is signed by Cranmer and a large number of Bishops and Divines, and contains the following passage: "In the New Testament there is no mention made of any degrees or distinctions in orders, but only of Deacons or Ministers, and of Priests or Bishops."§

---

* Bur. vol. I. p. 372. † Bur. vol. I. Par. 1, pp. 372–374.

‡ Hist. vol. I. Par. 2, Add. No. 1 and 4.

§ The Papists, to avoid the charge of having created a new *order* in the ministry, contend that Bishops and Priests are of the same *order*, the Pope alone constituting the third order. This point was hotly debated in the Council of Trent. On the part of the Pope it was contended, that all ecclesiastical authority was derived from St. Peter, who alone derived his authority from CHRIST. And those who, with the Archbishops of Grenada and Paris, held that all the Apostles, and con-

The Institution of a Christian Man was compiled from these papers,* and published the same year. This book contains the paragraph we have copied from the foregoing "declaration," and is one of the authorities usually cited by Anti-Churchmen. With how much fairness it can be thus quoted, our readers can judge, when we tell them, that this book, compiled from these documents, and signed by Cranmer and thirty-six of the most learned of the clergy, established the Romish doctrines of "Transubstantiation, communion in one kind, celibacy of the clergy, auricular confession, seven sacraments, and purgatory."† In all things they proved themselves staunch Papists, save in the single item of the *Pope's supremacy,* and perhaps the subject of monastic vows. This, therefore, was the opinion of these men as Romanists, not as Reformers, and the man who quotes them as such, is either too ignorant to write, or too dishonest to be trusted.

The next document in point of chronology, cited to prove the Anti-Episcopal notions of the English Reformers, bears date in 1540. The history of that paper is as follows. In 1539, the King proposed six questions to the clergy relative to points of doctrine; in answer to which, they asserted the doctrines of "Transubstantiation, communion in one kind, celibacy of the clergy, sacrifice of the mass, auricular confession," &c.‡ Upon these answers the act of Parliament, called "the bloody hill," was passed, an act which sent Protestants and Romanists to execution upon the same hurdle.

---

sequently, all Bishops, derived their authority from Christ, were told, that they thus took away the authority of the Pope, and that it was idle to pretend that the Pope was head of the Church, and yet to hold that there was authority in the Church not derived from him. Fra. Paolo. Hist. Coun. Tr. L. vii.

* Strype, Ann. B. 1, c. 41, p. 315, and App. No. 88.

† Strype, Ann. pp. 311, 315. Bur. vol. I. Par. 2, pp. 375–398.

‡ Srype, Ann. B. 1, c. 47, pp. 361, 362.

The complaints under this act, caused a new commission to be issued the same year, to re-examine the various points of disputed doctrine. Seventeen questions were proposed for consideration. Those who wish to see the whole paper, will find it in Burnet.* That summary is sufficient to show, that these men were then *Romanists*, and hence those opinions are no evidence of what they thought as *Reformers*.

The next paper usually cited in proof, bears date 1543, and is drawn from a work entitled, "*The Necessary Erudition of a Christian Man.*" This book was merely a revision of the "Institution," of which we have spoken,† revised and corrected by the King.‡ The book was somewhat enlarged, and the doctrine of purgatory omitted. In other respects, it taught the same doctrines as the *Institution*, and in common with that asserted, that Bishops and Priests were of the same order, and this is the last we hear of that opinion. With this book, published five years before the death of Henry VIII., and seven years before the compilation of the Book of Common Prayer, ends the chain of authorities by which the Reformers of the English Episcopal Church are to be proved Presbyterian. If, therefore, these publications are pertinent to prove what were the opinions of the Reformers on one point, they are pertinent on another, and if they prove any thing, they prove that the Reformers of the English Church believed in *transubstantiation, seven sacraments, sacrifice of the mass, auricular confession, celibacy of the clergy, monastic vows, communion in one kind;* they prove in fact, that the English Church was not reformed, and that it is still Roman Catholic. They prove this, or they prove nothing to the purpose for which they are so often quoted.

* Hist. Ref. vol. I. Par. 2, pp. 256-303. Strype, B. i. p. 357, App. No. III. p. 300.

† Strype, p. 377.

‡ Hallam, Cons. Hist. Eng. vol. I. pp. 79, 110.

Having examined the books published *before* the reign of Edward VI., usually cited to prove the Presbyterianism of the English Reformers, we shall endeavor to ascertain what were the opinions of the Reformers of the Episcopal Church, concerning THE CHURCH, *and its ministry;* and for this purpose, we shall only quote from authoritative documents, published in the reign of Edward and Elizabeth. Our chief authority shall be the book of Common Prayer. It will be borne in mind, that a distinct recognition of any *principle*, or point of doctrine, IN A PRAYER, is conclusive evidence that those who composed or adopted *that* prayer, believed the "principle" so recognized, to be *certain truth.*

THE CHURCH. "Art. 19. The visible Church of Christ *is a Congregation* of faithful men, *in the which* the pure word of GOD is preached, and *the sacraments be duly ministered, according to Christ's ordinance* in all those things that of necessity are requisite to the same."

OF THE MINISTRY. "Art. 23. *It is not* LAWFUL for any man to take upon himself the office of public preaching, or ministering the sacraments in the congregation, *before he be* LAWFULLY *called and sent*, to execute the same. And those we ought to judge *lawfully called and sent*, which be *chosen and called* to this work *by men who have public authority* given unto them in the congregation, *to call and send ministers into the Lord's vineyard.*"

THE MINISTRY DIVINELY INSTITUTED. *Collect at the ordination of a Deacon.*—"ALMIGHTY GOD, who by Thy divine Providence hast appointed *divers orders of ministers* IN THY CHURCH." *Collect at the ordination of a Priest.*—"ALMIGHTY GOD, giver of all good things, who by Thy HOLY SPIRIT hast appointed *divers orders of ministers* IN THY CHURCH." *Prayer at the consecration of a Bishop.*—"ALMIGHTY GOD, giver of all good things, who by Thy HOLY SPIRIT hast appointed *divers orders of ministers* IN THY CHURCH."

THE MINISTRY CONSISTS OF THREE ORDERS. *Litany.*—" That it may please Thee to illuminate all *Bishops, Priests, and Deacons,* with true knowledge and understanding of Thy word." *Collect at ordaining a Deacon.*—" And didst inspire thine Apostles to choose into *the order of Deacons,* the first martyr, Saint Stephen, with others, mercifully behold these Thy servants, now called to *the like office* and administration." *Collect at ordaining a Priest.*—" Mercifully behold these Thy servants, now called to *the office of the Priesthood.*" *Prayer at the consecration of a Bishop.*—" Mercifully behold this Thy servant, now *called to the* work and *ministry of a Bishop.*" *Litany at the ordination of Deacons or Priests.*—" That it may please Thee to bless these Thy servants, now to be admitted to the *order of Deacons,*" [or *Priests.*] *Litany at the ordination of a Bishop.*—" That it may please Thee to bless this, our brother elected, [to *the office of Bishop,*] and to send Thy grace upon him." *Preface to the Ordinal.*—" It is evident unto all men, diligently reading holy Scripture and ancient authors, that from the Apostles' time there have been these orders of ministers in CHRIST's Church—*Bishops, Priests, and Deacons.*"

BISHOPS SUPERIOR TO THE OTHER CLERGY.—This follows from the above, for, if GOD has " appointed divers *orders* of ministers in his Church," the different kinds of ministers so divinely constituted and appointed, of necessity belong to the " divers orders ;" and the *first* order must be *superior* to the second, or any subsequent order, so that Bishops must be superior to every other order. This superiority is recognized throughout the whole Liturgy. *Prayer for the clergy and people,* used both in the morning and evening service.—" Send down upon our BISHOPS and *other* clergy, and upon the congregations committed to their charge, the healthful spirit of Thy grace." The same superiority is recognized in the *Litany,* in the *Form of consecration of a Bishop,* and *ordaining Priests and Deacons*, in the *Order of confirmation*, in the *Rubric in the communion service*, in the thirtieth article, and in numerous other places. Indeed, this distinction of *order* between Bishops and Priests, is uniformly kept in sight, throughout the *Liturgy* and *Articles*.

WHO "LAWFULLY CALLED AND SENT?"—"Art. 36. The Book of consecration of Bishops, and ordaining of Priests and Deacons, *as set forth by the General Convention of this Church, in* 1792, [in the English Prayer Book, *lately set forth in the time of King Edward the Sixth*, with which the American Book agrees in every important particular, except in slight verbal alterations,] doth contain all things necessary to such consecration and ordering. . . . . Whosoever are consecrated or ordered according to said form, we decree all such to be rightly, orderly, and *lawfully consecrated and ordered*." *Preface to the Ordinal*, established by the foregoing *Article*.—"It is evident unto all men, diligently reading holy Scripture and ancient authors, that from the Apostles' time there have been these *orders* of ministers in CHRIST'S Church—BISHOPS, PRIESTS, and DEACONS. Which offices were evermore had in such reverend estimation, that no man might presume to execute any of them, except he were first called, tried, examined, and known to have such qualities as were requisite for the same; and also by public prayer, with imposition of hands, were approved and admitted thereto *by lawful authority*." The "lawful authority" here meant, is, of course, the authority prescribed by the *Ordinal*, that is, *the Bishop*. We learn, therefore, from the foregoing, what were the opinions of the framers of our Liturgy, that is, of the *Reformers of the English Church*, AS REFORMERS, concerning THE CHURCH, *and its ministry*, and also what is the opinion of the Church itself. They were as follows:—

The visible Church of CHRIST *is a congregation* of faithful men, *in the which* the pure word of GOD *is preached*, and the sacraments be duly ministered, *according to* CHRIST'S *ordinance;* that by the ordinance of CHRIST, no man may take upon himself the office of public preaching, or ministering the sacraments, before he is lawfully called and sent to do the same; that by the same ordinance, the ministry, by which the word is to be preached and the sacraments administered, is made to consist of three distinct orders, called Bishops, Priests, and Deacons; that these three orders, so divinely constituted, have existed in the Church of CHRIST from the time of the Apostles; that by the same authority by which these three orders exist, power and authority to call and send men to preach the word and administer the sacraments, is vested in the Bishop alone.

But notwithstanding the certainty of this conclusion, there are some who still persist in urging other reasons, to prove the very things we have so clearly disproved. The principal of these we shall mention. Thus it is said:—

1. That "Dr. Bancroft, chaplain to Archbishop Whitgift, [first] divided off the Bishops from the body of the Presbyters, and advanced them into a superior order by divine right, in a sermon at St. Paul's Cross, January 1, 1588." Those who know what the Book of Common Prayer teaches, know this can not be true; but all may not know, that *in the sermon referred to, there is not one word on the subject.**

2. That "those who had been ordained in foreign Churches, in the reign of Mary, were admitted in Elizabeth's reign to their ministerial offices and charges, and to legalize this, an act of Parliament was passed the thirteenth Elizabeth, allowing of ordination of Presbyters without a Bishop." No such act was ever passed by the British Parliament. The act referred to, is entitled, *An act to reform* CERTAIN DIS-

---

* So says Hallam, Const. Hist. Eng. vol. I. p. 504, who says he had read it.

ORDERS *touching the ministers of the Church.** The first section enacts, that every minister under the degree of Bishop, who had received ordination or consecration *by any other form than that prescribed by the Ordinal of Edward VI.*, should, in a certain limited time, subscribe to the articles of religion, confessions, &c. &c., prescribed by law, and in default thereof, should be deprived. One of the things they were thus required to sign, was the Preface to the Ordinal. The second section of the same act declares, that any minister who teaches or preaches any thing contrary to those articles, shall be deprived, and there is not, in the whole chapter, one word about, or one allusion to ordination by Presbyters.

3. "That Archbishop Grindal commissioned a Presbyterian minister to preach in his Diocese." This case of itself proves, that the English Church did not allow his orders, for if it had, there would have been no need of a commission. Further, for this very act and other irregularities, the Archbishop was suspended.†

4. "That ministers from abroad, who had received only Presbyterian ordination, were received in their ecclesiastical character by the Reformers, without re-ordination." These lists usually include the names of "Calvin, Knox, Fagius, Bucer, Tremellius, Peter Martyr, Ochinus, Travers, Whittingham, John A Lasco," &c. Of each of these separately.

Of CALVIN. And (1) he never visited England, and, therefore, could not have been admitted to their pulpits; and (2) *he never was in Priest's orders*,‡ and, therefore, could not have been acknowledged as a minister of Christ.

---

* Stat. 13 Eliz. c. 12, pp. 546, 547.

† Strype, Life Grind.

‡ Beza, Life Cal. Spon, Hist. Geneva, iii. p. 243, cited in Bayle, Hist. and Crit. Dict. vol. II. p. 264. Leti, Hist. Gen. vol. III. p. 41, in Bayle, ubi. sup. Maimbourg, Hist. Calvinism, p. 64, ib.

KNOX was *Episcopally* ordained in the Romish Church, before becoming a Reformer, and was, therefore, upon the same footing with the rest of the Reformers.*

FAGIUS. Of Fagius little is known, as he died very soon after he arrived in England.†

BUCER was a Dominican Friar, and Episcopally ordained, before joining the Reformers.‡

TREMELLIUS, an Italian Monk, was Episcopally ordained a Priest, before becoming a Reformer.§

PETER MARTYR had been Episcopally ordained in the Romish Church, before becoming a Reformer.||

OCHINUS had received orders in the Romish Church, and was at one time Father Confessor to Pope Paul III.¶

Of TRAVERS, it is sufficient to say, that "Archbishop Whitgift silenced him, and ultimately removed him, by means of the High Commission Court, *as unqualified for ministering in the Church of England, from want of Episcopal ordination.*"**

WHITTINGHAM. As for Whittingham, "he seems to have had merely what is termed, among Dissenters, *a call*, from the English refugees at Geneva, and to have been set apart for the ministry, by some of them, not in orders, in a private house. * * * * A solemn adjudication of this case was precluded by the Dean's [Whittingham's] death; but Archbishop Whitgift declared soon after, that *he would have been*

---

* Rob. Scot. vol. I. p. 238. Biog. Univers. vol. XXII. p. 499. Encyc. Am. vol. VII. p. 341. M'Crie's Life Knox, p. 8.

† Bur. vol. II. p. 116.

‡ Encyc. Am. vol. II. p. 206.

§ Bossuet, Hist. Prot. cit. in Trav. Irish Gent. p. 241, n. Strype, Ann. B. ii. c. 18, p. 387.

|| Encyc. Am. vol. VIII. p. 312. Bow. Lett. vol. I. p. 204.

¶ Churchm. xiii. 47.

** Soames's Elizabethan Religious History, p. 444.

deprived, had he lived, without 'especial grace and dispensation.' "*

John A Lasco had never received Episcopal ordination, and was never received into Episcopal pulpits. But Edward and Cranmer, desirous of patronizing eminent Reformers, though they did not adopt Episcopacy, issued a commission, authorizing A Lasco and four other foreigners, to preach to their countrymen, in certain chapels erected for the purpose.

It has also been said that the consecration of Scotch Bishops, in the time of James I., who before had only received Presbyterian ordination, was an acknowledgment of Presbyterian ordination. But this inference does not follow, for we have seen, that both in the Churches of Alexandria and Rome, even *laymen* were elected to the Bishopric, and consecrated without passing through the intermediate orders.

Thus much for this charge, which our readers will see by this time, is wholly unfounded. The Episcopal Church never has renounced the divine institution of Episcopacy, nor has she, as a Church, done any act that amounts to an acknowledgment of the orders of any one who has not been Episcopally ordained.

---

* Soames's Elizabethan Religious History, pp. 232–3.

APPENDIX.

Consecration of Archbishop Parker.

About fifty years after the death of Archbishop Parker, a story was made up by some of the Papists, denying that Parker was consecrated. This story became the subject of controversy, and is thus described by Rev. John Lingard, D. D., the Roman Catholic historian of England, in the following *note*, Hist. Eng., vol. VII. p. 293, Am. Ed., p 422, Paris Ed.

"It may, perhaps, be expected that I should notice a story which was once the subject of acrimonious controversy between the divines of the two communions. It was said that Kitchin and Scorey, with Parker and the other Bishops elect, met in a tavern called the Nag's Head, in Cheapside; that Kitchin, on account of a prohibition from Bonner, refused to consecrate them, and that Scorey, therefore, ordering them to kneel down, placed the Bible on the head of each, and told him to rise up Bishop. The facts that are really known, are the following. The Queen, from the beginning of her reign, had designed Parker for the Archbishopric. After a long resistance, he gave his consent; and a congé d'élire was issued to the Dean and Chapter, July 18, 1559. He was chosen August 1. On September 8, the Queen sent her mandate to Tunstall, Bishop of Durham, Bourne of Bath and Wells, Pool of Peterborough, Kitchin of Llandaff, Barlow, the deprived Bishop of Bath under Mary, and Scorey of Chichester, also deprived under Mary, to confirm and consecrate the Archbishop elect. (Rym. xv. 541.) Kitchin had conformed; and it was hoped that the other three, who had not been present in Parliament, might be induced to imitate his example. All three, however, refused to officiate; and, in consequence, the oath of supremacy was tendered to them, (Rym. xv. 545;) and their refusal to take it was followed by deprivation. In these circumstances no consecration took place; but three months later, (December 6,) the Queen sent a second mandate, directed to Kitchin, Barlow, Scorey, Coverdale, the deprived Bishop of Exeter under Mary, John, suffragan of Bedford, John, suffragan of Thetford, and Bale, Bishop of Ossory, ordering them, or any four of them, to confirm and consecrate the Archbishop elect: but with an additional clause, by which she, of her supreme royal authority, supplied whatever deficiency there might be according to the statutes of the realm, or the laws of the Church, either in the acts done by them, or in the person, state, or faculty of any of them, such being the necessity of the case, and the urgency of the time. (Rym. xv. 549.) Kitchin again appears to have declined the office. But Barlow, Scorey, Coverdale, and Hodgskins, suffragan of Bedford, confirmed the election on the 9th; and consecrated Parker on the 17th. The ceremony was performed, though with a little variation, according to the Ordinal of Edward VI. Two of the consecrators, Barlow and Hodgskins, had been ordained Bishops according to the Roman Pontifical, the other two according to the Reformed Ordinal. (Wilk. Con. iv. 198.) Of this consecration on the 17th of December, there can be no doubt: perhaps, in the interval between the refusal of the Catholic prelates, and the performance of the ceremony, some meeting may have taken place at the Nag's Head, which gave rise to the story."

This note called forth an attack in the *Birmingham Magazine*, by an anonymous writer, signing himself " T. H.," to which Rev. Dr. Lingard made the following reply:

" Mr. Editor,—In your last number, a correspondent, under the signature of T. H., has called on me to show why I have asserted, (Hist. Eng. VII. p. 293,) that Archbishop Parker was consecrated on the 17th of December, 1559. Though I despair of satisfying the incredulity of one who can doubt after he has examined the documents to which I have referred, yet I owe it to myself to prove to your readers the truth of my statement, and the utter futility of any objection which can be brought against it.

" The matter in dispute is, whether Parker received, or did not receive, consecration on the 17th of December; but the following facts are, and must be admitted on both sides: 1st. That the Queen, having given the royal assent to the election of Parker, by the Dean and Chapter of Canterbury, sent, on September 9, a mandate to six prelates to confirm and consecrate the Archbishop elect; and that they demurred, excusing, as would appear from what followed, their disobedience by formal exceptions on points of law. 2d. That on the 6th of December, she issued a second commission to seven Bishops, ordering them, or any four of them, to perform that office, with the addition of a sanatory clause, in which she supplied, by her supreme authority, all legal or ecclesiastical defects, on account of the urgency of the time, and the necessity of the thing—'temporis ratione et rerum necessitate id prostulante;'—words which prove how much the Queen had this consecration at heart; and certainly not without reason, for at that time, with the exception of Llandaff, there was not a Diocese provided with a Bishop; nor, as the law then stood, could any such provision be made without a consecrated Archbishop, to confirm and consecrate the Bishops elect. 3d. That four out of the seven Bishops named in the commission, (they had been deprived or disgraced under Queen Mary, but had now come forward to offer their services, and solicit preferment in the new Church,) having obtained a favorable opinion from six counsel learned in the law, undertook to execute the commission, and confirmed Parker's election on the 9th of December.

"Now, these facts being indisputable, what, I ask, should prevent the consecration from taking place? The Queen required it; Parker, as appears from his subsequent conduct, had no objection to the ceremony; and the commissioners were ready to perform it, or rather under an obligation to do so; for by the 25th of Henry VIII., revived in the last Parliament, they were compelled, under the penalty of præmunire, to proceed to the consecration within twenty days after the date of the commission. Most certainly all these preliminary facts lead to the presumption that the consecration did actually take place about the time assigned to it, the 17th of December, a day falling within the limits I have just mentioned.

"In the next place, I must solicit the attention of your readers to certain indisputable facts, subsequent to that period. These are:—1st. That on the 18th (and the date is remarkable) the Queen sent to Parker no fewer than six writs addressed to him, under the new style of Matthew, Archbishop of Canterbury, and Primate and Metropolitan of all England, and directing him to proceed to the confirmation and consecration of six Bishops elect, for six different Sees. This was the first time during the six months which had elapsed since his election, that any such writ had been directed to him. What, then, could have happened, just before the 18th, to entitle him to this new style, and to enable him to confirm and consecrate Bishops, which he could not do before? The obvious answer is, that he himself had been consecrated on the 17th. 2d. That on the 21st, he consecrated four new Bishops; on the 21st of January, five others; two more on the 2d, and two on the 24th of March. Can we suppose that so much importance would be attached to consecration given by him, if he had received no consecration himself? or, that the new Church would have been left so long without Bishops at all, if it had not been thought necessary that he, who was by law to consecrate the others, should previously receive that rite? 3d. That afterwards, at the same time with the new prelates, he obtained the restoration of his temporalities—a restoration which was never made till after consecration. 4th. That he not only presided at the convocation, but sat in successive Parliaments, which privilege was never allowed to any but consecrated Bishops. In my judgment, the comparison of these facts, with those that preceded the 17th of December, forms so strong a case, that I should not hesitate to pronounce in favor of the consecration, even if all direct and positive evidence respecting it had perished.

"But there exists such evidence in abundance. That Parker was consecrated on the 17th of December, is asserted, 1st, by Camden, (i. 49;) 2d, by Godwin, (De Præs. p. 219;) 3d, by the Archbishop himself in his work, (De Antiquitate Brittanicæ Ecclesiæ,) published in 1572, three years before his death; or, if that book be denied to be his, in his diary, in which occurs the following entry in his own hand: '17th Dec. Ann. 1559, consecratus sum in Archepiscopum Cantuariensem. Heu! Heu! Domine Deus, in quæ tempora servasti me!' (Strype's Parker, App. 15.) And 4th, by the Archiepiscopal Register, a record which details the whole proceeding, with the names of the Bishops, of the Chaplains, and of the official witnesses. In truth, it descends to so many minute particulars, that I think, Mr. Editor, it must be the model after which are composed the descriptions of consecrations, ordinations, and dedications, which we have the pleasure of perusing in your pages. In one respect only must it yield the superiority to them. It names not either the organist or the singers.

"Now to this mass of evidence, direct and indirect, what does your correspondent oppose? That Harding and Stapleton, and the more ancient Catholic controvertists, denied that Parker was a Bishop? That is, indeed, true; but I always understood that their objections (which is certainly the case with respect to the two passages quoted in your last number) referred to the validity, not to the *fact* of his consecration; and if Dr. Milner has chanced to assert to the contrary, I fear that he wrote it hastily, and without consideration. I am not aware of any open denial of the fact, till about fifty years afterwards, when the tale of the foolery supposed to have been played at the Nag's Head, was first published. In refutation of that story, Protestant writers appealed to the Register; their opponents disputed its authority; and the consequence was, that in 1614, Archbishop Abbot invited Colleton, the Archpriest, with two or three other Catholic missionaries, to Lambeth, and submitted the Register to their inspection, in presence of six of his own Episcopal colleagues. The details may be seen in Dodd, ii. 277, or in Godwin, p. 219.

"Your correspondent assures us that the Register contains 'so many inaccuracies and points at variance with the history of the times, as manifestly prove a forgery.' Were it so, there still remains sufficient evidence of the fact. But what induces T. H. to make this assertion? Has he examined into all the circumstances of the case? Or does he only take for granted the validity of the several objections which Dodd, without expressing any opinion of his own, has collected from different controvertists? However that may be, I have no hesitation in saying, that all those objections are founded on misconception or ignorance; that the Register agrees in every particular with what we know of the history of the times; and that there exists not the semblance of a reason for pronouncing it a forgery."

Epistles of Ignatius.

Among the authorities quoted in this volume, is Ignatius, Bishop of Antioch. He is important, both for the early date and fullness of his writings; and it has been found the easiest way to dispose of him is, to deny the authenticity and genuineness of his epistles. It is agreed, that Ignatius was Bishop of Antioch, a distinguished man and Christian, sentenced to death by Trajan, and was sent to Rome to die, A. D. 107, or 116; on his way, he wrote several epistles to several different Churches. It is also agreed, that we have two copies of seven epistles purporting to have been written by Ignatius; that the longer copy teaches Arianism, the shorter, the Divinity of Christ; that Eusebius had, when he wrote, A. D. 305, the same number of epistles, having the same directions as those we possess. Now it has been repeatedly shown, to our entire satisfaction, *that Ignatius wrote seven epistles to seven Churches; that they taught the doctrine of the Trinity; that the shorter copy is the same as that of Eusebius, Athanasius, Jerome, and other orthodox men of that age, in this respect.*

But this conclusion has been assailed with great violence. The opponents are of two classes: (1,) the Arian and Socinian, who finds his notions of the Trinity contradicted by that copy which has by far the greatest claim to authenticity; and (2) the anti-Episcopalian, who finds his views of the existence and authority of Bishops in that primitive age, controverted by them. Yet there are many non-Episcopalians who speak differently. MOSHEIM says: "The seven shorter epistles are, by most writers, accounted genuine. . . . To this opinion I cheerfully accede." Dr. MURDOCK says: "Moderate men, of various sects, especially Lutherans, are disposed to admit the genuineness of the epistles in their shorter form, but to regard them as interpolated and altered." This is the opinion of the leading German historians; as NEANDER, (Allgm. Gesch. Christ. Rel. I., B. III., Abth. 1107,) and J. E. C. SCHMIDT, (Handb. Christ. Kirch., I. Theil. §§ 47, 119.) J. C. I. GIESELER (Text-Book, Ecc. Hist. Div. I. § 33) places them among the genuine writings. A common opinion among good scholars now is, that *the seven shorter epistles of Ignatius are genuine, but interpolated.* But if these epistles are *interpolated*, can we quote them as authority? Certainly not, until we have ascertained the *true text.* Nor is this a difficult task, as has been shown by SCHMIDT, (Christ. Kirch. I., § 47. Versuch über gedop. Recens. Briefe Ign. in Henckes Mag. Relig. Bd. III. S. 91.) Thus, if we compare the two copies, and reject from each things not contained in the other, what remains will be genuine. That is, where they agree in phraseology, there is no reason to suspect either has been altered, and this may be set down as *the certain text.* Where the longer merely *expands the idea* of the shorter, the text of the shorter is *the highly probable text.* Where the only difference is, that the longer changes the language of the shorter, teaching another doctrine, the text of the shorter is *the probable text.* Finally, when either contains passages not in the other, and not relating to doctrine, that must be regarded as *probably spurious.* In this volume, Ignatius is never quoted as authority, except from the *certain text.*

Here we might leave this subject, inasmuch as no objection can be made against *the passages we have quoted;* but it may be well to add a few facts, in answer to some other objections, showing their futility. All the objections which can be urged with any plausibility, were brought together in the [monthly] *Christian Spectator*, published at New Haven, vol. V., No. 8; the chief of which we shall notice.

Objection 1. "The account of the martyrdom of Ignatius, which has been defended as ancient and authentic, disagrees with the relation Eusebius has given of his progress to Rome." (P. 393.)

We have compared both carefully, and cannot find a single point of disagreement or contradiction.

Objection 2. "If the larger epistles be claimed as genuine, their Arianism militates against their genuineness; if the smaller, their opposition to that doctrine [which did not arise till the 4th century] equally proves them supposititious." (P. 393.)

The expressions said to be directed against the Arians, are:—

(1.) "JESUS CHRIST OUR GOD." This occurs *twice* in the Epistle to the Ephesians, and is found *once* in most of the other epistles. Salutation to Eph.: "*Jesus Christ our God;*" c. 18: "*Our God Jesus Christ.*" Compare with this—Tit. ii. 10: "*God our Saviour;*" Tit. ii. 13: "*Our great God and Saviour Jesus Christ;*" Tit. iii. 4: "*God our Saviour.*" If the occurrence of this expression *twice in eighteen sections* of Ignatius's Epistle to the Ephesians, proves that spurious, what shall be said of St. Paul's Epistle to Titus, when the same expression occurs *three times in nine verses?*

(2.) "BY THE BLOOD OF GOD." Ign. Ep. Eph. c. i.: "*By the blood of God.*" Acts xx. 28: "*The Church of God, purchased by his own blood.*"

(3.) "There is one physician, both carnal and spiritual, create and uncreate, GOD MANIFEST IN THE FLESH." Ign. Ep. Eph. c. 7: "*God manifest in the flesh.*" 1 Tim. iii. 16: "*God manifest in the flesh.*" These are all the passages cited, which are said to be directed against Arianism, and *all are scriptural!*

Objection 3. "The word *Bishop* (*Episkopos*) was not used to distinguish the *President*, (*Proestos*,) or *Messenger*, (*Angelos*,) in their respective churches, from the other *Presbyters*, (*Presbuteroi*,) who were equally Bishops until long after the death of Ignatius." (P. 394.) For an answer to this objection, see pp. 147–152, 185, 199, 248–253, of this work.

Objection 4. "Many of the terms used in these epistles appear to be of later adoption than the days of this venerable martyr." (P. 395.) The terms cited and objected to, are:—

(1.) "The Church is called Catholic." See ante, p. 29, in reply.

(2.) "A place of worship is called *a temple*, ναον, having *one altar*, θυσιαστήριον." (P. 395.)

This occurs in the certain text of the Epistle to the Magnesians, (c. 7:) "Wherefore come ye all together, as unto one temple (*naon*) of GOD, as unto one altar (*thusiasterion.*)" It will probably be sufficient to reply that this language is copied from the Bible. (Luke i. 22, 23. Acts vii. 48; xvii. 24. Heb. xiii. 13, &c.)

(3.) "The Eucharist is called *the flesh* (σαρκά) of JESUS CHRIST, which suffered for our sins; and also, the *bread* (ἄρτος) of GOD." (P. 395.)

This language is from the certain text of the Epistle to the Romans, (c. 7:) "I delight not in the food of corruption, nor in the pleasures of this life; I desire the bread of GOD, the heavenly bread, the bread of life, which is the flesh of JESUS CHRIST, the Son of GOD." Like the rest, too, the expressions cited by the objector, are both from the Bible. "And he took *bread*, (*artos*,) saying, This is my *body*, (*soma*.)" (Mat. xxvi. 26. Mark xiv. 22. Luke xxii. 19. 1 Cor. xi. 24.)

(4.) "But the favorite and predominant expression appears to be—'*Be in subjection unto the Bishop*,' to which is also added, '*as unto the grace of God*.'" (P. 395.) See, in reply to this, pp. 207–210, 248–252, of this work.

Objection 5 is, in substance;—"It is denied in these epistles, that JESUS CHRIST proceeded from *Sigé*, (σιγῆς,) *silence*, one of the *Eons* of the Valentinians, which heresy was first preached after the death of Ignatius." This language occurs in the Epistle to the Magnesians, (c. 8:) "There is one GOD, who hath manifested himself by JESUS CHRIST his Son, who is his (eternal) Word, (not coming forth from *silence*, (*Sigé*,)) who was in all things well pleasing to him that sent him." The words in the parenthesis in this quotation, belong to the *doubtful text* of Ignatius, and are, therefore, to be rejected. Consequently, the objection falls to the ground. Should they be retained, however, it were easy to show that the objection is groundless.

Objection 6. "The language is not such as we should expect from the venerable martyr." (P. 394, 395.)

It is easy to make this assertion, but it would be hard to prove it. To our minds it seems the most natural and proper language imaginable. See, on this point, pp. 34, 239, 240, 248–252, of this work.

Those who wish to pursue the inquiry further, will find an article on the subject by the writer, in New York Review, vol. I. pp. 367–383. The scholar will also consult the *Vindication* of Bp. Pearson, printed originally in a separate work, and reprinted in Le Clerc's Apostolic Fathers.

EDITIONS OF THE PRINCIPAL AUTHORS CITED, OR REFERRED TO, IN THIS VOLUME.

Adam's Rom. Antiq. 8vo. N. Y. 1833.
Ambrose. 2 vols. fol. Paris, 1575.
American Bib. Repository. (Period. N. Y.)
Anacharsis the Younger, Travels of. 5 vols. 24mo. Paris, 1822.
Ancient Universal Hist. 21 vols. 8vo. Lond., 1747–1754.
Apostolic Canons. See *Le Clerc.*
" Constitution. See *Le Clerc.*
Assemani Bibliotheca Orientalis. 4 vols. fol. Rome, 1719–1728.
" History of Nestorian Patriarchs. 4to. Rome, 1745.
" Collection of Liturgies. See *Pusey.*
" Oriental Chronicle. See *Byzantine Historians,* XVII.
Athanasius. 2 vols. fol. Cologne, 1686.
Aucher's Armenian Dictionary. 2 vols. 8vo. Venice, 1821.
Augustin. 11 vols. fol. Paris, 1686.
Baptist Advocate. (Periodical, N. Y.)
Barnabas. See *Le Clerc.*
Barnes. See *Episcopacy Tested by Scripture.*
Bausobre's History of Manicheism. 2 vols. 4to. Amsterdam, 1734.
Baronius' Annals. 12 vols. fol. Antwerp, 1610–1629.
Basil. 3 vols. fol. Paris, 1618.
Bayle's Hist. and Crit. Dic. 5 vols. fol. Lond., 1734.
Bede, Ecc. Hist. fol. Canterbury, 1722.
" Trans. 8vo. Lond., 1840.
Beza's Life of Calvin. 12mo. Phil., 1836.
Bingham's Antiquities. 2 vols. fol. Lond., 1798.
Bloomfield on N. T. 2 vols. 8vo. Boston, 1837.
Bosworth's Anglo-Saxon Dic. 8vo. Lond., 1838.
Bowden's Letters to Dr. Miller. 2 vols. 12mo. N. Y. 1831.
Bowyer's Hist. of the Popes. 4 vols. 4to. Lond., 1748.
Brett on Liturgies. 8vo. Lond., 1720.
Burnett's Hist. Reformation. 6 vols. 24mo. Lond., 1825.
Buttman's Greek Gram. 8vo. Andover, 1833.
Byzantine Historians. 28 vols. fol. Venice, 1729–1733.
Calvin. See *Potter.*
Camden's Britannia. 3 vols. fol. Lond., 1789.
Canon of Wells. See *Wharton.*
Castell's Heptagloten Lexicon. 2 vols. fol. Lond., 1669.
Chronicle of Lichfield. See *Wharton.*
Chrysostom. 10 vols. fol. Paris, 1621.
Clement of Rome. See *Le Clerc.*
" Trans. 12mo. N. Y. 1834.
Coke on Littleton. fol. Lond., 1789.
Coleman's Primitive Church. 12mo. Boston, 1844.
Congregational Catechism. 24mo. New Haven, 1844.
Crabbe's Hist. Eng. Common Law. 8vo. Burlington, 1831
Cristodulos. See *Jarvis.*
Cyprian. fol. Bremen, 1698.
" Trans. 2 vols. 8vo. Oxford, 1839, 1844.
Cyril of Jerusalem. fol. Oxford, 1703.

Dunstan's Annals. See *Saxon Chronicle.*
Dupin's Hist. Ecc. Writers. 5 vols. fol. Lond., 1696.
Dutch Book of Common Prayer. 12mo. Amsterdam, 1838
" Dictionary. 8vo. Amsterdam, 1741.
" " 8vo. " 1642.
Ecchellensis. See *Byzantine Historians*, XVII.
Elfric's Annals. See *Saxon Chronicle.*
" Epistles. See *Wilkins.*
Encyclopedia Americana. 13 vols. 8vo. Phil., 1836.
Ephrem of Syria. 6 vols. fol. Rome, 1737–1746.
Episcopacy tested by Scripture. 12mo. N. Y. 1835.
Ethiopian Version. See *Walton.*
Eusebius' Ecc. Hist. 8vo. Phil., 1838.
" Demonstration Evang. fol. (*no date.*)
Eutychius' Annals. See *Jarvis.*
Fabricius Codex. Apoc. N. T. 3 vols. 12mo. Hamburg, 1719.
Fontenelle's Hist. of Oracles. 8vo.
Forcellini Lat. Lex. 2 vols. 4to. Lond., 1828.
Gallia Christiana. 11 vols. fol.
Gases, Greek Lexicon. 3 vols. 4to. Venice, (*no date.*)
Gerard's Elem. Bib. Criticism. 8vo. Boston, 1823.
Gesenius, Thesaurus Heb. and Chal. 3 vols. 4to. Leipsic, 1729–1842.
Gibbon's Dec. and Fall. 4 vols. 8vo. N. Y. 1831.
Gieseler's Ecc. Hist. 3 vols. 8vo. Phil., 1836.
Gildas, Epistles and History. 8vo. Lond., 1841.
Girald of Cambria. See *Ussher.*
Golius, Arab. Lex. fol. Lyons, 1651.
Godwin's Lives of English Bishops. fol. Canterbury, 1743.
Graveson's Ecc. Hist. 9 vols. fol. Augsburgh, 1738.
Gregory Nazianzen. 2 vols. fol. Paris, 1630.
" Nyssen. 3 vols. fol. Paris, 1638.
" Thaumaturgus. fol. Paris, 1622.
Guthries' Hist. Eng. 3 vols. fol. Lond., 1744.
Hallam's Constitutional Hist. Eng. 3 vols. 8vo. Boston, 1829.
Hammond on N. T. fol. Lond., 1659.
Harduin's Councils. 12 vols. fol. Paris, 1715.
Hargrave. See *Coke.*
Harris' Ethiopia. 8vo. N. Y. 1844.
Hegesippus. See *Eusebius.*
Henry Huntingdon, Hist. Eng. fol. Lond., 1596.
Hermas. See *Le Clerc.*
Hesychius. 4to. Lyons, 1668.
Hilarion. See *Gases.*
Hilary. fol. Paris, 1693.
Horne's Introduction O. and N. Test. 2 vols. 8vo. Phil., 1835.
Hug's Introduction N. T. 8vo. Andover, 1836.
Ignatius. See *Le Clerc.*
Ingulph, Hist. Croyland. fol. Lond., 1596.
Irenæus, Against Heresy. fol. Oxford, 1702.
Jahn's Bib. Archeology. 8vo. N. Y., 1832.
Jarvis, S. F., in Chron. Church, vol. 4. 4to., 1840
Jerome. 3 vols. fol. Paris, 1609.

Joceline of Furness. See *Ussher.*
John of Tinmouth. See *Ussher.*
Josephus. 2 vols. 4to. Boston, 1823.
Justin Martyr. fol. Lond., 1722.
Kirschius' Syriac Lexicon. 12mo. Hofæ, 1789.
Le Bas, Life of Wickliffe. 18mo. N. Y., 1832.
Le Clerc, Apostolic Fathers. 2 vols. fol. Antwerp, 1698.
Lemprier's Classical Dictionary. 8vo. N. Y., 1832.
Leti's Hist. Geneva. See *Bayle.*
Lingard's Hist. Ang. Sax. Church. 8vo. Phil., 1841.
" Hist. Eng. 8 vols. 8vo. Phil., 1827.
Livy. fol. Lyons, 1553.
Locke, On the Epistles. 8vo. Cambridge, 1832.
Ludolf's Ethiopian Lex. and Gram. 4to. Lond., 1661.
Maimbourg's Hist. Calvinism. See *Bayle.*
Mason's Vindication Church Eng. fol. Lond., 1728.
Matthew Paris. fol. Lond., 1640.
" Wm. Rishanger's Continuation. fol. Lond., 1640.
Michaelis' Edition of Castell's Syr. Lex. 2 vols. 4to. Gottingen, 1788.
Mosheim's Ecc. History. 3 vols. 8vo. New Haven, 1832.
Muratori, Annals of Italy. 12 vols. fol. Genoa, 1773–1778.
" Italian Writers. 31 vols. fol. Milan, 1723–1738.
Neander's History of Christianity. 4 parts, 8vo. 1825–1828.
New Englander. (Periodical. New Haven.)
New York Review. (Periodical. N. Y.)
Nicephorus' Ecc. Hist. 2 vols. fol. Langius, (*no date.*)
Nicholas' Annals. See *Saxon Chronicle.*
O'Brien's Hiberno-Celtic Dictionary. 8vo. Dublin, 1832.
Onderdonk. See *Episcopacy Tested by Scripture.*
Osbern's Annals. See *Saxon Chronicle.*
Oriental Chronicle. See *Byzantine Historians*, XVII.
Origen. 2 vols. fol. Basle, 1571.
Owen's Welsh Dictionary. 2 vols. 4to. Lond., 1793.
Paley's Horæ. Paulinæ. 8vo. Phil., 1831.
Palmer's Origines Liturgicæ. 2 vols. 8vo. Oxford, 1836.
Pamelius' Notes on Tertullian. fol. Cologne, 1617.
Papius. See *Eusebius.*
Patrick, Life of St. 12mo. Baltimore, (*no date.*)
Patriarchate of Britain. 12mo. Lond., 1839.
Petheram's History Ang. Sax. Lit. 8vo. Lond., 1840.
Peyron's Coptic Grammar. 8vo. Turin, 1841.
Phlegmund's Annals. See *Saxon Chronicle.*
Photius' Bibliotheca. fol. Geneva, 1612.
Pliny's Epistles. 2 vols. 8vo. Lond., 1796.
Poole's Synopsis of the Critics. 5 vols. fol. Lond., 1669.
Polycarp. See *Le Clerc.*
Polycrates. See *Eusebius.*
Pond, on the Church. 18mo. Boston, 1837.
Potter, on Church Government. 8vo. Phil., 1824.
Procopius. See *Byzantine Historians*, II.
Pusey, on Holy Baptism. 8vo. N. Y., 1839.
Quarterly Christian Spectator. (Periodical. N. H.)

Ralph Baldwin. See *Ussher.*
Remaldus' Annals. See *Saxon Chronicle.*
Renaudot, Hist. Pat. Alex. 4to. Paris, 1713.
Robinson's (J.) Grecian Antiquities. 8vo. Lond., 1827.
" (E.) Greek Lexicon. 8vo. Boston, 1836.
" " Calmet's Bib. Dic. 8vo. Boston, 1833
Robertson's Hist. Scotland. 2 vols. 8vo.
Roger Hoveden. fol. Lond., 1596.
Roger Wendover. 4 vols. 8vo. 1843.
Rymer's Fœdera. 20 vols. fol. Lond., 1703–1735.
Saxon Chronicle. 4to. Oxford, 1692.
Schmidt, Church Hist. 6 vols. 8vo.
Schroder's Thesaurus Lingua Armeniacæ, 4to.
Scoto-Celtic Dic. 2 vols. 4to. Edinburgh, 1836
Selden. See *Jarvis.*
Septuagint. 8vo. Leipsic, 1824.
Severus of Ashmonia. See *Jarvis.*
Socrates, Ecc. Hist. 8vo. Lond., 1844.
Sozomen, Ecc. Hist. fol. Cambridge, 1683.
Spelman's English Councils. 2 vols. fol.
Spon, Hist. Geneva. See *Bayle.*
Statutes of the [Eng.] Realm. 8 vols. fol. Lond., 1810–1819.
Stigand's Annals. See *Saxon Chronicle.*
Stillingfleet. 6 vols. fol. Lond., 1710.
Storr and Flatt, Elem. Bib. Theol. 2 vols. 8vo. Andover, 1826.
Strype's Annals. 3 vols. fol. Lond., 1720–1723.
" Elizabeth. fol. Lond., 1709.
" Life of Grindal. fol. Lond., 1710.
Suidas' Greek Lex. fol. Venice, 1514.
Suicer, Thesaurus Eccles. 2 vols. fol. Utrecht, 1746.
Syriac Version. See *Walton.*
Tertullian. fol. Paris, 1675.
Theodoret, Ecc. Hist. fol. Mayence, 1689.
Thornton. See *Cyprian.*
Tittman's Synonymes N. T. 18mo. Edinburg, 1838.
Tyschius' Syriac. Lex. 12mo. Rostock, 1793.
Utrecht, Hist. of Bishops. See *Bosworth.*
Ussher's Primordia. 4to. Dublin, 1639.
Valpey's Etymological Dic. Lat. Lang. 8vo. Lond., 1828.
Vander Kemp's Catechismus. 4to. Rotterdam, 1728.
Walsh's Lives of the Popes. 8vo. Lond., 1769.
Walter of Monmouth. See *Ussher.*
Walton's Polyglott. 5 vols. fol. Lond., 1657.
Wansleb. See *Ludolf.*
Whately's Kingdom of Christ. 12mo. N. Y., 1842.
Wharton's Angli-Sacra. 2 vols. fol. 1691.
Wickliffe, Life of. See *Le Bas.*
Wilkin's English Councils. 2 vols. fol.
William of Malmsbury. fol. Lond., 1596.
William Rishanger. See *Matthew Paris.*
Wulstan's Annals. See *Saxon Chronicle.*
Zahn's Mœso-Gothic Gram., Lex., and N. T. 4to. Weisenfels, 1805

GENERAL INDEX

www.ingramcontent.com/pod-product-compliance
Lightning Source LLC
LaVergne TN
LVHW020556110826
845149LV00002B/289

* 9 7 8 1 4 1 8 1 8 8 3 9 9 *